Mastering JXTA

Building Java Peer-to-Peer Applications

Mastering JXTA

Building Java Peer-to-Peer Applications

Joseph D. Gradecki

Wiley Publishing, Inc.

Publisher: Robert Ipsen
Editor: Robert M. Elliott
Managing Editor: John Atkins
Book Packaging: Ryan Publishing Group, Inc.

Copyeditor: Elizabeth Welch
Proofreader: Nancy Sixsmith
Compositor: Gina Rexrode
Technical Editor: Stan Ng

Library of Congress Cataloging-in-Publication Data:

ISBN: 0-471-25084-8

Printed in the United States of America

10 9 8 7 6 5 4 3 2 1

I would like to dedicate this book to my loving wife and our three won-
derful boys. I thank God each day for providing me such a great family.
Thank you for supporting me.

CONTENTS

I would like to acknowledge several folks. First, Tim Ryan for everything he does to support the writing of this book and his friendship. Second, Liz Welch for her diligent editing of this manuscript. Third, Stan Ng for his technical editing and keeping me straight on the use of the JXTA software.

Joseph D. Gradecki is a software engineer at Comprehensive Software Systems, where he works on its SABIL product, an enterprise-level securities processing system. He has built numerous dynamic enterprise applications using Java, C++, servlets, JSPs, Resin, MySQL, BroadVision, XML, and other technologies.

Joe has also built many P2P distributed computing systems in a variety of languages, including Java/JXTA, C/C++, and Linda. He holds Bachelor's and Master's degrees in Computer Science, and is currently pursuing a Ph.D. in Computer Science. Joe also regularly teaches Java and OOP courses at Colorado Technical University.

Introduction

Many of us tend to think of the Internet, and most other networks, as inherently client-server systems. Web developers spend a lot of time building powerful sites that serve information and services to the thousands of browser clients that visit them. But peer-to-peer (P2P) applications like KaZaA, Napster, and SETI have demonstrated the true power of the Internet: the millions of information stores—common PCs—sitting idle on desks around the world. Peer-to-peer technologies harness the CPUs and storage devices of these PCs to produce huge data stores, communications systems, and processing engines.

Due to a lack of standards and toolkits, early P2P application developers spent much of their time reinventing the wheel—building the same system "plumbing" for each new app they wrote. Developers at Sun created the JXTA specification to solve this problem. The specification is a basic building block from which developers can produce applications that

- Allow sharing of resources between peers without a central server
- Use idle cycles of desktop machines for solving complex problems
- Expose Web services to be used by other peers

What's In This Book

This book contains a complete discussion of the latest JXTA specification and the Java binding. As with any new technology, a number of components form the foundation of the specification. This book explains each of the core components and protocols of JXTA, and includes comprehensive examples to back up the concepts. Some of the concepts discussed in this book are

Peers—An application, executing on a computer, that has the ability to communicate with similar peer applications

Peer groups—A logical grouping of peers

Modules—Code that is made available by a peer or peer group for use by another peer or peer group.

Pipes—Communication channels created between peers

Services—Predefined functionality that can be utilized by peers

Advertisements—XML-based messages used to publish information between peers

Following a complete discussion of the specification, this book provides many code examples and full P2P applications written in Java. After reading *Mastering JXTA*, you will have a foundation in P2P programming and, more important, you will have several examples and full-blown applications to use as a springboard for your own creations. One of the major examples in this book builds a framework for distributed computations using JXTA. Using a generic work class, you can build P2P applications that will pass computational work to be done to peers and accumulate the results. Another example will show you how to build a comprehensive, three-tier storage system; this system allows data to be sent from client peers to business peers to database peers. The database peer connects to a MySQL database to store the data.

One of the major goals of this book is demonstrating how to develop P2P applications by stepping you through the process of building a comprehensive application framework that you can reuse to develop your own applications.

You can find the code in this book at www.wiley.com/compbooks/gradecki. The code for each chapter is located in a separate file so that you can quickly find what you need. The JXTA Java Reference Implementation can be found at www.jxta.org. You will also need the Java SDK, which you can find at www.javasoft.com.

Who Should Read This Book

This book assumes that you are new to JXTA and P2P concepts, but have programming experience with Java. To quickly understand some of the more complex examples in this book, you will need to be familiar with Java interface implementation, anonymous inner classes, and callbacks.

If you want to know how to build sophisticated, Java-based, peer-to-peer applications, then this book is for you.

Book Organization

This book is organized into three parts. Part I is a comprehensive overview of P2P, the JXTA specification, and the JXTA architecture and its components. Part II discusses the JXTA protocols, which are the core of the specification; you must understand the protocols in order to build robust P2P applications using a binding language. Finally, Part III takes all of the concepts learned in Parts I and II and applies them to many small examples and two large applications: a distributed computational engine and a robust storage service. Let's take a look at each of the chapters making up the three parts of the book.

Part I: JXTA Overview

Chapter 1: Introduction to Peer-to-Peer

This chapter provides the uninitiated with a comprehensive overview of what P2P is, where it came from, and how it's been used. We look to the past in order to understand that the concepts of a P2P network are really quite old. Next, we examine the various architectures that can be created when a P2P system is developed. Finally, we look into the more common P2P systems—such as Usenet, Napster, Gnutella, Instant Messaging, and distributed.net—to understand what you can do with peer-to-peer.

Chapter 2: An Overview of JXTA

This chapter is the fundamental chapter in the book. We describe the JXTA system, starting with its short history. Then we examine the JXTA architecture, which consists of three layers: the core layer, the services layer, and the application layer. We describe each of the layers in detail, and explain the components needed in each layer. The layers rely on several JXTA technologies, which are described next. These technologies are

- Peer
- Group
- Advertisement
- Protocols
- Pipes

- Services
- Rendezvous peers

Finally, we include an overview of how you can use JXTA in networks that have firewalls and peers that use a NAT address. Because XML is used throughout JXTA, an overview of XML is also provided for those who are new to that technology.

Chapter 3: JXTA Shell

One of the easiest ways to experience the JXTA system is through the JXTA shell. The JXTA shell is an interactive application that allows a command-line interface to the JXTA network; it is modeled after a Unix shell, and includes a number of commands for manipulating the shell presence on the network. Some of the commands we discuss are whoami, peers, env, share, and search, among many others. We provide a comprehensive overview of the shell and how to use it on the network. We cover all of the commands in the shell, along with helpful examples, and conclude with a discussion on writing shell scripts and user-defined classes.

Chapter 4: Using myJXTA

In order to further explain the code necessary to write JXTA P2P applications, this chapter focuses on the InstantP2P application, which you can download from the JXTA project web site. We examine major features of this application, including

- Chatting with InstantP2P in a group
- Using one-to-one chatting
- Searching for files in a group
- Sharing your own files

We discuss each of these features as well as the code used to implement them.

Chapter 5: JXTA Advertisements

One of the core concepts in JXTA is that of the *advertisement*. All resources, such as peers, groups, pipes, and services, rely on the advertisement to represent themselves on the JXTA network. This chapter provides a complete view of the JXTA advertisement based on the latest specification. For each of the different advertisements—including peer, peer group, module class, module specification, module implementation, pipe, peer info, and rendezvous—we offer complete descriptions, along with discussions of how the advertisements are created and used within the network.

Part II: JXTA Protocols

Chapter 6: Peer Discovery Protocol

This chapter provides a detailed view of the Peer Discovery Protocol (PDP), which is used for all discovery of advertisements from peers. A peer uses the PDP for resource queries, and will receive zero or more responses. In this chapter, we describe the messages received from a query as well as how to perform a PDP query. In addition, we briefly discuss how the protocol was implemented, and the features available for those peers that want to build and use their own discovery mechanism.

Chapter 7: Peer Resolver Protocol

The Peer Resolver Protocol is a generic query protocol designed to allow peers to query either specific peers or peers within a peer group. In this chapter, we examine the protocol specification and how it is used to implement a number of the JXTA protocols. We also cover the message formats and how to use the protocol. At the end of the chapter, you'll find a discussion of how the protocol is implemented.

Chapter 8: Peer Information Protocol

In any peer-to-peer environment, information about peers must be readily available. The Peer Information Protocol is a powerful mechanism for obtaining information about a peer once it has been discovered. In this chapter, we examine the protocol. As in the other protocol chapters, we cover the query and response messages, along with specific implementation details.

Chapter 9: Peer Endpoint Protocol

The JXTA network is designed to allow for routing between peers. There are times when one peer needs to send a message to another peer and they are not "directly" connected. In these situations, a relay peer will be used. In this chapter, we dive into the details behind the Peer Endpoint Protocol. We cover all of the query and response messages as well as implementation details.

Chapter 10: Pipe Binding Protocol

When peers want to communicate by sending more than advertisements, a pipe is necessary. The Pipe Binding Protocol provides the details behind pipes, endpoints, and transport mechanisms. In this chapter, we discuss all of these concepts and examine the various messages being transferred between peers.

Chapter 11: Rendezvous Protocol

The Rendezvous Protocol allows for the propagation of messages within a P2P system. In this chapter, we cover the Rendezvous Protocol, which is used by both the Peer Resolver and Pipe Binding Protocols.

Chapter 12: Developing a JXTA Application

This chapter provides the details behind building JXTA P2P applications. Using the information gathered from the first two parts of the book, this chapter guides you through the development of both command-line and GUI-based Java applications. You will learn how to build JXTA P2P applications using a simple-to-understand skeleton. We expand the skeleton to include creating and joining peer groups with both secure and non-secure membership rules.

Chapter 13: JXTA Pipes

One of the primary reasons to build a P2P system is to facilitate the transfer of information between the peers. The peers and services are made known to each other through advertisements, and information is transfer through a pipe. The concept is the same as that found in the Unix system, in which a pipe connects two commands. In this chapter, we explain the pipes used in JXTA, and illustrate with examples.

Part III: JXTA Implementation

Chapter 14: Content Sharing and the Content Management Service (CMS)

The Content Management Service (CMS) is a perfect example of an add-on to the JXTA network using a service. This software allows for easy sharing, access, and retrieval of all kinds of content in the JXTA networks. As you'll learn in this chapter, by using simple commands peers can implement the CMS and instantly be able to share content with other peers.

Chapter 15: Implementing Security

As noted in Chapter 12, the level of security provided in the default Java binding for JXTA is weak. Most of the security found in JXTA is located in the JXTACryptoSuite, which we discuss in detail. The default weak authentication code for group membership is expanded to include much stronger algorithms. Finally, we address the issue of security along the network transport.

Chapter 16: Peer Monitoring and Metering

As peers are developed and deployed, the issue of monitoring and metering will arise. In this chapter, each of these issues are addressed. On the topic of monitoring, we present code that allows a P2P system to keep track of the peers in the group, when they joined the group, when they left the group, and when sudden peer death occurs.

Chapter 17: Configuring NAT and Firewall Peers

Of particular importance to enterprise systems is how to handle firewall and Network Address Translation (NAT). In this chapter, we explain how to configure peers that use a NAT address and/or exist behind a firewall. We present code that you can use to build a simple peer to be used as a gateway or rendezvous peer.

Chapter 18: Using Endpoints for Low-level Communication

Under the high-level pipe component is a lower-level mechanism for communicating between peers. Endpoints represent portals into and out of individual peers and can be used as a low-level communication channel. This chapter will explore endpoints and present code for using them in peers.

Chapter 19: Building a Generic Framework for Distributed Computing

This chapter builds an application like SETI or distributed.net using the JXTA framework. We examine the process of building a framework system, in which computationally complex algorithms can be distributed to peers on the networks that choose to subscribe.

Chapter 20: Building an Encrypted, High-Availability Storage System

Imagine building an encrypted remote storage service in which clients can sign up and store vital records. In this chapter, we build such a system, and explore topics such as using replication among peers and handling integration with backend databases.

Part IV: JXTA Reference

Appendix A: Installing JXTA and Compiling JXTA Applications

Appendix A provides a guide for installing and using the JXTA system. Information covered in the appendix includes

- Finding JXTA
- Finding the ancillary installs you need
- Downloading the files
- Installing on Windows
- Installing on Linux
- Installing on Solaris
- Obtaining daily builds for the latest code

Appendix B: JXTA API

Appendix B provides a complete listing of the current JXTA API, along with descriptions.

Appendix C: Current Add-on JXTA Services

Since JXTA is a core technology, a number of complementary systems have been developed that can be "bolted" onto a P2P system. In this appendix, we look at some of those services and their current status.

Appendix D: Latest JXTA Projects

Anyone who has taken the time to look at the JXTA web site will find a number of projects. This chapter details the most important of those projects and how services provided by the projects can be utilized in other applications.

Appendix E: JXTA Resources

Appendix E covers the latest information about the Project JXTA web site, and provides listings of other web sites that can be used for resource purposes. We also include a number of mailing lists aimed at developers who want to remain in the loop of JXTA development.

Appendix F: JXTA Bindings

Appendix F covers the current language bindings of the JXTA specification. While Java was the first, a number of other bindings have been created using most of the recent and popular languages.

Appendix G: Other Peer-to-Peer Implementations and Toolkits

In this appendix, we examine some of the other P2P implementations and toolkits. We discuss both commercial and open-source systems.

Mastering JXTA

Building Java Peer-to-Peer Applications

Introduction to Peer-to-Peer

The early developers of ARPANET and the Internet allowed themselves to dream about a day when computers around the world would be linked together to share resources in a peer-to-peer fashion. In 1962, one of those early dreamers, J.C.R. Licklider of MIT, wrote a now-famous series of memos in which he described an "Intergalactic Network" of interconnected computers. His vision led to the creation of the Network Control Program (NCP), the first "host-host" networking protocol and the precursor to TCP/IP.

The host-host concept—which we now call peer-to-peer—was crucial in developing the Internet. Every computer on the network was an equal: Each computer could access the resources of any other computer on the network while making its own resources available. Communication among hosts was also equal: No computer was seen as a client or component of another, and all computers shared more-or-less equal bandwidth access to one another.

Several events have conspired to change the Internet landscape from primarily peer-to-peer to the now more familiar client-server architecture. The Internet has gradually become more commercial, and corporations build firewalls around their information to control access. Millions of people "log on" to the Internet using desktop computers that cannot match the power of the servers that form the backbone of the Internet. And many popular Internet applications and services, including the World Wide Web and FTP, are based on a client-server architecture.

In the last few years, however, peer-to-peer (P2P) technology has once again had a profound effect on the Internet and the distribution of information and resources. P2P is being aggressively hyped in the media, but there are a wide variety of opinions as to what exactly P2P is:

- Clay Shirky (Internet consultant, writer, and speaker) once said that "P2P is a class of applications that takes advantage of resources—storage, cycles, content, human presence—available at the edges of the Internet."

- Li Gong of Sun Microsystems wrote that "The term peer-to-peer networking is applied to a wide range of technologies that greatly increase the utilization of information, bandwidth, and computing resources in the Internet. Frequently, these P2P technologies adopt a network-based computing style that neither excludes nor inherently depends on centralized control points."

- Ed Dumbill of XML.com said, "P2P is whoever says they're P2P."

Right now Mr. Dumbill's definition seems to be winning the popular vote. One of the purposes of this chapter is to help you formulate your own answer to the question, "What is P2P?" The next section begins our discussion of peer-to-peer technology with a quick review of network topologies. In the final section, we look at Napster, Morpheus, instant messaging, and Usenet from a P2P perspective; and then discuss some of the legal, technical, and security issues that have arisen from the use of these and similar applications.

What Is a Peer-to-Peer Architecture?

If we take a moment to consider the Internet itself, we will see that there are millions of computers connected in the network at any given time. All of the computers are theoretically connected to one another, and information stored on any of the systems can be accessed. As a whole, the topology or layout of the computers on the Internet is a grouping of machines spread out in various locations. Within each of the groups or subnets, computers will be visible to other computers on the subnet and sometimes to the outside Internet.

Some of the computers will be servers and host information. The machines at Yahoo! that serve up contents are *web servers*. Browsing to Yahoo! on your local computer turns the machine into a *client*. This type of client-server interaction is happening for hundreds of thousands of computers at the same time. While a client machine is browsing to Yahoo!, it could also be sharing a local drive with group members. In this situation, the machine will become a server to any client that tries to access files on the local drive.

In most peer-to-peer systems, the division between a server and a client is blurred. The computer itself might be connected to other computers using a token-ring topology, but a peer-to-peer system might have a completely different architecture. The peers could all be communicating with a central server, like Napster.

In most cases, peers will be connected to one another over the Internet using either the TCP or HTTP protocol. As you probably already know, TCP/IP is the fundamental protocol for transferring information over the Internet. The HTTP protocol is built on top of TCP/IP and allows communication between computers using port 80. HTTP is very popular for peer-to-peer systems because most organizations keep port 80 clear on their firewalls for web browser traffic.

Several network topologies can be used for connecting P2P systems. In this section, we discuss the major P2P network topologies in order to explain how information can be transmitted between peers effectively.

The Hierarchical Topology

One of the most common topologies is the *hierarchy*. Every time you type a website URL into your browser, you are using a system called DNS, or Domain Name Server. This system is set up in a hierarchy, with root servers at the very top levels. The hierarchy topology looks like Figure 1.1. For several years now, critics have called for an overhaul of the DNS architecture because the root servers represent a single point of failure. However, because the entire system is based on replication and the chance of the DNS system going down is very small, no real work has occurred in this area.

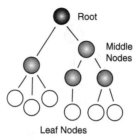

Figure 1.1 The hierarchy network topology.

The Ring Topology

Token Ring is a network topology that uses the concept of passing a single token around to the computers connected in a ring pattern. When a machine receives the token, it can send information out onto the network. The ring topology isn't used much anymore for common networks, but does provide an interesting pattern for load-balancing a single-server system or hierarchy. The top rung of a hierarchy topology could actually be a ring of servers that balance the network requests. Figure 1.2 shows what a ring topology looks like.

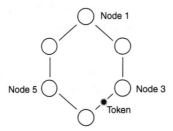

Figure 1.2   The ring network topology.

The Client-Server, or Centralized, Topology

By far the most common topology is the *client-server*, or *centralized*, topology. The terminology of client-server has been with us for many years; more recently, the term *centralized* has been used to describe a system in which a single computer, the server, makes services available over the network. Client machines contact the server when the services are needed. Obviously, the more clients in the system, the larger the server must be. At some point, the server will need to be replicated in order to handle the traffic volume from all clients. Figure 1.3 shows an example of the centralized topology.

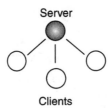

Figure 1.3   The client-server, or centralized, network topology.

The Decentralized Topology

The *decentralized* topology is a network topology that comes closest to being truly peer-to-peer. There is no central authority, only individual computers that are able to connect and communicate with any of the other computers on the network. When a packet of information starts its travels on the Internet, it is basically traveling through a decentralized topology. Information within the packet itself tells each computer where to send the packet next. Figure 1.4 shows an example of a decentralized network topology. Basically, all of the peers in the system act as both clients and servers, handling query requests and downloads while also making media searches and download request themselves. The KaZaA and Gnutella applications use this decentralized topology for their P2P systems.

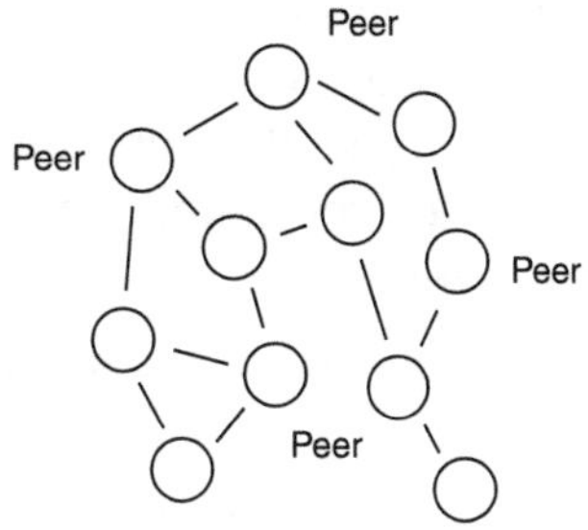

Figure 1.4   The decentralized network topology.

The Hybrid Topology

In the *hybrid* topology shown in Figure 1.5, we have an example of a situation where the individual computers are considered clients when they need information. The client that needs information will contact a central server (the centralized servers are distributed in the example shown in Figure 1.5) to obtain the "name" of another client where the requested information is stored. The requesting client will then contact the client with the information directly. With the hybrid, a computer can be either a client or a server. This is the topology used for the Napster system—individual peers contact a localized server for searching and proceed to contact peers directly for media downloading.

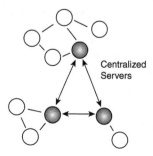

Figure 1.5   The hybrid network topology.

Examples of Peer-to-Peer Systems

This section describes several well-known peer-to-peer applications. We briefly examine how each one shares resources and services so that by the end of this section you'll have a clearer idea of what functional, real-world P2P really means.

Napster

Napster is the software that thrust the peer-to-peer concept into the limelight. As you probably know, Napster was developed to allow the sharing of MP3 music files created from CDs and other sources. Later in the chapter, we briefly discuss why Napster isn't the peer-to-peer powerhouse it once was, but for now let's look at how Napster works:

1. A prospective user downloads the Napster peer software from a Napster primary or mirror web site.

2. Once installed and launched, the peer software attempts to connect to a central Napster server, where the user is required to choose a username and password.

3. The user can have the peer software search his or her local hard drive for MP3 files to share with others. If this option is selected, the user's hard drive will be searched and the names of any media files will be transferred to the central server. Note that only the file*names* are transferred.

4. The user can search for media in the Napster network. The peer software will transfer the search string to the central server, which will return a list of files found and connection information about the peer computers where the files reside, including the username, the IP address, the port to connect to, the connection speed, and the file size.

5. The Napster peer making the request will attempt to directly contact the Napster peer on the remote computer where the target file resides. At this point, the central server is no longer involved in the file transfer.

For Napster, the central server is just a large database containing a list of all files found in all clients in the network. The system worked very well, and many of the peers who had a fast connection to the Internet were typically slammed with file requests. If your system was being swamped with requests to download files, you could set a limit to allow only N number of active downloads at any one time. If a new download request came into the peer, the peer would respond with a message indicating that the download request was added to the queue. The queue would automatically keep track of all download requests and move them into an active state as older download requests finished.

From this explanation, it is clear that the Napster system uses a hybrid topology. Without the centralized server, all of the peers in the system would have media to share and also want to search for media, but they wouldn't know about one another. The centralized server is responsible for keeping a database of all peers and what they have to share available to all peers in the network.

Gnutella

As Napster became successful, other P2P products such as Gnutella were created to enable information sharing. One feature that distinguishes Gnutella is that it uses the HTTP protocol to transfer information. HTTP is used by web browsers to contact web servers, so in a sense a Gnutella peer is actually a transparent web site "server" with links for each of the pieces of media being shared. A Gnutella peer contacts a Gnutella "server" in much the same way that a standard web browser contacts a web server.

The topology for Gnutella is decentralized, and there is no centralized authority. So, if there is no central authority, how does a peer obtain a list of the media files available in the network?

The real key to Gnutella is its search capability. With no central server, the peers need to be able to determine what files are available in a fashion that is both quick and effective. The search mechanism works by creating a search packet with a *max hops* value that indicates the maximum number of times the search packet will be propagated in the Gnutella network before it is returned to the peer that originated it. So, if a packet has a max hops value of 3, the packet will be allowed to be propagated throughout the Gnutella network a maximum of three peers away from its peer of origin. As each peer receives the packet, it decrements an internal counter. When the internal counter reaches zero, the search packet is no longer forwarded to other peers.

When a peer requests a search, the search packet is sent to all the peers that the requesting peer knows about. Those peers will immediately send all media file descriptions matching the search string in the packet back to the requesting peer; the peers will then forward the search packet to all the peers they know about.

The search process does have a problem in that you can never be sure your search packet reaches a peer that has the information you want. Further, the process of broadcasting the search packet to all known peers has a predictable consequence of using high bandwidth. If you increase the maximum hops allowed for the search, you might find your information, but there will also be a penalty in search time. In addition, when the search result is sent back to the originator, it must pass back through the same sequence of peers it initially traveled. Figure 1.6 shows an example of passing a search request between three sites.

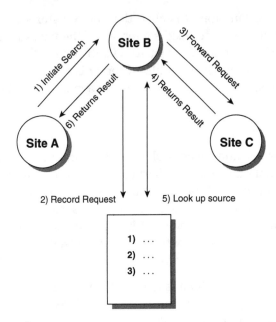

Figure 1.6 The Gnutella search process.

In this example, Site A is requesting all files that match the phrase *Rush*. Site A sends the search packet to Site B. Site B creates a list of the items requested by Site A (assigning a unique request number to the search packet), sends any matches it has locally back to Site A, and then forwards the search packet to Site C. If Site C has any matching files, the results will not be directly sent to Site A, but instead to Site B. When Site B receives the results from Site C, it checks its list, sees that Site A originally requested the information, and forwards it to Site A.

Morpheus/KaZaA

Another file-sharing system, called Morpheus, was developed by MusicCity to replace a central server system with a decentralized system. Morpheus is based on FastTrack's P2P Stack, also used in the KaZaA file-sharing system. Morpheus and KaZaA aren't limited in their sharing of file types. You will find audio, video, images, documents, and even software in the two applications' networks. The two systems have improved the technologies involved in file download and search on a decentralized system by allowing for file restarts during download and by keeping lists of multiple peers who have the same file available.

Although the peers are basically decentralized, a central server is still used for providing username/password functionality and maintaining the overall network. In addition, the systems use a pure hybrid topology, as shown earlier. When a peer logs on, it is associated with a peer hub. These peer hubs are responsible for maintaining a list of the media files on their peers, and assisting in the search requests between peers and peer hubs. If you are a peer on the network, and you have high bandwidth and a good deal of CPU power, your peer can be elected a peer hub automatically; however, you can select an option to not become a peer hub.

The hub peers are very important to the overall efficiency of the P2P network. Individual peers don't need to send requests to every peer in the network or worry about a max hops value—they send requests to their hub peer. The hub peer can quickly answer requests with information about media residing on the other peers in the hub. At the same time, the hub peers can contact other hub peers to find even more results. The amount of network traffic involved in a search is drastically reduced.

Media is transferred between peers on a purely peer-to-peer basis with no intermediary peers propagating them. The files are transferred using HTTP in order to reach peers behind firewalls. It should be noted that all transfers display the IP address of the machines involved in the transfer.

Usenet

One of the oldest peer-to-peer systems, Usenet is based on a hybrid topology in which server nodes will be contacted for information from clients, and the server nodes will communicate with one another to ensure widespread distribution of information. The server nodes in Usenet are really the peers in the network. They have information to share and also request updates as needed from other peers. For the most part, the server nodes will all contain the same information if they choose to keep all newsgroups. Figure 1.7 shows an example of how the server nodes communicate to keep one another up-to-date.

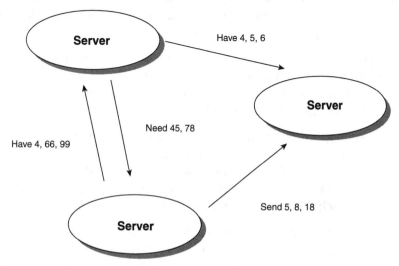

Figure 1.7   The Usenet server message-sharing process.

Client applications will connect to the server peers to obtain a listing of title messages available. When a message is selected, the actual data behind the title will be sent. It is obvious from this description that the developers of Usenet built an early prototype of a peer-to-peer system.

Instant Messaging

Instant messaging systems, such as AOL Instant Message (AIM) and Yahoo! Instant Message, typically work in a topology in which central servers are used to coordinate your group of connections. When you log into an instant messaging service, the server will keep a temporary list of your contacts. The server will check to see if any of your contacts is currently logged into the system. If so, the IP and port information for the instant messaging client on the contact will be provided to your client, and your client information will be provided to the contact. From that point on, all communication between you and the contact will be in a peer-to-peer fashion.

Extreme Peer-to-Peer: Distributed Computational Engines

Several years ago, a tremendous piece of software was created that revolutionized the way Grand Challenge and computationally complex problems were solved. This software follows the traditional habit of building larger and larger supercomputers to solve problems. While distributed.net (www.distributed.net) wasn't the first system to use the idle CPU cycles of machines on a network, they are certainly the biggest. Using client software that runs as a background process in a "nice" mode, distributed.net has announced its intention to break RSA Labs' 56-bit secret-key code in response to a challenge put forth by RSA Labs.

When installed, the client software contacts a central server and requests packets of encrypted data that it will attempt to decrypt using a brute-force algorithm. When those packets have been processed, the results are sent to the central authority and a new set of packets is retrieved.

The resulting computation power and magnitude of machines involved is enormous. For example, there are on average 33,000 participants active on any given day. All of those participants have a minimum of one computer, and some are using entire labs. The participants are working through 92,141,082 keys per second, which equates to roughly .01% of the entire keyspace every day.

When the popularity of distributed.net rose, another group decided to use the same principle in the search for extraterrestrials. SETI@home (which stands for Search for Extraterrestrial Intelligence) produced a client that works in much the same way. The client receives signal data from the SETI installation, and applies an algorithm to the information. The results are sent back to a central server, and more data is retrieved for processing. Figure 1.8 shows the transfer part of the system, which can be loosely called a peer-to-peer network.

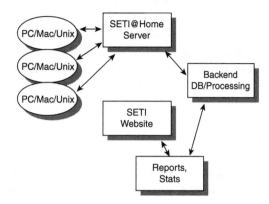

Figure 1.8   A traffic example within SETI.

Warnings

While peer-to-peer systems offer great benefits in resource distribution, communication, and problem solving, developers and users alike should be aware of unresolved issues involved in using them. In this section, we briefly discuss four broad issues to raise your awareness level and spur your own conversations and research.

Workplace Policies

Recently, there was a case in which a university system administrator installed a distributed computational engine on some of the computers under his control. When the university found out, he was charged with theft. In effect, he had stolen both CPU utilization and bandwidth of those computers. While there is much argument over the dollar figures provided by the university, you must be careful about how machines in your care are used.

The company I work for has a strict policy: No peer-to-peer systems or software shall operate on company computers. Before using a peer-to-peer system at work, check with those who make and enforce the policy.

Intellectual Property

One of the major faults commonly associated with the Internet is that it enables users to inappropriately distribute copyrighted material quickly and on a global basis. This issue has caused many heated arguments among consumers, distributors, copyright owners, artists, civil libertarians, and others; but it all comes down to what the law says about intellectual property. If you buy something and offer it for sale or give it away, there is usually no problem because the property has been transferred to another individual (one notable exception to this is software that is typically licensed, not purchased). If you buy something and make a copy of it, and then you offer that copy for sale or give it away, you are no longer transferring the property you purchased—instead, you are transferring a copy and keeping the original. The law says this is theft, and this is ultimately why Napster failed. Be careful what you offer to other peers in a peer-to-peer system.

Bandwidth Costs

Peer-to-peer applications eat bandwidth for lunch, and as we all know, there are no free lunches. In many cases, a peer-to-peer application will be in violation of an ISP's service agreement because it can act as a server. ISPs put these policies in place to guard their precious bandwidth.

In addition to the bandwidth costs, there is a real concern for peer-to-peer systems that use broadcast mechanisms to locate other peers. As messages propagate across the Internet, more and more "garbage" broadcast packets are bouncing off the infrastructure. There have even been cases of denial of service occurring because of the volume of broadcast messages occurring on a network. In some cases, it might be preferable for peer-to-peer applications to operate on private networks with a limited connection to the "outside world."

Security

Internet applications are known for security holes. What kind of access does a remote peer have to your computer when it makes a request to the peer software you are running? Do you really know what information is gathered and sent to some remote server? What about the application itself? Is it secure? Buggy? Does it contain a Trojan horse? Most recently, it was released that the KaZaA client contained a stealth application designed to use the spare CPU cycles of the machine it was installed on. The stealth nature of the application allowed it to process work undetected by the computer's owner. These are all questions and situations that you must ask when using peer-to-peer software. And as a developer, you have a responsibility to ensure that the peer-to-peer applications you create are secure.

Summary

This chapter has enumerated several clear and not-so-clear examples of peer-to-peer applications. Most of the applications, which allow the sharing of information over the Internet, have had a profound effect on society. Sometimes, the effect is to challenge the norm, and in other cases, it provides the ability to get more work done through increased communication. Throughout this book, we will learn about the tools available and necessary to build peer-to-peer systems.

CHAPTER 2

An Overview of JXTA

J XTA is a peer-to-peer platform specification developed in the Apache open-source model by Sun Microsystems under the direction of Bill Joy and Mike Clary. Some of the basic goals of the platform are

- Peers should be able to discover one another.
- Peers should self-organize into peer groups.
- Peers should advertise and discover network resources.
- Peers should communicate with one another.
- Peers should monitor one another.
- The platform should not require the use of any particular computer language or operating system.
- The platform should not require the use of any particular network transport or topology.
- The platform should not require the use of any particular authentication, security, or encryption model.

The overriding tenet for JXTA was to create a platform with enough standardized functionality to enable open-source and commercial developers to create interoperable services and applications. To facilitate this tenet as well as the other goals, the platform was not created based on one software language over another. The platform was created through a design process, and the result was a specification that describes the major points of the system and provides implementation information.

The entire JXTA system is modeled using a small number of protocols for handling JXTA services. The protocols can be implemented using any language, thus allowing heterogeneous devices to exist and communicate with one another in a huge peer-to-peer system. Currently, there are six protocols in the system:

Peer Resolver Protocol (PRP)—Used to send a query to any number of other peers and to receive a response.

Peer Discovery Protocol (PDP)—Used to advertise content and discover content.

Peer Information Protocol (PIP)—Used to obtain peer status information.

Pipe Binding Protocol (PBP)—Used to create a communication path between peers.

Peer Endpoint Protocol (PEP)—Used to find a route from one peer to another.

Rendezvous Protocol (RVP)—Used to propagate messages in the network.

In Figure 2.1, the six different protocols are shown in their relationships to each other. The illustration further shows how a Java reference implementation can be built between the Java JRE and an application.

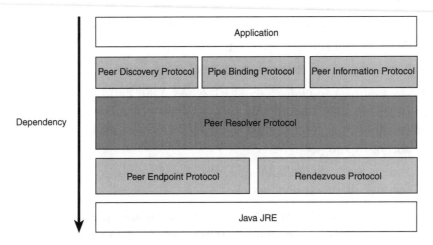

Figure 2.1 JXTA specification protocols hierarchy.

These six protocols are all that is needed for individual peers to exist in a decentralized peer-to-peer environment that is self-forming and that has no need for a centralized server. Peers have the ability to exist on private networks behind firewalls, and can be assigned Internet addressable IP addresses or an address through the Network Address Translation process. Network assumptions in the protocols were kept to a minimum to allow implementations on a variety of transport mechanisms. The protocols allow peers to

- Advertise content they would like to share
- Discover content they are interested in
- Form and join peer groups, both public and private
- Assist in the routing and forwarding of messages transparently

The protocols and the entire JXTA specification do not specify languages that must be used for implementation. As one would expect, Sun chose to do the *initial reference implementation* in Java.

NOTE

By using Java as the first implementation language for JXTA, Sun has made the toolkit available to a large audience on many different platforms. You can find the current binding on the JXTA website; Appendix A contains full installation instructions.

The JXTA Architecture

In order for the JXTA protocols to work together to form a complete system, an architecture must be in place. Figure 2.2 shows the architecture defined for the JXTA specification.

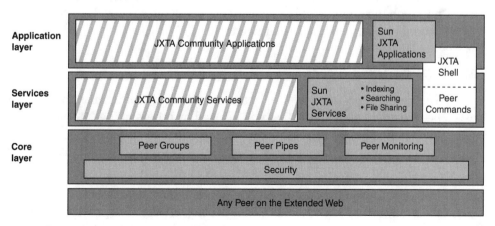

Figure 2.2 The JXTA peer-to-peer architecture.

The Core Layer

The *core layer* is where the code for implementing the protocols is found. The protocols provide the functionality for peers, peer groups, security, and monitoring; as well as all the message-passing and network protocols.

Sitting over the protocols is a universal peer group called the WorldPeerGroup. When a peer starts executing, it will automatically become part of the World-PeerGroup, and will have access to peer group functionality or services already implemented. This functionality allows the peer to perform discoveries, join and create other peer groups, and exchange messages using pipes.

The Services Layer

A service is a functionality, built on top of the core layer, that uses the protocols to accomplish a given task. The *services layer* can be divided into two areas: essential and convenient. To illustrate this difference, consider two services: a service that provides membership and a service that translates messages from AOL Instant Messenger (AIM) to MSN Messenger. The membership service is an essential service in a peer-to-peer environment. In the JXTA architecture, all peers automatically join a default group called the NetPeerGroup. This peer group provides basic services, but not all peers will want to be part of the big umbrella group at all times. By using a membership function, peers can join smaller private groups, and interact only with other known peers. On the other hand, the instant messaging translator service is a convenient service because a peer does not have the inherent need to translate messages between AIM and MSN.

All of the services that could be created will allow peer-to-peer applications to be written more quickly and, more important, allow the sharing of code the likes of which haven't been seen. In fact, the entire Microsoft .NET system is based on the concept of having services available so they don't have to be reinvented by every company that needs them.

The Application Layer

The *application layer* is where you come into the picture as the developer of peer-to-peer applications that will be used by others in the Internet community. The application layer hosts code that pulls individual peers together for a common piece of functionality—for instance, to perform the computational modeling of a new virus or to decipher an encrypted code.

One of the important points to remember is that the line between the layers in the architecture is not rigid. If you develop a peer that provides functionality, one peer might see your peer's functionality as a service that fits into a niche needed by the peer, but another might see it as a complete application without pulling in other pieces. For the JXTA specification and related bindings to be successful, developers need to fill out the application layer.

Major JXTA Technologies

This section is an overview of the major technologies and concepts used in JXTA. We discuss these technologies in greater depth throughout the remainder of the book.

IDs

As you would expect in a peer-to-peer system, the resources of the system have to be referenced in some manner. A simple name isn't enough because resources could have identical names. There could easily be two peer groups called "Home Office" or 1,000 files named me.jpg. JXTA solves this problem with a JXTA ID, also referred to as a URN, which is a unique string used for the identification of six types of resources:

- Peers
- Peer groups
- Pipes
- Content
- Module classes
- Module specifications

String Format

The JXTA ID consists of three parts. It is important to note that the URN and JXTA portions of the ID are *not* case-sensitive, but the data portion of the ID *is* case-sensitive.

- Namespace identifier—jxta
- Format specifier—urn
- ID—unique value

The entire ID can be specified by using the following Augmented Backus-Naur Form shown in Listing 2.1.

```
<JXTAURN>     ::= "urn:" <JXTANS> ":" <JXTAIDVAL>

<JXTANS>      ::= "jxta"

<JXTAIDVAL>   ::= <JXTAFMT> "-" <JXTAIDUNIQ>
```

Listing 2.1 The JXTA URN specification. (continues)

```
<JXTAFMT>    ::= 1 * <URN chars>

<JXTAIDUNIQ> ::= 1 * <URN chars>

<URN chars>  ::= <trans> | "%" <hex> <hex>

<trans>      ::= <upper> | <lower> | <number> | <other> |
                 <reserved>

<upper>      ::= "A" | "B" | "C" | "D" | "E" | "F" | "G" | "H" |
                 "I" | "J" | "K" | "L" | "M" | "N" | "O" | "P" |
                 "Q" | "R" | "S" | "T" | "U" | "V" | "W" | "X" |
                 "Y" | "Z"

<lower>      ::= "a" | "b" | "c" | "d" | "e" | "f" | "g" | "h" |
                 "i" | "j" | "k" | "l" | "m" | "n" | "o" | "p" |
                 "q" | "r" | "s" | "t" | "u" | "v" | "w" | "x" |
                 "y" | "z"

<hex>        ::= <number> | "A" | "B" | "C" | "D" | "E" | "F" |
                 "a" | "b" | "c" | "d" | "e" | "f"

<number>     ::= "0" | "1" | "2" | "3" | "4" | "5" | "6" | "7" |
                 "8" | "9"

<other>      ::= "(" | ")" | "+" | "," | "-" | "." |
                 ":" | "=" | "@" | ";" | "$" |
                 "_" | "!" | "*" | "'"

<reserved>   ::= "%" | "/" | "?" | "#"
```

Listing 2.1 The JXTA URN specification. (continued)

Examples

The peer IDs in Figure 2.3 are valid JXTA IDs, created and displayed using the program in Listing 2.2. This program will come in handy later when we create advertisements to publish new resources and services.

```
Creator                                                                    _ □ ×
PeerGroupID is: urn:jxta:uuid-22A4394EDA7E41EE9AFA86378795B37902
PeerID is: urn:jxta:uuid-22A4394EDA7E41EE9AFA86378795B379DA9EDFBB119742E4990FA4F1BAC463E203
CodatID is: urn:jxta:uuid-22A4394EDA7E41EE9AFA86378795B3795B1D12F51FD0438883EA9732750EA9D201
ModuleClassID is: urn:jxta:uuid-ACF3B5EFCFFB47A0AA1F80184C78ADEE05
ModuleSpecID is: urn:jxta:uuid-ACF3B5EFCFFB47A0AA1F80184C78ADEE82BC6A7CE09E47C29BD68B9C822A236706
PipeID is: urn:jxta:uuid-22A4394EDA7E41EE9AFA86378795B379861288FC722B427EA5E19F22FCEC594204
```

Figure 2.3 Sample peer IDs.

```java
import java.io.*;
import java.awt.*;
import java.awt.event.*;
import javax.swing.*;

import net.jxta.document.*;
import net.jxta.peergroup.*;
import net.jxta.exception.*;
import net.jxta.impl.peergroup.*;
import net.jxta.id.*;
import net.jxta.discovery.*;
import net.jxta.pipe.*;
import net.jxta.protocol.*;
import net.jxta.platform.*;
import net.jxta.endpoint.*;
import net.jxta.peer.*;
import net.jxta.codat.*;

public class PeerGroupIDCreator extends JFrame {

    private JTextArea displayArea;

    public static void main(String args[]) {
        PeerGroupIDCreator myapp = new PeerGroupIDCreator();

        myapp.addWindowListener (
          new WindowAdapter() {
            public void windowClosing(WindowEvent e) {
              System.exit(0);
            }
          }
        );

        myapp.run();
    }

    public PeerGroupIDCreator() {
      super("Creator");

      Container c = getContentPane();

      displayArea = new JTextArea();
      c.add (new JScrollPane(displayArea), BorderLayout.CENTER);

      setSize(300,150);
      show();
```

Listing 2.2 The code for generating IDs. (continues)

```
    PeerGroupID myNewPeerGroupID = (PeerGroupID)
      net.jxta.id.IDFactory.newPeerGroupID();
    displayArea.append("PeerGroupID is: " + myNewPeerGroupID +
      "\n");

    PeerID myNewPeerID = (PeerID)
      net.jxta.id.IDFactory.newPeerID(myNewPeerGroupID);
    displayArea.append("PeerID is: " + myNewPeerID + "\n");

    CodatID myCodatID = (CodatID)
      net.jxta.id.IDFactory.newCodatID(myNewPeerGroupID);
    displayArea.append("CodatID is: " + myCodatID + "\n");

    ModuleClassID myModuleClassID = (ModuleClassID)
      net.jxta.id.IDFactory.newModuleClassID();
    displayArea.append("ModuleClassID is: " + myModuleClassID
      + "\n");

    ModuleSpecID myModuleSpecID = (ModuleSpecID)
      net.jxta.id.IDFactory.newModuleSpecID(myModuleClassID);
    displayArea.append("ModuleSpecID is: " + myModuleSpecID +
      "\n");

    PipeID myNewPipeID = (PipeID)
      net.jxta.id.IDFactory.newPipeID(myNewPeerGroupID);
    displayArea.append("PipeID is: " + myNewPipeID + "\n");
  }

  public void run() {
  }
}
```

Listing 2.2   The code for generating IDs. (continued)

Specific IDs

The IDs for peers, peer groups, pipes, and content are fairly self-explanatory, but the Module Class ID and Module Spec ID deserve a little more detail. Both of these IDs deal with a JXTA technology called a *module*. We discuss modules in detail later in the chapter, so for now, consider a module to be an implementation of some named functionality.

Typically, functionality is based on a specification that describes and/or names the desired features. JXTA has a method of publishing a specification to a peer group, which must contain an ID called the Module Spec ID. No code—only a specification—is involved here. When a developer creates an implementation based on the specification, that implementation is advertised with a Module Impl ID. The container used for the advertisement of the implementation will also contain the Module Spec ID of the specification being implemented. If several implementations of the same specification exist, all of the implementation containers will have different Module Impl IDs but the same Module Spec ID.

Well-Known IDs

There are three reserved IDs in the JXTA specification:

- NULL ID
- World Peer Group ID
- Net Peer Group ID

The ABNF for these IDs is:

```
<JXTAJXTAURN>       ::= "urn:" <JXTANS> ":" <JXTAJXTAFMT> "-"
                        <JXTAJXTAFMTID>

<JXTAJXTAFMT>       ::= "jxta"

<JXTAJXTAFMTID>     ::= <JXTANULL> | <JXTAWORLDGROUP> | <JXTANETGROUP>

<JXTANULL>          ::= "Null"

<JXTAWORLDGROUP> ::= "WorldGroup"

<JXTANETGROUP>      ::= "NetGroup"
```

Java Binding for IDs

Our previous discussions have focused on how the specification defines IDs. The Java binding builds an ID based on a Universal Unique Identifier (UUID), which is a 128-bit hexadecimal number that functions as a unique identifier for each object. The last two hex characters of the ID define the type of ID being encoded. The current values can be seen in the ABNF for the Java binding of IDs:

```
<JXTAUUIDURN>       ::= "urn:" <JXTANS> ":" <JXTAUUIDFMT> "-"
                        <(1*(<hex> <hex>)) <JXTAUUIDIDTYPE>

<JXTAUUIDFMT>       ::= "uuid"

<JXTAUUIDIDTYPE> ::= <CODATID> | <PEERGROUPID> | <PEERID> |
                        <PIPEID> | <MODULECLASSID> | <MODULESPECID>

<CODATID>           ::= "01"

<PEERGROUPID>       ::= "02"
```

```
<PEERID>          ::= "03"

<PIPEID>          ::= "04"

<MODULECLASSID>   ::= "05"

<MODULESPECID>    ::= "06"
```

The Peer

The most common and widely understood component of any P2P system is the peer. A *peer* is simply an application, executing on a computer device, that has the ability to communicate with other peers. For the entire system to work, it is fundamental that the peer have the ability to communicate with other peers. Obviously, with this definition, a wide variety of applications can be considered P2P.

One computer system might be host to any number of peers. In fact, if you consider the systems presented in the first chapter, your own computer might be using its extra CPU cycles for distributed.net while at the "same time" performing a query on the Gnutella network. Shortly, you will be developing JXTA peers. All of the peers will be executing on the same computer, but each will interact in different P2P systems.

In the client-server paradigm, clients contact a central server that stores data and delivers services. In peer-to-peer systems, all peers can be clients, servers, or both. In file-sharing P2P systems, many peers in the network share their own files while at the same time pulling new files from distant peers. A single peer can function both as a "client" (to request information from other peers) and as a "server" (to answer requests from other peers).

As you begin to dig deeper into the definition of a peer, you will discover other characteristics, including

Peer identity—A peer needs to be known.

Peer membership—A single peer isn't much use.

Peer transport—Peers must communicate to survive.

For the purposes of JXTA, a peer "is any networked device . . . that implements the core JXTA protocols." This is the definition in the specification, but you should note that a single "networked device" can have any number of JXTA peers executing on it. The peers could all be implementing different service code or participating in a computational complex algorithm. By using the term *networked device*, the creators of JXTA are also stating that peers are not limited to computers that sit on a desk but also extend from mainframes to the smallest PDAs and devices that we might not normally think of as "computers."

Some of the other capabilities and features of JXTA peers include

A JXTA peer could volunteer to implement a module specification and lend its host computer to some task. In JXTA, any peer can implement a specification regardless of the binding used by the peer. All of the peers that implement the same specification are interchangeable and transparent to the peer using the peer's service.

Peers can—but are not required to—share content within a peer group.

Peers have the ability to discover other peers and content using all of the network transport protocols implemented by the specification binding; however, the peer will use the defined JXTA message format for all communications.

Peers are not required to remain on the JXTA network for any known period. A peer that is using the services of another peer cannot be guaranteed that a peer will remain on the network until its services are no longer needed.

Peers are not required to have direct communication or live directly on the Internet. Peers may use the services of a routing or rendezvous peer for communicating on the network.

Peer Groups

If several peers get together to share files or work on a large, computationally intensive problem, they have formed a *group*. The formation of a group is usually attributed to several things:

- Membership to a shared system using a username/password
- Common transport
- Access to a centralized server

In the first case, the group is formed when peers log into a group with a predetermined username/password or one picked by the peer itself. In some cases, the group is defined by one of the peers publishing the information necessary to join. If the peer publishes its own username/password, the group would be considered private because not all peers would potentially know about the group.

In the second case, the transport system used to connect peers and exchange information can produce a group in itself. Take, for example, Napster and Gnutella; these two systems are unable to communicate between themselves because the network transport is different and the format of the messages exchanged between peers is unique. The potential to create an even larger group of peers is lost because the individual peers don't know how to communicate with each other. We have seen this in the instant messaging world as well; AOL, Microsoft, and Yahoo! all have proprietary systems, and if you want to communicate with someone on each system, you must have three individual clients.

Finally, a group is formed when all of the peers are required to log into a centralized server in order to be a part of the group. Although the log will require a username and password, the group hasn't been set up by an individual peer but by the network itself.

Joining a group can provide many benefits that a single peer would have to implement itself. The group will have features—commonly called services—which each peer can take advantage of. The JXTA network has one umbrella peer group called the WorldPeerGroup. Because the WorldPeerGroup is the default group that all new peers automatically join on the JXTA network, a JXTA peer has a number of services immediately available to it, including discovery, advertisements, and pipes, among others. The current implementation includes code for creating and joining new peer groups in a public and private format. The public peer group doesn't require a username or password, but a private one does. Any peer can create either type of peer group for whatever purpose it desires.

You might think there is a common peer group server on the network somewhere. There really isn't, because the Java realization of the JXTA specification has all of the default peer group functionality built in. This means that one or more peers can be launched in a network completely cut off from the Internet and still function. The default peer group exists by name, and its functionality is contained within all peers by default.

Peer groups have a number of services, which have been defined as a core set by the specification. Those services listed in the current specification are

Discovery Service—Allows searching for peer group content.

Membership Service—Allows the creation of a secure peer group.

Access Service—Permits validation of a peer.

Pipe Service—Allows creation and use of pipes.

Resolver Service—Allows queries and responses for peer services.

Monitoring Service—Enables peers to monitor other peers and groups.

Peer groups have the option of creating and implementing additional services as desired.

Advertisements

When peers and peer groups have services that they want to make known to the P2P network, they use an advertisement. An *advertisement* is an XML-based document that describes JXTA resource and content. All of the protocols use advertisements to pass information. An example of a pipe advertisement is:

```
<?xml version="1.0" encoding="UTF-8"?>
<jxta:PipeAdvertisement>
    <Name>JXTA-CH20EX1</Name>
    <Id>urn:jxta:uuid-
9CCCDF5AD8154D3D87A391210404E59BE4B888209A2241A4A162A10916074A9504</Id>
    <Type>JxtaUnicast</Type>
</jxta:PipeAdvertisement>
```

All advertisements are hierarchical in nature and will contain elements specific to the advertisement type. Of particular importance is the ID of the resource, which will be used to identify the resource being advertised.

Modules

Peer groups provide the basic functionality needed for a P2P system, but at some point you will want to create additional features or services usable by all peers. You might want to expand on the base JXTA specification and provide better, stronger, faster resources; or you may need to provide new services, such as a distributed storage system. A module is one of the ways the functionality can be provided. A *module* is simply a piece of functionality designed to be "downloaded" or obtained outside the core JXTA implementation. In most cases, a P2P group will advertise a specification that tells about the functionality needed. The specification will be propagated through the JXTA network. A peer can discover the specification and want to use the new functionality.

This might sound a little strange, considering the fact that we are talking about software, but imagine for a moment that a peer that has some task to perform. A developer could write code to perform the task directly in the peer, yet also use services provided in the JXTA network. The situation could evolve like this: The peer begins execution by first requesting data from all peers. The peer has been programmed to execute some functionality on the incoming data, yet the functionality as written in the peer is expensive. Therefore, it performs a key-word search within the network to find if any peers have implemented the desired functionality. If a module is found within the network that handles that functionality, the peer could be programmed to use the less "expensive" functionality. Granted, a fairly large and sophisticated network would be needed for this type of scenario, but it isn't beyond reason.

The specification doesn't actually provide the functionality; it only supplies the information about it. Another peer and its associated human developer can build a service using the specification and publish an implementation advertisement. The *implementation advertisement* tells the network that a service is available at a specific peer that implements the functionality described in the specification. One of the goals of a P2P system is that multiple peers can have implementations of the same specification. The implementations could be in different languages, yet still provide the same service. This specification/implementation paradigm allows for redundancy of services so that functionality is still available in the network when peers are overloaded or unavailable. We cover modules in detail in Chapter 12, where we will build a specification and its implementations.

Transport Mechanisms and Pipes

When a peer wants to communicate with other peers, it must use some sort of network transport. The *network transport* is the protocol used to send information over the wires connecting all the peers. In all cases, the peers will be connected to a computer network. The network itself will likely be an Ethernet system. Ethernet, a protocol that dictates how information is passed from one network card to another, is really the barebones network transport. However, because of the housekeeping involved, another protocol was created, called the Transmission Control Protocol (TCP). The job of TCP is to manage the Ethernet packets of information being sent from one machine to another. On top of TCP is the Internet Protocol (IP). IP is primarily concerned with routing, and describes the steps necessary to route packages across the Internet from one machine to another. When you activate a peer call FTP, it is using TCP/IP to transfer data from one machine to another.

It is fair to say that all P2P systems use TCP/IP as a network transport because all of them allow peers to exist on the Internet. Without TCP/IP, Internet traffic isn't possible, so these protocols must exist. Now, with that out of the way, let's look at networks more closely to see how many of the various P2P systems are able to operate.

For communication to occur using TCP/IP from a computer application, a set of sockets is used. The socket on the transmitting computer binds to a socket on the receiving computer using a port. There are many common ports on a computer, including 20/21 (for FTP), 80 for (HTTP), and others. The ports below 1024 are generally reserved for system use, and those above 1024 can be used by any application. So, when a peer wants to communicate with another peer, it will ultimately create a socket connection to the remote peer. A port will be specified in the connection process and communication will begin.

For simplicity's sake, we will say that the information passed between the machines is sent in a message. The message will contain information about the sender and receiver, as well as the data to be transmitted. Don't confuse this high-level message with the low-level packets TCP/IP and Ethernet are handling to make network communication possible.

With this background knowledge, we can discuss the two primary network transport differences between all P2P systems. Basically, these two differences keep peers belonging to different systems from communicating with each other. The differences are

- The high-level network protocol
- The message format

The High-Level Network Protocol

Given the fact that all communication will occur using TCP/IP, what do some systems do above and beyond that? The answer is HTTP and security. HTTP is a protocol, much like FTP or other Internet protocols, that defines how information should be passed from one machine to another, and specifies which port should be used for the communication. HTTP is the protocol used by the World Wide Web over port 80. All common web servers bind to port 80 on the machine they are executing. TCP/IP traffic, which arrives at port 80, will be consumed by the web server, and the information in the traffic will be parsed using the HTTP protocol. Because HTTP is built on top of TCP/IP, the information will also include the IP address of the machine that originated the transfer; this allows the web server to send a response back to the originator.

If a P2P system uses the HTTP protocol for sending information between peers, then to all of the machines in the route from peer 1 to peer 2, the message will look like a request from a browser to a web server. This is important to those peers who are behind firewalls because firewalls will generally reduce the number of ports open between the outside and inside networks, but they allow HTTP port 80. This is the primary reason for using HTTP as a network protocol on top of TCP/IP (we will discuss this in detail later).

If a system doesn't use HTTP, but simply relies on TCP/IP, it can choose from any number of ports to send data to a remote peer. Whether the peers use HTTP or not, the format of the message is also important.

The Message Format

The HTTP protocol dictates a specific format for requesting information from a web server as well as sending the response back to the browser; however, our peers aren't web servers and browsers (but they probably could be if we wanted because there is nothing within the JXTA specification to prohibit a peer implementing the functionality necessary for either a Web server or a browser). When a P2P system uses HTTP or just TCP/IP for information transfer, a predefined message format will be used. Napster does, Gnutella does, AIM does, and so does JXTA. The sending peer is responsible for putting its information into the correct format so that the receiving peer will be able to find the information easily.

The primary reason all of the numerous peers in use today cannot communicate with one another is the message format. If you want your AIM Instant Messaging application to "see" Yahoo! peers, it will need to know the message format to talk with Yahoo!'s central server and with the individual peers. Wouldn't the industry be revolutionized if a specification were created that had a common message format?

Pipes

The JXTA specification takes the concept of using a *pipe* as its communication mechanism from the Unix operating system and its shell. Information is put in one end of the pipe, and it comes out at the other end. Through the pipes, messages can be sent between peers without having to know anything about the underlying infrastructure. As long as a pipe is involved, peers don't need to worry about the network topology or where a peer is located on the network in order to send messages. Pipes use the concept of an *endpoint* to indicate the input and output points of communication; a *channel* is the connection between the endpoints.

The Java implementation of the specification has three pipe types:

Unicast—One-way, not secure, and unreliable

Unicast secure—One-way, secure, and unreliable

Propagating—Propagating pipe, not secure, and unreliable

The unicast pipes connect one peer to another for one-way communication. The propagating pipe connects an output pipe to multiple input pipes. We will cover pipes in detail in Chapter 13.

Services

By far, one of the most hyped concepts in recent months is the service. The concept of services in JXTA goes above and beyond the simple web service and extends to functionality that needs to exist in a decentralized network. Password verification and authentication, purchasing systems, and money handlers are just a few of the services needed. Because there are two primary entities in a P2P system—the peer and the peer group—both should be expected to have services available for all to use.

Peer Group Services

Depending on the implementation of the system, peer groups might have services available that peers can take advantage of. Some of the more common services include group startup, discovery, and membership. When a new peer group is put into existence, there are usually a number of startup activities that have to take place in order to let other peer groups know about the new group. Once the new peer group has been established, peers should have the ability to not only find the peer group, but also find other peers within the group. Discovery is paramount to any P2P system, and we will discuss this issue in detail shortly. When a peer finds a new group that it would like to belong to, the peer group should have a membership service available.

Within a JXTA peer group, a number of high-level or core services are available. These services include the ability to propagate advertisements throughout the network, creation of pipes, and discovery.

Peer Services

In most cases, the primary service that an individual peer will make available is the sharing of content. A peer will let the group know what types of content it has available for sharing. The peer will also use the services of the group to find content it is interested in. Specialized peers can be created to provide services that aren't supplied by the group. For example, a peer could be created to serve as an intermediary between a customer and a store for the purpose of credit card validation. Customers would provide their credit card to a secure peer, and the store could provide the order. Customers wouldn't have to give their credit card information to the store directly, and the store wouldn't have to worry about stolen cards because the intermediary peer would handle all the details. Customers would get their merchandise, and the store would get paid.

All JXTA peers have the ability to share content with other peers. The content is published using a peer group service, and a peer can query for content using a discovery service. When a JXTA peer wants to provide direct paths of communication, it will advertise the existence of a pipe service. Other peers can find the pipe and communicate one-on-one as needed.

Discovery

Discovery is the process of one peer searching for another peer—in the same peer group—that contains the desired content. In the example about the customer, store, and clearinghouse peers, we have a situation that illustrates the importance of discovery. Suppose a retail store creates a peer on a local P2P network to sell encrypted data storage. Also on the network is a peer that needs encrypted storage. These two peers must be able to discover each other's existence before they can exchange content. The content can be an image, a text file, or any other type of media available for sharing. In addition, peers will want to be able to locate services created using the modules described earlier. There are three basic discovery arenas:

- Local
- Direct
- Propagated

Local

Wouldn't it be great if all a peer had to do was open the yellow pages and instantly be able to find the service or content it needs? JXTA peers have a sort of yellow pages functionality available through the use of a *local cache* of advertisements. The first time a peer is executed, the local cache is generally empty, though you can seed a peer's cache with information about other known peers. When a peer initiates a search, it checks its own cache first, as shown in step 1 of Figure 2.4. If the search comes up positive from the cache, that peer has the option of connecting to the peer listed in its cache. If the necessary information isn't found in the local cache, a remote discovery will be attempted, as shown in steps 2 and 3 of the illustration. As a peer performs searches and discovers new advertisements, it will populate its cache with this information.

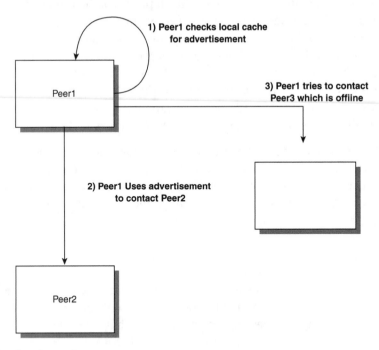

Figure 2.4 A local cache and peer contact.

There are times when a peer's own local cache is the only place it can search for content—for example, when the peer doesn't have direct access to an outside network or the Internet, or in the event of a failure of a remote site that has the ability to search for content. In these situations, the peer cannot use any of the other types of discovery.

Many peers will have a local cache, whether they are directly attached to the Internet or not. The cache has the obvious advantage of enabling quick searches for content. However, the local peer cannot be 100 percent confident of the status of the peer found in the local cache. The remote peer might not be available, or the peer may no longer have the information found in the search (some peers rotate their content). In either case, the local peer will have to resort to a more expansive discovery.

If a peer has a local cache and is not directly connected to the Internet, you will need to seed its cache initially with information about peers with services or content available. Obviously, the seeded information could become quickly out-of-date and increasingly worthless.

To solve the problem of a stale cache, you can associate a time-to-live parameter with the cached information. When the time-to-live value expires, the entity is removed from the cache and destroyed. It is hoped that the peer will have the ability to reseed its cache at some point.

Direct

When a peer exists on a network with other peers, the discovery process gets a little easier. Using a number of different methods, the peer will contact each of the peers on its network, and discover what services or content they have available. Fortunately, TCP/IP has a protocol for just this type of discovery—*broadcast* or *multicast*. A peer can send out a discovery request along with search criteria in a broadcast message. All of the peers on the local network will receive the message and respond appropriately. Figure 2.5 shows an example of a direct discovery.

For obvious reasons, the multicast protocol works only on your local subnet and is not allowed to traverse routers to the Internet. For discovery outside the local network, another method must exist. The JXTA specification allows direct discovery using the multicast or broadcast feature of the TCP/IP network protocol. For the most part, though, direct and indirect discovery processes (which we will explain next) will occur at the same time if both the TCP and HTTP protocols are utilized under JXTA.

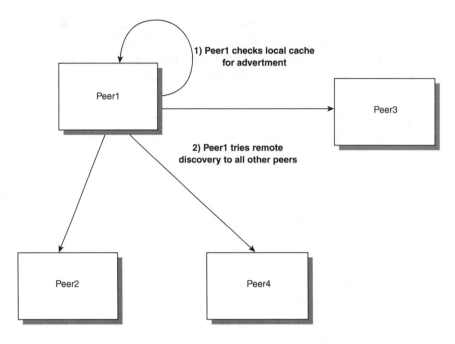

Figure 2.5 The direct discovery of services.

Propagated

Discovering peers outside your local network requires the use of a *rendezvous* peer. The rendezvous peer serves primarily as a place where a peer can go to find other peers. The rendezvous peer will cache all of the peers it comes in contact with over the course of time. It can also be used as an intermediary for discovery operations.

A peer can contact a rendezvous peer and request that it perform a search. This capability is a big advantage for those peers on a local network that have the ability to get outside the network; they can use the rendezvous peer to perform discovery outside the network. Figure 2.6 shows an example of using the rendezvous peer for discovery.

If there are a number of rendezvous peers on the network, a large discovery can take place in a short amount of time; each of the rendezvous peers will forward discovery requests to one another as well as other peers. Those peers will send the discovery request to other peers and probably even rendezvous peers. But what happens if one peer gets a discovery request it has already seen and forwards it to other peers who have already seen it, and so on? The answer again is a time-to-live parameter. When a peer receives a discovery request, it can decrement the parameter. When the parameter gets to zero, the request is thrown out. This keeps a discovery request from living in the network forever.

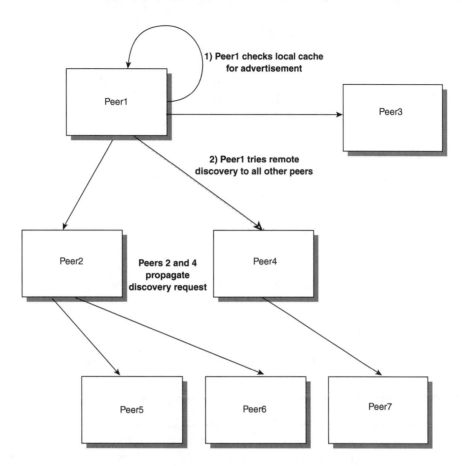

Figure 2.6 A propagation discovery request.

But what about the case where a peer has already seen a request? By keeping a list within the discovery-request message of peers that have already seen the request, a peer can easily check and discard a message it has already seen. This allows a request to exist in the network efficiently.

The JXTA specification has defined a number of protocols that are combined to allow discovery requests to be propagated to any of the peers on the JXTA network. Individual peers will obtain a discovery, check their own advertisements, and send the query request to all the peers it knows about. Special rendezvous peers can be used that know about many more peers than individual peers know about. Rendezvous peers will contact other rendezvous peers, and in short order, a query will have propagated throughout a JXTA peer group. You should note that queries are specific to the group to which a peer currently belongs.

Handling Private Networks

As mentioned before, not all applications execute on machines that are directly connected to the Internet. A P2P system that wants to take into consideration the many peers existing on a private network will need to handle two situations: firewalls and NATs.

Firewalls

The job of a *firewall* is to restrict the TCP/IP traffic coming from the Internet into a private network, and many times also restrict the traffic going from the private network to the Internet. A network administrator will "lock down" all of the ports TCP/IP traffic could use to send data. When required services such as e-mail and possibly the web server need to be allowed access through the firewall, those specific ports will be opened for traffic. Ports can also be opened that allow traffic to go from the private network to the Internet, but not the reverse.

Firewalls are often the reason applications such as streaming media players don't work within a private network. The ports used to transfer the data are typically locked down. The same thing can occur with peers in a P2P system; the ports needed for communication are locked.

One of the ways system designers have gotten around this situation is by using the HTTP protocol to send data through the same port a browser would use to send a request to a web server. Because the port is already open, the firewall doesn't know the data isn't destined for a web server, but instead a P2P network. The remote peer is able to respond to the peer behind the firewall using a response protocol defined in the HTTP protocol. The firewall allows the response to go through the wall to the appropriate peer. In this type of situation, peers outside the firewall will not be able to find the internal peer.

A relay peer solves this problem by becoming a bridge between the internal peers and the peers on the Internet. When a peer on the Internet wants to send a message to the internal peer, it will contact the relay peer with the message. The peer will hold onto the message until the internal peer sends a request to the relay peer. Now that the relay peer has the ability to send a response to the internal peer, it will put in the message from the Internet peer. When the internal peer gets the message, it has the ability to send messages directly to the Internet peer because it now has an address for it. Some systems do not allow this direct connection and still require the internal peer to communicate with Internet peers using the router.

NATs

A NAT isn't a small insect but a TLA (three-letter acronym) for *Network Address Translation*. All computers on an internal network need IP addresses in order to communicate on the corporate network as well as on the Internet. However, getting an IP address can be expensive over time, and not all internal computers need to have a "real" IP address. The Internet protocols keep a number of IP addresses out of circulation for use in internal networks. These addresses are in the IP groups 10.x.x.x, 192.168.x.x, and 172.16.x.x. The address can be assigned to any computer on an internal network that doesn't have direct access to the Internet. Typically, these computers will be behind a router that prohibits the internal computer from accessing the Internet. While this is all good for the internal network and the pocketbook, it doesn't help the internal computers get to the Internet.

The NAT process allows the router to translate the internal addresses to a real IP address. The router will be assigned a real IP address, which will be used to communicate with the outside Internet. When an internal machine requests access to the Internet, its request will be wrapped by the router and the router's IP address will be used in place of the internal address. When a response from a request arrives at the router, it will check for the wrapper and the response will be forwarded to the internal computer.

This could pose something of a problem for the peer on the internal network, especially when a firewall is in place as well. But the situation isn't all bad. All of the work is done by the router performing the NAT; the peer system doesn't need to do anything. The internal peer must communicate with the P2P system just as if a firewall were in place by using the router and rendezvous peers for discovery requests and pulling information from Internet peers.

The JXTA specification allows for peers to be located behind firewalls by incorporating the use of the HTTP protocol and enabling communication to occur over all ports defined for a system. If communication needs to occur over port 80, only a small change is needed to a peer's configuration. Peers can also have IP addresses through Network Address Translation without any problem. *Gateway peers* allow access to the JXTA network from a peer located on an internal network. The gateway peer is responsible for delivering advertisements from the internally bound peer to the outside network.

Summary

With the major component of a P2P system and a review of the JXTA specification behind us, we are ready to investigate some of the major applications built using JXTA. The next chapter will show how to use the JXTA Shell and provide many examples of using its built-in commands.

CHAPTER 3

JXTA Shell

One of the goals of the JXTA team was to create tools that would have a familiar feel to developers. To partially achieve this goal, the team created the JXTA shell, an interactive application that provides direct access to the JXTA network in much the same way that a Unix shell provides direct access to the operating system. Through a series of commands, the shell enables you to interact with the network and provide information about it. As with the Unix shell, commands are loaded when executed, and the shell can be extended. In this chapter, we take an in-depth look at how to use the JXTA shell.

Executing the Shell

You can execute the shell in one of two ways. If you installed JXTA on a Windows system using the instructions in Appendix A, the shell will have an icon under the Start menu. In addition, for both Windows and Unix, you can find the shell in a directory called Shell. There will be either a BAT or a SH script file for starting the shell application. Once started, the shell will display a configuration screen. See Appendix A for instructions on filling out this screen.

After you've entered the correct information, the shell application window will appear, as shown in Figure 3.1 (this could take as long as 60–120 seconds).

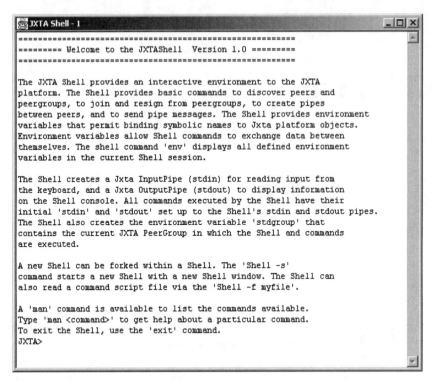

Figure 3.1 JXTA shell's main window.

The shell application begins with an explanation of what the application is all about. At the end of the text is the shell command prompt, JXTA>, which indicates that the user can now enter a command. In the rest of this chapter, we will run through the various commands available in the shell.

Shell Commands

In both the Windows Command Prompt window and a Unix shell, you can use a number of built-in commands to perform some simple operations. The JXTA shell leans toward the Unix side of things, which features a mix of both simple and complex commands. The following section lists the commands available in the current implementation of the JXTA shell. Each of the commands is presented with its available options, as well as some sample output where appropriate.

Shell

The Shell command is used to create a new shell from the command prompt of another shell. A new shell lets us perform an operation without disrupting the

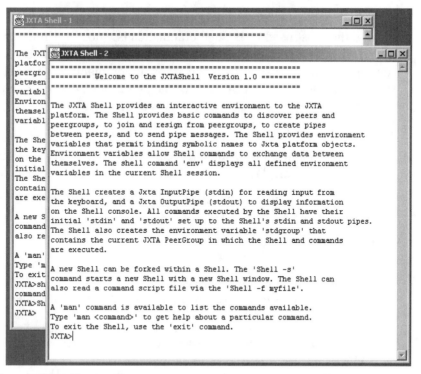

Figure 3.2 One shell invoking another.

current commands in the original shell. The format of the command is

```
Shell [-f filename] [-s]
```

The –f option allows a Shell command to execute commands from a file you specify. The –s option indicates the new shell should fork a new window and environment. The –s option is appended to the Shell command to force a new shell window to appear. The –f option is used to both create a new shell and execute commands. For example, the command Shell –f batch will execute the commands within a file called batch, located in the same directory in which the shell was first started

Figure 3.2 shows what happens when one shell invokes another using the command

```
Shell —s
```

The shell is case-sensitive, so be sure to enter *Shell –s* instead of *shell –s*.

If you want specific commands to be executed each time the shell is initiated, you can place them in a file called $HOME/.jshrccan. These commands will be executed once the shell is completely set up, but before a command prompt is provided.

whoami

One of the most-used Unix shell commands is whoami. Under Unix, this command will display a string giving the name of the user currently logged into the machine. The JXTA shell uses the whoami command to show either the peer advertisement of the current user, or the peergroup advertisement of the group currently logged into. The format of the command is:

```
whoami [-g][-l]
```

The –g option is used to display the current peer group advertisement. The –l option is used to display the entire peer or peer group advertisement.

By default, the command only displays consolidated information. The output of the command when using no options is:

```
JXTA>whoami
<Peer>JosephGradecki</Peer>
<PeerId>urn:jxta:uuid-9616261646162614A787461503250339
1329E2072D241499211AE2F2CB657BC03</PeerId>
<TransportAddress>tcp://12.254.21.182:9701/</TransportAddress>
<TransportAddress>jxtatls://uuid-
9616261646162614A7874615032503391329E2072D241499211AE2
F2CB657BC03/TlsTransport/jxta-WorldGroup</TransportAddress>
<TransportAddress>jxta://uuid-
9616261646162614A7874615032503391329E2072D241499211AE2
F2CB657BC03/</TransportAddress>
<TransportAddress>http://JxtaHttpClientuuid-
9616261646162614A7874615032503391329E2072D241499211AE2
F2CB657BC03/</TransportAddress>
JXTA>
```

The command will show only the important information about the peer, including its ID, name, and the input/output connections available on the peer. The output of the command using the –g option is:

```
JXTA>whoami -g
<PeerGroup>NetPeerGroup</PeerGroup>
<Description>NetPeerGroup by default</Description>
<PeerGroupId>urn:jxta:jxta-NetGroup</PeerGroupId>
JXTA>
```

The output of the command using the –l option is:

```
JXTA>whoami -l
jxta:PGA :
      GID : urn:jxta:jxta-NetGroup
      MSID : urn:jxta:uuid-DEADBEEFDEAFBABAFEEDBABE000000010206
      Name : NetPeerGroup
      Desc : NetPeerGroup by default
JXTA>
```

env

The env command displays all of the current environment variables and their associated values. Environment variables are created from the output of a JXTA shell command, and will be illustrated in later sections. The command does not have any parameters and will display a listing like this:

```
JXTA>env
stdout = Default OutputPipe (class
net.jxta.impl.shell.ShellOutputPipe)
SHELL = Root Shell (class net.jxta.impl.shell.bin.Shell.Shell)
consout = Default Console OutputPipe (class
net.jxta.impl.shell.ShellOutputPipe)
History = History (class
net.jxta.impl.shell.bin.history.HistoryQueue)
stdgroup = Default Group (class
net.jxta.impl.peergroup.ShadowPeerGroup)
stdin = Default InputPipe (class
net.jxta.impl.shell.ShellInputPipe)
consin = Default Console InputPipe (class
net.jxta.impl.shell.ShellInputPipe)
Shell = Root Shell (class net.jxta.impl.shell.bin.Shell.Shell)
JXTA>
```

peers

The shell can be used to find or discover other peers in the current peer group. The format of the peers command is:

```
peers [-r][-p peername][-n limit][-a tagname][-v tagvalue] [-f]
```

The simplest version of the command is to execute

```
peers
```

This command will display all of the peers in the local cache of the peer. For example:

```
JXTA>peers
peer0: name = Florin
peer1: name = JXTA.ORG 237
peer2: name = joe2jake
peer3: name = JosephGradecki
peer4: name = pauld
JXTA>
```

If it's been awhile since peers have been discovered with the shell, we can execute the command peers –r to send a remote discovery to the JXTA network. The *remote discovery* is a request to all peers in the network to return information about themselves. For example:

```
JXTA>peers -r
peer discovery message sent
JXTA>
```

Not what you expected? The peers –r command just sends the request to the network. To see the results of the discovery request, execute the peers command again to see if any additional peers have been found. All of the peers found will be placed in the local cache of the shell and given a number. If you are aware of a specific rendezvous peer in the network, it can be specified using the –p option, as in

```
peers -p myRendezvous
```

Here, *myRendezvous* is the name of the peer.

Many times, a discovery needs to be narrowed to find specific peers. We can use the –a option to specify an element within a peer advertisement to be used as a search name. The –v option is used to specify the value of the element used for the search. For example:

```
JXTA>peers -a name -v a*
```

This command will attempt to find peers in the network where the name element of the peer's advertisement has a value of * (where * is a wildcard).

At some point, the local cache might have stale or old peer advertisements in it. We can flush the cache by using the –f option.

Finally, we can limit the total number of peers returned from the remote discovery request by using the –n option. For example, the following command will return 10 peers from the local cache:

```
JXTA>peers -n 10
```

groups

The shell also provides a way to search for new groups in the JXTA network: the groups command. The format of this command is:

```
groups [-r][-p peername][-n limit][-a tagname][-v tagvalue] [-f]
```

Notice that the format of the command is the same as that of peers, and it works the same way. Here's an example of submitting a group search request, along with the results:

```
JXTA>groups -r -a name -v m
JXTA>groups
group0: name = MyShareGroup
group1: name = MuzzleGroup
group2: name = mdc-test
group3: name = momo
```

mkadv

As we discuss later in the book, the *advertisement* is the file tool the JXTA specification uses for configuration information. The advertisement is an XML document that is both human-readable and able to be parsed by the computer. The shell environment uses the mkadv command to build advertisements dynamically for new peer groups, or *pipes* (which are used for peer communication). The format of the mkadv command is:

```
mkadv [-g|p] [-t type] [-d doc] name
```

The –g option is used to create a new peer group. If the –d option isn't used, the peer group advertisement will be a clone of the current group. The –p option specifies that a pipe advertisement should be created. The –t option is used for pipe advertisements and specifies the type of pipe; the values are *JxtaUnicast*, *JxtaUnicastSecure*, and *JxtaPropagate*. The –d option specifies the name of a document that contains the XML advertisement in use. Finally, *name* is the name to be used for the new pipe or peer group.

Creating a Peer Group Advertisement

The mkadv command creates an advertisement object based on an advertisement XML document found on the local file system of the computer or by using a clone advertisement. Creating an advertisement for a new peer group can be done in two ways. First, we can create a new peer group advertisement based on the current peer group or the NetPeerGroup. The command is:

```
JXTA>Mynewpeergroupadv = mkadv —g myGroup
```

We can create the group by using a peer group advertisement pulled from a file using the importfile command (which we discuss later in this chapter). For example:

```
JXTA>importfile —f myDoc groupfileadv
JXTA>Mynewgroup = mkadv —g —d myDoc
```

The file with the peer group advertisement is called *groupfileadv*. The contents of the file are read into the shell variable, *myDoc*. The mkadv command builds a new peer group advertisement using the *myDoc* variable, as specified by the –d option in the command.

Creating a Pipe Advertisement

Creating a pipe can only be done using an advertisement pulled from a file on the local machine. An example of the command is:

```
JXTA>mkadv —p —t JxtaUnicast inputPipe
```

This command will build a new pipe advertisement as specified by the –p option. The –t option tells the system to use a JxtaUnicast type. The name of the pipe will be *inputPipe*. At this time, the shell does not support building a pipe advertisement.

mkpgrp

If a new peer group is needed, we can use the mkpgrp command. This command can create a new peer group by using an advertisement or by cloning the NetPeerGroup advertisement. The format of the command is:

```
mkpgrp  [-d doc] [-m policy] groupname
```

The –d option tells the command the document that contains the peer group advertisement; the document is the environment variable with the advertisement. The –m option specifies the policy to use in the new peer group, and wasn't implemented in the current shell. The *groupname* is the name to be used for the new group.

To create a new peer group that is a clone of the current peer group, we use the following command:

```
JXTA>mkpgrp myGroup
JXTA>groups
group0: name = myGroup
JXTA>
```

Notice that the new group is in the local cache of the peer. A peer group can be created with an advertisement located in a document by using this code:

```
JXTA>importfile –f myDoc groupfileadv
JXTA>mynewgroup = mkadv –g –d myDoc
JXTA>mkpgrp –d mynewgroup myGroup
```

Here, the advertisement is read from a local file and placed in an environment variable called *myDoc*. Next, a peer group advertisement object is created with the mkadv command using the document in the environment variable. Finally, the peer group is created with the group advertisement.

join

Once peer groups are discovered using the groups command, a specific group can be joined using the join command. The format of the command is:

```
join [-r] [-d doc] [-c credential] [groupname]
```

The –r option tells the new group to use the current peer as a rendezvous peer. The –d option specifies the advertisement of the peer group to join. The –c option allows a credential to be provided to the group being joined. The *groupname* is the name of the group to join. The group should be in the local cache.

A peer group can be joined by either specifying the name of the group or providing the peer group advertisement using the –d option. For example:

```
JXTA>join myGroup
Stopping rdv
Enter the identity you want to use when joining this peer
group (nobody)
lIdentity : JosephGradecki
JXTA>
```

Listing Join Status

If we want to list all groups in the local cache and learn whether or not they are joined, we can specify the join command by itself. For example:

```
JXTA>join
 Unjoined Group : myGroup
JXTA>
```

chpgrp

A peer can join as many groups as it wants, but there can be only one default group. The chpgrp command allows the default group to be changed. The format of the command is:

```
chpgrp group
```

The *group* is the name of the group to join. If the current default peer group is NetPeerGroup, it can be changed with this command:

```
JXTA>chpgrp myGroup
```

leave

Any peer group that has been joined can also be left. The format for the leave command is:

```
leave [-k]
```

The –k option tells the system to delete and remove the peer group from the JXTA network, if possible. When a peer group is left using the leave command, the default peer group is reset to be the NetPeerGroup.

search

We can use the search command to find advertisements in the JXTA network. The format of the command is:

```
search [-n limit] [-p peername] [-f] [-r] [-a] [-v]
```

The –n attribute limits the total number of advertisements found before the command returns. The –p attribute searches for advertisements at a specific peer. The –f attribute will flush the local cache of advertisements. The –r attribute will force a remote propagated search. We use the –a attribute to specify a search using an element of the advertisement. And finally, the –v attribute is used with the –a attribute for the search value.

If executed by itself, the search command will find only those advertisements in the local cache. The –a and –v options allow searching based on an element of the advertisement. A common example is searching on the name element using a pattern such as *apple*. To perform a search for *jpg* in the name element, the command would look like this:

```
Jxta>search -r -a name -v jpg
```

The shell will put all of the found advertisements in the local cache using environment variables named *adv#*. For example:

```
JXTA>search
JXTA Advertisement adv0
JXTA Advertisement adv1
JXTA Advertisement adv2
JXTA Advertisement adv3
JXTA Advertisement adv4
JXTA Advertisement adv5
JXTA Advertisement adv6
JXTA Advertisement adv7
JXTA>
```

To see the contents of an advertisement, use the cat command:

```
JXTA> cat adv0
```

mkpipe

The shell has the capability to create input and output pipes based on a given pipe advertisement. The mkadv command is used to create the pipe advertisement, and the mkpipe command is used to build the pipe. The format of the command is:

```
mkpipe -i|o pipeadv
```

The –i option creates an input pipe; the –o option creates an output pipe. The *pipeadv* is the pipe advertisement to use when creating the pipe.

The command is quite simple to use. Here's an example of building a pipe:

```
JXTA>InputPipeAdv = mkadv -p
JXTA>InputPipe = mkpipe -I InputPipeAdv
```

Once the input pipe is created, we can use the recv command to receive a message from a peer that connects to the input pipe.

mkmsg

A message is the container used to receive data from a pipe or to send data out a pipe. A message container is built using the mkmsg command, whose format is as follows:

```
mkmsg
```

If the command is used by itself from a command prompt, a new container is created and assigned an environment variable using the format *env#*. In many cases, you will create a message and provide a name with the following command:

```
JXTA>AMessage = mkmsg
```

The message is now ready for data, and can be sent to another peer or used for receiving data. The put, send, and recv commands will use the new message container.

put

We use the put command to store data in a message container. The format of the command is:

```
put msg tag document
```

The *msg* is the message container. The *tag* is the data tag used to store the data. The *document* is the data to be stored in the data tag. An example of using the command is:

```
JXTA>Amessage = mkmsg
JXTA>put Amessage "newData" "this is the data"
```

get

Once a message has been received from a pipe using the recv command, we can use the get command to extract data from the message. The format of the command is:

```
get msg tag
```

The *msg* is the message container. The *tag* is the data tag to extract the data from.

An example of using the get command is:

```
JXTA>InputPipeAdv = mkadv —p
JXTA>InputPipe = mkpipe —i InputPipeAdv
JXTA>Amessage = recv InputPipe
JXTA>Thedata = get Amessage newData
```

send

The basic format for the send command is:

```
send outputpipe msg
```

The *outputpipe* is the pipe to be used to send the message. The *msg* is the message container. An example of using the send command is:

```
JXTA>OutputPipeAdv = mkadv —p
JXTA>OutputPipe = mkpipe —o OutputPipeAdv
JXTA>Importfile —f  datafile dataDocument
JXTA>Amessage = mkmsg
JXTA>put  Amessage newData dataDocument
JXTA>send OutputPipe Amessage
```

recv

The recv command is used to accept a message from an input pipe. The format of the command is:

```
recv [-t timeout] inputpipe
```

The —t option is used to limit the amount of time the shell will wait for a message on the pipe. The *inputpipe* is the input pipe to used for reception of a message.

An example of using the recv command is:

```
JXTA>InputPipeAdv = mkadv —p
JXTA>InputPipe = mkpipe —i InputPipeAdv
JXTA>Amessage = recv InputPipe
```

man

Because the shell application is constantly changing, the man command is extremely valuable. The format of the command is:

```
man [commandname]
```

The *commandname* is the name of the command that we want to find more information about. We can list all of the current commands in the application by executing the man command by itself. In the current application, the man command produces:

```
JXTA>man
The 'man' command is the primary manual system for the JXTA Shell.
The usage of man is:

    JXTA> man <commandName>
```

```
    For instance typing
     JXTA> man Shell
             displays man page about the Shell
```

The following is the list of commands available:

```
cat         Concatane and display a Shell object
chpgrp      Change the current peer group
clear       Clear the shell's screen
env         Display environment variable
exit        Exit the Shell
exportfile  Export to an external file
get         Get data from a pipe message
grep        Search for matching patterns
groups      Discover peer groups
help        No description available for this ShellApp
history     No description available for this ShellApp
importfile  Import an external file
instjar     Installs jar-files containing additional Shell commands
join        Join a peer group
leave       Leave a peer group
man         An on-line help command that displays information about a
specific Shell command
mkadv       Make an advertisement
mkmsg       Make a pipe message
mkpgrp      Create a new peer group
mkpipe      Create a pipe
more        Page through a Shell object
peerconfig  Peer Configuration
peerinfo    Get information about peers
peers       Discover peers
put         Put data into a pipe message
rdvserver   No description available for this ShellApp
rdvstatus   Display information about rendezvous
recv        Receive a message from a pipe
search      Discover jxta advertisements
send        Send a message into a pipe
set         Set an environment variable
setenv      Set an environment variable
share       Share an advertisement
Shell       JXTA Shell command interpreter
sql         Issue an SQL command (not implemented)
sqlshell    JXTA SQL Shell command interpreter
talk        Talk to another peer
uninstjar   Uninstalls jar-files previously installed with 'instjar'
version     No description available for this ShellApp
wc          Count the number of lines, words, and chars in an object
who         Display credential information
whoami      Display information about a peer or peergroup
```

```
JXTA>
```

As you look through the commands, you'll notice that several are not implemented at this time. You can learn more information about a command by executing the man command, followed by that command's name.

importfile

Files on the current file system can be brought into the shell using the importfile command. The format of the command is:

```
importfile -f filename [env]
```

The –f option specifies the location of the file. The *filename* is the name of the file to be loaded. The *env* option is the name of the environment variable for storing the file's contents.

exportfile

The contents of an environment variable can be exported to a file using the exportfile command. The format of the command is:

```
exportfile -f filename [env]
```

The –f option specifies the location of the file. The *filename* is the name of the file to use on the file system. The *env* option is the environment variable that will be exported.

Here's an example:

```
JXTA>exportfile -f c:/shell/myFile variableToExport
```

version

We can learn the current version of the shell application by executing the version command. For example:

```
JXTA>version
jxta version 1.0 (build 41e, 12-03-2001)
JXTA>
```

clear

To clear the screen of the current shell application, execute the clear command.

exit

To terminate the shell, use the exit command. There are no options to the command, and the application will be terminated once the command is executed.

Writing New Shell Commands

As mentioned at the beginning of the chapter, the shell is extensible. New commands can be added very easily. The code in Llisting 3.1 shows a new command called tank.

```
package net.jxta.impl.shell.bin;

import net.jxta.Impl.shell.ShellEnv;
public class tank extends ShellApp {
  private ShellEnv myEnv;
  public int startApp(String []args) {
    myEnv = getEnv();

    System.out.println("tank");
    return ShellApp.appNoError;

  }
  public void stopApp() {
  }
}
```

Listing 3.1 A new shell command.

The code in Listing 3.1 should be placed in the bin directory of the shell in order for the shell application to find the new command. All new commands are required to extend ShellApp. ShellApp is a framework for new commands that includes two methods: startApp() and stopApp(). These two methods must be overridden in any new command. The startApp() method is appropriately called when the user enters a command. When the command has finished its work, it will call the stopApp() method to perform any necessary housekeeping. The primary work of the new command should be contained in the startApp() method or called from startApp().

Summary

This chapter has provided a comprehensive view of the JXTA shell application. We covered all of the commands available in the shell, as well as the process of building commands that aren't included in the shell itself. When you're developing JXTA applications, the JXTA shell can be a useful tool for finding the peer application and making sure it is executing in the network appropriately.

Using myJXTA

When the JXTA specification and Java binding were first introduced, an application called InstantP2P (later called myJXTA) was also provided to teach many of the key concepts of the specification/binding. myJXTA has the following functions:

- One-to-one chat
- Group chat
- Resource sharing
- Searching
- Document downloading

myJXTA has taken on a life of its own, and has its own project page off the main JXTA web site at http://myjxta.jxta.org/servlets/ProjectHome. This chapter discusses the features of myJXTA, and also provides pointers to the code where you can see the implementations of those features. Because the source code to the myJXTA application is available, you can study and reuse many of the common functions desirable in a peer-to-peer application.

In addition, the myJXTA application can be considered a peer within the JXTA network. As a peer, it will have a name visible to other peers in the network and share the common NetPeerGroup upon execution. Being a part of the NetPeer-Group enables the application to publish advertisements, create pipes, and exchange content.

Downloading myJXTA

The myJXTA application is installed when you download the JxtaInst.exe application (see Appendix A). After you've installed the application, click Start, Programs, JXTA to see an entry called myJXTA. Click on the entry to launch the myJXTA application. If you right-click on the listing and select Properties, you will find that the application is stored in a directory called <root>/JXTA_Demo/ InstantP2P. There is no source code in this directory; it contains only the application executables. You can find the application in a similar directory after a Linux/Unix installation, often in the path /usr/local/JXTA_Demo/InstantP2P.

You can find the source for this application at http://download.jxta.org/stable-builds/index.html, and the instructions for building the myJXTA application are located at http://instantp2p.jxta.org/build.html. I recommend you install both the application executable file and the source code; both will be referenced in this chapter.

Executing myJXTA

When you first execute the application, you'll see a splash screen like the one shown in Figure 4.1. As you can see, a few options are available:

Quit—The application will quit.

Quit & Reconfigure—The application will quit, but will allow the reconfiguration window to be displayed when the application is started again.

Just Wait—If this is the first time the application has been executed, the configuration window will appear; otherwise, the application will continue to connect to the JXTA network.

Proceed Anyway—This command will launch the application, even if the appropriate JXTA network peers haven't been contacted.

Executing myJXTA for the First Time

The first time you start myJXTA, you will need to configure it. Figure 4.2 shows the first Configurator dialog box. You *must* provide a valid peer name; because the application is a peer within the default peer group, it needs a name. This name will be put into a peer advertisement and then distributed within the network and made available upon request by another peer. You don't need a unique name; it serves only as a human-readable identifier for peers.

Next, click the Security button; you will see the dialog box shown in Figure 4.3. Each peer must have a personal security name and password, so fill in the

Figure 4.1 The myJXTA splash screen.

Figure 4.2 Enter a peer name in the myJXTA Configurator dialog box.

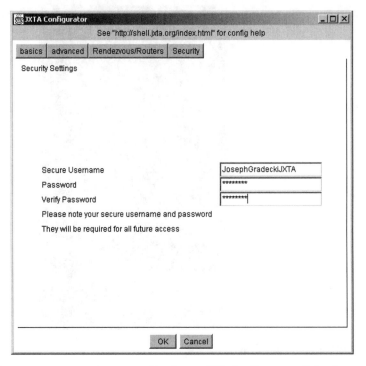

Figure 4.3 Entering a username and password in the myJXTA Configurator dialog box.

appropriate values. Make the username and password something you will remember; the system won't allow you to start the application without the correct values. For simplicity's sake, the peer name and the secure peer name can be the same. The secure peer name and password are used only on the local machine (and stored only in a file locally as well). Once you've entered the username and password, click the OK button to continue.

You can find the code for the splash screen and the JXTA network connection in the instantp2p.java file in the root directory /binding/java/src/net/ jxta/instantp2p/desktop. Located in the file is the InstantP2P class, which contains the application's main() method. The constructor of the class handles most of the GUI details through object instantiation and configuration. The main() method includes a call to a class method called startJxta(). Within startJxta() is the code for joining the default peer group and handling the splash status bar graphic:

```
statusBar.setPercentage(.50);
netPeerGroup = PeerGroupFactory.newNetPeerGroup();
statusBar.setPercentage(1.0);
```

After the peer is joined to the peer group, an attempt is made to contact one of the rendezvous peers. At this point, the splash screen remains on the screen, giving the user the ability to continue with the application without having

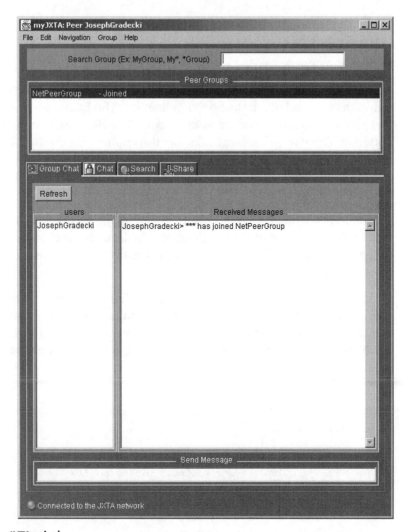

Figure 4.4 myJXTA window.

contacted a rendezvous peer. The run() method will execute once a peer is found or the user clicks to continue without waiting. (Note that this doesn't mean the attempt to contact the rendezvous peer isn't still occurring; however, it will no longer block waiting on the attempt.) The code in the run() method will finish the setup of the main application GUI and make it visible.

myJXTA Window

After several seconds, the application tries to connect to the NetPeerGroup. (As you'll recall, *NetPeerGroup* is the name of the default peer group that all JXTA peers will initially join.) The myJXTA window will appear, as shown in Figure 4.4. The functionality provided by the myJXTA application is found in three areas:

- Menu bar
- Dialog box tabs
- Search panel

On the menu bar, the File menu allows the user to create and accept chat invitations as well as launch the Shell application. The Edit menu includes the ability to save the session and activate sharing. The Help menu contains the About option, which you can select to display the application version. The Navigation menu duplicates the tabs in the dialog box; and you use the Group menu to create, join, and leave groups. We discuss both the File and Group menu items in detail a little later.

The dialog box tabs—Group Chat (the default), Chat, Search, and Share—are located in the center of the application. The Search panel is located at the top of the application; it is visible in all tabs. We also discuss these features later in this chapter.

Within the instantp2p.java file mentioned earlier, the menu and buttons are created, and appropriate ActionListeners are built. A specific actionPerformed() method is created to handle the menu item events; the code is shown in Listing 4.1. Notice that for each menu event, a specific method is called to handle the request.

```
        if (item == exit) {
            exitInstantP2P();
        } else if (item == prefs) {
            //net.jxta.impl.peergroup.ConfigDialog config =
            //      new net.jxta.impl.peergroup.ConfigDialog (
            //              application.getAdvertisement());
            //  config.setVisible ( true );
        } else if (item == sharingPrefs) {
          setSharingPreferences();
        } else if (item == about) {
            String[] str = new String[1];
            str[0] = "myJXTA Version: " + Version.version;
            getDialog().setText(str);
        } else if (item == addGroup) {
            addNewGroup();
        } else if (item == joinGroup) {
            joinGroup();
        } else if (item == leaveGroup) {
            leaveGroup();
/*          } else if (item == refresh) {
```

Listing 4.1 The myJXTA code for handling menu events. (continues)

```
        refreshGroup(); This is broken and redundant with
           search */

      } else if (item == shell) {
         runShell();
      } else if (item == invite) {
       invite();
   } else if (item == accept) {
     accept();
      }
   }
```

Listing 4.1   The myJXTA code for handling menu events. (continued)

Group Chat

When the myJXTA application launches, the default tab is Group Chat, as shown in Figure 4.4. All of the users who are part of the currently selected group in the Peer Groups panel will be displayed in the users panel on the left. The right panel contains the messages being constantly sent by users in the group. As peers join and leave the group, indicator messages will be displayed. To send a message to the group, simply enter text in the Send Message text area.

If you want to view the chat in other groups, just click on any of the groups listed in the Peer Groups panel. Notice that when you're switching to other peer groups, you will not see any of the chat history, but only the chat that occurs while you are viewing the group chat.

The code for the group chat can be found in the GroupChat.java file in the <root directory where you installed source>/binding/java/src/net/jxta/instantp2p/. When an object is instantiated from the GroupChat class, one of the first things the constructor does is create a separate thread to contain the instantiation. This allows the object to constantly be aware of new peers entering the Net-PeerGroup, and display their peer name and chat in the Group Chat tab.

All communication received by this peer during the group chat is funneled to the pipeMsgEvent() method. This method receives information about the sender as well as the sender's message (see Listing 4.2).

```
   public void pipeMsgEvent(PipeMsgEvent event) {
         Message msg = event.getMessage();
```

Listing 4.2   The myJXTA code for handling group peer discussions. (continues)

```
    try {
String        sender = getTagString(msg,
  SENDERNAME, "anonymous");
String      groupname = getTagString(msg,
  SENDERGROUPNAME, "unknown");
String senderMessage = getTagString(msg,
  SENDERMESSAGE, null);
String msgstr;
if (groupname.equals(group.getPeerGroupName()) ) {
    //message is from this group
    msgstr = sender + "> " + senderMessage;
} else {
    msgstr = sender + "@" + groupname + "> " +
    senderMessage;
}

for (int i = 0; i < applisteners.size(); i++) {
      ChatListener cl = (ChatListener)
        applisteners.elementAt(i);
      cl.chatEvent(msgstr);
}
 updateList(sender);
} catch (Exception e) {
  e.printStackTrace();
}
}
```

Listing 4.2 The myJXTA code for handling group peer discussions. (continued)

When a peer enters a message in the Send Message control box, the code found in sendMsg() is executed:

```
public void sendMsg(String gram) {
      try {
          Message msg = pipe.createMessage();
          msg.setString(SENDERMESSAGE, gram);
          msg.setString(SENDERNAME, userName);
          msg.setString(SENDERGROUPNAME,
            group.getPeerGroupName());
          queue.push(msg);
      } catch (Exception ex) {
            ex.printStackTrace();
      }
}
```

This code accepts message text in the form of a String object. The text along with the peergroup name and username of the current peer is inserted into a Message object and placed on a queue to be sent to other peers.

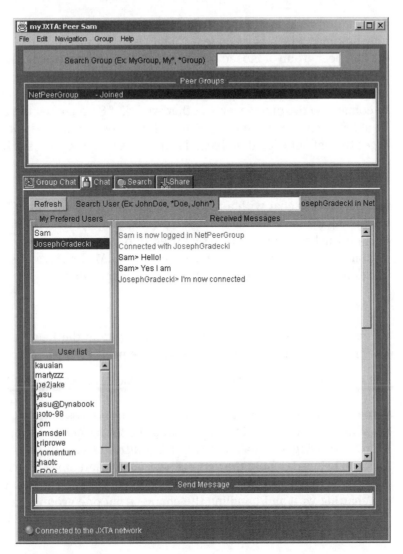

Figure 4.5 The myJXTA Chat window.

Chat

If you click on the Chat tab, you'll see the window shown in Figure 4.5. The Chat functionality in the application is designed to allow a chat session between two users. The chat session will be secure, but both of the peers need to be in the same group.

Chatting with a User

Chatting with a user is very simple; just locate his or her peer name in the User List panel of the known peer group, and double-click on it. When you do, the application will first attempt to find the user in the current peer group. (There may be times when users appear in the User List panel, but they have left the current peer group or closed their application.) Once the peer has been located, a connection will be made with the remote peer. After the connection is established, messages can be sent. It should be noted that each peer will be required to connect to the other peer. In other words, if Sam connects to Joe, Sam will be able to send secure messages to Joe, but Joe will not be able to send messages to Sam until Joe double-clicks on Sam's name in the User List panel.

Changing Users

It is possible to chat with a number of users at the same time. To do this, just double-click on another user in the User List panel of the current group. A connection will be attempted with that user; if found, a one-way connection will be established. The new user will be placed in your My Preferred Users list. Simply click on a user to send a message to that user specifically.

Changing Groups

If you join a group and then click on that group in the Peer Group panel, the User List panel will refresh to display all the peers in the new group.

You can find the code for the one-to-one chat in the chat.java file in the <root directory where you installed source>/binding/java/src/net/jxta/instantp2p/. As in the case of the group chat, the one-to-one chat class places itself in a thread when instantiated. Recall that numerous one-to-one chat sessions can occur, so it isn't surprising to see a number of array attributes for the class. These attributes will be used to hold the various peer names and pipes. The majority of the code in the Chat class handles administration tasks, such as changing users you are chatting with and handling the change from one group to another. One of the most important methods is processMessage(), which handles a new message when it arrives at the peer (see Listing 4.3).

```
protected void processMessage(Message msg) {
  String messageID;
  byte[] buffer = null;

  String srcPeerAdvWireFormat = msg.getString (SRCPEERADV);
  PeerAdvertisement srcPeerAdv = null;
  try {
    if (srcPeerAdvWireFormat != null) {
      srcPeerAdv = (PeerAdvertisement)
        AdvertisementFactory.newAdvertisement(
```

Listing 4.3 The processMessage() method handles new chat messages as they arrive at the peer. (continues)

```
             new MimeMediaType("text/xml"),
             new ByteArrayInputStream(
             srcPeerAdvWireFormat.getBytes()));

        discovery.publish(srcPeerAdv, DiscoveryService.PEER);
      }
    } catch (Exception e) {
}

String srcPipeAdvWireFormat = msg.getString (SRCPIPEADV);
  PipeAdvertisement srcPipeAdv = null;
  try {
    if (srcPipeAdvWireFormat != null) {
      srcPipeAdv = (PipeAdvertisement)
        AdvertisementFactory.newAdvertisement(
        new MimeMediaType("text/xml"),
        new ByteArrayInputStream(
        srcPipeAdvWireFormat.getBytes()));

      discovery.publish(srcPipeAdv, DiscoveryService.ADV);
    }
  } catch (Exception e) {
}

String groupId = msg.getString (GROUPID);
PeerGroup group = null;
if (groupId != null) {
  group = getGroup (groupId);
}

String sender = null;
String groupname = null;
String senderMessage = null;
// Get sender information
try {
  sender = getTagString(msg, SENDERNAME, "anonymous");
  groupname = getTagString(msg, SENDERGROUPNAME, "unknown");
  senderMessage = getTagString(msg, SENDERMESSAGE, null);

  String msgstr;
  if (groupname.equals(manager.getSelectedPeerGroup()
    .getPeerGroupName()) ) {
    //message is from this group
    msgstr = sender + "> " + senderMessage +EOL ;
  } else {
    msgstr = sender + "@" + groupname + "> "
      + senderMessage +EOL;
```

Listing 4.3 The processMessage() method handles new chat messages as they arrive at the peer. (continues)

```
      }

    if (senderMessage != null) {
      messageBoard.displayMessage( msgstr, sender);
    }
    // If there is a PipeAdvertisement piggy backed
    //into the message
    // create a new buddy.

    if ((srcPipeAdv != null) && (group != null)) {
      PipePresence p  =  getPipePresence (group, myPipeAdvt);
      if (p != null) {
        p.addOnlineBuddy (sender, srcPipeAdv);
      }
    }
  } catch (Exception e) {
    messageBoard.error(e.getMessage());
  }
  // Process any Chat commands

  String cmd = msg.getString (COMMAND);
  if (cmd == null) {
    // Nothing to do
    return;
  }

  if (cmd.equals (PING) && (group != null)) {
    // This is a PING request. We need to reply ACK
    OutputPipe op = null;
    Vector dstPeers = new Vector (1);
    dstPeers.add (srcPeerAdv.getPeerID());
    try {
      op = group.getPipeService().createOutputPipe (scPipeAdv,
           dstPeers.elements(),
           PipeTimeout);
      if (op != null) {
        // Send the ACK
        Message rep = pipes.createMessage();
        rep.setString (COMMAND, ACK);
        rep.setString (GROUPID, groupId);
        rep.setString (SENDERNAME, myName);
        op.send (rep);
      } else {
      }
    } catch (Exception ez1) {
      // We can't reply. Too bad...
    }
}
```

Listing 4.3 The processMessage() method handles new chat messages as they arrive at the peer. (continues)

```
    }

    if (cmd.equals (ACK) && (group != null)) {
        // This is a ACK reply. Get the appropriate PipePresence
        PipePresence p  =  getPipePresence (group, myPipeAdvt);
        if (p != null) {
          p.processAck (sender);
        }
      }
    }
```

Listing 4.3   The processMessage() method handles new chat messages as they arrive at the peer. (contiued)

Notice where the method compares the tag of the received message to determine what to do with the message. The action could be to display the contents of the message because it was sent to the current peergroup, or it could be a ping message which requires an acknowledgment message be returned to the caller. This type of processing will be shown again in Chapter 15, where we examine the default password membership service and have to process various messages from peers.

Search

Clicking the Search tab displays the search features that enable a peer in a group to find resources that have been made available by other peers. Figure 4.6 shows an example of searching in the default peer group for the text string "html". As you can see, several different filenames have been identified. If you click on any of the filenames, you will see the dialog box shown in Figure 4.7.

You can save the file at the given path or browse to place the file in a different location. If you just want to view the file, click the View button to launch a viewer (if you have one on your system).

You can find the code for the search functionality in the files Search.java, SearchListener.java, SearchManager.java, and SearchResult.java in the <root directory where you installed source>/binding/java/src/net/jxta/instantp2p/. The Search.java file handles the basic mechanics of the search functionality by searching through the instantiation of SearchListener objects as well as canceling currently executing searches. When a search result occurs, the advertisement sent back from each of the peers will include not only the name of the content but a pipe advertisement that the local peer can use to obtain the content. The result is handled in the SearchResult class, located in the SearchResult.java file. The SearchManager class (which is located in the SearchManager.java file) does quite a bit of work when dealing with the shared content the local peer has provided to the peer group. When a request from

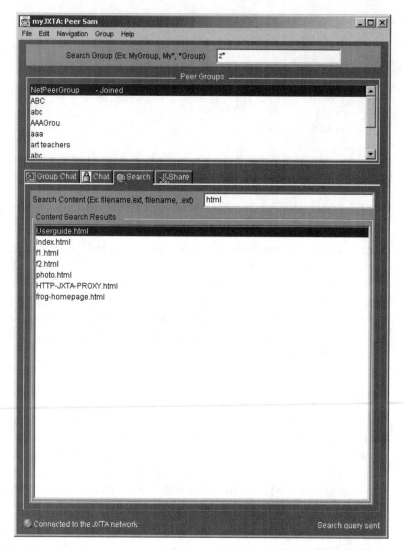

Figure 4.6 Performing a search.

Figure 4.7 Saving and viewing a search result.

another peer arrives at the local peer, SearchManager will check to see if any of the local shared content matches the search text. If there is a match, an output pipe will be opened, and an advertisement will be created and sent to the requesting peer.

Share

Clicking the Share tab will open the window shown in Figure 4.8. The Share part of the application allows contents to be shared among the peers in a group. Content is added to the Share Content panel at the bottom of the GUI. When you click the Add button, you'll see a Select File dialog box, which lets you add content. If you want to remove any of the pieces of content, just highlight the entry and click the Remove Content button.

You can find the code for the share functionality in the LocalContentTab.java file in the <root directory where you installed source>/binding/java/src/ net/jxta/instantp2p/desktop. The code for the local content isn't too complex; it simply handles the adding and removing of content from the Share tab's display panel.

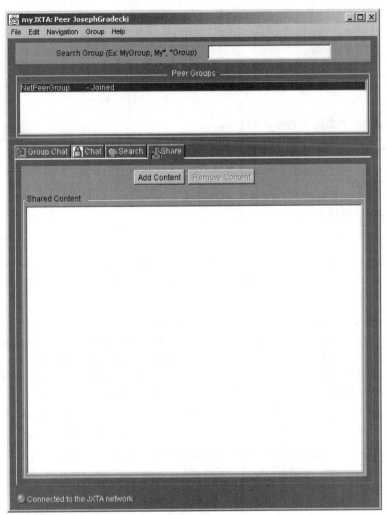

Figure 4.8 The myJXTA Share window.

Using the File Menu

The File menu contains three commands. The first, called Shell, opens a Shell application to the JXTA network (see Chapter 3 for a complete discussion of the shell's functionality). The second and third commands are called Create Invite and Accept Invite. The Create Invite command will create a peer advertisement that can be sent to other users. A user who receives a peer advertisement can use the Accept Invite command to load the peer advertisement from the local drive.

You can find the code for the File menu functionality in the instantp2p.java file in the <root directory where you installed source>/binding/java/src/ net/jxta/instantp2p/desktop. The code for starting a new peer group shell can be found in the same file. For invite( ) and accept( ) functionality, the final code resides in the PeerGroupPanel.java file, located in the same directory. The invite( ) method pulls information about the local peer and peer group, and saves the information to the local disk. The code is a good example of using disk operations within JXTA. The accept( ) method contains code for pulling an advertisement from the disk and building appropriate JXTA objects from it.

Using the Group Menu

The Group menu contains three separate commands all related to dealing with peer groups. The commands are

- Create New Group
- Join Group
- Leave Group

The Create New Group command allows a new peer group to be advertised and created in the JXTA network. When you choose this command, you'll see the window shown in Figure 4.9.

To create a new peer group, enter the desired name of the group in the provided space. By default, the new peer group will act as a rendezvous, but can be turned off if you desire. If you click OK at this point, the new peer group will be visible to all who discover it. There are no restrictions for joining the group. If you select the Create Private Group check box, you'll have to supply a password for the group. After you click OK, the new peer group will be available only to those peers who know the password to the group.

In either case, the new peer group will appear in the Peer Groups panel at the top of the application. You will not be automatically joined to the group because you created it.

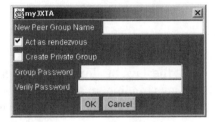

Figure 4.9 Creating a new peer group.

If you want to join a group, that group must appear in the Peer Group panel. Click on the group you want to join, and select the Join Group command from the Group menu. Either you will be joined to the group, or a dialog box will appear asking you for the password to the group. In either case, a Joined label will indicate the joined group after the peer group name in the Peer Group panel.

When you have finished with a group, just highlight it in the panel, and choose Leave Group from the Group menu to resign from the group.

You can find the code for the Group menu commands in the PeerGroupPanel. java file in the <root directory where you installed source>/ binding/java/src/ net/jxta/instantp2p/desktop. The code for creating new peer groups, joining groups, and leaving groups can be found in that file.

Searching for a Group

If you look at Figure 4.8 again, you will see that quite a few peer groups are listed in the top panel of the application. We discovered the peer groups by placing search text with an asterisk (*) wildcard in the Search Group text area at the top of the myJXTA application. A discovery is attempted against peer group advertisements in the JXTA network based on the search text. All of the peer groups found will be listed in the panel. If you click on one of the groups, you can join it using the Join Group command on the Group menu.

You can find the code for the group search functionality in the PeerGroup-Panel.java file in the <root directory where you installed source>/binding/ java/src/net/jxta/instantp2p/desktop. The code for building the search panel is in this file.

Summary

This chapter has been an overview of the myJXTA sample application provided by the developers of the Java binding. The application introduces the full capabilities of the JXTA Java binding. In addition, we supplied pointers to the underlying source code that provides the functionality in the application. Reusing the source code from the application gives us a foundation on which we can build new and innovative programs. Next, we will begin looking into the details behind the JXTA specification and Java implementation with a discussion of JXTA advertisements.

CHAPTER 5

JXTA Advertisements

The advertisement is the primary tool the JXTA protocols use for making general peer, peer group, and resource configuration information available to the network, peers, and peer groups. The advertisement is a container that can be passed from peer to peer using a common format. To provide a generalized format, the JXTA team chose to implement the advertisement using XML, thus providing an easily expandable and hierarchical representation of information needed by all peers to support the JXTA network. In this chapter, we discuss the major advertisements, as well as the code needed to pull advertisements from files or to build them on the fly programmatically.

Core Advertisements

The core advertisements defined in the current specification include the following:

- Peer advertisement
- Peer group advertisement
- Module class advertisement
- Module specification advertisement
- Module implementation advertisement
- Pipe advertisement
- Rendezvous advertisement (discussed in Chapter 11)

An XML-Based Format

Instead of creating yet another configuration description format, the JXTA team chose to format the advertisement using XML. This section contains a brief introduction to XML; if you are already familiar with XML, you can safely skip ahead.

The JXTA team selected XML as the configuration description language because XML is the following:

- Independent of any language
- Self-describing
- Extensible
- Strongly typed

Because of these important features, XML is a format that can be shared between implementations of the JXTA specification, regardless of how the protocols have been coded. XML is plain text, and parsing engines are widely available. Listing 5.1 contains a simple XML document.

```
<?XML  VERSION="1.0"?>
<root>
     <elem1>
           value
     </elem1>
     <elem2 attrib="value2">
           value3
     </elem2>
</root>
```

Listing 5.1   A simple XML document.

All XML documents must begin with a processing instruction:

```
<?XML VERSION="1.0"?>
```

An XML parser uses this instruction to confirm that the document it is starting to work with is indeed a XML document. A hierarchy of elements follows the instruction. An XML element is denoted by a text string enclosed in < > symbols. Here's an example of an element pair:

```
<address>
</address>
```

Note the use of the / symbol for the ending element. If you are familiar with HTML, this syntax won't be new to you. Although the JXTA specification has defined a number of specific elements for advertisements, XML's extensibility enables you to define your own elements as well. The JXTA system will simply ignore additional elements; you will need to parse the XML document on your own to find the elements.

XML is hierarchical, which means you can nest elements within other elements, as in the following:

```
<account>
      <name>
      </name>
</account>
```

Elements are allowed to contain a value, which is either a string value or another element. For example:

```
<account>
      <name>
            John Smith
      </name>
</account>
```

In this case, the value of the <account> element is the <name> element, and the <name> element has a string value. You can have any number of subelements within a parent element:

```
<account>
      <name>John Smith</name>
      <address>123 S. Anywhere Street></address>
      <city>Nowhere</city>
</account>
```

All XML documents must have a high-level root element, which means that all documents will consist of a minimum of three lines. For example:

```
<?XML VERSION="1.0">
<root>
</root>
```

Here are some important XML rules to keep in mind:

- The document must be well formed; elements must have matching beginning and ending elements.
- Attribute values must be enclosed with double quote characters.
- Documents must contain one and only one root element.

Peer Advertisements

The peer advertisement has a twofold purpose. The first is to identify the peer to outside entities, such as peer groups or other peers. This public part of the peer advertisement is made available to convey information, such as its name,

ID, the endpoint addresses currently available on the peer, and other elements that are placed in the advertisement by current group services. The second purpose of a peer advertisement is to hold local configuration information that isn't published.

Listing 5.2 shows the JXTA specification-defined elements of a peer advertisement. These elements are defined in the advertisement:

Name—The name of the peer is taken from the name provided when the peer was first configured (see Chapter 4 for information about configuring a peer with myJXTA).

Desc—You can supply a description string in the peer advertisement for the primary purpose of having text available for searching. Note that you have to separate the keywords in the description by spaces, and the terms don't have to be unique—in other words, the description string for one advertisement might match or be close to the same as another advertisement.

PID—Each peer in a JXTA network will have a unique ID, as described in Chapter 2. It is imperative that the PID be unique in order for the JXTA protocols to be able to locate peers.

GID—The group ID (GID) is the name of the group to which the peer belongs (in formal notation).

Svc—This element contains information relevant to the peer, including its certificate and transports that it supports.

Dbg—This element corresponds to the Debug option found on the Advanced tab of the Configuration window. The value is used to display some level of debugging during the execution of the peer. At a high level, all types of messages will be displayed at the command prompt or terminal window from where the peer was executed.

```
<xs:complexType name="PA">
      <xs:element name="Name" type="xs:string" minOccurs="0"/>
      <xs:element name="PID" type="JXTAID"/>
      <xs:element name="GID" type="JXTAID"/>
      <xs:element name="Desc" type="xs:anyType" minOccurs="0"/>
      <xs:element name="Dbg" type="xs:token" minOccurs="0"/>
      <xs:element name="Svc" type="jxta:serviceParams" minOccurs="0"
maxOccurs="unbounded"/>
</xs:complexType>

<xs:simpleType name="JXTAID">
      <xs:restriction base="xs:anyURI">
```

Listing 5.2 The specification-defined structure of a peer advertisement. (continues)

```
              <pattern value="([uU][rR][nN]:[jJ][xX][tT][aA]:)+\-+"/>
        </xs:restriction>
</xs:simpleType>

<xs:complexType name="serviceParam">
        <xs:element name="MCID" type="JXTAID"/>
        <xs:element name="Parm" type="xs:anyType"/>
</xs:complexType>
```

Listing 5.2   The specification-defined structure of a peer advertisement.

Listing 5.3 shows an example of a "real" peer advertisement. Notice the <parm> element, which includes information specific to the peer, such as available endpoints into the peer. The values in Listing 5.3 include two endpoints and their related protocols (TCP as well as the Transport Layer Security protocols).

```
<?xml version="1.0"?>
<!DOCTYPE jxta:PA>
<jxta:PA xmlns:jxta="http://jxta.org">
        <PID>
                urn:jxta:uuid-5961626164616261
  4A787461503250336027A230B57E4EBBB32DA84EAC3588F003
        </PID>
        <GID>
                urn:jxta:jxta-NetGroup
        </GID>
        <Name>
                JosephGradeckiClient
        </Name>
        <Svc>
                <MCID>
                        urn:jxta:uuid-DEADBEEFDEAFBABA
FEEDBABE0000000805
                </MCID>
                <Parm>
                        <Addr>
                                tcp://12.254.21.182:9702/
                        </Addr>
                        <Addr>
                                jxtatls://uuid-5961626164
6162614A787461503250336027A230B57E4EB
BB32DA84EAC3588F003/TlsTransport/jxta-WorldGroup
                        </Addr>
                        <Addr>
                                jxta://uuid-59616261646
```

Listing 5.3   A valid peer advertisement. (continues)

```
162614A787461503250336027A230B57E4EBBB32DA84EAC3588F003/
                         </Addr>
            </Parm>
      </Svc>
      <Svc>
            <MCID>
                      urn:jxta:uuid-DEADBEEFDEAFB
ABAFEEDBABE0000000105
            </MCID>
            <Parm>
                  <RootCert>
                             MIICVDCCAb2gAwIBAgIBATANBgkqhkiG9w0BAQUFADByMRUw
EwYDVQQKEwx3d3cuanh0YS5vcmcxCzAJBgNVBAcTAlNGMQswCQYDVQQGEwJVUzEg
MB4GA1UEAxMXSm9zZXBoR3JhZGVja2lDbGllbnQtQ0ExHTAbBgNVBAsTFEZBNjY2
QTQxRjg2NDAwNjlCN0NBMB4XDTAxMTIxMTA1MzMwNVoXDTExMTIxMTA1MzMwNVow
cjEVMBMGA1UEChMM
d3d3Lmp4dGEub3JnMQswCQYDVQQHEwJTRjELMAkGA1UEBhMCVVMxIDAeBgNVBAMT
F0pvc2VwaEdyYWR1Y2tpQ2xpZW50LUNBMR0wGwYDVQQLExRGQTY2NkE0MUY4NjQw
MDY5QjdDQTCBmzALBgkqhkiG9w0BAQEDgYsAMIGHAoGBAIwUgZp16K4D1q82iIm5
iXojbUznV+dtwjZnqXhqtvVOoP7JNTRPiK/fNGUTGDVrJTohlPJmVkwEj1HLbx27
3jmiVNGvkLbDM+sFG+ZaTAwjuOmfDei81aiYnKx1fKSz+MQ8OAnQwUeBPHYW611k
IwhXxJ/mJCvjtFy/PzyuNFy7AgERMA0GCSqGSIb3DQEBBQUAA4GBAA4oO0HH1f7a
bB2O0hsceRi2IjQtL8d6ZXAbHSa93VMRoYQ2gI68ORAbN1ZErRKFX3u1XgSq7oxF
6UP8Jnm0D5S/8cSsEigN46pTiSo8RifniqOaD6RnW8qZZJea4y968A6NYtZfH44z
EDzrh7OhEX8KvMDoopTR3hcrqTVVuwBn
                        </RootCert>
                  </Parm>
            </Svc>
</jxta:PA>
```

Listing 5.3   A valid peer advertisement. (continued)

You can obtain all of the information from a peer advertisement by using the methods associated with the PeerAdvertisement object. The most important methods are as follows:

String getAdvertisementType( )—Returns a string representing the type of the current advertisement.

String getDescription( )—Returns the description string found in the peer advertisement.

ID getID( )—Returns the ID associated with the peer advertisement for unique identification.

ID getPeerID( )—Returns the ID of the peer associated with this advertisement.

String getName( )—Returns the name of the peer.

PeerGroupID getPeerGroupID( )—Returns the ID of the group the peer is currently associated with.

StructuredDocument getServiceParam(ID key)—Returns the element found in the <parm> hierarchy that matches the parameter key.

Hashtable getServiceParams( )—Returns all of the elements found in the <parm> hierarchy.

The PeerAdvertisement object also includes the appropriate setter methods corresponding to these getter methods.

Peer Group Advertisements

A peer group advertisement is created for all peer groups in the JXTA network. As with peers, the advertisement describes the group, and provides other information necessary for creating a new group. To create a new peer group, you must create an advertisement and provide it to a current group. This is one of the reasons that all peers are part of a default peer group. Listing 5.4 shows the definition of a peer group advertisement as outlined in the specification. Within the peer group advertisement are the following elements:

GID—A unique peer group ID.

MSID—The Module Specification ID, which defines the basic functionality necessary for a peer group. You can locate any number of implementations of the functionality in the JXTA network by using the MSID of the peer group.

Name—The name of the peer group.

Desc—A description string useful for searching.

Svc—A list of services available from this peer group as well as the attributes necessary for the services. A peer group advertisement can include any number of Svc elements.

```
<xs:complexType name="PGA">
     <xs:element name="GID" type="JXTAID"/>
     <xs:element name="MSID" type="JXTAID"/>
     <xs:element name="Name" type="xs:string" minOccurs="0"/>
     <xs:element name="Desc" type="xs:anyType" minOccurs="0"/>
     <xs:element name="Svc" type="jxta:serviceParam"
  minOccurs="0" maxOccurs="unbounded"/>
</xs:complexType>
```

Listing 5.4   The specification definition of a peer group advertisement.

Module Class Advertisements

When a peer is expected to provide some type of functionality to a peer group, a number of advertisements will be used to publish this fact. At the top level of the necessary advertisements is the module class advertisement. This advertisement is designed to be a high-level announcement of pending functionality. It could be considered analogous to a package in the Java language. The package describes and contains some level of functionality, and acts as a high-level descriptor, just as the module class advertisement does. Listing 5.5 shows the specification's definition of the module class advertisement. In the specification, the elements are:

MCID—The Module Class ID is an ID created to be unique and to represent this module.

Name—The name of the module class.

Desc—A description of the class.

```
<xs:complexType name="MCA">
     <xs:element name="MCID" type="JXTAID"/>
     <xs:element name="Name" type="xs:string" minOccurs="0"/>
     <xs:element name="Desc" type="xs:anyType" minOccurs="0"/>
</xs:complexType>
```

Listing 5.5   The module class advertisement.

Listing 5.6 shows an example of a valid module class advertisement. Notice that the advertisement is quite simple. The most important part of the advertisement is the MCID, which you must use when providing a specification and an implementation to the JXTA network. The module class advertisement also has the purpose of associating an ID to the functionality a peer wants to put into the peer group. All of the functionality will be tied to the ID placed within the advertisement.

```
<?xml version="1.0"?>

<!DOCTYPE jxta:MCA>

<jxta:MCA xmlns:jxta="http://jxta.org">
     <MCID>
             urn:jxta:uuid-401A2D3C453F4893A6A48684B9DE6B9B05
     </MCID>
     <Name>
```

Listing 5.6   A valid module class advertisement. (continues)

```
              JXTAMOD:JXTA-CH15EX2
       </Name>
       <Desc>
              Service 1 of Chapter 15 example 2
       </Desc>
</jxta:MCA>
```

Listing 5.6 A valid module class advertisement. (continued)

Module Specification Advertisements

After a module class advertisement has been published to the JXTA network, it should normally be followed up by a module specification advertisement (MSA). The MSA has two purposes:

- Provides references to documentation describing how to implement the services of the module class.

- Provides an instance of a class discoverable by remote peers and containing information about how to obtain the code behind a class.

The MSA is a human-readable advertisement designed to provide information about a module class. The specification of the class is defined in the advertisement. Listing 5.7 shows the definition of the advertisement as given in the specification. The elements of the advertisement include those listed here in the order found in the specification:

Name—The name of the specification this advertisement is describing.

Desc—A description string that can be searched by other entities.

MSID—A unique ID used by the JXTA network.

CRTR—A string representing the creator of this specification.

SURI—A URI that points to an actual specification. This could be a URL to a web server, for instance.

Vers—A string representing the version of the specification. This value is mandatory.

Parm—Parameters that can be retrieved by the receiver of the advertisement.

Pipe—A pipe advertisement that may be used to communicate with a peer that implements this module specification.

Proxy—An optional Module Spec ID of a module that can be used to communicate with the module of this specification.

Auth—The Module Spec ID of a module that may be required for authentication before using modules of this specification.

```
<xs:complexType name="MSA">
    <xs:element name="MSID" type="JXTAID"/>
    <xs:element name="Name" type="xs:string" minOccurs="0"/>
    <xs:element name="Crtr" type="xs:string" minOccurs="0"/>
    <xs:element name="SURI" type="xs:anyURI" minOccurs="0"/>
    <xs:element name="Vers" type="xs:string"/>
    <xs:element name="Desc" type="xs:anyType" minOccurs="0"/>
    <xs:element name="Parm" type="xs:anyType" minOccurs="0"/>
    <xs:element name="PipeAdvertisement"
  type="jxta:PipeAdvertisement" minOccurs="0"/>
    <xs:element name="Proxy" type="xs:anyURI" minOccurs="0"/>
    <xs:element name="Auth" type="JXTAID" minOccurs="0"/>
</xs:complexType>
```

Listing 5.7 The module specification advertisement definition.

The valid advertisement is shown in Listing 5.8.

```
<?xml version="1.0"?>

<!DOCTYPE jxta:MSA>

<jxta:MSA xmlns:jxta="http://jxta.org">
    <MSID>
            urn:jxta:uuid-69D41BB186FF4E1AB9E
AAB40F1BC6EDC0F0F6A0680D54A7A8A85BD1C68BF2B06
    </MSID>
    <Name>
            JXTASPEC:JXTA-CH15EX2
    </Name>
    <Crtr>
            gradecki.com
    </Crtr>
    <SURI>
            &lt;http://www.jxta.org/CH15EX2>
    </SURI>
    <Vers>
            Version 1.0
    </Vers>
    <jxta:PipeAdvertisement>
            <Id>
                    urn:jxta:uuid-9CCCDF5AD8154D3D8
7A391210404E59BE4B888209A2241A4A162A10916074A9504
            </Id>
            <Type>
                    JxtaUnicast
```

Listing 5.8 A valid module specification advertisement. (continues)

```
            </Type>
            <Name>
                    JXTA-CH15EX2
            </Name>
        </jxta:PipeAdvertisement>
    </jxta:MSA>
```

Listing 5.8   A valid module specification advertisement. (continued)

Module Implementation Advertisements

An advertisement isn't much good without implementations. The module implementation advertisement (MIA) is designed to be published when an implementation of a specification has been created. This advertisement is used to tell peers where to find the implementation. The MIA references the ID of the MSA so that peers can find implementations based on the ID of the specification. As one might expect, there can be a whole host of implementations of a single specification.

The MIA contains all of the information necessary to execute the implementation. As you'll see in a moment, the elements <Code> and <PURI> contain the class of the code and the download location, respectively. Depending on the implementation desired, the <Code> element might contain some other kind of execution information. Listing 5.9 shows the advertisement as defined in the JXTA specification; Listing 5.10 contains a valid advertisement.

The elements of the advertisement are as follows:

Name—The name of the specification this implementation is based on.

Desc—A description of the implementation. This is an optional name that can be associated with a specification. The name does not have to be unique unless it is obtained from a centralized naming service that guarantees name uniqueness.

Proxy—An element used to hold a URL through which communication should be directed. Some organizations don't use port 80 for communication, but instead use an IP address and port 8080 to act as a proxy.

MSID—The Module Spec ID from the MSA of the specification this implementation is based on. This is a mandatory field.

Comp—An element with required information about the environment this implementation can execute.

PURI—The location of the package, if not found in the code on the client's machine.

Code—Information needed for a peer to load and execute the code. This could be the entire code.

Parm—Parameters for the implementation.

Prov—A string with information about the provider of this implementation.

```
<xs:complexType name="MIA">
      <xs:element name="MCID" type="JXTAID"/>
      <xs:element name="Comp" type="xs:anyType"/>
      <xs:element name="Code" type="xs:anyType"/>
      <xs:element name="PURI" type="xs:anyURIv minOccurs="0"/>
      <xs:element name="Prov" type="string" minOccurs="0"/>
      <xs:element name="Desc" type="xs:anyType" minOccurs="0"/>
      <xs:element name="Parm" type="xs:anyType" minOccurs="0"/>
</xs:complexType>
```

Listing 5.9 A module implementation advertisement definition.

```
<?xml version="1.0"?>

<!DOCTYPE jxta:MIA>

<jxta:MIA xmlns:jxta="http://jxta.org">
      <MSID>
              urn:jxta:uuid-DEADBEEFDEAF
BABAFEEDBABE000000010306
      </MSID>
      <Comp>
              <Efmt>
                      JDK1.4
              </Efmt>
              <Bind>
                      V1.0 Ref Impl
              </Bind>
      </Comp>
      <Code>
              net.jxta.impl.peergroup.StdPeerGroup
      </Code>
      <PURI>
              http://www.jxta.org/download/jxta.jar
      </PURI>
      <Prov>
              sun.com
      </Prov>
      <Desc>
              General Purpose Peer Group Implementation
```

Listing 5.10 A valid module implementation advertisement. (continues)

```
                </Desc>
                <Parm>
                    <Svc>
                        <jxta:MIA>
                            <MSID>
                                    urn:jxta:uuid-DEADBEEF
DEAFBABAFEEDBABE000000060106
                            </MSID>
                            <Comp>
                                <Efmt>
                                        JDK1.4
                                </Efmt>
                                <Bind>
                                        V1.0 Ref Impl
                                </Bind>
                            </Comp>
                            <Code>

net.jxta.impl.rendezvous.RendezVousServiceImpl
                            </Code>
                            <PURI>

http://www.jxta.org/download/jxta.jar
                            </PURI>
                            <Prov>
                                    sun.com
                            </Prov>
                            <Desc>
                                    Reference
Implementation of the Rendezvous service
                            </Desc>
                        </jxta:MIA>
                    </Svc>
                    <Svc>
                        <jxta:MIA>
                            <MSID>
                                    urn:jxta:uuid-DEAD
BEEFDEAFBABAFEEDBABE000000030106
                            </MSID>
                            <Comp>
                                <Efmt>
                                        JDK1.4
                                </Efmt>
                                <Bind>
                                        V1.0 Ref Impl
                                </Bind>
                            </Comp>
```

Listing 5.10 A valid module implementation advertisement. (continues)

```
                                      <Code>

net.jxta.impl.discovery.DiscoveryServiceImpl
                                      </Code>
                                      <PURI>

http://www.jxta.org/download/jxta.jar
                                      </PURI>
                                      <Prov>
                                              sun.com
                                      </Prov>
                                      <Desc>
Reference Implementation of the DiscoveryService service
                                      </Desc>
                          </jxta:MIA>
                  </Svc>
                  <Svc>
                          <jxta:MIA>
                              <MSID>
urn:jxta:uuid-DEADBEEFDEAFBABAFEEDBABE000000050106
                              </MSID>
                              <Comp>

                                      <Efmt>
                                              JDK1.4
                                      </Efmt>
                                      <Bind>
                                              V1.0 Ref Impl
                                      </Bind>
                              </Comp>
                              <Code>

 net.jxta.impl.membership.NullMembershipService
                              </Code>
                              <PURI>

http://www.jxta.org/download/jxta.jar
                              </PURI>
                              <Prov>
                                      sun.com
                              </Prov>
                              <Desc>
                                      Reference Implementation of the
MembershipService service
                              </Desc>
                          </jxta:MIA>
                  </Svc>
                  <Svc>
```

Listing 5.10 A valid module implementation advertisement. (continues)

```
                        <jxta:MIA>
                                <MSID>
                                        urn:jxta:uuid-
DEADBEEFDEAFBABAFEEDBABE000000070106
                                </MSID>
                                <Comp>
                                        <Efmt>
                                                JDK1.4
                                        </Efmt>
                                        <Bind>
                                                V1.0 Ref Impl
                                        </Bind>
                                </Comp>
                                <Code>

  net.jxta.impl.peer.PeerInfoServiceImpl
                                </Code>
                                <PURI>

http://www.jxta.org/download/jxta.jar
                                </PURI>
                                <Prov>
                                        sun.com
                                </Prov>
                                <Desc>
                                        Reference Implementation of the
Peerinfo service
                                </Desc>
                        </jxta:MIA>
                </Svc>
                <Svc>
                        <jxta:MIA>
                                <MSID>
                                        urn:jxta:uuid-
DEADBEEFDEAFBABAFEEDBABE000000020106
                                </MSID>
                                <Comp>
                                        <Efmt>
                                                JDK1.4
                                        </Efmt>
                                        <Bind>
                                                V1.0 Ref Impl
                                        </Bind>
                                </Comp>
                                <Code>

net.jxta.impl.resolver.ResolverServiceImpl
```

Listing 5.10 A valid module implementation advertisement. (continues)

```
                                       </Code>
                                       <PURI>

http://www.jxta.org/download/jxta.jar
                                       </PURI>
                                       <Prov>
                                                 sun.com
                                       </Prov>
                                       <Desc>
                                                 Reference Implementation of the
ResolverService service
                                       </Desc>
                              </jxta:MIA>
                 </Svc>
                 <Svc>
                              <jxta:MIA>
                                       <MSID>
                                                 urn:jxta:uuid-
DEADBEEFDEAFBABAFEEDBABE000000040106
                                       </MSID>
                                       <Comp>
                                                 <Efmt>
                                                           JDK1.4
                                                 </Efmt>
                                                 <Bind>
                                                           V1.0 Ref Impl
                                                 </Bind>
                                       </Comp>
                                       <Code>
                                                 net.jxta.impl.pipe.PipeServiceImpl
                                       </Code>
                                       <PURI>

http://www.jxta.org/download/jxta.jar
                                       </PURI>
                                       <Prov>
                                                 sun.com
                                       </Prov>
                                       <Desc>
                                                 Reference Implementation of the
PipeService service
                                       </Desc>
                              </jxta:MIA>
                 </Svc>
                 <App>
                              <jxta:MIA>
                                       <MSID>
```

Listing 5.10 A valid module implementation advertisement. (continues)

```
                                          urn:jxta:uuid-
DEADBEEFDEAFBABAFEEDBABE0000000C0206
                              </MSID>
                              <Comp>
                                   <Efmt>
                                          JDK1.4
                                   </Efmt>
                                   <Bind>
                                             V1.0 Ref Impl
                                   </Bind>
                              </Comp>
                              <Code>

  net.jxta.impl.shell.bin.Shell.Shell
                              </Code>
                              <PURI>

  http://www.jxta.org/download/jxta.jar
                              </PURI>
                              <Prov>
                                        sun.com
                              </Prov>
                              <Desc>
                                        JXTA Shell reference implementation
                              </Desc>
                         </jxta:MIA>
               </App>
          </Parm>
</jxta:MIA>
```

Listing 5.10   A valid module implementation advertisement. (continued)

Pipe Advertisements

The final advertisement we will look at is the pipe advertisement, which has the job of informing one peer how to establish a connection with another peer. Listing 5.11 shows the schema for the pipe advertisement, and Listing 5.12 shows a sample pipe advertisement. The elements of the advertisement are:

Name—The name of the pipe.

Type—The type of the pipe:

- xtaUnicast

- JxtaUnicastSecure

- JxtaPropagateSecure

Id—The ID of the pipe.

```
<xs:element name="PipeAdvertisment" type="jxta:PipeAdvertisment"/>

<xs:complexType name="PipeAdvertisement">
    <xs:element name="Name" type="xs:string" minOccurs="0"/>
    <xs:element name="Id" type="JXTAID"/>
    <xs:element name="Type" type="xs:string"/>
</xs:complexType>
```

Listing 5.11   A pipe advertisement schema.

Another peer will discover the pipe advertisement of a remote peer in a number of ways:

- From a file on the local machine
- Through an already established pipe
- In a module specification advertisement

```
<?xml version="1.0"?>
<jxta:PipeAdvertisement>
  <Id> UUID </Id>
  <Type> type of the pipe </Type>
  <Name> optional symbolic name that can be used by
     any search engine </Name>
</jxta:PipeAdvertisement>
```

Listing 5.12   A sample pipe advertisement.

Displaying an Advertisement

During the process of debugging a JXTA application, the capability to display the contents of an advertisement is invaluable. Fortunately, the code that displays the contents is quite simple. Listing 5.13 shows the code that you can use for any advertisement class. The code creates a PipeAdvertisement object in the first line. In the next line, a StructuredTextDocument object is created using the getDocument() method of the advertisement. The code will pull the advertisement as XML, based on the getDocument() method's parameter. A StructuredTextDocument object contains a method called sendToStream(), which outputs the contents of the document object into the specified stream object. Subsequently, the advertisement will appear in the terminal window or the command prompt from where the application is started.

```
PipeAdvertisement aPipeAdv = new PipeAdvertisement();
StructuredTextDocument aDoc = (StructuredTextDocument)
  aPipeAdv.getDocument(new MIMETYPE("text/xml"));
try {
  aDoc.sendToStream(System.out);
} catch(Exception e) {}
```

Listing 5.13 Display advertisement code.

Creating an Advertisement

At some point, a peer will need to create an advertisement for a service or pipe. As we mentioned earlier, there are several ways to obtain an advertisement. One way is to receive the advertisement from another peer in a pipe. In this case, the pipe advertisement is already built.

Another way a peer can obtain an advertisement is to pull it from the local file system. The code in Listing 5.14 shows how to pull an advertisement from the local file system into an object.

```
PipeAdvertisement myPipeAdvertisement = null;

try {
  FileInputStream is = new
    FileInputStream("service1.adv");
  myPipeAdvertisement = (PipeAdvertisement)
    AdvertisementFactory.newAdvertisement(new
    MimeMediaType("text/xml"), is);
} catch (Exception e) {
    System.out.println("failed to read/parse pipe
        advertisement");
      e.printStackTrace();
    System.exit(-1);
}
```

Listing 5.14 Code to pull an advertisement from a local file system.

The code assumes that the advertisement is already in a valid XML format. The code begins by creating a null PipeAdvertisement object. Next, a FileInput-Stream object is created using the filename of the advertisement that will be pulled. The code starting in Line 7 uses a class called AdvertisementFactory to build a new advertisement object based on data fed to it. In this case, the data is of XML type, and thus the first parameter to the newAdvertisement() method of the factory is the data type. The second parameter is where the information for the advertisement can be found. If any of these steps fail, an exception will be raised. Once the code finishes successfully, the PipeAdvertisement object will have valid information from the data file.

Building an Advertisement from Scratch

There will be times when you have to create a new advertisement on the fly. The code in Listing 5.15 shows the steps for building a new advertisement using all code and no data files.

```
ModuleSpecAdvertisement myModuleSpecAdvertisement =
  (ModuleSpecAdvertisement)AdvertisementFactory.

  newAdvertisement(ModuleSpecAdvertisement.
  getAdvertisementType());

myModuleSpecAdvertisement.setName(
  "JXTASPEC:JXTA-CH15EX2");
myModuleSpecAdvertisement.setVersion("Version 1.0");
myModuleSpecAdvertisement.setCreator("gradecki.com");
myModuleSpecAdvertisement.setModuleSpecID(
  IDFactory.newModuleSpecID(myService1ID));
myModuleSpecAdvertisement.setSpecURI(
  "<http://www.jxta.org/CH15EX2>");
myModuleSpecAdvertisement.setPipeAdvertisement(
  myPipeAdvertisement);
```

Listing 5.15   Code for building an advertisement.

The code in Listing 5.15 starts by calling the newAdvertisement() method of the AdvertisementFactory class. The exact method called is an overloaded method, which accepts the type of advertisement needed. The parameter to the method is obtained using the getAdvertisementType() method of the desired advertisement class. After the advertisement object has been created, the individual methods of the advertisement class are called with appropriate parameter values. The methods will basically fill in the values of specific elements in the advertisement. After all of the necessary methods are called, a valid advertisement object will have been populated.

Summary

Advertisements are the main information-dissemination tool for the JXTA system. Most all of the advertisements covered in this chapter are designed to be manipulated by a JXTA application and the developer. The next six chapters discuss the underlying protocols defined in the JXTA specification. Each of these protocols include their own advertisements for encapsulated communication between protocols and peers.

CHAPTER 6

Peer Discovery Protocol

The Peer Discovery Protocol (PDP) is a protocol designed to allow for the discovery of advertisements published by peers within a peer group. As we saw in the previous chapter, we use advertisements to describe and make available a wide variety of resources, including other peers, peer groups, and ordinary content. All resources must have an advertisement associated with them.

The PDP works in conjunction with a peer group, and is implemented as a discovery service. In the Java reference implementation, the DiscoveryService class allows peers associated with a particular group to publish and discover advertisements. The NetPeerGroup, the default group that all peers belong to, provides a discovery service to all peers without individual peers having to write their own service. When developers create their own peer group, the new group will typically be derived from the NetPeerGroup, thus enabling the new group to have publish and discovery services. The designers of the discovery protocol have written the specification and the Java reference implementation in a manner that allows the basic discovery service and PDP to serve as a basis for more intelligent and high-level discovery services.

This chapter, and all the other protocol chapters in this book, takes a twofold approach to presenting information about the JXTA protocols. First, we explain the protocol as it is defined in the specification. Second, we discuss the Java reference implementation for the protocol. It is not our intention to provide all of the code necessary to use the protocol—you can find most of that information in later chapters. Here, we want to provide insights into the reference implementation, and examine how the functionality is defined.

PDP Protocol Overview

The PDP works on two basic levels: local (within the requesting peer's own cache) and remote (across the network). In both cases, the requesting peer calls an exposed method of the discovery service implemented by a language binding of the JXTA specification. The methods have the following parameters:

- An element name to use as a search key
- A value for the search key
- A value indicating the number of returned responses desired

The discovery service, which implements the PDP, packages the information provided as parameters into a PDP query message represented as XML (see the section "The PDP Query Message Format"). We will examine the discovery service in detail later in this chapter.

In the case of a remote query, the requesting peer sends a query message to other peers on the network, including rendezvous peers, using the Peer Resolver Protocol (which we discuss in Chapter 7). Each peer that receives the query message will examine its advertisements to see if any match the search key and its associated value. If a match is found, the matching advertisement is returned to the requesting peer. The requesting peer has the option of using any of the returned advertisements.

In the case of a local query, the discovery service will check in the local cache of the peer to find any advertisements that match the request. The local cache contains advertisements sent from other peers, as well as advertisements created by the local peer. The discovery service doesn't need to build a query message when searching the local cache—the code can simply perform a search of the data structure used for holding the local cache. All of the obvious concerns exist with the local cache, including stale advertisements and peers that are no longer connected to the network. The local cache will also be populated with the advertisements found during any remote discoveries. In both the local and remote queries, results will be returned from peers with matching resource using a response message (see the section "The PDP Response Message Format").

The local cache is maintained in a directory called cm, which is located in the root directory in which a peer's application was started. Within the cm directory are a number of subdirectories, as shown in the following diagram. At the lowest level of the cache are the XML advertisements.

```
/cm
        /info-jxta-NetGroup
/info-jxta-WorldGroup
/jxta-NetGroup
        /Adv
        /Groups
        /Peers
                uuid-5949438393849202093484509398 2092
                uuid-9023083248484932098209209202 0200
        /private
        /public
        /tmp
/jxta-WorldGroup
```

Within the cm directory are the peer groups the peer has contacted. The system doesn't allow the mixing of advertisements across peer groups (notice the separate Adv, Peers, and Groups directories). In the publishing and discovery of advertisements, these three directories will be used as key parameters in the methods implementing the discovery of publishing.

In many cases, a discovery will return advertisements that aren't of the type being searched for. This is a normal operation for the JXTA network, and it enables the system to propagate advertisements effectively. For this reason, all advertisements found will need to be cast to the appropriate type and rejected if the cast is not successful.

In summary, a service that implements the PDP will follow these basic steps:

1. Receives a request for discovery, either local or remote, from an application.

2. For a local discovery, searches the local cache of the peer for the desired key/value.

3. For a remote discovery, builds a query message, and forwards it to all known peers.

4. Places responses from the query message in the local cache based on their type, and subsequently places them in the appropriate directory on the hard drive.

The PDP Query Message Format

The XML in Listing 6.1 shows the format required for a PDP query message. The elements are defined as follows:

Type—The advertisement type to be explicitly searched during the query. Its values are the following:

PEER—An advertisement that includes information about an individual peer

GROUP—An advertisement that includes information about a group

ADV—All advertisements

Threshold—The maximum number of advertisements to be returned by each peer.

PeerAdv—The advertisement of the peer performing the discovery request.

Attr—The <element> name that should be searched in all advertisements. An obvious example is the <name> element.

Value—The search string to be matched using the Attr element. The value can contain a wildcard character (*) at either end (or both ends of) the value string. A value of * will draw any advertisement of the specified type, although an implementation may choose to match no advertisement. If the Attr and Value elements are not present, peers will return a random number of advertisements up to the stated Threshold value.

```
<xs:element name="DiscoveryQuery" type="jxta:DiscoveryQuery"/>

<xs:complexType name="DiscoveryQuery">
    <!-- this should be an enumeration -->
    <xs:element name="Type" type="xs:string"/>
    <xs:element name="Threshold" type="xs:unsignedInt" minOccurs="0"/>
    <xs:element name="PeerAdv" type="jxta:PA" minOccurs="0"/>
    <xs:element name="Attr" type="xs:string" minOccurs="0"/>
    <xs:element name=vValue" type="xs:string" minOccurs="0"/>
</xs:complexType>
```

Listing 6.1 PDP query message XML format.

PDP Response Message Format

The XML in Listing 6.2 shows the format of a PDP response message. The elements in the response message are the following:

Type—The advertisement type returned in the <response> element.

Count—The total number of <response> elements in the response message.

PeerAdv—The peer advertisement of the responding peer.

- **Expiration**—An attribute of the <response> element that indicates the total number of milliseconds until expiration of the returned advertisement.

Attr—The element used in the search for the enclosed advertisements.

Value—The search string this response message relates.

Response—The <count> element noted previously indicates the total number of response advertisements that will appear under this element.

- **Expiration**—An attribute of the <response> element that indicates the total number of milliseconds until the expiration of the returned advertisement.

```
<xs:element name="DiscoveryResponse" type="jxta:DiscoveryResponse"/>

<xs:complexType name="DiscoveryResponse">
    <!-- this should be an enumeration -->
    <xs:element name="Type" type="xs:string"/>
    <xs:element name="Count" type="xs:unsignedInt" minOccurs="0"/>
    <xs:element name="PeerAdv" type="xs:anyType" minOccurs="0">
        <xs:attribute name="Expiration" type="xs:unsignedLong"/>
    </xs:element>
    <xs:element name="Attr" type="xs:string" minOccurs="0"/>
    <xs:element name="Value" type="xs:string" minOccurs="0"/>
    <xs:element name="Response" type="xs:anyType" maxOccurs="unbounded">
        <xs:attribute name=vExpiration" type="xs:unsignedLong"/>
</xs:element>
</xs:complexType>
```

Listing 6.2   PDP response message XML format.

Java Binding of the PDP

In the remainder of this chapter, we will look at the code necessary to perform discovery operations as defined in the Java binding of the JXTA specification. The classes necessary to implement discovery within a peer group, and ultimately a peer, are as follows:

- net.jxta.discovery.DiscoveryService
- net.jxta.discovery.DiscoveryListener
- net.jxta.impl.discovery.DiscoveryServiceImpl
- net.jxta.impl.discovery.DiscoveryServiceInterface

Discovery Service

The heart of the discovery implementation is the discovery service. The service has a twofold purpose: publishing of new advertisements and querying for advertisements. To support these purposes, the following methods are available:

- public Enumeration getLocalAdvertisements(int type, String attribute, String value);
- public int getRemoteAdvertisements(String peerid, int type, String attribute, String value, int threshold);
- public void getRemoteAdvertisements(String peerid, int type, String attribute, String value, int threshold, DiscoveryListener listener);
- public void publish(Advertisement advertisement, int type);
- public void publish(Advertisement adv, int type, long lifetime, long lifetimeForOthers);
- public void remotePublish(Advertisement adv, int type);
- public void remotePublish(Advertisement adv, int type, long lifetime);

A discovery service is a core service provided with the NetPeerGroup or any other group created using the NetPeerGroup as a default implementation. To obtain a discovery service object, simply use the getDiscoveryService() method belonging to the PeerGroup object obtained when the peer first joined a group. For example:

```
PeerGroup netPeerGroup; //holds a peergroup object associated
  with the NetPeerGroup
DiscoveryService myDiscoveryService =
  netPeerGroup.getDiscoveryService();
```

All of the initialization work required by the discovery service will be handled internally with the object. The discovery service interacts with the other protocols to both push and publish new advertisements in the current peer group. If a peer needs to publish or query advertisements in another peer group, it will have to obtain a PeerGroup object and instantiate a DiscoveryService object specific to that group.

Publishing Advertisements

Before advertisements can be queried, some advertisements must exist in the peer group. All peers will have advertisements cached relating to themselves as well as their peer group, but an application will also want to publish advertisements about resources available in the group. As we mentioned earlier, four methods are available for publishing advertisements:

```
public void publish(Advertisement advertisement, int type);
public void publish(Advertisement adv, int type, long
  lifetime, long lifetimeForOthers);
public void remotePublish(Advertisement adv, int type);
public void remotePublish(Advertisement adv, int type, long
  lifetime);
```

The methods can be grouped in terms of local publishing and remote publishing. All published advertisements have a default lifetime and a default expiration expressed in milliseconds. The current Java binding sets these values as the following:

```
public final static long DEFAULT_LIFETIME = 1000 * 60 * 60 *
  24 * 365;
public final static long DEFAULT_EXPIRATION = 1000 * 60 * 60 * 2;
```

The overloaded publishing methods allow the lifetime and expiration to be specified. In the case of the publish() method with a parameter called lifetimeForOthers, all peers who discover this advertisement will hold onto the advertisement for the number of milliseconds specified in lifetimeForOthers. This is because the peer that originally published the advertisement will republish the advertisement using the same time frame.

Local Publishing

An advertisement that is published locally will be placed in the cache of the executing peer and use a multicast transport, if available, to disseminate the advertisement to other peers. If the TCP transport is available, all peers on the local network will receive a copy of the published advertisement. The two methods available for a local publish are the following:

```
public void publish(Advertisement advertisement, int type);
public void publish(Advertisement adv, int type, long
  lifetime, long lifetimeForOthers);
```

In the first case, the advertisement will be published using the default lifetime and expiration values. In the second method, the lifetime and expiration (lifetimeForOthers) can be specified using milliseconds. Consider the code in Listing 6.3, which builds a ModuleClassAdvertisement object and publishes it locally.

```
ModuleClassAdvertisement myService1ModuleAdvertisement =
  (ModuleClassAdvertisement)
  AdvertisementFactory.newAdvertisement
  (ModuleClassAdvertisement.getAdvertisementType());

myService1ModuleAdvertisement.setName("JXTAMOD:JXTA-CH15EX2");
myService1ModuleAdvertisement.setDescription("Service 1 of
  Chapter 15 example 2");
myService1ID = IDFactory.newModuleClassID();
myService1ModuleAdvertisement.setModuleClassID(myService1ID);

try {
```

Listing 6.3 A local publishing example. (continues)

```
    myDiscoveryService.publish(myService1ModuleAdvertisement,
DiscoveryService.ADV);
                } catch (Exception e) {
        System.out.println("Error during publish of Module
Advertisement");
        System.exit(-1);
      }
    }
```

Listing 6.3   A local publishing example. (continued)

The Java binding requires that the publish() method be enclosed in a try block—it will throw an exception if there is any problem with the publishing.

Remote Publishing

An advertisement that is published remotely will be placed in the local cache, as well as broadcast to the current peer group using all available transports. This means that the advertisement will be delivered to all remote rendezvous peers using HTTP or TCP (depending on which protocol is available). Obviously, advertisements that are remotely published get the widest audience. Two methods are available for publishing remote advertisements:

```
public void remotePublish( Advertisement adv, int type );
public void remotePublish( Advertisement adv, int type, long
   lifetime );
```

To use the methods, just place them within a try block. For example:

```
try {
   myDiscoveryService.publish(myService1ModuleAdvertisement,
   DiscoveryService.ADV);
   myDiscoveryService.remotePublish(myService1ModuleAdvertisement,
   DiscoveryService.ADV);

            } catch (Exception e) {
        System.out.println("Error during publish of Module
   Advertisement");
        System.exit(-1);
      }
    }
```

The discovery service will create an Advertisement object from the information provided as parameters to the methods. The Advertisement will be sent to all known peers, as well as any currently configured rendezvous peers. In the examples preceding, it should be noted that we don't have to call publish() and then remotePublish() if the peer application does not need to publish advertisement to all remote peers. Remember that publish() uses only multi-cast protocols that will not allow publishing over HTTP.

Discovering Advertisements

The other primary functionality provided in the DiscoveryService object is querying for advertisements that meet a particular criterion. Three methods are available for finding advertisements in a peer group:

```
public Enumeration getLocalAdvertisements( int type,
   String attribute, String value );
public int getRemoteAdvertisements( String peerid, int type,
   String attribute, String value, int threshold );
public void getRemoteAdvertisements( String peerid, int type,
   String attribute, String value, int threshold,
   DiscoveryListener listener );
```

The getLocalAdvertisements() method is responsible for pulling advertisements from the local cache of the current peer only. All of the advertisements found in the cache matching the type, attr, and value specified in the method will be returned in an Enumeration object.

Both of the getRemoteAdvertisements() methods will send a propagated query message to all possible peers to find matching advertisements up to the specified threshold. When a remote peer finds a match, the advertisement will be returned to the requesting peer. The returned advertisement will be placed in the local cache, where a call to getLocalAdvertisements() will find it. Optionally, a listener object can be attached to the getRemoteAdvertisements() method, which will be called when any remote advertisement is returned that relates to the query.

Checking Advertisements

The advertisements are pulled from the local cache and placed into an Enumeration object. The Enumeration object consists of numerous XML elements, which in turn make up the advertisements. A loop is typically used to move through the Enumeration object. For example, the following code will loop through the Enumeration, looking for the start of a pipe advertisement and then determining its name:

```
TextElement singleElement = null;
TextElement childElements = null;

while (elements.hasMoreElements()) {
  singleElement = (TextElement) elements.nextElement();
  if (singleElement.getName().equals("jxta:PipeAdvertisement")) {
     childElements = (TextElement)singleElement.getChildren();
```

```
        while (childElements.hasMoreElements()) {
          tempElement = (TextElement) childElements.nextElement();
          if (tempElement.getName().equals("Name")) {
            //do something
            // check value with tempElement.getValue()
          }
        }
      }
    }
```

The code begins by checking to make sure there are elements in the current Enumeration. If elements are available, the name of the current element is checked; if the name is jxta:PipeAdvertisement, then a valid PipeAdvertisement is the current element. Because the code is XML, it must obtain the child elements of the current element in order to process them. Within the code, a loop is used to look at each of the child elements of the pipe advertisement and determine if the <Name> element is found, the value associated with the element is compared against the text passed to the method. The code will loop through all of the elements of each PipeAdvertisement element found in the Enumeration.

A Local Query

The code necessary to query the current cache for an advertisement is shown in Listing 6.4. The code starts by defining a local Enumeration object to hold any of the advertisements found in the cache. Next, a try block is created, and a call is made to the method getLocalAdvertisements(), using the appropriate parameters. The discovery service will use the information to pull appropriate advertisements from the local cache. No query message is sent on the network or to other peers—all advertisements are pulled from the cache only.

```
Enumeration localEnum;
try {
  localEnum = myDiscoveryService.getLocalAdvertisements(DiscoveryService.ADV,
  -name", -*group*");

  if (localEnum != null) {
    while (localEnum.hasMoreElements()) {
Element elem = localEnum.nextElement();
    }
  }
} catch (Exception e) {}
```

Listing 6.4 Local cache advertisement query code.

A Remote Query

A remote query is performed using the getRemoteAdvertisements() methods. The code in Listing 6.5 shows an example of requesting a remote discovery. The code is very basic—the only thing required is a call to the method using the appropriate parameters. The discovery service will create a query message using the parameter information and cause the message to be propagated within the JXTA network if the appropriate network protocols are available. All of the peers that receive the query message have the option of responding with advertisements matching the desired criteria. The advertisements are returned to the original peer and placed in the local cache. At this point, the peer would make a call to getLocalAdvertisements() using the same search criteria to find any returned advertisements.

```
try {
        myDiscoveryService.getRemoteAdvertisements(null,
  DiscoveryService.ADV, --name", --Group*", null);
} catch(Exception e) {}
```

Listing 6.5 Remote query discovery code.

Using an Asynchronous Listener

At the same time the getRemoteAdvertisements() functionality is placing a new response advertisement in the local cache, it also has the capability to call a method asynchronously when a new response appears. The functionality to do this callback is a *listener*, which works the same way as a button listener on a Java GUI screen. Your application can use the listener functionality in one of two ways. First, it can specify on the class line that it implements DiscoveryListener—the interface used to implement the remote query callback mechanism. The class declaration would look similar to this:

```
public class Client implements DiscoveryListener {
  // code to implement listener goes here
  }
```

The DiscoveryListener interface requires a single method be available based on the following prototype:

```
public void discoveryEvent(DiscoveryEvent e);
```

If the application states that it implements the interface, one of the methods must be discoveryEvent(). We will discuss the contents of this method in a moment.

The second way to implement DiscoveryListener is to use an inner anonymous class. The inner anonymous class is used to build a self-contained object, which will handle all of the incoming advertisements from a given query. Listing 6.6 shows an example.

The primary part of the code in Listing 6.6 is the creation of a new DiscoveryListener object. After the instantiation of the object, the discoveryEvent() method is created, along with the code necessary to handle a response message.

```
        DiscoveryListener myDiscoveryListener = new
DiscoveryListener() {
        public void discoveryEvent(DiscoveryEvent e) {
            Enumeration enum;
            String str;

            DiscoveryResponseMsg myMessage = e.getResponse();
            enum = myMessage.getResponses();
            str = (String)enum.nextElement();

            try {
              ModuleSpecAdvertisement myModSpecAdv =
(ModuleSpecAdvertisement) AdvertisementFactory.newAdvertisement(new
MimeMediaType("text",
  "xml"), new ByteArrayInputStream(str.getBytes()));
                PipeAdvertisment myPipeAdvertisement =
myModSpecAdv.getPipeAdvertisement();

            } catch(Exception ee) {
                ee.printStackTrace();
                System.exit(-1);
            }
        }
    };
```

Listing 6.6 DiscoveryListener inner anonymous class.

DiscoveryEvent Method

The DiscoveryEvent() method will be called each time a new discovery response is received. The parameter passed to the method is a DiscoveryEvent object, which contains a DiscoveryResponseMsg object. The Msg object is pulled from the DiscoveryEvent using the getResponse() method. An enumeration of the responses from the remote query is obtained by calling the getResponse() method of the DiscoveryResponseMsg object. Now, the advertisements returned can be parsed and processed as desired.

Assigning the Listener

After a listener object is created, it should be attached to the DiscoveryService object. There are basically two ways to perform the attachment. The first is by using an overloaded version of getRemoteAdvertisements():

```
myDiscoveryService.getRemoteAdvertisements(null,
  DiscoveryService.ADV, searchKey, searchValue, 1,
  myDiscoveryListener);
```

In this overloaded method, the DiscoveryListener object is passed to the discovery service as the last parameter and attached to the service. The second way to attach the listener is to use the addDiscoveryListener() method of the DiscoveryService object. The method is as follows:

```
public void addDiscoveryListener( DiscoveryListener
  listener );
```

If the listener is no longer needed, but the DiscoveryService object isn't destroyed, a listener can be removed with the following statement:

```
public boolean removeDiscoveryListener( DiscoveryListener
  listener );
```

Flushing Advertisements

One of the ancillary functions available through a DiscoveryService object is the capability to flush the cache of all current advertisements. Although a user can flush the advertisement quite easily by removing the /cm subdirectory found in the directory where the peer is executed, programmatically a peer can use the flushAdvertisements() method. The prototype for the method is as follows:

```
public void flushAdvertisements( String id, int type );
```

The id parameter is a valid document, peer, or peer group ID value. The type parameter is PEER, GROUP, or ADV. For the most part, the local cache will handle advertisements that have expired; however, if the expiration threshold of an advertisement hasn't been reached, but the peer that originally published the advertisement cannot be reached, the developer may want to flush the advertisement. For example:

```
flushAdvertisement(aPipeAdvertisement.getID().toString(),
    DiscoveryService.ADV);
```

This code will flush the advertisement associated with the object aPipeAdvertisement. It could be that all attempts were made to use the advertisement, but that all failed, so it will be flushed. Notice the use of the toString() method. The first parameter to the flushAdvertisement () method is a string, so the ID of the advertisement must be converted.

As you might expect though, there can be many reasons an advertisement appears to be "bad." The peer associated with the advertisement could be rebooting, or a network segment may be down. The peer itself could be down for several days, or perhaps permanently. Great care should be taken when flushing advertisements; however, all is not lost when one is flushed. The code just needs to perform a discovery to find new advertisements.

Summary

The Peer Discovery Protocol is essential to a JXTA application, which relies on resources being dynamically published to the group and discovered by other peers. As a core mechanism, the PDP provides the most basic and brute-force implementation for finding advertisements across any number of peers in a peer group. Peers and peer groups have the flexibility to use the basic mechanism, provide their own service, or extend the current one. Many of the services of the DiscoveryService class will be used in the next part of the book, in which we build JXTA applications. In the next chapter, the Peer Resolver Protocol will show how peers are able to find and communicate with each other without the use of a centralized server.

CHAPTER 7

Peer Resolver Protocol

When a peer needs to instantiate a query to other peers in the network, massive confusion would result if the peer just sent its own message to the other peers using whatever network protocol it had available. The JXTA specification defines a protocol called the Peer Resolver Protocol (PRP) with the purpose of laying out a framework for generic query and response communication between peers. The specification does not define any type of peer searching or discover service, but expects that such a service would be built using the framework. The service would be made available within a peer group.

The Java binding of the specification builds a resolver service using the PRP specification. The resolver service is directly associated with a peer group as a default or core service. The discovery service discussed in Chapter 6 is one of the beneficiaries of this service. The discovery service relies on the resolver service to handle the exchange of the query and response messages necessary for publishing and discovery.

An Overview of the PRP

The PRP is a set of generic query and response messages designed to facilitate a common messaging system among peers in the JXTA network. To reduce the amount of processing a service has to do, the messages are assigned and delivered to a specific handler on the peer. The *handler* is a name assigned to a definition that specifies the format of a message, as well as the response that can occur when a message of that type is received. For instance, a handler might use the rendezvous service to propagate a message to multiple peers or to send the message to a specific peer.

As you might expect, the discovery service will have a handler assigned to it that is designed to handle the discovery query and response messages. When the discovery service needs to send a query message, it passes the message to the PRP. The PRP will wrap the discovery query message in its own message, and send the new message to other peers. The PRP on the remote peers will receive the wrapper message and then forward the underlying message to the appropriate handler.

Handler Naming

The PRP uses the handler name to transfer messages arriving at, or leaving from, the peer to a specific endpoint service. (We cover the *endpoint service*, which handles low-level communication, in Chapter 9.) A listener is used to connect an endpoint service to a handler name. All of the details are currently handled by the Java binding's implementation of a resolver service. The current specification states that all PRP bindings must use a common format for naming. The format is a string concatenation of the service name, the ID of the peer's group, and a unique value. The ABNF for the handler name is shown in Listing 7.1.

```
<JXTARSLVRRSQRY>    ::= <JXTARSLVRNAM> <JXTAIDVAL> <JXTARSLVRQRYTAG>

<JXTARSLVRRSRSP>    ::= <JXTARSLVRNAM> <JXTAIDVAL> <JXTARSLVRRSPTAG>

<JXTARSLVRQRYTAG> ::= "ORes"

<JXTARSLVRRSPTAG> ::= "IRes"

<JXTARSLVRNAM>      ::= "jxta.service.resolver"

<JXTAIDVAL>         ::= JXTA ID
```

Listing 7.1   Listener naming syntax ABNF.

Only two listeners are currently defined for the PRP.

For queries:

```
jxta.service.resolver[group unique Id string]ORes
```

For responses:

```
jxta.service.resolver[group unique Id string]IRes
```

Although the service will be unique on a specific peer, all peers within a group will use the same service. Obviously, we can create a group that doesn't use the default resolver service implementation. In this situation, the query and response messages should still be the same because they are defined by the specification. However, we could create other handlers with unique messages and handler names.

Resolver Query Messages

As we discussed in Chapter 6, when a discovery service has to send a query to peers within a group, it will put the query into its own message format. The message will be given to the resolver service for delivery to other peers, and the resolver service will wrap the discovery message into its own message. Listing 7.2 shows the XML used for the resolver query message; the elements of the message are the following:

Credential—The credential object of the query peer.

SrcPeerID—The ID of the query peer.

HandlerName—A string that the receiving resolver service will use to determine how the enclosed query will be processed.

QueryID—A JXTA ID of the query; it must be used in response messages to identify the query.

Query—A string, in our case the discovery message, which represents the query.

```
<xs:element name="ResolverQuery" type="jxta:ResolverQuery"/>

<xs:complexType name="ResolverQuery">
    <xs:element name="Credential" type="xs:anyType" minOccurs="0"/>
    <xs:element name="SrcPeerID" type="xs:anyURI"/>
    <!-- This could be extended with a pattern restriction -->
    <xs:element name="HandlerName" type="xs:string"/>
    <xs:element name="QueryID" type="xs:string" minOccurs="0"/>
    <xs:element name="Query" type="xs:anyType"/>
</xs:complexType>
```

Listing 7.2 Resolver query message format.

Listing 7.3 shows an example of a query executed from the myJXTA application; the query is searching for content containing the string jpg. The XML message begins with the ResolverQuery element. This is the root element for the message, and it indicates that the message was created by the resolver service. The elements after the root are those required by the resolver query message format, including the handler name, credential, query ID, ID of the peer that issued the query, and the query itself. The <query> element is used to hold the discovery query message and its elements. The message starts on line 14 and runs through line 24.

```
Line 1: <?xml version="1.0"?>
<!DOCTYPE jxta:ResolverQuery>
<jxta:ResolverQuery xmlns:jxta="http://jxta.org">
    <HandlerName>
        urn:jxta:uuid-DEADBEEFDEAFBABAFEEDBABE0000000305
    </HandlerName>
    <Credential>JXTACRED</Credential>
    <QueryID>0</QueryID>
    <SrcPeerID>
Line 10:    urn:jxta:uuid-59616261646162614A787
            4615032503304BD268FA4764960AB93A53D7F15044503
    </SrcPeerID>
    <Query>
        <?xml version="1.0"?>
        <!DOCTYPE jxta:DiscoveryQuery>
        <jxta:DiscoveryQuery xmlns:jxta="http://jxta.org">
            <Type>2/Type>
            <Threshold>25</Threshold>
            <PeerAdv>
                <?xml version="1.0"?>
                <!DOCTYPE jxta:PA>
Lne 20:                     ...just too big to show ...
                </jxta:PA>
            </PeerAdv>
            <Attr>Name</Attr>
            <Value>*jpg*</Value>
        </jxta:DiscoveryQuery>
    </Query>
</jxta:ResolverQuery>
```

Listing 7.3   Sample of a resolver query.

Resolver Response Messages

When a query is executed, the remote peers are more than likely (although not required) to reply to the query with a result. The remote peers will put the response into a discovery service response message, and the discovery service will pass the message to the resolver service to deliver to the requesting peer. The resolver service will then wrap the message into its own message format, which is shown in Listing 7.4. The elements in the response message are as follows:

Credential—The credential object of the query peer.

HandlerName—A string that the receiving resolver service will use to determine how the enclosed query will be processed.

QueryID—A JXTA ID of the query; it must be used in response messages to identify the query.

Response—A string-based response to the query. In the case of the discovery service, the response will be its specified message.

```
<xs:element name="ResolverResponse" type="ResolverResponse"/>

<xs:complexType name="ResolverResponse">
    <xs:element name="Credential" type="xs:anyType" minOccurs="0"/>
    <xs:element name="HandlerName" type="xs:string"/>
    <xs:element name="QueryID" type="xs:string" minOccurs="0"/>
    <xs:element name="Response" type="xs:anyType"/>
</xs:complexType>
```

Listing 7.4 Resolver service response message.

Listing 7.5 shows an example of a response message from a remote peer. You can see the wrapping of various core service messages in the message. On line 3, an element named ResolverResponse indicates that this XML document is a message created by the resolver service. This root element is followed by the elements specific to the resolver service response message, such as the handler name, the credential, the query ID, and the response.

Within the Response element resides the discovery response message (remember that the resolver service is just handling the messages between handlers). Line 14 is the start of this message. Notice that the message is a complete and valid XML document because it begins with the processing instruction <?xml version="1.0"?>. Lines 14 through 41 represent the entire discovery response message.

Embedded in the message are the required fields: Count (the number of responses), Type (the discovery type used—PEER, PEERGROUP, ADV (2)), PeerAdv (most of the peer advertisement is removed because it is very large), and the Response element. The responses for the discovery query begin on line 27. The responses are advertisements, and subsequently include their appropriate elements. Notice the expiration on the advertisement being returned. This particular advertisement is a pipe advertisement that includes the pipe type and the ID that a peer can use to connect with the response peer.

```
Line 1:<?xml version="1.0"?>
<!DOCTYPE jxta:ResolverResponse>
<jxta:ResolverResponse xmlns:jxta="http://jxta.org">
    <HandlerName>
        urn:jxta:uuid-DEADBEEFDEAFBABAFEEDBABE0000000305
    </HandlerName>
    <Credential>
        JXTACRED
    </Credential>
Line 10:    <QueryID>
        0
    </QueryID>
    <Response>
        <?xml version="1.0"?>
        <!DOCTYPE jxta:DiscoveryResponse>
        <jxta:DiscoveryResponse xmlns:jxta="http://jxta.org">
            <Count>1</Count>
            <Type>2</Type>
            <PeerAdv>
Line 20:            <?xml version="1.0"?>
                <!DOCTYPE jxta:PA>
                <jxta:PA xmlns:jxta="http://jxta.org">
                    too big to show.
                </jxta:PA>
            </PeerAdv>
            <Response Expiration="7200000">
                <?xml version="1.0"?>
                <!DOCTYPE jxta:PipeAdvertisement>
                <jxta:PipeAdvertisement xmlns:jxta="http://jxta.org">
Line 30:                <Id>
                    urn:jxta:uuid-59616261646162
    614E50472050325033D1D1D1D1D1D1D1D1D1D1D1D1D1D104
                    </Id>
                    <Type>
                        JxtaPropagate
                    </Type>
                    <Name>
                        JxtaInputPipe
                    </Name>
Line 40:                </jxta:PipeAdvertisement>
            </Response>
        </jxta:DiscoveryResponse>
    </Response>
</jxta:ResolverResponse>
```

Listing 7.5 A sample response message. (continued)

No Guarantees

We all know the adage that the only guarantees in life are death and taxes; JXTA messages aren't going to challenge that. As we've seen, the PRP is designed to wrap query messages from high-level components and deliver them to the JXTA network. As responses are available, the PRP provides them to the calling components. Unfortunately, there are no guarantees that a query message sent from the discovery service and resolved through the PDP will arrive at a destination; furthermore, there are no guarantees that a response will be generated from the query.

Java Binding of the PRP

The Java binding for the PRP is defined in the following files:

- net.jxta.protocol.ResolverQueryMsg.java
- net.jxta.protocol.ResolverResponseMsg.java
- net.jxta.protocol.GenericResolver.java
- net.jxta.protocol.QueryHandler.java
- net.jxta.protocol.ResolverService.java
- net.jxta.protocol.ResolverInterface.java

You can find the actual implementation of the definition in the corresponding files in the net.jxta.impl.resolver package; the Java Reference implementation includes the PRP as a peer group service called the resolver service. For all of the basic and fundamental query/response operations found in the JXTA specifications, all you need is the default resolver service in the NetPeerGroup peer group. As an application developer, you do not have to become involved with the details of using the service. However, if you develop a new service and want to take advantage of the resolver's query/response mechanism, the remaining sections of this chapter will show you some of the basic code.

GenericResolver is a base interface that defines the methods for sending and receiving query and response messages. The ResolverService interface, which is derived from GenericResolver, implements methods for registering and unregistering handlers based on the QueryHandler interface. QueryHandler will receive objects of types ResolverQueryMsg and ResolverResponseMsg when the resolver service has to invoke a specific handler.

Building a Handler

The process of implementing code that handles developer-defined query/ response messages begins with the development of a handler. The QueryHandler interface contains two methods (note that we don't show the exceptions):

- ResolverResponseMsg ProcessQuery(ResolverQueryMsg)
- void ProcessResponse(ResolverResponseMsg)

The processQuery() method will be called with an object of type Resolver-QueryMsg. The code within the method is responsible for creating a Resolver-ResponseMsg to send to the calling peer, and should have a response based on the query message received. The processResponse() method will receive a ResolverResponseMsg, and will perform actions based on the response.

The processQuery() method has a number of exceptions that will be thrown in specific cases. These exceptions are as follows:

DiscardException—This exception is thrown when there is no response to the query and the query should not be propagated to other peers for an answer.

NoResponseException—This exception is thrown when the handler has no response to the query.

ResendQueryException—This exception is thrown when the current peer has no response to the query, but wants to know the answer. The query message will be re-sent to other peers to obtain an answer.

IOException—This exception is thrown when the handler is unable to respond to the query due to an error.

So, let's say we want to build a peer that offers a service that automatically translates a phrase from one language to another. We *could* implement this service in the application part of the peer, but it is such a routine request that the service can be moved into core functionality. Just as in the case of the discovery service, our new service will need query and response messages. The query message is shown in Listing 7.6, and the response message is shown in Listing 7.7.

```
<?xml version="1.0"?>
<translate:TranslateQuery  xmlns:translate="http://jxta.org">
  <from> </from>
  <to> </to>
  <phrase> </phrase>
</translate:TranslateQuery>
```

Listing 7.6 Translation query message.

```
<?xml version="1.0"?>
<translate:TranslateResponse  xmlns:translate="http://jxta.org">
  <from> </from>
  <to> </to>
  <phrase> </phrase>
</translate:TranslateResponse>
```

Listing 7.7   Translation response message.

Based on these two messages, we need to build a QueryHandler object that will take the information provided in the query message, perform a translation, and return the new phrase in a response message. Listing 7.8 shows the code necessary to build a QueryHandler for our translation messages. As we discussed earlier, only two methods are available in the QueryHandler interface: processQuery() and processResponse().

The processQuery() method has four functions. First, the query message received needs to be parsed and the individual message pieces extracted. This parsing is accomplished using a loop and several conditional statements to pull out the to, from, and phrase strings. Next, the phrase has to be translated from the "from" language into the "to" language. Then, an XML document is created with the new phrase. Finally, a response object is created that wraps the new XML document. During the translation, the code should throw any of the exceptions listed earlier as appropriate. For instance, there could be languages that aren't recognized, and as such, the handler should not produce a response.

The processResponse() method is simple in that the only functionality is the parsing of the response message. The to, from, and phrase parts of the response are obtained and dealt with appropriately.

```
class TranslationHandler implements QueryHandler
{
    public ResolverResponseMsg processQuery(ResolverQueryMsg queryMsg)
        throws IOException, NoResponseException,
            DiscardQueryException, ResendQueryException
    {
        ResolverResponse responseMsg;
        String to = null;
        String from = null;
        String phrase = null;
        String newPhrase = null;
```

Listing 7.8   Translation QueryHandler. (continues)

```
//parse the query Message

StructuredTextDocument doc = (StructuredTextDocument)
   StructuredDocumentFactory.newStructuredDocument(
   new MimeMediaType("text/xml"), queryMsg.getQuery() );

Enumeration elements = doc.getChildren();
while (elements.hasMoreElements()) {
   TextElement element = (TextElement)
     elements.nextElement();
   if(element.getName().equals("to")) {
       to = element.getTextValue();
       continue;
   }
   if(element.getName().equals("from")) {
       from = element.getTextValue();
       continue;
   }
   if(element.getName().equals("phrase")) {
       phrase = element.getTextValue();
       continue;
   }
}



// Perform the translation and place the new phrase
// in the variable newPhrase

// Insert code here

// Build the response
Element element;
StructuredDocument doc = (StructuredTextDocument)
    StructuredDocumentFactory.newStructuredDocument(
    new MimeMediaType( "text/xml" ),
    "translate:TranslateResponse");

element = doc.createElement("to", to);
doc.appendChild(element);

element = doc.createElement("from", from);
doc.appendChild(element);

element = doc.createElement("phrase", newPhrase);
doc.appendChild(element);

responseMsg = new ResolverResponse("TranslateHandler",
```

Listing 7.8 Translation QueryHandler. (continues)

```
            "JXTACRED", queryMsg.getQueryId(),
            doc.toString());

    return responseMsg;
}

public void processResponse(ResolverResponseMsg responseMsg)
{

  String to = null;
  String from = null;
  String phrase = null;
  String newPhrase = null;

  try {
    StructuredTextDocument doc = (StructuredTextDocument)
      StructuredDocumentFactory.newStructuredDocument(
      new MimeMediaType("text/xml"),
      responseMsg.getResponse() );

    Enumeration elements = doc.getChildren();
    while (elements.hasMoreElements()) {
      TextElement element = (TextElement)
        elements.nextElement();

      if(element.getName().equals("to")) {
        to = element.getTextValue();
        continue;
      }
      if(element.getName().equals("from")) {
        from = element.getTextValue();
        continue;
      }
      if(element.getName().equals("phrase")) {
        phrase = element.getTextValue();
        continue;
      }
    }

    }
    catch (Exception e){
      // ignore
    }
  }
}
```

Listing 7.8   Translation QueryHandler. (continued)

Getting the Resolver and Registering a Handler

With the query and response messages created and a QueryHandler built, it is time to associate the handler with the resolver service. This is a twofold process. First, the resolver service has to be obtained from the peer group. The following code will handle this:

```
ResolverService resolver = currentGroup.getResolverService();
```

Next, the resolver service's register() method is called using an instance of the QueryHandler class built earlier as a parameter. The statement that performs the registration is the following:

```
TranslationHandler handler = new
    TranslationHandler();
resolver.registerHandler("TranslationHandler",
    handler);
```

The first parameter to the registerHandler() method is the name of the handler. Notice that this name is the same as that found in the instantiation of a ResolverResponse in the processQuery() method of the query handler. This name tells the resolver where to send query and response messages.

Sending a Query

After the handler is registered, a peer can send a query to the handler using the resolver. For example:

```
Element element;
StructuredDocument doc = StructuredTextDocument)
  StructuredDocumentFactory.newStructuredDocument(
  new MimeMediaType( "text/xml" ),
  "translate:TranslateResponse");

element = doc.createElement("to", "German");
doc.appendChild(element);

element = doc.createElement("from", "English");
doc.appendChild(element);

element = doc.createElement("phrase", "Have a good
  day");
doc.appendChild(element);


ResolverQuery query = new
  ResolverQuery("TranslationHandler","JXTACRED",
  netPeerGroup.getPeerID().toString(), doc.toString(),
  0);

resolver.sendQuery(null, query);
```

This code begins by creating a new XML document with the to, from, and phrase elements containing the information for the translation. Next, a new ResolverQuery object is instantiated using the name of the query handler, and the XML document is created. The message will be sent to other peers in the last line of the code, where the sendQuery() method is called. When the current peer receives a response from the query, the processResponse() method of the handler will be called, and the appropriate actions outlined in the code will be executed.

Summary

The Peer Resolver Protocol is another step in the progression toward exchanging information between peers. The Java binding's resolver service acts as a traffic director, pushing query and response messages to the proper handlers. The PRP is used by the Peer Discovery Protocol, but doesn't do the actual transmission of the query and response messages. This task is left to other protocols, as explained in upcoming chapters. Next, we look at the Peer Information Protocol, which has the singular purpose of providing information about a peer.

8

Peer Information Protocol

With most network-based applications, there is always the desire to know what the remote peers are doing. The desire could be to know just the peer's name, but might also include knowing how long the peer has been active, when the peer last sent a message, and even how much data has been transferred from the peer.

The JXTA specification includes a protocol called the Peer Information Protocol (PIP) to handle information requests about remote peers. Like most of the other JXTA protocols, the PIP is implemented by using a series of messages transferred between two or more peers. In Chapter 16, we'll use this protocol to implement peer monitoring.

The PIP is not a complete protocol at this time, and is changing with each new release of the specification. The information contained in this chapter, as well as Chapter 16, was accurate as of the time this book went to print, but may change as the JXTA specification matures in this area.

An Overview of the PIP

The JXTA specification declares that the PIP is optional in any binding; accordingly, the specification doesn't place any requirements on remote peers to respond to PIP messages. The PIP messages are sent via unreliable and non-secure pipes, which in themselves could prevent messages from getting to a remote peer. To handle the routing and transport of the PIP messages, the protocol is built on top of the Peer Resolver Protocol, which uses other protocols for actual message transport.

PIP Query Messages

The PIP uses a query message (shown in Listing 8.1) to request information from a remote peer. The elements of the message are as follows:

sourcePid—The ID of the requesting peer

targetPid—The ID of the destination peer

request—An optional request

The request element forms the basis of this message. If the element itself is empty, the destination peer will assume that the requestor wants only default information, and that information is returned based on the PIP response message (which we will cover in a moment). If the requesting peer is interested in additional information, a query message can be made a part of the element. The implementation of the PIP must be able to receive and process the information request appropriately.

```
<xs:element name="PeerInfoQueryMessage" type="jxta:PeerInfoQueryMessage"/>
<xs:complexType name="PeerInfoQueryMessage">
    <xs:element name="sourcePid" type="xs:anyURI"/>
    <xs:element name="targetPid" type="xs:anyURI"/>
    <xs:element name="request" type="xs:anyType" minOccurs="0"/>
</xs:complexType>
```

Listing 8.1   PIP query message format.

PIP Response Messages

When a peer receives a PIP response message, the peer resolver forwards the message to the appropriate handler, which is responsible for responding to the query. The elements in the message are as follows:

sourcePid—The ID of the requesting peer

targetPid—The ID of the destination peer

uptime—The time (in milliseconds) since the PIP service started execution on the remote peer

timestamp—Epoch time (in milliseconds) when the response message was created

traffic—The parent element for information about network traffic generated by this peer

- **lastIncomingMessageAt**—Epoch time (in milliseconds) since the remote peer last received a message
- **lastOutgoingMessageAt**—Epoch time (in milliseconds) since the remote peer last sent a message
- **in**—The parent element for incoming traffic information
  - **transport**—The number of bytes received at a specific endpoint address
- **out**—The parent element for outgoing traffic information
  - **transport**—The number of bytes sent to a specific endpoint address

response—The element that optionally contains information based on the corresponding request element of the query message

Listing 8.2 contains a sample PIP query sent to a remote peer. Listing 8.3 shows the remote peer's response to the PIP query.

```xml
<xs:element name="PeerInfoResponse" type="jxta:PeerInfoResponse"/>

<xs:complexType name="PeerInfoResponse">
    <xs:element name="sourcePid" type="xs:anyURI"/>
    <xs:element name="targetPidv type=vxs:anyURI"/>
    <xs:element name="uptime" type="xs:unsignedLong" minOccurs="0"/>
    <xs:element name="timestamp" type="xs:unsignedLong" minOccurs="0"/>
    <xs:element name=vresponse" type="xs:anyType" minOccurs="0"/>
    <xs:element name="traffic" type="jxta:piptraffic" minOccurs="0"/>
</xs:complexType>

<xs:complexType name="piptraffic">
    <xs:element name="lastIncomingMessageAt"
type="xs:unsignedLong" minOccurs="0"/>
    <xs:element name="lastOutgoingMessageAt"
type="xs:unsignedLong" minOccurs="0"/>
    <xs:element name="in" type="jxta:piptrafficinfo" minOccurs="0"/>
    <xs:element name="out" type="jxta:piptrafficinfo" minOccurs="0"/>
</xs:complexType>

<xs:complexType name="piptrafficinfo">
    <xs:element name="transport" type="xs:unsignedLong"
maxOccurs="unbounded">
        <xs:attribute name="endptaddr" type="xs:anyURI"/>
    </xs:element>
</xs:complexType>
```

Listing 8.2 PIP query message.

```
<?xml version="1.0"?>

<!DOCTYPE jxta:PeerInfoAdvertisement>

<jxta:PeerInfoAdvertisement xmlns:jxta="http://jxta.org">
        <sourcePid>
                urn:jxta:uuid-
59616261646162614A787461503250337CE1ACE17356403D8EECBE6B9D25351303
        </sourcePid>
        <targetPid>
                urn:jxta:uuid-
59616261646162614A787461503250337CE1ACE17356403D8EECBE6B9D25351303
        </targetPid>
        <uptime>
                22642
        </uptime>
        <timestamp>
                1010872452153
        </timestamp>
        <traffic>
                <in>
                </in>
                <lastIncomingMessageAt>
                        0
                </lastIncomingMessageAt>
                <out>
                </out>
                <lastOutgoingMessageAt>
                        0
                </lastOutgoingMessageAt>
        </traffic>
</jxta:PeerInfoAdvertisement>
```

Listing 8.3 Corresponding PIP response message.

Java Binding of the PIP

The Java binding of the PIP is defined in these files:

- net.jxta.peer.PeerInfoAdv.java
- net.jxta.protocol.PeerInfoAdvertisement.java
- net.jxta.peer.PeerInfoEvent.java
- net.jxta.peer.PeerInfoListener.java
- net.jxta.peer.PeerInfoService.java

- net.jxta.impl.peer.PeerInfoServiceImpl.java
- net.jxta.impl.peer.PeerInfoServiceInterface.java

The PIP service is created and a listener object attached to it; the listener is defined in the PeerInfoListener class. (See Chapter 16 for a working application that demonstrates these concepts.) When a query is sent, the listener object will wait for a response. When a response is returned, it is encapsulated in a Peer-InfoEvent object. The PeerInfoEvent object includes a method for extracting a PeerInfoAdvertisement object. Within the PeerInfoAdvertisement object are methods for extracting the various elements of the object without having to perform XML parsing.

Requesting Peer Information

All peers in the JXTA network have a peer ID associated with them. The peer ID is a unique identifier and is present in all peer advertisements. If a peer knows the advertisement or ID of another peer in the network, it can make a peer information request. The first step in requesting peer information is to obtain a reference to the PeerInfoService:

```
private PeerInfoService myPeerInfoService = null;
myPeerInfoService = netPeerGroup.getPeerInfoService();
```

Next, a request is made of the PeerInfoService object in the same manner as a query using the discovery service. The code is the following:

```
myPeerInfoService.getRemotePeerInfo(localPeerID,
peerInfoListener);
```

Two parameters to the getRemotePeerInfo() method provide all of the information necessary to request a PeerInfoAdvertisement from a remote peer. The first parameter is the ID of the remote peer from which information is requested. The second parameter is a listener that will be called when the remote peer returns a PIP response.

Building a Listener

The listener class for a PIP response is shown in Listing 8.4. A PIP listener is defined based on the PeerInfoListener interface, and requires a method called peerInfoResponse(). When the listener is activated, the peerInfoResponse() method will be executed and provided with a PeerInfoEvent object. One of the primary methods of the PeerInfoEvent object is getPeerInfoAdvertisement(). The return value of this method is a PeerInfoAdvertisement object, which allows access to its internal attributes using a series of methods.

```
PeerInfoListener peerInfoListener = new PeerInfoListener() {
  public void peerInfoResponse(PeerInfoEvent e) {
    PeerInfoAdvertisement adv = e.getPeerInfoAdvertisement();

  //displaying information from peer


  }
};
```

Listing 8.4 PIP listener.

Viewing the Information Returned

The PeerInfoAdvertisement object includes a number of methods for obtaining the information contained within the advertisement. These methods are:

Enumeration getIncomingTrafficChannels( )—Returns an enumeration of all incoming traffic channels

long getIncomingTrafficOnChannel(String channelName)—Returns the total bytes received on the specified channel

long getLastIncomingMessageTime( )—Returns a timestamp indicating when the last incoming message was received

long getLastOutgoingMessageTime( )—Returns a timestamp indicating when the last outgoing message was sent

Enumeration getOutgoingTrafficChannels( )—Returns an enumeration of all outgoing traffic channels

long getOutgoingTrafficOnChannel(String channelName)—Returns the total bytes sent on the specified channel

long getUptime( )—Returns the total uptime of the peer in milliseconds

The basic information about the peer can be displayed by calling the appropriate method. For example:

```
displayArea.append("Total Uptime in milliseconds - " +
adv.getUptime() + "\n");
```

For the channel traffic information, we must use an enumeration. This code will pull an enumeration for all the incoming channels on the remote peer and display the total bytes in each:

```
        Enumeration localInEnum =
adv.getIncomingTrafficChannels();
        while (localInEnum.hasMoreElements()) {
          String inChannelName = (String)localInEnum.nextElement();
```

```
        displayArea.append("Incoming Channel Bytes = " +
adv.getIncomingTrafficOnChannel(inChannelName) + "\n");
      }
```

Summary

The Peer Information Protocol is basically an ancillary protocol created within the JXTA specification for the monitoring and metering of JXTA peers. The current specification isn't completed as of this writing, but all indications point to a robust protocol in the future. In the next chapter, the Peer Endpoint Protocol (PEP) will be discussed. This is the protocol responsible for determining and finding a route between two peers that need to communicate.

CHAPTER 9

Peer Endpoint Protocol

All of the protocols we've covered up to this point deal with the manipulation and encapsulation of messages for transport to another peer; however, none of those protocols is able to perform the actual transportation of the messages. The Peer Endpoint Protocol (PEP) is responsible for determining a route between peers in the JXTA network. The endpoint service is a core service in the Java reference implementation that is responsible for implementing the PEP.

The PEP is designed to provide the communication channel between one peer and possibly several others. Located at the bottom of the protocol layer, the PEP handles many of the low-level details of communication.

An Overview of the Peer Endpoint Protocol

The PEP is responsible for providing a facade that makes two peers that don't have a direct connection to each other seem as if they do. This makes the JXTA network appear to be a many-to-many network topology. Having a separate protocol for this virtual connection means that the endpoint service doesn't need to know whether two peers are directly connected.

To accomplish this, the protocol defines a number of messages, consisting of queries and responses (in much the same way many of the other protocols do). The query and response messages are as follows:

Ping query—The endpoint service sends this message to determine whether a route exists between peers. In most situations, the connection will be a direct one and won't involve propagation. When a peer receives a ping query message, it responds to that message.

Ping response—When a peer receives a ping query, it sends a ping response message. The message will let the source peer know that a route is available between the peers.

Route query—If a peer needs to send a message to another peer, but doesn't have a direct route, it sends a route query message to the peer's directly connected peer looking for a route to the peer.

Route response—If a peer has a route to a target peer, the peer sends a route response to the requesting peer. In other words, the route response message is an answer to a route query message.

Each of the query and response messages contains a number of elements, including the following:

Source—The endpoint address of the source peer

Destination—The endpoint address of the potential destination peer

LastHop—The endpoint address of the last router to touch the message

NbOfHop—The total number of peers the message has touched

ForwardRoute—An optional list of endpoint address strings a peer would need to send a message to reach a destination peer

ReverseRoute—An optional list of endpoint address strings a peer would use to respond to a message sent from a source peer

Endpoint Service

The endpoint service is a core peer group service that provides transport functionality between peers using a JXTA transport protocol. The current JXTA transport protocols are as follows:

- HTTP Transport
- TCP Transport
- TLS Transport
- Beep Transport
- ServletHttpTransport

The JXTA transport protocols are responsible for the low-level communication over those specific channels. The endpoint service is used by other core services, such as the resolver and propagation services. By using the endpoint service, peers can be assured that messages sent on the JXTA network are using the network topology defined in the specification. We will see in Chapter 18 that there are ways to bypass the topology of the JXTA network and send "raw" messages using any topology necessary for a given task.

If you dig into the details of the endpoint service, it will become clear that the service is responsible only for sending messages from one peer to another. The peers can be local to each other or connected through relay peers. This makes sense because most of the JXTA transport protocols are designed for one-to-one communication between directly connected peers. The Peer Endpoint Protocol handles the process of making disconnected peers appear to be connected.

Sending a Message

When a message is ready to be sent from one peer to another, the endpoint service needs a source and destination in the form of an ID. The ID is constructed in the following format:

```
protocol://address_as_per_protocol/unique_name_of_recipient/
    unique_name_in_recipient_context
```

Based on the value of the protocol string, the endpoint service invokes an endpoint protocol, such as TCP or HTTP. The *address_as_per_protocol* value represents the machine that the message is being sent to. For the TCP protocol, this value would typically be an IP address. When the message arrives at the destination machine, a handler is invoked based on a concatenation of the *unique_name_of_recipient* and *unique_name_in_recipient_context* values.

Endpoint Protocols

Currently, five endpoint protocols are defined in the Java binding of the JXTA specification:

- HTTP Transport
- TCP Transport
- TLS Transport
- Beep Transport
- ServletHttpTransport

The protocols defined in the current Java implementation are all written to follow the endpoint protocol, but provide different functionality. All potential protocols must implement the following methods:

```
    public EndpointMessenger getMessenger (EndpointAddress dest);
    public void propagate (Message msg, String serviceName,
String serviceParams, String prunePeer);
    public boolean allowOverLoad();
    public String getProtocolName();
    public EndpointAddress getPublicAddress();
    public boolean isConnectionOriented();
    public boolean allowRouting();
    public boolean ping (EndpointAddress addr);
```

The two most important methods are getMessenger() and propagate(). Both methods accept an endpoint address that consists of the concatenated *unique_name_of_recipient* and *unique_name_in_recipient_context* values. The getMessenger() method is used to send a message from one peer directly to another without any type of routing needed, whereas the propagate() method is called when a message should be given to all local peers reachable from the current peer. Each of the individual transport implementations are responsible for overriding the methods above as well as for providing all of the code necessary for handling traffic to and from individual peers.

The actual Java implementations of the transport protocols can be found in these files:

- HttpTransport.java
- ServletHttpTransport.java
- TcpTransport.java
- TlsTransport.java
- BeepTransport.java

Java Binding of the Peer Endpoint Protocol

The Peer Endpoint Protocol is implemented in the Java binding within the file EndpointRouter.java. The purpose of the endpoint router is to get a message from point A to point B. With this task in mind, the router will do everything it can to minimize the amount of work necessary to accomplish the task. One of the tools the router uses to minimize the work is a *route cache*. When a route is needed between two peers, the endpoint router checks its internal cache to find the route. If a route is found, it will be used; if no route is found in the cache, a route query message is sent to the JXTA network.

All messages from the endpoint router use both the discovery and router services. These core services allow the query messages to be published and routed throughout the JXTA network. The method within the endpoint router that does the work of finding an address is the following:

```
public EndpointAddress getAddress(String pId)
```

This method accepts the ID of a peer and returns an endpoint address that can be used to communicate with the peer. The steps to finding a route are as follows:

1. Check to see whether the peer is directly connected; the endpoint router will attempt to reach the destination peer locally. If the peer is directly connected to the current peer, the route is found.

2. If no direct route exists, check the already routed routes. This step checks the cache for the route. If a route is found, it is used.

3. If the peer is not directly connected and no route is found in the cache, a query must be sent into the JXTA network to find a route. The code for building the query is in the findRoute() method.

This code snippet illustrates the building of a query message:

```
StructuredTextDocument doc = ( StructuredTextDocument )
StructuredDocumentFactory.newStructuredDocument(new
MimeMediaType("text/xml"),"jxta:EndpointRouter");

Element e = null;
e = doc.createElement(TypeTag, RouteQuery);
doc.appendChild(e);

e = doc.createElement(DestPeerIdTag, peer);
doc.appendChild(e);

e = doc.createElement(RoutingPeerAdvTag, localPeerAdv);
doc.appendChild(e);
```

After the query message is created, a resolver object is instantiated, and the query is sent throughout the network.

If a response is received for the query, the route listed in the response message will be added to the cache. The code will loop, trying to find the route, up to one minute. After a minute, the attempt is abandoned, and no route will be available to the peer. Note that most of this functionality is hidden within the endpoint service.

The code to perform this basic functionality is shown in Listing 9.1.

```
    EndpointService myEndpointService =
netPeerGroup.getEndpointService();

    EndpointAddress endpointAddress =
myEndpointService.newEndpointAddress(toAddress);
    endpointAddress.setServiceName("tempServiceName");
```

Listing 9.1 Obtaining and sending data through endpoints. (continues)

```
            endpointAddress.setServiceParameter("tempParams");

            if (myEndpointService.ping(endpointAddress)) {
               Message message = myEndpointService.newMessage();
Line 110:            message.setString("MessageText", "Just a String");

               try {
                  EndpointMessenger messenger =
   myEndpointService.getMessenger(endpointAddress);
                  messenger.sendMessage(message);
               } catch (IOException e) {
                  System.out.println("Error sending to endpoint");
               }
            } else {
               displayArea.append("No Endpoint Available\n");
         }
```

Listing 9.1 Obtaining and sending data through endpoints. (continued)

The code first obtains the endpoint service from the current peer group. Next, an endpointAddress object is instantiated. This object holds the ID—the toAddress parameter—of the peer to which a connection is being requested. After the address of the remote peer is known, a call is made to the ping() method of the endpointService object. The ping() method has the effect of putting into motion the sending of query messages in order to find a route between the requesting peer and the remote peer.

If the query is successful, an endpoint message will be created and sent to the remote peer; otherwise, an error message is displayed informing the user that no endpoint connection is available between the two peers. You can find additional code in Chapter 18, which shows all the steps necessary to use the Peer Endpoint Protocol and its implementation, the endpoint service, to send information between peers.

Summary

All of the JXTA protocols rely on the endpoint service, transport protocols, and the Endpoint Router Transport Protocol to send messages throughout the network. These protocols and service work together to send data in the network, as well as to find routes to both direct and remote peers. In the next chapter, we discuss the Pipe Binding Protocol. This protocol builds on the low-level functionality presented in this chapter to allow information to be passed through a higher level channel called a pipe.

CHAPTER 10

Pipe Binding Protocol

O ne of the most used protocols of the JXTA specification is the Pipe Binding Protocol (PBP). It is based on the assumption that a peer will create an input pipe and want to have remote peers connect to the pipe for information transfer.

The PBP defines a pipe, and specifies how the pipe can be used for communication between peers within a group. The pipe is an abstract communication channel built on an Internet transport protocol, such as HTTP or TCP/IP. Just as in the case of a Unix shell pipe, there are two ends to the pipe: an input, or receiving, end and the output, or sending, end.

Overview of the Pipe Binding Protocol

To facilitate the transfer of information down the pipe, the Pipe Binding Protocol is built on top of the Peer Endpoint Protocol (see Chapter 9). The PBP is a high-level service within the JXTA specification, and exists for the purpose of allowing messages to be passed from peer to peer. The PBP uses the Peer Resolver Protocol to obtain a path from one peer to another. The Peer Resolver Protocol will use the Rendezvous Protocol if it needs to propagate messages to a remote peer; it will use the Endpoint Protocol for more direct communication.

The current protocol specification outlines three different types of pipes:

Unicast—A one-way connection between two peers. The specification states that the Unicast pipe is unreliable and not secure. Most bindings will use TCP/IP for the Unicast pipe. In the specification and Java implementation, the descriptor for this pipe type is JxtaUnicast.

SecureUnicast—A one-way connection between two peers. The connection is secured using TLS for data encryption. In the specification and Java implementation, the descriptor for this pipe type is JxtaUnicastSecure.

Propagate—A one-to-many connection between a host peer and multiple remote peers. The connection is unreliable and not secure. In the specification and Java implementation, the descriptor for this pipe type is JxtaPropagate.

As we will see in Chapter 13, the Java binding contains reliable and bi-directional pipes, both of which are built on the one-way and unreliable pipes defined in the JXTA specification.

Pipe Advertisements

A peer uses a pipe advertisement to describe the characteristics of a pipe. As you might expect, the pipe advertisement encompasses all of the information necessary to describe a pipe. Listing 10.1 shows the format of a pipe advertisement (a full example found in Listing 10.4 will be discussed later in the chapter). The elements in the advertisement are the following:

Name—An optional name used for the pipe

ID—A JXTA ID for the pipe

Type—JxtaUnicast, JxtaUnicastSecure, or JxtaPropagate

```
<?xml version="1.0" encoding="UTF-8"?>
<jxta:PipeAdvertisement>
        <Name></Name>
        <Id></Id>
        <Type></Type>
</jxta:PipeAdvertisement>
```

Listing 10.1 Pipe advertisement format.

Pipe Binding Query Messages

The PBP has to perform quite a bit of work in order to connect two peers using a pipe. A peer will create an input pipe as well as a pipe advertisement. A remote peer will discover the pipe advertisement through a query or through information provided directly by the host peer. The remote peer cannot assume that the host peer actually has the pipe built and ready for communication; therefore, the peer sends a pipe resolver message to the host peer. The message format is shown in Listing 10.2; the elements of the message are:

MsgType—A value of either *Query* or *Answer*. A *Query* value occurs when a remote peer initially sends the message to a host peer. An *Answer* value occurs when the host peer responds to the remote peer's original request.

PipeID—The JXTA ID of the pipe being queried.

Type—The pipe type: JxtaUnicast, JxtaUnicastSecure, or JxtaPropagate.

Cached—A value of *false* means that the answer shouldn't come from the cache of the remote peer, but needs to be provided based on current data.

Peer—The peer ID of the host peer that should answer the query. If the value isn't present and the cached element has a value of *true*, an intermediary peer could respond to the query.

Found—A value of *true* indicates that the pipe was found on the remote peer

PeerAdv—The peer advertisement of the pipe

The PBP will use the answer message to build an appropriate output pipe to the remote peer.

```
<xs:element name="PipeResolver" type="jxta:PipeResolver"/>

<xs:complexType name="PipeResolver">
    <!-- should be an enumeration choice -->
    <xs:element name="MsgType" type="xs:string"/>
    <xs:element name="PipeId" type="JXTAID"/>
    <xs:element name="Type" type="xs:string" minOccurs="0"/>

    <!-- used in the query -->
    <xs:element name="Cached" type="xs:boolean" default="false"
minOccurs="0"/>
    <xs:element name="Peer" type="JXTAID" minOccurs="0"/>

    <!-- used in the answer -->
    <xs:element name="Found" type="xs:boolean" minOccurs="0"/>
    <!-- This should refer to a peer adv, but is instead a whole
doc -->
    <xs:element name="PeerAdv" type="xs:string" minOccurs="0"/>
</xs:complexType>
```

Listing 10.2 Pipe resolver message.

Java Binding

The Java binding of the PBP is implemented in the following files.

- PipeID.java
- PipeAdv.java
- PipeResolver.java
- PipeServiceImpl.java
- PipeServiceInterface.java

The protocol is implemented as the pipe service in the same manner as the other protocols. A pipe service is obtained through the peer group of which the peer is currently a member. The implementation of the pipe service is a core function within the default peer group provided with the JXTA Java binding. In order to use the PBP, a pipe service is obtained for the peer group with the code:

```
PipeService localPipeService = netPeerGroup.getPipeService();
```

The service itself provides the ability to create input and output pipes and create a message object to be sent through an output pipe. The methods for these operations are shown in Table 10.1.

Table 10.1 Pipe Operations and Corresponding Methods

OPERATION	METHOD
InputPipe	createInputPipe(PipeAdvertisement adv)
InputPipe	createInputPipe(PipeAdvertisement adv, PipeMsgListener listener)
OutputPipe	createOutputPipe(PipeAdvertisement adv, java.util.Enumeration peers, long timeout)
OutputPipe	createOutputPipe(PipeAdvertisement adv, long timeout)
void	createOutputPipe(PipeAdvertisement adv, OutputPipeListener listener)

Looking through the implementation, you will find that the pipe service is basically a wrapper around the PipeResolver class. The PipeService class provides the high-level functionality for such applications as creating pipes and messages. The PipeResolver class is responsible for all aspects of query/answer message handling as well as pipe advertisement discovery.

Creating a Pipe

As we mentioned earlier, the PBP is based on the assumption that a peer will create an input pipe and want to have remote peers connect to the pipe for information transfer. The pipe advertisement will provide information about the pipe's ID and type. Just creating the pipe advertisement doesn't inform other peers about the existence of the communication channel. The peer will need to use the discovery service to let other peers know about it.

The input pipe is created using one of the methods listed in Table 10.1. Each of the methods takes the pipe advertisement as a parameter. The Pipe Service implementation will build one of the three known pipe object types: JxtaUnicast, JxtaUnicastSecure, or JxtaPropagate. At this point, the pipe's input is bound to the peer that has created it. If the createInputPipe() method used accepts a listener, the peer application is required to pass an object that implements the PipeMsgListener interface. Otherwise, the polling functionality available in the pipe object can be used. The steps in using pipes typically are as follows:

- On the peer with an input pipe available:

    1. Get the PipeService object.

    2. Build the input pipe advertisement.

    3. Create an InputPipe listener.

    4. Create an input pipe.

    5. Publish the pipe advertisement.

- On the peer with an output pipe:

    1. Discover the pipe advertisement.

    2. Build an output pipe.

From a code standpoint, the first step is to obtain the pipe service. This is done with the following statement:

```
PipeService pipeService = netPeerGroup.getPipeService();
```

In this example, the object netPeerGroup has been previously assigned when the peer was first booted into the JXTA network.

Two different pipes are available: the input and output pipes. For the most part, an output pipe is created in response to an input pipe created on a remote peer. The remote peer will advertise the existence of the pipe using an advertisement—specifically, the pipe advertisement. Listing 10.3 shows an example of a pipe advertisement. The advertisement can be built using the code in Listing 10.4, which assigns a unique ID, a pipe name, and the pipe type.

```
<?xml version="1.0"?>

<!DOCTYPE jxta:PipeAdvertisement>

<jxta:PipeAdvertisement xmlns:jxta="http://jxta.org">
    <Id>
        urn:jxta:uuid-
59616261646162614E5047205032503331BE4F9EC1D941BBBDA18B3273791A9D04
    </Id>
    <Type>
        JxtaPropagate
    </Type>
    <Name>
        bipipe2.end1
    </Name>
</jxta:PipeAdvertisement>
```

Listing 10.3   Sample pipe advertisement.

```
    PipeAdvertisement pipeAdv =
(PipeAdvertisement)AdvertisementFactory.newAdvertisement(PipeAd
vertisement.getAdvertisementType());
    pipeAdv.setName("JXTA:KEYRECEIVE");
    pipeAdv.setType("JxtaUnicast");
    pipeAdv.setPipeID((ID) net.jxta.id.IDFactory.
newPipeID(netPeerGroup.getPeerGroupID()));
```

Listing 10.4   Sample code to build a pipe advertisement.

Receiving Information

Before an input pipe is created, there must be a way to receive information through the pipe. Two methods are available: synchronous and asynchronous. The PipeMsgListener interface allows PipeMsgEvent events to be received asynchronously. An object that implements the interface must include a method called public void pipeMsgEvent(PipeMsgEvent event). This method will be called when information is received through the input pipe. For the synchronous method, a poll() method is available on the pipe.

Polling for Information on the Input Pipe

When an input pipe is created (as described in the next section), the easiest way to get a message from the pipe is to call the pipe's poll() method. For example:

```
Message newMessage = inputPipe.poll(30000);
```

The parameter to the poll() method is a timeout period in milliseconds. The system will block up to the timeout period or until a message is received.

Building a Listener Event Class

A better situation could be the use of a callback object. When a message arrives at the pipe, a specific method will be called within a listener object. The format of the required listener is shown here:

```
PipeMsgListener pipeListener = new PipeMsgListener() {
    public void pipeMsgEvent(PipeMsgEvent event) {
     try {
      Message msg = event.getMessage();
     } catch (Exception e) {
       e.printStackTrace();
       return;
      }
    }
};
```

The listener is an interface called PipeMsgListener and requires the pipeMsgEvent() method (defined above). When the method is called, a PipeMsgEvent object is passed to the method, which has a method called getMessage(). The method returns the message sent through the pipe.

Building the Pipe

Both the input and output pipes require an advertisement in order to be built. For the most part, the output pipe will be created when a pipe advertisement is discovered using the discovery service. This process is described in the upcoming section "Discovering an Input Pipe." For the input pipe, the CreateInputPipe() method of the pipe service is used to build the necessary pipe. The code will use the listener event class and advertisement built earlier.

```
InputPipe inputPipe = pipeService.createInputPipe(pipeAdv, new
inputPipeListener());
```

This code builds a new input pipe with its specifics based on the pipeAdv pipe advertisement and assigned a new Listener object.

Advertising the Pipe

Once the input pipe has been established on the local peer, the pipe advertisement can be advertised. In fact, the input pipe doesn't have to be established for the advertisement to be published—the remote peer will find out the pipe isn't available when it tries to connect to it.

A remote peer will discover the pipe advertisement and attempt to build an output pipe using the advertisement. The pipe service begins the process of attempting to determine whether the pipe is available on the peer advertising it and creating the necessary connection. The process involves the pipe service sending a query message to the peer that might have an input pipe available. The pipe service of the input pipe peer will process the query and determine the current state of the input pipe, and an answer message will be returned to the querying peer. If an input pipe is available, the newly created output pipe is bound to the input pipe, and then information can begin flowing between the peers.

The code to publish the advertisement might look like the following:

```
discoveryService.publish(pipeAdv, DiscoveryService.ADV);
discoveryService.remotePublish(pipeAdv, DiscoveryService.ADV);
```

Discovering an Input Pipe

The discovery of a pipe advertisement is based on the code presented in Chapter 6, and won't be repeated here. The following statement builds an Output-Pipe object based on a valid pipe advertisement received from the discovery service:

```
OutputPipe =
pipeService.createOutputPipe(discoveredPipeAdv, TIMEOUT_VALUE );
```

Summary

The Pipe Binding Protocol is the protocol used by the JXTA system to create and administer pipes. Pipes allow communication between peers within the JXTA network and are fundamental to the entire system. Various implementation classes are available that keep the application developer out of the details when creating and using pipes. In the next chapter, we discuss the Rendezvous Protocol, which allows messages to be propagated between peers in the network.

CHAPTER 11

Rendezvous Protocol

The Rendezvous Protocol is designed to propagate messages between peers within a group. An implementation of the protocol specification allows a peer to use a rendezvous service for message propagation and rely on the service itself for administering the propagation. Some of the administration includes monitoring the time-to-live variable in each message and ensuring that messages are not caught in loops.

The transport mechanisms used by the Java binding of the specification are HTTP and TCP/IP. For the most part, these mechanisms aren't designed to send information from one machine to several other machines. The transports are basically one-to-one (with the exception of the TCP/IP multicast mechanism). The rendezvous protocol was created to facilitate the transportation of messages to multiple peers within the JXTA network.

A *rendezvous peer* is simply a peer that decides to propagate messages that it receives. You can designate a peer as a rendezvous peer by selecting the Rendezvous checkbox on the configuration screen or by dynamically invoking the appropriate service. At the same time, a peer can download available rendezvous peers on the configuration screen or dynamically discover the peers.

When a peer uses the discovery service to find advertisements in the JXTA network, that service uses the resolver service implemented based on the Peer Resolver Protocol. The resolver service will have the choice of using either the Peer Endpoint Protocol or the Rendezvous Protocol, or both. By using the Rendezvous Protocol and, subsequently, the rendezvous service, the discovery service will gain a much wider audience for a discovery or publish event.

When a peer is designated as a rendezvous peer, a listener will be invoked to listen for messages using the service name JxtaPropagate and a service parameter of a peer group ID. When a message is received through the listener, the peer will check its current peer group and propagate the message accordingly.

Rendezvous Advertisements

When a peer is either configured as a rendezvous or becomes one dynamically, it creates a rendezvous advertisement to advertise the rendezvous service to other peers in the group. The advertisement is described in Listing 11.1. The elements in the advertisement are the following:

Name—An optional name for the rendezvous peer

RdvGroupID—The peer group ID with which this rendezvous peer is associated

RdvPeerID—The peer ID of this rendezvous peer

```
<?xml version="1.0" encoding="UTF-8"?>
<jxta:RdvAdvertisement>
      <Name> name of the rendezvous peer</Name>
      <RdvGroupId> PeerGroup UUID </RdvGroupId>
      <RdvPeerId>Peer ID of the rendezvous peer</RdvPeerId>
</jxta:RdvAdvertisement>
```

Listing 11.1   Rendezvous advertisement format.

Message Propagation

As mentioned earlier, the Rendezvous Protocol must be aware of the messages being propagated around the network in order to keep garbage from accumulating. The housekeeping is accomplished by embedding a rendezvous propagate message within the message being propagated throughout the network. The message is shown in Listing 11.2; the elements of the message are as follows:

MessageId —A JXTA ID associated with the message

DestSName—A string representing the name of the destination

DestSParam—A string representing any parameters associated with the destination

TTL—The time-to-live integer for the message

Path—The URI where the message has already visited

```
<xs:element name="RendezVousPropagateMessage"
type="jxta:RendezVousPropagateMessage"/>

<xs:complexType name="RendezVousPropagateMessage">
    <xs:element name="MessageId" type="xs:string"/>
    <!-- This should be a constrained subtype -->
    <xs:element name="DestSName" type="xs:string"/>
    <xs:element name="DestSParam" type="xs:string"/>
    <xs:element name="TTL" type="xs:unsignedInt"/>
    <xs:element name="Path" type="xs:anyURI" maxOccurs="unbounded"/>
</xs:complexType>
```

Listing 11.2   Rendezvous propagate message.

The Java Binding

The Java binding of the Rendezvous Protocol is defined in the following class files:

- RendezvousEvent.java
- RendezvousListener,java
- RendezVousManager.java
- RendezVousMonitor.java
- RendezVousService.java
- Rendezvous.java
- RendezVousPropagateMessage
- RendezVousServiceImpl.java
- RendezVousServiceInterface.java

Dynamic Rendezvous Service Implementation

A peer can take advantage of the rendezvous service implemented by a default peer group through a call to the peer group object:

```
RendezVousService netPeerGroup.getRendezVousService();
```

NOTE

Notice the use of the capital V character in the RendezVousService call; this is a potential source for a number of syntax errors.

Three different methods are associated with the RendezVousService object for sending propagated messages within a peer group:

```
public void propagate (Message msg, String serviceName,
String serviceParam, int defaultTTL);

public void propagateInGroup (Message msg, String serviceName,
String serviceParam, int defaultTTL, String prunePeer);

public void propagateToNeighbors (Message msg, String serviceName,
String serviceParam, int defaultTTL, String prunePeer);
```

The methods take a Message object and propagate the message through the network. Associated with each message is a serviceName that represents the handler responsible for the interpretation of the method. A new listener or handler can be added to the RendezVousService object with the following method:

```
void addPropagateListener(java.lang.String name, EndpointListener
listener);
```

This method will add a listener using the specified name. When a message is received with the same serviceName, the listener method is called. The listener is responsible for parsing the message.

Finding Rendezvous Peers Dynamically

The discovery service can be used to locate rendezvous peers dynamically during the execution of a peer. The discovery request code is

```
myDiscoveryService.getRemoteAdvertisements( null,
  DiscoveryService.ADV,
  netPeerGroup.getPeerGroupID().toString(),
  100, myListener );
```

This code publishes a query into the current peer group, and looks for all advertisements with an element named RdvGroupID and a value of the current peer group. The myListener() method is called when any rendezvous advertisements are found. The advertisements can be used to connect to the rendezvous peer.

Connecting to Rendezvous Peers

Connecting to a rendezvous peer basically means that the rendezvous peer is added to the querying peer's list of known rendezvous peers. The current list of rendezvous peers could have been found dynamically or by using the configuration screen.

There are two ways to connect to a remote rendezvous peer: sending a raw connect advertisement or via a method of the RendezVousService. In either case, the rendezvous service will pass a rendezvous connect message, as shown in Listing 11.3. The message consists of a <jxta:Connect> element wrapping the local peer's advertisement denoted by the <jxta:PA> advertisement. In Listing 11.3, the peer advertisement has not been shown due to its enormous size.

The following method is the most common way to send the connect advertisement to the remote peer:

```
public void connectToRendezVous (PeerAdvertisement adv);

<jxta:Connect xmlns:jxta="http://jxta.org">
<jxta:PA xmlns:jxta="http://jxta.org">
      //Peer Advertisement
</jxta:PA>
</jxta:Connect>
```

Listing 11.3   Rendezvous connect message.

When either the connect message is sent to the remote rendezvous peer or the connectToRendezVous() method is called, the remote rendezvous peer will respond with a RendezvousAdvertisementReply message (shown in Listing 11.4). The message will be handled by the requesting peer's rendezvous service. The most important part of the message is the ConnectedLease element, which indicates how long the requesting peer will be kept in the remote rendezvous peer's list of peers to send propagated messages to.

```
<jxta:RdvAdvReply xmlns:jxta="http://jxta.org">
<jxta:PA xmlns:jxta="http://jxta.org">
   // Peer Advertisment of the peer granting the lease
</jxta:PA>
</jxta:RdvAdvReply>
<jxta:ConnectedPeer xmlns:jxta="http://jxta.org">
   // ID
</jxta:ConnectedPeer>
<jxta:ConnectedLease xmlns:jxta="http://jxta.org">
  value in milliseconds that the lease Is granted for
</jxta:ConnectedLease>
```

Listing 11.4   RendezvousAdvertisementReply message.

Disconnecting from a Rendezvous Peer

When a peer is finished being part of a rendezvous chain, whether the rendezvous was created dynamically or through the configuration screen, it can disconnect by either sending a disconnect advertisement (as shown in Listing 11.5) or by calling the following method:

```
public void disconnectFromRendezVous (PeerID peerID);

<jxta:Disconnect xmlns:jxta="http://jxta.org">
<jxta:PA xmlns:jxta="http://jxta.org">
  //Peer Advertisement of the peer requesting the disconnection
</jxta:PA>
</jxta:Disconnect>
```

Listing 11.5 A disconnect message.

Summary

The Rendezvous Protocol is an important part of the JXTA specification. The protocol allows messages to be propagated between peers using a transport that isn't designed for propagated messages. As a go-between protocol, the Rendezvous Protocol is used by the Peer Discovery Protocol and the Resolver Protocol. This section of the book has covered the protocol outlined in the JXTA Specification as well as Java code from the reference implementation. In the next part of the book, the Java reference implementation will be used to build peer-to-peer applications.

CHAPTER 12

Developing a JXTA Application

In the first two parts of this book, we covered the structure and theory behind JXTA. We begin this third part with the process of developing JXTA applications. We have two primary goals in this chapter:

- To demonstrate the process for building and executing simple JXTA command-line and GUI applications
- To explain how to create independent peer groups

To accomplish these goals, we build two peers that can connect and transmit information to each other through pipes. The first peer will advertise the existence of a pipe using three separate advertisements: the module class advertisement, the module specification advertisement, and the pipe advertisement. Once the advertisements have been published to the JXTA network, we create an input pipe to accept messages. The second peer will join the JXTA network, locate the advertisements, create an output pipe, and then connect its output pipe to the first peer's input pipe. Once the connection is successful, the second peer will transmit data to the first peer. In other words, the two peers provide the following functionality:

- Initialize the Java JXTA reference implementation
- Connect to the JXTA network and its default peer group
- Obtain internal services for publishing, discovery, and pipe functionality
- Communicate information between peers

In the final section of this chapter, we add functionality that enables the peers to create and join groups outside the global NetPeerGroup.

The Basic Structure for JXTA Applications

In this section, we examine the process for building a basic structure for writing JXTA applications. The JXTA applications in this book all begin with the basic structure of a Java application, including a class and a main() method, as well as a launchJXTA() method for performing basic initialization (as shown in Listing 12.1).

The code for Chapter 12 as well as the other chapters in the book can be found on the companion website at the URL www.wiley.com/compbooks/Gradecki.

```
Line 1:        import net.jxta.peergroup.PeerGroupFactory;
Line 2:        import net.jxta.exception.PeerGroupException;
Line 3:        import net.jxta.impl.peergroup.Platform;
Line 4:        import net.jxta.impl.peergroup.GenericPeerGroup;
Line 5:        import net.jxta.peergroup.PeerGroup;
Line 6:        public class Example1 {
Line 7:
Line 8:            static PeerGroup netPeerGroup = null;
Line 9:
Line 10:           public static void main(String args[]) {
Line 11:               Example1 myapp = new Example1();
Line 12:               System.out.println ("Launching JXTA");
Line 13:
Line 14:               myapp.launchJXTA();
Line 15:
Line 16:               System.out.println ("Terminating Application");
Line 17:               System.exit(0);
Line 18:           }
Line 19:
Line 20:           /*
Line 21:            *  Default Constructor
Line 22:            */
Line 23:           public void Example1() {
Line 24:           }
Line 25:
Line 26:           /*
Line 27:            *  Private method for starting the JXTA platform.
Line 28:            */
Line 29:           private void launchJXTA() {
Line 30:           }
Line 31:       }
```

Listing 12.1 Basic Java skeleton for a JXTA application.

You can compile and execute the code in Listing 12.1 by using the instructions in Appendix A. When executed, the application will simply print:

```
Launching JXTA
Terminating Application
```

The output will appear immediately after the application executes because there is no code in the launchJXTA() method. The application code simply begins executing in the main() method, where an object of type Example is instantiated and the launchJXTA() method is called. After control returns to main(), the application is terminated.

Connecting to the JXTA Network

To enable our application to become a peer and connect to the JXTA network, we add the code from Listing 12.2 to the launchJXTA() method.

```
Line 1: try {
Line 2:    netPeerGroup = PeerGroupFactory.newNetPeerGroup();
Line 3: } catch (PeerGroupException e) {
Line 4:     System.out.println("Unable to create PeerGroup - Failure");
Line 5:     e.printStackTrace();
Line 6:     System.exit(1);
Line 7: }
```

Listing 12.2   Connecting to the JXTA network.

Before reading the following discussion, take the time to add Listing 12.2 to the application; then compile and run it. If all goes well, you will see one of two possible outcomes:

1. If this is the first time you have executed the application, you will be asked to configure the peer just as you did when you executed the JXTA shell. At a minimum, you will need to enter a peer name and a security name. The application will then connect to the JXTA network.

2. If this isn't the first time you have executed the application, you will be asked to enter your sign-in name and password. The application will then connect to the JXTA network.

Of particular importance to us is what the code is doing when the launchJXTA() method is called. Because this code is fundamental to other code that we will add to the application, the initial connection to the JXTA network is embedded in a try catch block. Lines 1 and 3 set up the block, and in line 2 an attempt is made to connect to the network using the information provided in the configuration window when it was first displayed.

All JXTA applications (peers) want to be a part of a peer group, so one of the first things an application will do is create a default peer group by calling the newNetPeerGroup() method. In turn, this method creates a default peer group with the name NetPeerGroup. As a general rule, all JXTA applications will belong to this peer group. The group itself provides a number of services for finding and creating additional groups.

If the method call is successful—which means the current peer was able to connect to a rendezvous router and to the default group NetPeerGroup—a Peer-Group object is returned. This object is stored in a static variable called netPeerGroup. If for some reason the method call fails, it will throw a Peer-GroupException, which will cause the catch block to execute and exit the application.

When the peer joins the NetPeerGroup group, the ID of the group, as well as the group advertisement, is assigned. The next section explains how to view these properties.

Viewing Peer Group Information

Once a peer connects to the JXTA network, a call to the newNetPeerGroup() method will reveal a number of properties from the PeerGroup object. In this section, we discuss methods that we can use to obtain information about our peer in the default NetPeerGroup peer group (see Appendix B for the complete PeerGroup API):

getPeerGroupID()—Returns the ID of the group associated with this PeerGroup object

getPeerGroupName()—Returns the name of the group associated with this PeerGroup object

getPeerID()—Returns the ID of the peer in this peer group

getPeerName()—Returns the name of the peer in this peer group

To use these methods, we make two changes to our sample program from Listings 12.1 and 12.2. First, in the main() method, we replace the line

```
myapp.launchJXTA();
```

with

```
myapp.launchJXTA();
myapp.getJXTAInfo();
```

Second, we add the following getJXTAInfo() method code immediately after the launchJXTA() method:

```
public void getJXTAInfo() {
    System.out.println("This Peer's ID in the group : " +
```

```
netPeerGroup.getPeerID().toString());
    System.out.println("This Peer's Name in the group : " +
netPeerGroup.getPeerName());
    System.out.println("The Peergroup's ID : " +
netPeerGroup.getPeerGroupID().toString());
    System.out.println("The Peergroup's name : " +
netPeerGroup.getPeerGroupName());
  }
```

After compiling and executing the revised application, you should see something similar to the following output:

```
Launching JXTA
This Peer's ID in the group : urn:jxta:uuid-
59616261646162614A78746150325033078319 2C4C59465BB731B8AD1A67F6C403
This Peer's Name in the group : JosephGradecki
The Peergroup's ID : urn:jxta:jxta-NetGroup
The Peergroup's name : NetPeerGroup
Terminating Application
```

As evidenced by the information returned, our application has become a peer in the NetPeerGroup peer group. Note that the peer name and ID are pulled from our JXTA configuration information we supplied when the application was first executed. Once the peer connects to the peer group, various IDs and names will be displayed.

Viewing Peer Group Advertisement

To view advertisements from the peer's current peer group, simply add the code from Listing 12.3 to our application. You should add this code where class methods are located. In addition, a call to the method getAdvertisements() should be placed in either the main() or constructor method.

```
public void getAdvertisements() {
  PeerGroupAdvertisement  myPeerGroupAD;
  Document advertisementDocument;

  myPeerGroupAD = netPeerGroup.getPeerGroupAdvertisement();
  System.out.println("\n\nPeerGroup Advertisement:" +
myPeerGroupAD.toString());
  System.out.println("PeerGroup Advertisement Type:" +
myPeerGroupAD.getAdvertisementType());
  System.out.println("PeerGroup Advertisement Description:" +
myPeerGroupAD.getDescription());
```

Listing 12.3   Code for viewing a peer group advertisement. (continues)

```
    advertisementDocument = myPeerGroupAD.getDocument(new
MimeMediaType("text/xml"));
    try {
      advertisementDocument.sendToStream(System.out);
    } catch(IOException e) {
      System.exit(1);
    }
  }
```

Listing 12.3   Code for viewing a peer group advertisement. (continued)

Now add the following code at the top of our sample application in order to resolve classes used in the getAdvertisements() method:

```
import java.io.*;
import net.jxta.document.Document;
import net.jxta.document.MimeMediaType;
import net.jxta.protocol.PeerGroupAdvertisement;
```

Now when you run the application, you will see output similar to this:

```
PeerGroup Advertisement:net.jxta.impl.protocol.PeerGroupAdv@7e121c
PeerGroup Advertisement Type:jxta:PGA
PeerGroup Advertisement Description:NetPeerGroup by default
<?xml version="1.0"?>

<!DOCTYPE jxta:PGA>

<jxta:PGA xmlns:jxta="http://jxta.org">
        <GID>
                urn:jxta:jxta-NetGroup
        </GID>
        <MSID>
                urn:jxta:uuid-DEADBEEFDEAFB
                  ABAFEEDBABE000000010206
        </MSID>
        <Name>
                NetPeerGroup
        </Name>
        <Desc>
                NetPeerGroup by default
        </Desc>
</jxta:PGA>
```

The first three lines of output show generic information about the advertisement, including the name of the advertisement, the type (PGA = Peer Group Advertisement), and the description. Following the first three lines is the XML representation of the actual advertisement. As we know, advertisements are designed to publish available peers, groups, and/or services. As we can see from the advertisement for the NetPeerGroup, no services are available or provided by the peer group itself; however, this doesn't mean there aren't peers in the group that have services available. Before we start looking for services in the group, let's provide our own.

Building a Peer to Offer Services

The code from the previous section instantiates a peer that can then become a member of the default NetPeerGroup peer group. In this section, we add a simple pipe service where messages can be sent. This peer has all of the basic parts needed for communication with another peer. The class name is called sender because it sends out an advertisement for a communication channel. Once the peer is executed, the advertised pipe remains open and available, regardless of whether any remote peers need it. The steps to be performed are:

1. Obtaining group services
2. Building and publishing a module class advertisement
3. Building a pipe advertisement
4. Building and publishing a module specification advertisement
5. Waiting for messages

Figure 12.1 shows the completed peer. Each time a remote peer sends data to this peer, the data will be displayed in the GUI windows (as shown in Figure 12.2).

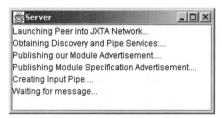

Figure 12.1 Completed service peer.

Figure 12.2 Service peer receives data.

NOTE

To obtain the complete code for the service peer found in Listing 12.4, go to www.wiley.com/compbooks/Gradecki, download the file for Chapter 12, and look in the /jxtawiley/chapter12/example2/sender directory.

For the remainder of this section, the code in Listing 12.4 will be referenced by line number. This source code is based on the examples found in Listings 12.1, 12.2, and 12.3 that we discussed earlier in the chapter; however there are two primary changes. First, we include code to support the advertising and support of the peer's service. Second, we've changed the code to allow the use of a Java GUI instead of a command-line operation. The GUI components cause the following to occur:

- All of the System.out.println statements for non-error strings are changed to displayArea.append() methods. The displayArea is a JtextArea placed on the window of the application.

- GUI code is added to the constructor for the application.

- Class now extends JFrame.

```
Line 1: import java.io.*;
import java.awt.*;
import java.awt.event.*;
import javax.swing.*;

import net.jxta.document.Document;
import net.jxta.peergroup.PeerGroup;
import net.jxta.peergroup.PeerGroupFactory;
import net.jxta.exception.PeerGroupException;
Line 10:  import net.jxta.document.AdvertisementFactory;
import net.jxta.impl.peergroup.Platform;
import net.jxta.impl.peergroup.GenericPeerGroup;
import net.jxta.id.ID;
import net.jxta.id.IDFactory;
import net.jxta.discovery.DiscoveryService;
import net.jxta.pipe.PipeService;
import net.jxta.protocol.ModuleClassAdvertisement;
import net.jxta.platform.ModuleClassID;
import net.jxta.document.StructuredDocumentFactory;
Line 20: import net.jxta.document.StructuredTextDocument;
import net.jxta.document.StructuredDocument;
import net.jxta.document.StructuredDocumentUtils;
import net.jxta.document.MimeMediaType;
```

Listing 12.4   A peer that offers a pipe service. (continues)

```
import net.jxta.protocol.PipeAdvertisement;
import net.jxta.document.Element;
import net.jxta.protocol.ModuleSpecAdvertisement;
import net.jxta.endpoint.Message;
import net.jxta.protocol.PeerGroupAdvertisement;
import net.jxta.pipe.InputPipe;
Line 30: import net.jxta.pipe.PipeMsgListener;
import net.jxta.pipe.PipeMsgEvent;

public class sender extends JFrame {

    static PeerGroup netPeerGroup = null;
    private DiscoveryService myDiscoveryService = null;
    private PipeService myPipeService = null;
    private ModuleClassID myService1ID = null;
    private InputPipe myPipe = null;
Line 40:    private JTextArea displayArea;

    public static void main(String args[]) {
        sender myapp = new sender();

        myapp.addWindowListener (
          new WindowAdapter() {
            public void windowClosing(WindowEvent e) {
              System.exit(0);
            }
Line 50:          }
        );

        myapp.launchJXTA();
        myapp.getServices();
        myapp.buildModuleAdvertisement();
myapp.buildModuleSpecificationAdvertisement(myapp.createPipeAdvertisement());
        myapp.run();
    }

Line 60:    public sender() {
        super("sender");

        Container c = getContentPane();

        displayArea = new JTextArea();
        c.add (new JScrollPane(displayArea), BorderLayout.CENTER);

        setSize(300,150);
        show();
Line 70:    }
```

Listing 12.4   A peer that offers a pipe service. (continues)

```
    public void run() {
      displayArea.append("Waiting for message...\n");
    }

    private void launchJXTA() {
        displayArea.append("Launching Peer into JXTA Network...\n");
        try {
            netPeerGroup = PeerGroupFactory.newNetPeerGroup();
Line 80:        } catch (PeerGroupException e) {
            System.out.println("Unable to create PeerGroup - Failure");
            e.printStackTrace();
            System.exit(1);
        }
    }

    private void getServices() {
      displayArea.append("Obtaining Discovery and Pipe Services....\n");
      myDiscoveryService = netPeerGroup.getDiscoveryService();
Line 90:      myPipeService = netPeerGroup.getPipeService();
    }

    private void buildModuleAdvertisement() {
      ModuleClassAdvertisement myService1ModuleAdvertisement =
(ModuleClassAdvertisement) AdvertisementFactory.newAdvertisement
(ModuleClassAdvertisement.getAdvertisementType());

      myService1ModuleAdvertisement.setName("JXTAMOD:JXTA-CH15EX2");
      myService1ModuleAdvertisement.setDescription("Service 1 of Chapter 15
example 2");

      myService1ID = IDFactory.newModuleClassID();
Line 100:      myService1ModuleAdvertisement.setModuleClassID(myService1ID);

      displayArea.append("Publishing our Module Advertisement....\n");
      try {
         myDiscoveryService.publish(myService1ModuleAdvertisement,
DiscoveryService.ADV);
        myDiscoveryService.remotePublish(myService1ModuleAdvertisement,
DiscoveryService.ADV);
      } catch (Exception e) {
        System.out.println("Error during publish of Module Advertisement");
        System.exit(-1);
      }
Line 110:    }

    private PipeAdvertisement createPipeAdvertisement() {
```

Listing 12.4 A peer that offers a pipe service. (continues)

```
      PipeAdvertisement myPipeAdvertisement = null;

      try {
        FileInputStream is = new FileInputStream("service1.adv");
        myPipeAdvertisement = (PipeAdvertisement)AdvertisementFactory.
newAdvertisement(new MimeMediaType("text/xml"), is);
      } catch (Exception e) {
          System.out.println("failed to read/parse pipe advertisement");
Line 120:             e.printStackTrace();
          System.exit(-1);
      }

      return myPipeAdvertisement;
    }

    private void buildModuleSpecificationAdvertisement(PipeAdvertisement
myPipeAdvertisement) {


Line 130:
      ModuleSpecAdvertisement myModuleSpecAdvertisement =
(ModuleSpecAdvertisement) AdvertisementFactory.newAdvertisement
(ModuleSpecAdvertisement.getAdvertisementType());

      myModuleSpecAdvertisement.setName("JXTASPEC:JXTA-CH15EX2");
      myModuleSpecAdvertisement.setVersion("Version 1.0");
      myModuleSpecAdvertisement.setCreator("gradecki.com");
      myModuleSpecAdvertisement.setModuleSpecID(IDFactory.newModuleSpecID
(myService1ID));
      myModuleSpecAdvertisement.setSpecURI("<http://www.jxta.org/CH15EX2>");
myModuleSpecAdvertisement.setPipeAdvertisement(myPipeAdvertisement);

Line 140:      displayArea.append("Publishing Module Specification
Advertisement....\n");
      try {
myDiscoveryService.publish(myModuleSpecAdvertisement,
DiscoveryService.ADV);
myDiscoveryService.remotePublish(myModuleSpecAdvertisement,
DiscoveryService.ADV);
      } catch (Exception e) {
          System.out.println("Error during publish of Module Specification
Advertisement");
          e.printStackTrace();
          System.exit(-1);
      }
```

Listing 12.4   A peer that offers a pipe service. (continues)

```
Line 150:        createInputPipe(myPipeAdvertisement);
    }

    private void createInputPipe(PipeAdvertisement myPipeAdvertisement) {
      displayArea.append("Creating Input Pipe....\n");

      PipeMsgListener myService1Listener = new PipeMsgListener() {
        public void pipeMsgEvent(PipeMsgEvent event) {
          Message myMessage = null;
          try {
            myMessage = event.getMessage();
Line 160:
            String myMessageContent;

            myMessageContent = myMessage.getString("DataTag");
            if (myMessageContent != null) {
              displayArea.append("Message received: " + myMessageContent +
"\n");
              displayArea.append("Waiting for message...\n");
              return;
            } else {
              displayArea.append("Invalid tag\n");
Line 170:              return;
            }
          } catch (Exception ee) {
              ee.printStackTrace();
              return;
          }
        }
      };

      try {
Line 180:        myPipe = myPipeService.createInputPipe(myPipeAdvertisement,
myService1Listener);
      } catch (Exception e) {
          System.out.println("Error creating Input Pipe");
          e.printStackTrace();
          System.exit(-1);
      }
    }
}
```

Listing 12.4 A peer that offers a pipe service. (continued)

Obtaining Group Services

When our peer from Listing 12.4 connects to the NetPeerGroup peer group (or any other group, for that matter), it becomes a peer in the group with the ability to provide or request services. For our example, we provide a pipe through which other peers can communicate or exchange data.

A peer must execute two primary operations in order to provide a service: publish the existence of the service and provide the mechanism to perform the work of the service. For each of these operations, the JXTA group we have joined provides group-level services in the form of the discovery service and the pipe service; thus, our peer will need to instantiate an object of each service. The code to handle the instantiation is found in the following lines:

- Lines 87 through 91 create a method called getServices().
  - Line 89 instantiates an object named myDiscoveryService from the current group by using the getDiscoveryService() method.
  - Line 90 instantiates an object named myPipeService from the current group by using the getPipeService() method.
- Lines 15 through 16 import the correct JXTA code for the calls made in lines 89 and 90.
- Lines 36 through 37 declare variables to hold the objects instantiated in lines 89 and 90.
- Line 54 makes the method call to getServices() once the peer has communicated with the JXTA network.

Building and Publishing the Module Class Advertisement

In order for a peer to offer a service to other peers, it must create several advertisements. The first is the module class advertisement, which is a shell advertisement used to indicate that a service is available. The second type of advertisement, the module class advertisement, provides the specifics of the service available. The module class advertisement has a specific format defined in the JXTA specification (Chapter 5 describes these advertisements in detail).

In Listing 12.4, lines 93 through 110 handle the creation and functionality for the module class advertisement. Line 94 instantiates the advertisement using the JXTA advertisement factory. The parameter to the factory is the advertisement type returned using the static method getAdvertisementType() from the ModuleClassAdvertisement class.

Line 96 assigns a name to the service. In this case, the name JXTASPEC:JXTA-EXAMPLE is optional; during debugging, a meaningful name is helpful because the name of the advertisement can be displayed.

Line 97 adds a description for the service. A remote peer searching for a service can access this description, so you'll want to include relevant keywords.

Lines 99 and 100 create a new module class ID and assign it to the advertisement for this specific service. The ID will uniquely identify the class module to other peers.

Lines 104 and 105 are the key to making the new service known to other peers in the group. Line 104 publishes the advertisement in the local cache, and line 105 publishes the advertisement to the group. It should be noted that if you are part of a group other than NetPeerGroup, the advertisement published with the remotePublish() method will only go to the group of which your peer is currently a member. An advertisement that must be published to the NetPeerGroup will have to use the getParent() method of the current group to obtain the parent group. For our example, if either of the publishing methods fails, any exception thrown will be caught and the application will be closed.

Lines 17 through 23 contain imports necessary for the creation and publishing of the advertisement. Line 55 makes the actual method call to build the module class advertisement.

Building the Pipe Advertisement

Two more advertisements are necessary in order to give other peers the ability to discover and use our service: the module specification advertisement and the pipe advertisement. We just built the module class advertisement, whose primary purpose is to publish a module class ID and provide searchable keywords. Once a peer finds the module class advertisement, it will try to retrieve the module specification advertisement (MSA), which acts as a container for the actual service.

Within the MSA are *service advertisements*. The service advertisements publish the existence of a service that a remote peer can take advantage of. In most cases, the service advertisements will be an input pipe advertisement, which the remote peer will use to build a pipe connection. Because a service advertisement is needed to build the MSA, we will create it next.

The service that will be exposed by our peer is an input pipe that accepts text messages from another peer. There are three key elements to the advertisement (for details of the pipe advertisement specification, refer to Chapter 5, Listing 5.11):

name—Even though the name is optional, it is still good practice to include it in the advertisement. You will notice that the name of the pipe is the same as the name used in the module class advertisement.

ID—The ID of the pipe uniquely identifies the pipe.

type—The type dictates what can be done with the pipe.

For our purposes, the pipe is kept in a file in the same directory as the application—this is not necessary, but doing so provides the ability to change the ID or pipe type without recompiling the application. Listing 12.5 shows the contents of the pipe advertisement file named service1.adv.

```
<?xml version="1.0" encoding="UTF-8"?>
<jxta:PipeAdvertisement>
    <Name>JXTA-EXAMPLE</Name>
    <Id>urn:jxta:uuid-
9CCCDF5AD8154D3D87A391210404E59BE4B888209A2241A4A162A10916074A9504</Id>
    <Type>JxtaUnicast</Type>
</jxta:PipeAdvertisement>
```

Listing 12.5   Pipe advertisement (service1.adv).

With the pipe advertisement description file created, the code for building the internal representation begins. The following line descriptions refer to Listing 12.4.

Lines 112 through 125 define a method called createPipeAdvertisement(), which handles all of the details for pulling in the pipe service advertisement defined in the service1.adv file. The outcome of the method is a PipeAdvertisement object; this object will subsequently be passed to a method called buildModuleSpecificationAdvertisement().

Line 113 declares a local variable, which will ultimately point to a new pipe advertisement. Line 116 opens an input stream to the local file called service1.adv.

Line 117 uses the advertisement factory to instantiate a new advertisement object. The object is based on the XML in the service1.adv file. Note the use of the MimeMediaType object to specify to the factory that the advertisement should be built from data presented in XML format.

Once the object has been created by the factory, it is cast to a PipeAdvertisement object. Line 124 returns the new PipeAdvertisement object to the caller.

Line 56 is the method call to createPipeAdvertisement(). The call is actually a parameter to the buildModuleSpecificationAdvertisement() method.

Building and Publishing the Module Specification Advertisement

As we mentioned earlier, the module class advertisement is just a "courtesy" advertisement that can be searched by other peers looking for specific services. The pipe advertisement we created in the previous section is more concrete because it defines the name, type, and ID for a specific service. The final advertisement we need to build is the module specification advertisement, the purpose of which is to specify services described by the module class advertisement. Once a peer has found a necessary service, it will pull the MSA and locate the embedded service. Our code needs to build the MSA, embed the pipe advertisement, and publish the advertisement.

Lines 127 through 148 define the buildModuleSpecificationAdvertisement() method, which creates the MSA, embeds the pipe advertisement, and publishes the advertisement. Line 130 uses the advertisement factory to instantiate a new ModuleSpecAdvertisement object. A call to the getAdvertisementType() method of the MSA class ensures that the correct advertisement object is generated.

Lines 132 through 135 fill in the details of the advertisement object. Most of the information is optional, including the name of the spec, the creator, and the Supported Universal Resource Identifier or SURI. The module's version is a required component. In the call to setModuleSpecID(), a new ModuleSpecID is built that is based on the ID of the module class advertisement we created earlier. By using the previous ID, the code links the ModuleAdvertisement and the ModuleSpecAdvertisement objects.

Lines 142 and 143 perform the publishing of the advertisement to the local and remote systems so that other peers can find our service. If any problems are found with the publishing, an exception will be caught and the program ended.

Line 150 makes a call to a private method of the peer to build the actual InputPipe object we've just advertised. By putting the method call in the method that builds and publishes the MSA, we are assured that the pipe will be available if a remote peer discovers our advertisement and tries to send information.

Line 56 contains the method call to buildModuleSpecificationAdvertisement(). The single parameter to the method is the PipeAdvertisement object returned from the call to buildPipeAdvertisement().

Waiting for Messages

The last statement in the buildModuleSpecificationAdvertisement() method is a call to createInputPipe(). The createInputPipe() method is an essential component in the overall system because it creates the input pipe that will receive string data from other peers. As you might expect, the input pipe works on an asynchronous basis. Our peer has no idea when information will be received from another peer in the system; for this reason, we have to decide how to monitor the pipe for incoming data.

We have two choices. The first is to use the waitForMessage() method defined for input pipes. A simple piece of code illustrates this:

```
while (true) {
  Messsage myMessage;
  Try {
     MyMessage = myInputPipe.waitForMessage();
  } catch(Exception e) {}
  do something with message
}
```

In this code snippet, an infinite loop is both pulling messages from the input pipe and processing the messages. The call to waitForMessage() is blocked until a message arrives at the input pipe. In most situations, we try to avoid the use of an infinite loop because it will put the CPU at 100 percent usage. However, in this case, the waitForMessage() method will block and not allow the infinite loop to pull 100 percent CPU. Of course, this method isn't very elegant and is thus not in keeping with the purpose of Java.

The second and better choice for handling the asynchronous nature of an input pipe is through a listener. Fortunately, we have defined a listener interface called PipeMsgListener. We will be using the listener and an anonymous class to handle all of the communication that occurs with our input pipe. The code for the listener will be explained as we walk through the createInputPipe() method. Lines 153 through 188 define this method.

Lines 156 through 177 create an object that implements the PipeMsgListener interface by using an anonymous inner class. When using the pipe listener, the pipeMsgEvent() method must be overridden with the functionality to be executed when a new message appears on the pipe. The pipe message from a remote peer (another machine or on the same machine) will be encapsulated in a PipeMsgEvent object. The PipeMsgEvent object is the parameter to the listener's pipeMsgEvent() method. When the method fires, an attempt is made to pull a message object from the event using the getMessage() method provided by the PipeMsgEvent class.

Once the message object has been obtained, the string contents of the message can be pulled using the getString() method, as shown in line 163. Of particular importance is the key value provided as a parameter to the method. In our case, we are using a key value of DataTag. Because we are in a peer-to-peer environment, anyone could be sending data to our input pipe, so the key value can be used to discard message objects that aren't appropriate for our service. When the client side of our peer-to-peer application is created later in the chapter, it will need to use the DataTag key when sending messages to the server. In this sample program, the message received from the client is printed in the server's content pane.

Line 180 attempts to create an inputPipe object and assign the resulting object to the myPipe object attribute. If the attempt is not successful, an exception will be thrown. The exception will be caught locally and the application exited.

Putting It All Together

All of the major functionality for the sender peer that is providing a service has been described in the previous sections. We need only add four primary methods to complete the application and tie everything together.

Lines 42 through 58 define the main() method of the application. The code within the main() method instantiates a new application object, starts the JXTA environment, calls the appropriate methods defined earlier for creating and publishing the necessary advertisements, and finally calls the run() method of the application object.

Lines 60 through 70 define the default constructor for the application class. The only code found in the constructor is the code that builds the GUI components of the application.

Lines 72 through 74 define the run() method of the application class. Since we are building a GUI-based Java application, we need to invoke the run() method so that the internal Java event loop is started. The application will continue to run until the GUI window closes.

Lines 76 through 85 define the launchJXTA() method. This method uses the same code as that created in our command-line examples earlier in the chapter.

With the code in place, executing the application will cause an initial application GUI to be displayed, along with the JXTA configuration window or login dialog box. After the correct information or login is provided, the application will connect to the NetPeerGroup group, advertise our input pipe service, and await messages. Now we need to look at building a peer that will find our service and send messages.

Building a Peer for Using Services

The sender peer from the previous section advertises the existence of an input pipe through which data can be transferred. In this section, we build a receiver peer with the necessary components for discovering and using the sender peer's pipe. In simple terms, a receiver peer joins the default NetPeerGroup peer group, searches for the sender peer's advertisement, and then uses the pipe by sending data to it.

When executed, the receiver peer displays the GUI shown in Figure 12.3. When the user clicks on the Send Data button, a message is sent through the peer's output pipe to the input pipe of the sender peer that published the pipe advertisement. The sender peer will receive the message and display its contents.

The client peer will need to execute a few steps into order to use the pipe published by the sender peer. These steps are as follows:

1. The receiver peer will attempt to find the advertisement in the local cache.

2. When that attempt fails, a remote discovery request is sent by the receiver peer using the Discovery Service.

3. The module specification advertisement is obtained from the remote discovery request.

4. The receiver peer obtains the pipe advertisement from the module specification advertisement.

5. The receiver obtains the pipe data from the pipe advertisement.

6. The receiver creates the pipe advertisement.

7. The receiver creates the output pipe, and uses it to send data to the sender peer.

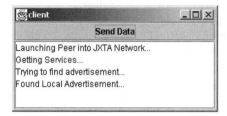

Figure 12.3   Receiver peer's GUI.

Code for the Receiver Peer

The code for our client peer appears in Listing 12.6. We describe the code in this section.

```
Line 1:import java.io.*;
import java.awt.*;
import java.awt.event.*;
import javax.swing.*;

//For Local Search
import java.util.Enumeration;

Line 10:import net.jxta.document.Document;
import net.jxta.peergroup.PeerGroup;
import net.jxta.peergroup.PeerGroupFactory;
import net.jxta.exception.PeerGroupException;
import net.jxta.document.AdvertisementFactory;
import net.jxta.impl.peergroup.Platform;
import net.jxta.impl.peergroup.GenericPeerGroup;
import net.jxta.id.ID;
import net.jxta.id.IDFactory;

Line 20://For Getting Services
import net.jxta.discovery.DiscoveryService;
import net.jxta.pipe.PipeService;

//build Spec Adv
import net.jxta.document.MimeMediaType;
import net.jxta.document.StructuredTextDocument;
import net.jxta.protocol.ModuleSpecAdvertisement;
import net.jxta.protocol.DiscoveryResponseMsg;

Line 30://build pipe adv
import java.net.MalformedURLException;
import java.net.URL;
import net.jxta.protocol.PipeAdvertisement;
import net.jxta.pipe.PipeID;
import net.jxta.document.TextElement;
import net.jxta.pipe.OutputPipe;
import net.jxta.endpoint.Message;

import net.jxta.discovery.DiscoveryListener;
Line 40:import net.jxta.discovery.DiscoveryEvent;

import net.jxta.document.Advertisement;
```

Listing 12.6 Receiver peer. (continues)

```
public class receiver extends JFrame{

    static  PeerGroup netPeerGroup = null;
    private DiscoveryService myDiscoveryService = null;
    private PipeService myPipeService = null;
Line 50:    private PipeAdvertisement myPipeAdvertisement = null;
    private OutputPipe myOutputPipe;
    private JTextArea displayArea;
    private JButton   sendButton;
    String  valueString = "JXTA-EXAMPLE";

        private final static MimeMediaType XMLMIMETYPE = new
MimeMediaType("text/xml");


    public static void main(String args[]) {
Line 60:        receiver myapp = new receiver();

        myapp.addWindowListener (
          new WindowAdapter() {
            public void windowClosing(WindowEvent e) {
              System.exit(0);
            }
          }
        );

Line 70:        myapp.launchJXTA();
        myapp.getServices();
        myapp.findAdvertisement("Name", "JXTASPEC:JXTA-CH15EX2");
        myapp.run();
    }


    public receiver() {
      super("receiver");

Line 80:    Container c = getContentPane();

      sendButton = new JButton("Send Data");
      sendButton.addActionListener(
        new ActionListener() {
          public void actionPerformed(ActionEvent e) {
            sendData();
          }
        }
```

Listing 12.6 Receiver peer. (continues)

```
        );
Line 90:        c.add(sendButton, BorderLayout.NORTH);

        displayArea = new JTextArea();
        c.add(new JScrollPane(displayArea), BorderLayout.CENTER);

        setSize(300,150);
        show();
    }

    public void run() {
Line 100:        displayArea.append("Click on Button to send data...\n");
    }

    private void launchJXTA() {
        displayArea.append("Launching Peer into JXTA Network...\n");
        try {
            netPeerGroup = PeerGroupFactory.newNetPeerGroup();
        } catch (PeerGroupException e) {
            System.out.println("Unable to create PeerGroup - Failure");
            e.printStackTrace();
Line 110:            System.exit(1);
        }
    }

    private void getServices() {
        displayArea.append("Getting Services...\n");
        myDiscoveryService = netPeerGroup.getDiscoveryService();
        myPipeService = netPeerGroup.getPipeService();
    }

Line 120:        private void findAdvertisement(String searchKey, String
searchValue) {
        Enumeration myLocalEnum = null;
        displayArea.append("Trying to find advertisement...\n");

        try {
          myLocalEnum = myDiscoveryService.getLocalAdvertisements
(DiscoveryService.ADV, searchKey, searchValue);

          if ((myLocalEnum != null) && myLocalEnum.hasMoreElements()) {
            displayArea.append("Found Local Advertisement...\n");
```

Listing 12.6 Receiver peer. (continues)

```
                ModuleSpecAdvertisement myModuleSpecAdv = (ModuleSpecAdvertise-
ment)myLocalEnum.nextElement();
Line 130:
              myPipeAdvertisement = myModuleSpecAdv.getPipeAdvertisement();
            createOutputPipe(myPipeAdvertisement);
          }
        else {
          DiscoveryListener myDiscoveryListener = new DiscoveryListener() {
            public void discoveryEvent(DiscoveryEvent e) {
              Enumeration enum;
              PipeAdvertisement pipeAdv = null;
              String str;
Line 140:
              displayArea.append("Found Remote Advertisement...\n");
              DiscoveryResponseMsg myMessage = e.getResponse();
              enum = myMessage.getResponses();
              str = (String)enum.nextElement();

              try {
                ModuleSpecAdvertisement myModSpecAdv = (ModuleSpecAdvertise-
ment) AdvertisementFactory.newAdvertisement(XMLMIMETYPE, new ByteArrayInput-
Stream(str.getBytes()));
                myPipeAdvertisement = myModSpecAdv.getPipeAdvertisement();

Line 150:                  createOutputPipe(myPipeAdvertisement);
              } catch(Exception ee) {
                  ee.printStackTrace();
                  System.exit(-1);
              }
            }
          };

          displayArea.append("Launching Remote Discovery Service...\n");
          myDiscoveryService.getRemoteAdvertisements(null,
DiscoveryService.ADV, searchKey, searchValue, 1, myDiscoveryListener);
Line 160:          }
      } catch (Exception e) {
          System.out.println("Error during advertisement search");
          System.exit(-1);
      }
  }
```

Listing 12.6 Receiver peer. (continues)

```
    private void createOutputPipe(PipeAdvertisement myPipeAdvertisement) {
      boolean noPipe = true;
      int count = 0;
Line 170:
      myOutputPipe = null;
      while (noPipe && count < 10) {
        count++;
        try {
          myOutputPipe = myPipeService.createOutputPipe(myPipeAdvertisement,
100000);
          displayArea.append("Output Pipe Created...\n");
          noPipe = false;
        } catch (Exception e) {
          System.out.println("Unable to create output pipe");
Line 180:              System.exit(-1);
        }
      }

      if (count >= 10) {
        System.out.println("no Pipe");
        System.exit(-1);
      }
    }

Line 190:    private void sendData() {
      String data = "Hello my friend!";

      Message msg = myPipeService.createMessage();
      msg.setString("DataTag", data);

      try {
        myOutputPipe.send (msg);
      } catch (Exception e) {
          System.out.println("Unable to print output pipe");
Line 200:             e.printStackTrace();
          System.exit(-1);
      }

      displayArea.append("message \"" + data + "\" sent to the Server\n");
    }
}
```

Listing 12.6 Receiver peer. (continued)

Getting Services

Just as the sender peer needed services of the peer group, so does the receiver peer. Lines 114 through 118 are identical to the code in the sender peer where discovery and pipe service objects are obtained and stored in attributes for later use. The call to the getServices() method is found in line 71.

Finding the Advertisement through Discovery

As we discussed in earlier chapters, the sender peer uses an *advertisement* to communicate to the world that it has a service available. You will also recall that each peer has a local cache that stores advertisements as they are discovered in the various peer groups. When a peer needs to access a service, it first checks its local cache for the advertisement. If it doesn't find the advertisement in the local cache, it initiates a remote discovery query. Our client peer code does exactly this type of operation. A method called findAdvertisement() is created that accepts a name-value pair indicating how the advertisement should be found. In our case, the name is denoted by the Name variable; the value is the name of our module class.

First, the receiver will try to find the advertisement in the local cache. Lines 125 through 132 handle the discovery of a cached local advertisement. The primary statement is line 125, where a call is made to the getLocalAdvertisements() method. Using the parameters provided—including our search name-value pair—the method searches for advertisements that match the appropriate values. If an appropriate advertisement is found, an Enumeration object is returned. Before the code does any work with the object, the object must pass the test of being non-null and having a number of elements associated with it. If the conditions are met, the Enumeration object is passed to the obtainPipeAdvertisement() method, where the specific PipeAdvertisement object will be extracted.

If the advertisement isn't found locally, a remote discovery is attempted. A remote discovery is accomplished through the Discovery Service, and attempts to find advertisement on peers within the JXTA network. The primary component is a listener for the discovery service. Recall that the discovery service is asynchronous. We don't want to force our application to wait for the discovery to complete, so an anonymous class listener is created.

Lines 135 through 156 handle the creation of the discovery service listener. As we mentioned earlier, the functionality of the listener is built using an inner anonymous class. First, we create an object of type DiscoveryListener. The functionality behind the resulting object is the definition of the DiscoveryEvent object, as defined in the interface specification. When a remote discovery attempt is made, the system returns a DiscoveryEvent object to the method. The first task is to determine if the data found is an actual advertisement.

Line 1421 pulls a message from the DiscoveryEvent object provided to the listener. Line 1423 attempts to obtain an Enumeration object from the message by using a call to the getResponses() method. If there is a valid response from the discovery service, the response will be provided as an Enumeration object.

Line 144 converts the Enumeration object to a string in an attempt to build a valid advertisement. Line 147 contains the actual attempt to build an advertisement from the XML. In this line, a call is made to the advertisement factory. Instead of trying to build a generic advertisement, the code creates a stream object from the discovered strings. If an advertisement is made successfully, an attempt is made to cast the advertisement to a module specification advertisement so we can pull out the pipe information.

Line 147 makes a call to the getPipeAdvertisement() method, which attempts to pull the pipe advertisement from the MSA. Line 150 builds an output pipe with the pipe advertisement found in line 147.

If any of the attempts to pull out the advertisement or the MSA fail, an exception will be thrown. For the sample code in this chapter, the exception is ignored and no output pipe is created. The code we described earlier does the majority of the work for remote advertisement discovery; however, the code does have to be launched.

Lines 158 through 164 are invoked when a local discovery fails. The code consists of a single call to the getRemoteAdvertisement() method on line 158, where our key-value pair along with the listener object are passed to the discovery service. The method will set up our listener object before starting the process of discovering an advertisement that matches our search criteria.

In either local or remote discovery, what we are ultimately discovering is the MSA. This advertisement is important to us because the input pipe advertisement is embedded in it.

Building an Output Pipe

The pipe advertisement obtained from the MSA provides all the information needed for the JXTA system to build a connection between the sender and receiver peers. After the advertisement is obtained, either in the local cache or through remote discovery, a call is made to the createOutputPipe() method.

Lines 167 through 188 contain the code for the createOutputPipe() method. This method makes 10 attempts to create the connection between the remote

InputPipe object described in the PipeAdvertisement object and a newly created OutputPipe object. The code will wait for 10 seconds after each attempt to make the connection.

Line 175 contains the call to the pipe service method createOutputPipe(). If a connection between the input and output pipes is successful, an OutputPipe object is returned. The object is stored in a class attribute for use by the sendData() method.

Lines 178 through 180 will be called if there is a problem with the internal system during the connection attempt. Lines 184 through 187 check the total number of connection attempts. If a connection could not be created after 10 attempts, an error will be generated and the application stopped.

Sending a Message through a Pipe

At this point in the receiver application, all of the components have been discovered and connected to allow communication between the sender and receiver peers. The last thing to do is send data to the sender.

Lines 190 through 206 contain the code for a method called sendData(). This method sends a message through the client peer's output pipe, and is received by the input pipe of the server.

Lines 193 and 194 instantiate a new message object and then set the string attribute, which is basically a name-value pair. You will recall from our discussion of the server code that only messages received through the input pipe will be accepted if the key value of DataTag is associated with a message. Line 194 sets both the key and value pair using the DataTag key and a specified string for the data.

Line 197 uses the send() method associated with the OutputPipe object to push the message object out the client pipe. If the method fails, the application will stop.

Application Basics

Finally, there are a couple of methods associated with the receiver application that set up the GUI and begin the event loop. In lines 78–97, the constructor receiver() does the work of setting up the GUI for the application. One of the primary components created is a button on the GUI. The button is associated with the sendData() method, so that each time the button is clicked, a message is sent to the sender peer.

The run() method is called when the GUI has been created and the JXTA network contacted.

Creating a New Peer Group

Now that we've covered the basics of building peers and transferring information between them, let's look at how we enable our peers to build and join a private peer group. A private peer group has all of the same functionality as the NetPeerGroup, but a password is required to join a private peer group.

A new peer group is created using a series of steps consisting of:

1. Obtaining a unique PeerGroup ID
2. Establishing a Module Implementation Advertisement specifying services from the NetPeerGroup
3. Creating a PeerGroup Advertisement
4. Creating a new PeerGroup
5. Advertising the existence of the new peer group
6. Joining the new peer group

Creating a Peer Group ID

Let's tackle the creation of a new peer group ID. The code in Listing 12.7 creates a unique peer group ID, and displays the ID in the GUI window. This new ID is used as the ID for the peer group we are trying to create. The code in Listing 12.7 is executed only a single time for each application being built. The ID created will be hard-coded into all application code in order for it to be used each time the peers are executed. By using the same peer group ID for our new group each time the peer application is executed, we avoid cluttering the JXTA network with many advertisements, each with a different ID, that refer to the same peer group. This simple step greatly decreases stress on the JXTA network.

```java
import java.io.*;
import java.awt.*;
import java.awt.event.*;
import javax.swing.*;

import net.jxta.peergroup.*;
import net.jxta.exception.*;

public class PeerGroupIDCreator extends JFrame {

    private JTextArea displayArea;
```

Listing 12.7 Code for creating a peer group ID. (continues)

```
    public static void main(String args[]) {
        PeerGroupIDCreator myapp = new PeerGroupIDCreator();

        myapp.addWindowListener (
          new WindowAdapter() {
            public void windowClosing(WindowEvent e) {
              System.exit(0);
            }
          }
        );

        myapp.run();
    }

    public PeerGroupIDCreator() {
      super("Creator");

      Container c = getContentPane();

      displayArea = new JTextArea();
      c.add (new JScrollPane(displayArea), BorderLayout.CENTER);

      setSize(300,150);
      show();

      PeerGroupID myNewPeerGroupID = (PeerGroupID)
net.jxta.id.IDFactory.newPeerGroupID();
      displayArea.append("PeerGroupID is: " + myNewPeerGroupID);
    }

    public void run() {
    }

}
```

Listing 12.7   Code for creating a peer group ID. (continued)

Creating a Module Implementation Advertisement

When creating a new peer group, you must also create a new advertisement that indicates that the new group will be using a peer group implementation already in the system. From our early discussions, we know the NetPeerGroup implements the basic services of a peer group. The NetPeerGroup can be used as the basis for other peer groups, and provides a good starting point for our group. By using the specification and default implementation provided by the NetPeerGroup, we automatically have access to the discovery and pipe services within our new group. So, the first step in creating our new peer group is to copy the implementation advertisement from the NetPeerGroup. Since we are creating a peer group that implements the same functionality as the default NetPeerGroup, the only thing we need from the implementation advertisement is the module spec ID associated with it.

Recall that all advertisements need a module spec ID, which is usually published with an MSA. A module implementation advertisement publishes information about an implementation of a module class that is advertised using the MSA. By using the same module spec ID as the one found in the NetPeerGroup, we are signaling that our new group uses the same implementation. Our new group is just reusing an implementation already created. In line 108 of Listing 129, the Module Spec ID from the NetPeerGroup implementation is used as the Module Spec ID for the new peer group being created. The NetPeerGroup implementation is obtained in line 99.

Creating a Group Advertisement

The next step is to build the group advertisement representing our new group. The group advertisement requires the following:

PeerGroupID—Obtained from the PeerGroupIDCreator code in Listing 12-5

ModuleSpecID—Obtained from the module implementation advertisement by using the getModuleSpecID( ) method

GroupName—Can be any string

Description—Can be any string

After the advertisement is built, it is published to both the local and remote JXTA network. Note that the advertisement is being published in the NetPeerGroup using its associated discovery service.

Because we already have the advertisement for our new group, we could go ahead and just create the group. Instead, for learning purposes, we will go through the exercise of trying to locate the group advertisement we just published before creating the group.

Creating a New Peer Group

Creating a new group is done by using a single method called newGroup( ), found in the PeerGroup class. The NetPeerGroup allows new groups to be created using the method. Note that only one of the peers in the system should create the new group.

Once the new group has been created, our peer joins the group. Joining a new group can be simple or complex—it all depends on the membership requirements of the group. In other words, does the group require a username and password to join? For our first example, there are no such requirements because we are using the default services of the NetPeerGroup, which, as you know, can be joined by any peer that joins the JXTA network. Our next example will expand on this work to build a private peergroup.

Joining a new peer group is fairly easy when no logins are involved. The sequence of steps is:

1. Build an authenticated credential.

2. Obtain the membership service from the peer group.

3. Apply for membership using the membership service's authenticator.

4. Check to see if everything was filled out in our credentials.

5. Join the group.

For our current example, the membership service uses a null implementation; therefore, not much work is involved during any of these steps (but we must follow them in order). In the next section, we build a peer group that requires a login and password, and all of these steps will be expanded.

Listing 12.8 contains the code for creating and joining a new peer group. This code performs the steps we just described, including creating and advertising a new group as well as joining the group itself.

```
Line 1: import java.io.*;
import java.awt.*;
import java.awt.event.*;
import javax.swing.*;
import java.net.*;
import java.util.Enumeration;

import net.jxta.peergroup.*;
import net.jxta.exception.*;
Line 10: import net.jxta.id.IDFactory;
import net.jxta.protocol.*;
import net.jxta.discovery.*;
import net.jxta.document.*;
import net.jxta.credential.*;
import net.jxta.membership.*;

public class Example3 extends JFrame {
```

Listing 12.8 Creating, advertising, and joining a new group. (continues)

```
      private static PeerGroup netPeerGroup = null,
Line 20:                              wileyHowGroup = null,
                        discoveredWileyHowGroup = null;
    private static PeerGroupID wileyHowGroupID;
    private DiscoveryService myDiscoveryService = null;
    private JTextArea displayArea;

      private final static MimeMediaType XMLMIMETYPE = new
MimeMediaType("text/xml");

    public static void main(String args[]) {
        Example3 myapp = new Example3();
Line 30:
        myapp.addWindowListener (
          new WindowAdapter() {
            public void windowClosing(WindowEvent e) {
              System.exit(0);
            }
          }
        );

        myapp.run();
Line 40:    }

    public Example3() {
      super("Creator");

      Container c = getContentPane();

      displayArea = new JTextArea();
      c.add (new JScrollPane(displayArea), BorderLayout.CENTER);

Lien 50:       setSize(300,150);
      show();

      launchJXTA();
      getServices();
      wileyHowGroupID = createPeerGroupID("jxta:uuid-
DCEF4386EAED4908BE25CE5019EA02");
      wileyHowGroup = createPeerGroup(wileyHowGroupID, "wileyHowGroup",
"Experimentation Group");

      joinGroup(wileyHowGroup);
    }

Line 60:    public void run() {
```

Listing 12.8 Creating, advertising, and joining a new group. (continues)

```
    }

    private void launchJXTA() {
        displayArea.append("Launching Peer into JXTA Network...\n");
        try {
            netPeerGroup = PeerGroupFactory.newNetPeerGroup();
        } catch (PeerGroupException e) {
            System.out.println("Unable to create PeerGroup - Failure");
            e.printStackTrace();
Line 70:            System.exit(1);
        }
    }

    private void getServices() {
      displayArea.append("Obtaining Discovery Service....\n");
      myDiscoveryService = netPeerGroup.getDiscoveryService();
    }

    PeerGroupID createPeerGroupID(String myStringID) {
Line 80:      PeerGroupID tempPeerGroupID = null;

      try {
        tempPeerGroupID = (PeerGroupID) IDFactory.fromURL(new URL("urn", "",
myStringID));
      } catch (Exception e) {
        e.printStackTrace();
        System.exit(-1);
      }

    displayArea.append("Valid PeerGroupID has been created from
StringID\n");
Line 90:      return tempPeerGroupID;
    }

    PeerGroup createPeerGroup(PeerGroupID myPeerGroupID, String myPeerGroup-
Name, String myPeerGroupDescription) {
        PeerGroupAdvertisement wileyHowGroupAdvertisement;
        PeerGroup tempPeerGroup = null;
        ModuleImplAdvertisement myGroupImpl = null;

        try {
          myGroupImpl = netPeerGroup.getAllPurposePeerGroupImplAdvertisement();
Line 100:      } catch (Exception e) {
          e.printStackTrace();
          System.exit(-1);
        }
```

Listing 12.8 Creating, advertising, and joining a new group. (continues)

```
       wileyHowGroupAdvertisement = (PeerGroupAdvertisement)
AdvertisementFactory.newAdvertisement(PeerGroupAdvertisement.getAdvertise-
mentType());
       wileyHowGroupAdvertisement.setPeerGroupID(myPeerGroupID);
       wileyHowGroupAdvertisement.setModuleSpecID
(myGroupImpl.getModuleSpecID());
       wileyHowGroupAdvertisement.setName(myPeerGroupName);
Line 110:      wileyHowGroupAdvertisement.setDescription
(myPeerGroupDescription);
       displayArea.append("New Peer Group Advertisement has been created\n");

       try {
         myDiscoveryService.publish(wileyHowGroupAdvertisement,
myDiscoveryService.GROUP, PeerGroup.DEFAULT_LIFETIME, PeerGroup.
DEFAULT_EXPIRATION);
         myDiscoveryService.remotePublish(wileyHowGroupAdvertisement,
myDiscoveryService.GROUP, PeerGroup.DEFAULT_EXPIRATION);
       } catch (Exception e) {
         e.printStackTrace();
Line 120:        System.exit(-1);
       }
       displayArea.append("New Peer Group Advertisement has been
published\n");

       try {
         tempPeerGroup = netPeerGroup.newGroup(wileyHowGroupAdvertisement);
       } catch (Exception e) {
         e.printStackTrace();
         System.exit(-1);
       }
Line 130:        displayArea.append("New Peer Group has been created\n");

       return tempPeerGroup;
    }

    void joinGroup(PeerGroup myLocalGroup) {
       StructuredDocument myCredentials = null;
       try {
         AuthenticationCredential myAuthenticationCredential =
new AuthenticationCredential(myLocalGroup, null, myCredentials);
         MembershipService myMembershipService =
myLocalGroup.getMembershipService();
Line 140:        net.jxta.membership.Authenticator myAuthenticator =
myMembershipService.apply(myAuthenticationCredential);
         if (!myAuthenticator.isReadyForJoin()) {
           displayArea.append("Authenticator is not complete\n");
           return;
         }
```

Listing 12.8 Creating, advertising, and joining a new group. (continues)

```
                myMembershipService.join(myAuthenticator);
                displayArea.append("Group has been joined\n");
            } catch (Exception e) {
                displayArea.append("Authentication failed - group not joined\n");
                e.printStackTrace();
Line 150:            System.exit(-1);
            }
        }
    }
```

Listing 12.8   Creating, advertising, and joining a new group.

The code in Listing 12.8 has a number of primary components that are related to the steps necessary to create a new peer group. In the sections that follow, we discuss the code for each of these components.

main() Method

The main() method is executed when the application starts. Line 29 begins the normal creation of the application object (called Example3). Line 39 fires the run() method, which causes the application to loop on its internal event loop.

Constructor

The majority of the work for setting up the object occurs in the constructor. Lines 43 through 51 do the work of creating the window and building a JTextArea control within it.

Line 53 calls the launchJXTA() method, where the work is performed to put the current peer into the NetPeerGroup group. Line 54 calls the getServices() method in order to obtain the discovery service from the NetPeerGroup group; the discovery service will be used to publish advertisements about our new peer group.

Line 55 calls the createPeerGroupID() method to build an internal Peer-GroupID object based on a string representation of an ID. Line 56 calls the createPeerGroup() method that does the actual work of building the advertisements necessary for the new group. Once built, the advertisements are published in the local cache and remotely. Line 57 calls the joinGroup() method to join the new peer group just created

createPeerGroupID() Method

As discussed earlier, when an advertisement is published repeatedly for the same resource, it is *not* desirable to build a new ID each time since this will clutter the cache and the JXTA network with basically identical advertisements. For this reason, we use a separate program to generate an ID. The ID is passed to the createPeerGroupID() method as a string parameter, and a "real" PeerGroupID is returned.

Line 83 does all of the work in this method by using the IDFactory to build a PeerGroupID object using the string ID and the string "urn" as a URL. If everything works, the method will return the new object; otherwise, the application will exit with an error.

createPeerGroup() Method

The createPeerGroup() method does the work required to build and publish the necessary advertisements for our new group. Line 99 obtains the default peer group implementation advertisement from the NetPeerGroup group so that we have a valid ModuleSpecID to use for our peer group advertisement.

Line 105 builds a new PeerGroupAdvertisement object. For this application, we are building the advertisement from scratch instead of reading it from a file. Line 106 assigns the PeerGroupID object created earlier to the advertisement.

Line 107 sets the ModuleSpecID of the new advertisement to be the same ID that the implementation advertisement obtains in line 99. Our peer group now is assumed to implement the default peer group services.

Line 108 sets the name of the peer group, line 109 sets the description of the peer group, and lines 113 through 114 publish the new peer group advertisement to the local cache and remotely.

Line 122 is an example of building the new group right away with the advertisement just created. There really isn't any reason to search for the peer group advertisement since our own application created it—this line of code just creates the new group.

joinGroup() Method

The final method in our code is the joinGroup() method, which does the work of joining a new peer group.

Line 133 creates a variable that holds a document; this document contains the identity of the peer trying to join the new group. Since our new group is using a null membership service, the identity will be null as well.

Line 135 creates a new AuthenticationCredential object based on the group being joined, the authentication method we want peers to use when joining the group (null in our case), and the credentials of the peer attempting to join.

Line 136 obtains the membership service of the group to be joined. Line 137 takes our AuthenticationCredential and gives it to the membership service of the group we are attempting to join. Success or failure is checked in line 138.

Line 138 determines whether all of the information needed for authentication to the new group was provided. If the credentials weren't all available, the group will not be joined.

Line 142 is executed when line 138 evaluates to false. This line does the work of actually joining the group—something of a formality since our credentials already checked out with the group.

A Peer that Discovers and Joins a New Peer Group

The peer group application created in the previous section did all of the work of creating a new peer group and advertising it. As a side note, the application also joins the group, although this step isn't exactly necessary. In this section, we build a peer that uses the peer group application—what this means is that this new peer will not create a peer group, but instead will discover another peer group's advertisement and join that group. In Listing 12.9, some of the code is the same as our previous application, but we've removed the code for building advertisements and added code for discovering the peer group advertisement.

The code for discovering a peer group advertisement is very similar to the code we discussed earlier for our receiver peer that enabled it to discover an MSA advertisement and use the message pipe service.

```
Line 1: import java.io.*;
import java.awt.*;
import java.awt.event.*;
import javax.swing.*;
import java.net.*;
import java.util.Enumeration;

import net.jxta.peergroup.*;
import net.jxta.exception.*;
Line 10: import net.jxta.id.IDFactory;
import net.jxta.protocol.*;
import net.jxta.discovery.*;
import net.jxta.document.*;
import net.jxta.credential.*;
```

Listing 12.9 Finding and joining a new peer group. (continues)

```
import net.jxta.membership.*;

public class Example3 extends JFrame {

    private static PeerGroup netPeerGroup = null,
Line 20:                          wileyHowGroup = null,
                             discoveredWileyHowGroup = null;
    private static PeerGroupID wileyHowGroupID;
    private DiscoveryService myDiscoveryService = null;
    private JTextArea displayArea;

        private final static MimeMediaType XMLMIMETYPE = new
MimeMediaType("text/xml");

    public static void main(String args[]) {
        Example3 myapp = new Example3();
Line 30:
        myapp.addWindowListener (
          new WindowAdapter() {
            public void windowClosing(WindowEvent e) {
              System.exit(0);
            }
          }
        );

        myapp.run();
Line 40:     }

    public Example3() {
      super("User");

      Container c = getContentPane();

      displayArea = new JTextArea();
      c.add (new JScrollPane(displayArea), BorderLayout.CENTER);

Line 50:      setSize(300,150);
      show();

      launchJXTA();
      getServices();
      findAdvertisement("Name", "wileyHowGroup");
    }

    public void run() {
    }
Line 60:
```

Listing 12.9 Finding and joining a new peer group. (continues)

```
      private void launchJXTA() {
          displayArea.append("Launching Peer into JXTA Network...\n");
          try {
              netPeerGroup = PeerGroupFactory.newNetPeerGroup();
          } catch (PeerGroupException e) {
              System.out.println("Unable to create PeerGroup - Failure");
              e.printStackTrace();
              System.exit(1);
          }
Line 70:  }

      private void getServices() {
        displayArea.append("Obtaining Discovery Service....\n");
        myDiscoveryService = netPeerGroup.getDiscoveryService();
      }

      private void findAdvertisement(String searchKey, String searchValue) {
        Enumeration myLocalEnum = null;
        PeerGroupAdvertisement localWileyHowGroupAdv = null;
Line 80:      displayArea.append("Trying to find advertisement...\n");

        try {
          myLocalEnum = myDiscoveryService.getLocalAdvertisements
(DiscoveryService.GROUP, searchKey, searchValue);

          if ((myLocalEnum != null) && myLocalEnum.hasMoreElements()) {
              displayArea.append("Found Local Advertisement...\n");
              PeerGroupAdvertisement myFoundPGA = null;
              while (myLocalEnum.hasMoreElements()) {
                  myFoundPGA = (PeerGroupAdvertisement) myLocalEnum.nextElement();
Line 90:            if (myFoundPGA.getName().equals(searchValue)) {
                    localWileyHowGroupAdv = myFoundPGA;
                    break;
                  }
              }

              if (localWileyHowGroupAdv != null) {
                  displayArea.append("Creating new group variable...\n");
                  wileyHowGroup = netPeerGroup.newGroup(localWileyHowGroupAdv);
                  joinGroup(wileyHowGroup);
Line 100:           }
          }
          else {
            DiscoveryListener myDiscoveryListener = new DiscoveryListener() {
              public void discoveryEvent(DiscoveryEvent e) {
                Enumeration enum;
                String str;
```

Listing 12.9 Finding and joining a new peer group. (continues)

```
                 displayArea.append("Found Remote Advertisement...\n");
                 DiscoveryResponseMsg myMessage = e.getResponse();
Line 110:             enum = myMessage.getResponses();
                 str = (String)enum.nextElement();

                 try {
                    PeerGroupAdvertisement myPeerGroupAdv =
(PeerGroupAdvertisement) AdvertisementFactory.
newAdvertisement(XMLMIMETYPE, new ByteArrayInputStream(str.getBytes()));

                    displayArea.append("Creating new group variable...\n");
                    wileyHowGroup = netPeerGroup.newGroup(myPeerGroupAdv);
                    joinGroup(wileyHowGroup);

Line 120:        } catch(Exception ee) {
                    ee.printStackTrace();
                    System.exit(-1);
                 }
              }
              };

             displayArea.append("Launching Remote Discovery Service...\n");
             myDiscoveryService.getRemoteAdvertisements(null,
DiscoveryService.GROUP, searchKey, searchValue, 1, myDiscoveryListener);
          }
Line 130:     } catch (Exception e) {
             System.out.println("Error during advertisement search");
             System.exit(-1);
          }
       }

    void joinGroup(PeerGroup myLocalGroup) {
       StructuredDocument myCredentials = null;
       try {
          AuthenticationCredential myAuthenticationCredential =
new AuthenticationCredential(myLocalGroup, null, myCredentials);
Line 140:        MembershipService myMembershipService =
myLocalGroup.getMembershipService();
          net.jxta.membership.Authenticator myAuthenticator =
myMembershipService.apply(myAuthenticationCredential);
          if (!myAuthenticator.isReadyForJoin()) {
             displayArea.append("Authenticator is not complete\n");
             return;
          }
          myMembershipService.join(myAuthenticator);
          displayArea.append("Group has been joined\n");
```

Listing 12.9 Finding and joining a new peer group. (continues)

```
    } catch (Exception e) {
      displayArea.append("Authentication failed - group not joined\n");
      e.printStackTrace();
      System.exit(-1);
    }
  }
}
```

Listing 12.9 Finding and joining a new peer group. (continued)

Much of the code in Listing 12.9 will look familiar; it includes code for the constructor and the main(), launchJXTA(), run(), and getServices() methods. The joinGroup() method is exactly the same as the code found in our application that creates a peer group shown in Listing 12.8.

The new method in this application is findAdvertisement(). In our previous examples, we had to find the module spec advertisement of a remote peer because it held a pipe advertisement we needed in order to use the remote pipe. This time, we have to locate the group advertisement. We use code from the previous example and modify it to handle a group advertisement instead of a module spec advertisement (we will discuss that code in detail shortly). Peers search for the group advertisement in both the local cache and remotely if needed. Once the current advertisement is found, the program creates a new group.

Lines 83 through 101 do the work to find the peer group advertisement in the local cache. You should note that in line 83, we changed the first parameter from the value DiscoveryServer.ADV (which is used to indicate general advertisements like pipe advertisements) to DiscoveryService.GROUP, which tells the service to look only at group advertisements.

Lines 88 through 94 contain a loop based on the elements in the Enumeration object returned by the call in line 83. For each of the advertisements found in the local cache, the name is compared to ensure that the correct advertisement is found. So, in order for this peer to join a peer group, it will need to know the name of the group it wants to join.

Lines 96 through 100 are executed when the appropriate advertisement has been found. Line 98 builds an internal PeerGroup object for the new group, and line 99 makes a call to the joinGroup() method for doing the official work of joining the group.

If the peer cannot find the advertisement for the new group in the local cache, lines 102 through 134 initiate a remote discovery query. Since the discovery process is asynchronous, a listener is created for when an advertisement is found.

Lines 103 through 125 contain the code behind the listener class. The first few lines of the code pull the event, message, and resulting Enumeration object from the parameter passed to the method.

Line 114 attempts to obtain a PeerGroupAdvertisement object from the Enumeration object created in the previous lines. If successful, a new PeerGroup object is created, and a call is made to the joinGroup() method.

Line 128 does the work of launching the remote discovery for the peer group advertisement. Notice the use of the DiscoveryService.GROUP parameter in order to ensure that the correct advertisement is found.

Creating a Secure Peer Group

We have discussed how to discover peers and advertisements, connect to pipes and transfer data, and build new peer groups. Up to this point, no authentication between peers, groups, and services has been required. Membership to the peer group was accomplished by creating credentials and attempting to authenticate the user with the membership service associated with the new peer group.

In our final application for this chapter, we build a secure peer group. Instead of the membership service being null, the secure peer group requires a peer to provide a specific username and password before being allowed to join. The big question is, where does the new membership service come from, and how does the new peer group know about it?

Using a Membership Service Implementation

Recall that we have a number of advertisements associated with a peer group. The first advertisement is called the module class specification, which is designed to let the community know about a new set of specifications that are available. The specification can be implemented and advertised using a module class implementation. The implementation advertisement includes a number of <Svc> elements, which look like this:

```
<Svc>
        <jxta:MIA>
                <MSID>
            urn:jxta:uuid-DEADBEEFDEAFBABAFEEDBABE000000050106
            </MSID>
            <Comp>
                <Efmt>
                    JDK1.4
```

```
            </Efmt>
            <Bind>
                V1.0 Ref Impl
            </Bind>
        </Comp>
        <Code>
          net.jxta.impl.membership.NullMembershipService
        </Code>
        <PURI>
          http://www.jxta.org/download/jxta.jar
        </PURI>
        <Prov>
          sun.com
        </Prov>
        <Desc>
          Reference Implementation of the MembershipService service
        </Desc>
      </jxta:MIA>
  </Svc>
```

Of particular importance are the MSID, Code, and PURI entries. As we know, all resources must have a unique MSID to identify the resource. The Code element indicates the Java class and the path to the class; and finally, the PURI element indicates where the code for this implementation can be found if not on the local client machine. The <Svc> element is embedded in the class implementation advertisement, and a peer can request a specific implementation based on the MSID of this advertisement. If the client peer doesn't have the code necessary for the implementation, it can be loaded based on the PURI.

Changing the Default Class Implementation Advertisement

For the secure peer group, we use an implementation coded by the JXTA team and incorporated into the jxta.jar file. In order to use this new service (which is called PasswdMembershipService), we have to build a class implementation advertisement for our new peer group that includes the information necessary for the new service in the <Svc> element. This seems simple, but the class implementation advertisement includes many standard peer group services. We will need to include all these services in our advertisement as well. The solution is to copy a default class implementation peer group advertisement and change the membership service element only. The code in Listing 12.10 (which we introduce in the next section) features a method called updateElementMSID(), which updates the MSID, Code, and Description elements for the new service. We don't need to change the PURI because the code is in the same JAR file as the null membership service.

The process of building our own class implementation advertisement involves these steps:

1. Copy a default class implementation advertisement for peer groups.

2. Locate the <Svc> element for the membership service.

3. Update the membership element with information on the PasswdMembershipService.

4. Change the MSID of the class implementation advertisement because it is no longer associated with the default advertisement.

5. Publish the new advertisement locally and remotely.

We will discuss these steps when we walk through the code in an upcoming section.

Code for a Secure Peer Group

The code in Listing 12.10 builds a secure peer group, and joins the new group. In the discussion of the code that follows, we examine three key areas: building and publishing the new implementation advertisement, building and publishing the peer group advertisement, and using the authenticateMe( ) method. In this code, we use the Java XML Pack from www.javasoft.com for manipulating the XML advertisements and the latest JDOM package from www.jdom.org. In order to execute this code, you have to install the Pack and JDOM. Both of the packages are easy to download and install if you follow the instructions provided at the respective sites.

The compile and execute commands also change with the new packages. The compile line follows; it assumes you have created an environment variable called JXTALIB that points to the location of the JXTA Java implementation libraries:

```
javac -d . -classpath %JXTALIB%/jxta.jar
;%JXTALIB%/log4j.jar;%JXTALIB%/beepcore.jar;%JXTALIB%/jxtasecurity.
jar;%JXTALIB%/org.mortbay.jetty.jar;%JXTALIB%/servlet.jar;%JXTALIB%/
cryptix-asn1.jar;%JXTALIB%/cryptix32.jar;%JXTALIB%/
jxtaptls.jar;%JXTALIB%/minimalBC.jar;c:/jdom/jdom.jar;c:/jdom/
xerces.jar Example4.java
```

The primary change in this command is the addition of the JAR files—c:/jdom/jdom.jar and c:/jdom/xerces.jar. Both the jdom and xerces JAR files are located in a directory called jdom. The execute command is:

```
java -classpath %JXTALIB%/jxta.jar;%JXTA
LIB%/log4j.jar;%JXTALIB%/beepcore.jar;%JXTALIB%/jxtasecurity.jar;%JXTALI
B%/org.mortbay.jetty.jar;%JXTALIB%/servlet.jar;%JXTALIB%/cryptix-
asn1.jar;%JXTALIB%/cryptix32.jar;%JXTALIB%/jxtaptls.jar;%JXTALIB%/mini-
malBC.jar;c:/jdom/jdom.jar;c:/jdom/xerces.jar; Example4
```

```
Line 1: import java.io.*;
import java.awt.*;
import java.awt.event.*;
import javax.swing.*;
import java.net.*;
import java.util.Enumeration;

import net.jxta.peergroup.*;
Line 10: import net.jxta.exception.*;
import net.jxta.id.IDFactory;
import net.jxta.protocol.*;
import net.jxta.discovery.*;
import net.jxta.document.*;
import net.jxta.credential.*;
import net.jxta.membership.*;
import net.jxta.platform.*;

import org.jdom.input.DOMBuilder;
Line 20: import org.jdom.output.XMLOutputter;
import org.w3c.dom.*;

import net.jxta.impl.membership.*;
import java.lang.reflect.Method;

public class Example4 extends JFrame {

    private static PeerGroup netPeerGroup = null,
                             wileyHowGroup = null,
Line 30:                               discoveredWileyHowGroup = null;
    private static PeerGroupID wileyHowGroupID;
    private DiscoveryService myDiscoveryService = null;
    private JTextArea displayArea;

        private final static MimeMediaType XMLMIMETYPE = new
MimeMediaType("text/xml");

    public static void main(String args[]) {
        Example4 myapp = new Example4();

Line 40:        myapp.addWindowListener (
          new WindowAdapter() {
            public void windowClosing(WindowEvent e) {
              System.exit(0);
            }
          }
        );
```

Listing 12.10 Secure peer group creator application. (continues)

```
                myapp.run();
        }
Line 50:
    public Example4() {
        super("Creator");

        Container c = getContentPane();

        displayArea = new JTextArea();
        c.add (new JScrollPane(displayArea), BorderLayout.CENTER);

        setSize(300,150);
Line 60:        show();

        launchJXTA();
        getServices();
        wileyHowGroupID = createPeerGroupID("jxta:uuid-
DCEF4386EAED4908BE25CE5019EA02");
        wileyHowGroup = createPeerGroup(wileyHowGroupID, "wileyHowGroup",
"Experimentation Group");
        joinGroup(wileyHowGroup);
    }

    public void run() {
Line 70:    }

    private void launchJXTA() {
        displayArea.append("Launching Peer into JXTA Network...\n");
        try {
            netPeerGroup = PeerGroupFactory.newNetPeerGroup();
        } catch (PeerGroupException e) {
            System.out.println("Unable to create PeerGroup - Failure");
            e.printStackTrace();
            System.exit(1);
Line 80:        }
    }

    private void getServices() {
        displayArea.append("Obtaining Discovery Service....\n");
        myDiscoveryService = netPeerGroup.getDiscoveryService();
    }

    PeerGroupID createPeerGroupID(String myStringID) {
        PeerGroupID tempPeerGroupID = null;
Line 90:
        try {
            tempPeerGroupID = (PeerGroupID) IDFactory.fromURL(new URL("urn", "",
```

Listing 12.10 Secure peer group creator application. (continues)

```
myStringID));
      } catch (Exception e) {
        e.printStackTrace();
        System.exit(-1);
      }

      displayArea.append("Valid PeerGroupID has been created from
StringID\n");
      return tempPeerGroupID;
Line 100:    }


    PeerGroup createPeerGroup(PeerGroupID myPeerGroupID,
String myPeerGroupName, String myPeerGroupDescription) {
      PeerGroupAdvertisement wileyHowGroupAdvertisement;
      PeerGroup tempPeerGroup = null;

      ModuleImplAdvertisement myGroupImpl = null;
      ModuleImplAdvertisement myNewImplAdv = null;
      try {
        myGroupImpl = netPeerGroup.getAllPurposePeerGroupImplAdvertisement();
Line 110:         StructuredTextDocument paramDoc =
(StructuredTextDocument)myGroupImpl.getDocument(XMLMIMETYPE);

        DOMBuilder builder = new DOMBuilder();
        org.jdom.Document doc = builder.build(paramDoc.getStream());

        org.jdom.Element membershipElement =
getElementMSID(getParamElement(doc.getRootElement()), "urn:jxta:uuid-
DEADBEEFDEAFBABAFEEDBABE000000050106");
        updateElementMSID(membershipElement, myGroupImpl);

        XMLOutputter outputter = new XMLOutputter();
        myNewImplAdv = (ModuleImplAdvertisement)AdvertisementFactory.
newAdvertisement(XMLMIMETYPE, new ByteArrayInputStream(outputter.
outputString(doc).getBytes()));
Line 120:
        if (!myNewImplAdv.getModuleSpecID().equals(PeerGroup.
allPurposePeerGroupSpecID)) {
          myNewImplAdv.setModuleSpecID(IDFactory.newModuleSpecID(myNewImplAdv.
getModuleSpecID().getBaseClass()));
        }
        else {
          myNewImplAdv.setModuleSpecID((ModuleSpecID)IDFactory.fromURL(new
URL("urn", "", "jxta:uuid-"+"DeadBeefDeafBabaFeedBabe00000001"+"05"+"06")));
        }
```

Listing 12.10 Secure peer group creator application. (continues)

```
Line 130:      myDiscoveryService.publish(myNewImplAdv, DiscoveryService.ADV,
PeerGroup.DEFAULT_LIFETIME, PeerGroup.DEFAULT_EXPIRATION);
     myDiscoveryService.remotePublish(myNewImplAdv, DiscoveryService.ADV,
PeerGroup.DEFAULT_EXPIRATION);

     } catch (Exception e) {
       e.printStackTrace();
       System.exit(-1);
     }

     wileyHowGroupAdvertisement = (PeerGroupAdvertisement) AdvertisementFac-
tory.newAdvertisement(PeerGroupAdvertisement.getAdvertisementType());
     wileyHowGroupAdvertisement.setPeerGroupID(myPeerGroupID);
Line 140: wileyHowGroupAdvertisement.setModuleSpecID(myNewImplAdv.getModule-
SpecID());
     wileyHowGroupAdvertisement.setName(myPeerGroupName);
     wileyHowGroupAdvertisement.setDescription(myPeerGroupDescription);

     StructuredTextDocument loginInfo = (StructuredTextDocument)
StructuredDocumentFactory.newStructuredDocument(new
MimeMediaType("text/xml"), "Parm");
     String loginString = "username" + ":" +
PasswdMembershipService.makePsswd("password") + ":";
     TextElement loginElement = loginInfo.createElement("login",
loginString);
     loginInfo.appendChild(loginElement);
     wileyHowGroupAdvertisement.putServiceParam(PeerGroup.membershipClassID,
loginInfo);

Line 150:      displayArea.append("New Peer Group Advertisement has been
created\n");


     try {
       myDiscoveryService.publish(wileyHowGroupAdvertisement,
myDiscoveryService.GROUP, PeerGroup.DEFAULT_LIFETIME, PeerGroup.DEFAULT_EXPI-
RATION);
       myDiscoveryService.remotePublish(wileyHowGroupAdvertisement,
myDiscoveryService.GROUP, PeerGroup.DEFAULT_EXPIRATION);
     } catch (Exception e) {
       e.printStackTrace();
       System.exit(-1);
Line 160:      }
     displayArea.append("New Peer Group Advertisement has been
published\n");

     try {
       tempPeerGroup = netPeerGroup.newGroup(wileyHowGroupAdvertisement);
```

Listing 12.10 Secure peer group creator application. (continues)

```
        } catch (Exception e) {
          e.printStackTrace();
          System.exit(-1);
        }
        displayArea.append("New Peer Group has been created\n");
Line 170:
        return tempPeerGroup;
    }

    org.jdom.Element getParamElement(org.jdom.Element theRootElement) {
        java.util.List elements = theRootElement.getChildren();
        java.util.Iterator itr = elements.iterator();
        org.jdom.Element currentElement = null;

        while (itr.hasNext()) {
Line 180:           currentElement = (org.jdom.Element)itr.next();
          if (currentElement.getName().equals("Parm"))
            return currentElement;
        }
        return null;
    }

    org.jdom.Element getElementMSID(org.jdom.Element theParamElement,
String theMatchingID) {
        java.util.List elements = theParamElement.getChildren(),
                    innerElements = null,
Line 190:                      tempList = null;
        java.util.Iterator paramItr = elements.iterator();
        org.jdom.Element returnElement = null,
                    localElement = null,
                    tempElement = null;

        while (paramItr.hasNext()) {
            returnElement = (org.jdom.Element)paramItr.next();
            if (returnElement.getName().equals("Svc")) {

Line 200:             tempList = returnElement.getChildren();
              tempElement = (org.jdom.Element)tempList.get(0);
              innerElements = tempElement.getChildren();

              java.util.Iterator svcItr = innerElements.iterator();
              while (svcItr.hasNext()) {
                localElement = (org.jdom.Element)svcItr.next();
                if (localElement.getName().equals("MSID") &&
localElement.getTextTrim().equals(theMatchingID))
                  return returnElement;
              }
Line 210:           }
```

Listing 12.10 Secure peer group creator application. (continues)

```
        }
        return null;
    }

    void updateElement(org.jdom.Element parentElement, String key, String
value) {
        java.util.List elements = parentElement.getChildren();
        java.util.Iterator Itr = null;
        org.jdom.Element tempElement = null;

Line 220:       Itr = ((org.jdom.Element)elements.get(0)).getChildren().
iterator();

        while (Itr.hasNext()) {
          tempElement = (org.jdom.Element)Itr.next();
          if (tempElement.getName().equals(key)) {
            tempElement.setText(value);
            return;
          }
        }
    }
Line 230:
    void updateElementMSID(org.jdom.Element membershipElement,
ModuleImplAdvertisement myGroupImpl) {
        updateElement(membershipElement, "MSID",
PasswdMembershipService.passwordMembershipSpecID.getURL().toString());
        updateElement(membershipElement, "Code",
PasswdMembershipService.class.getName());
        updateElement(membershipElement, "Desc", "Module Impl Advertisement for
the PasswdMembership Service");
    }


    void joinGroup(PeerGroup myLocalGroup) {
        StructuredDocument myCredentials = null;
Line 240:       try {
          AuthenticationCredential myAuthenticationCredential =
new AuthenticationCredential(myLocalGroup, null, myCredentials);
          MembershipService myMembershipService =
myLocalGroup.getMembershipService();
          net.jxta.membership.Authenticator myAuthenticator =
myMembershipService.apply(myAuthenticationCredential);

          authenticateMe(myAuthenticator, "username", "password");

          if (!myAuthenticator.isReadyForJoin()) {
            displayArea.append("Authenticator is not complete\n");
            return;
```

Listing 12.10 The secure peer group creator application. (continues)

```
Line 250:          }
        myMembershipService.join(myAuthenticator);
        displayArea.append("Group has been joined\n");
    } catch (Exception e) {
        displayArea.append("Authentication failed - group not joined\n");
        e.printStackTrace();
        System.exit(-1);
    }
  }

Line 260:    void authenticateMe(net.jxta.membership.Authenticator
theAuthenticator, String login, String password) {
    Method [] ourMethods = theAuthenticator.getClass().getMethods();

    try {
    for (int meth=0; meth<ourMethods.length; meth++) {
      if (ourMethods[meth].getName().equals("setAuth1Identity")) {
        Object [] authLogin = {login};
        Method aMethod = (Method)ourMethods[meth];
        aMethod.invoke(theAuthenticator, authLogin);
      }
Line 270:        else if
(ourMethods[meth].getName().equals("setAuth2_Password")) {
        Object [] authPassword = {password};
        Method aMethod = (Method)ourMethods[meth];
        aMethod.invoke(theAuthenticator, authPassword);
      }
    }
    } catch (Exception e) {
      e.printStackTrace();
      System.exit(-1);
    }
Line 280:    }
}
```

Listing 12.10 The secure peer group creator application. (continued)

A Secure Peer Group Advertisement

As in the previous example, a peer group advertisement will need to be published as well. The code for creating and publishing the advertisement is basically the same except for two places. The first difference is the ModuleSpecID that the peer group advertisement is associated with. Previously, the association was with the default class implementation advertisement, but now, since we want it associated with our new advertisement, we will use its ModuleSpecID instead. The second difference is the addition of a <Parm> element to the peer group advertisement. The element will appear as follows:

```
<Parm>
      <login>
            username:KDIekdI:
      </login>
</Parm>
```

The login element will state the login name necessary to join the secure peer group as well as an encrypted password.

Becoming Authenticated

Once the peer group has been published and discovered, a peer can join the group. The steps are as follows:

1. Build an authenticated credential.

2. Obtain the membership service from the peer group.

3. Apply for membership using the membership service's authenticator.

4. Authenticate the peer using the username and password.

5. Check to see if everything was filled out in our credentials.

6. Join the group.

This process differs from joining a non-secure peer group; in step 4, the method that implements the authentication is called authenticateMe(), and it accepts the authenticator object created in the previous step as well as the username and password. All of the work is performed in the authenticateMe() method. Before we look at the method, let's take a look at the PasswdMembershipService we have associated with this peer group.

The PasswdMembershipService code can be found in the jxta.jar file. The easiest way to view the file is to download the JXTA source and look in the directory <root directory>/platform/binding/java/impl/src/net/jxta/impl/ membership. One of the first things you will notice when reading through the file is a comment letting you know that this membership service code is not ready for production use. It is an example of how to write a membership service; we will actually look at this task in more detail in Chapter 15, "Implementing Security," so here we just want to hit the highlights of the code.

Move through the file until you come to the method isReadyForJoin(). The code is:

```
synchronized public boolean isReadyForJoin() {
      return ( (null != password) && (null != whoami) );
```

Notice the requirement for a user to be able to join this group; both the password and whoami objects must not be null. Just a few lines under these are two methods:

```
public void setAuth1Identity( String who ) {
    whoami = who;
}

public void setAuth2_Password( String secret ) {
    password = secret;
}
```

These three functions represent the beginning of the membership process for a client, setting the login and password, and checking to see if the membership is successful and ready to be joined.

Before we look at the work being done in the middle, consider the following snippet of code found in the init() method further down in the code:

```
if( aLogin.getName().equals( "login" ) ) {
  String etcPasswd = (String) aLogin.getTextValue( );

  int nextDelim = etcPasswd.indexOf( ':' );
  if( -1 == nextDelim )
    continue;

  String login = etcPasswd.substring( 0, nextDelim ).trim();
  int lastDelim = etcPasswd.indexOf( ':', nextDelim + 1 );
  String passwd = etcPasswd.substring( nextDelim + 1, lastDelim );

  LOG.info( "Adding login : '" + login + "' with encoded password : '" +
passwd + "'" );

  logins.put( login, passwd );
```

When the peer group is created, this code will execute and expect to find the one or more login/password combinations in the peer group advertisement. The code above will read the combinations and store them internally.

Now let's look at the middle part of the process for both the peer group and the client. When the client wanting to join the peer group has set the login and password, it will call the isReadyForJoin() method to be sure all fields required for membership have been filled out. If all of the fields are complete, the join() method is called. A code snippet for join() looks like this:

```
        if( !authenticated.isReadyForJoin() )
    throw new PeerGroupException( "Not Ready to join!" );

  if( !checkPasswd(
    ((PasswdAuthenticator)authenticated).getAuth1Identity(),
    ((PasswdAuthenticator)authenticated).getAuth2_Password() ) )
      throw new PeerGroupException( "Incorrect Password!" );
```

Another call to isReadyForJoin() is made and then an internal method, checkPasswd(), is called. This internal method checks the client provided login/password against the login/password combination(s) assigned in the peer group advertisement. If a match is not successful, an exception will be thrown; otherwise, the client will be allowed to join the group.

NOTE

We skipped a number of details in this discussion, but we cover those details in Chapter 18 when we build a more secure membership service. If the call to join() returns successfully, the client peer is considered joined to the new peer group.

New Class Implementation Advertisement Details

The majority of the changes from our previous example occur in the development of a new implementation advertisement for the peer group. As we mentioned previously, several steps must occur in order to build the new advertisement.

Step 1 takes place in lines 108 and 109, where a call is made to the method getAllPurposePeerGroupImplAdvertisement(). The call is made against the root peer group (or NetPeerGroup in our case, because that is the default group we joined when the application first executed). A ModuleImpleAdvertisement object is returned once the call completes; it contains quite a few default implementation <Svc> elements for a peer group. The remainder of the steps replace the null membership service with the password membership service. Line 109 uses the getDocument() method to pull a structured document in XML format from the advertisement. It should be noted that the StructuredDocument is a lightweight XML document. An XML-lite engine is used to handle the data structures behind the document but it isn't very powerful—the implementation of the StructuredDocument does not support all of the functionality normally found in an XML document. The intent of this document is to act like an XML document, but not to provide all of the functionality found in other XML implementations, such as JDOM.

Step 2 is accomplished by putting the advertisement into a DOM object and using appropriate controls to find the <Svc> element associated with the default membership service. Line 111 instantiates a DOMBuilder object from the JDOM package. (As we mentioned earlier, you need to install both the Java XML Pack and JDOM in order for this code to work correctly.) Once the DOMBuilder is instantiated, a JDOM document is built using the advertisement's structured document and the build() method of the DOMBuilder object. This is all accomplished on line 112. Line 114 makes a call to a helper method, getElementMSID(), which is defined in lines 182 through 208. The method searches through the entire XML document until the <Svc> element is found that is associated with the membership service. The method will return either an Element object referencing the element or a null object.

Now let's see how steps 3 and 4 are accomplished. Once the <Svc> element has been found, a call is made to the helper method updateElementMSID(), which is defined in lines 225 through 230. This method makes three updates to the membership element.

The MSID of the <Svc> element is changed from the ModuleSpecID of the default null membership implementation to the ModuleSpecID of the password membership service. This is a key step because our new peer group will reference this implementation advertisement, which in turn references the password membership service instead of the default null service.

The Code element is changed to the implement for the password membership service.

The description element is changed to something more appropriate for describing the functionality of the service.

Step 5 begins on line 117 with the instantiation of an XMLOutputter object used to pull the XML from our XML document. Line 118 instantiates a new ModuleImplAdvertisement using the XML from the DOM document. The final update before the advertisement is published is to change the ModuleSpecID of the new ModuleImplAdvertisement. The ModuleSpecID should be different from the ModuleSpecID of the default implementation advertisement. Finally, the new advertisement is published both locally and remotely. The ID in line 117 should be changed to a unique ID based on the output from Listing 12.5.

Peer Group Advertisement Details

Before a peer can use the new peer group, it needs to discover a peer group advertisement. The code for the peer group advertisement resembles the code in our previous example shown in Listing 12.8; however, we have changed the ModuleSpecID to that of the implementation advertisement we built in the previous section, and added a Parm section.

Lines 135–146 build the peer group advertisement, line 135 obtains a generic advertisement object, and line 136 sets the peer group ID to be that of our new peer group.

Line 136 fills in the ModuleSpecID of the peer group advertisement. (As we explained, it will be the same as the ModuleSpecID of the new implementation advertisement.) Line 137 sets the name of the peer group, and line 138 sets the description of the peer group.

Lines 140 through 144 build a small XML document with a root element of <Parm> and a single element of <login>. The value of the <login> element is "required login string":"required password string". Notice how the cleartext password in the code is converted to an encoded password before being put in the element value. Finally, the document is added to the peer group advertisement by using the putServiceParam() method.

After the peer group advertisement is complete, it is published locally and remotely.

authenticateMe() Method Details

You will recall from our discussion of the authentication process that before we can call the join() method for the new peer group, we need to fill in the required fields of the membership service. These fields specify the login and password values. The methods that need to be called are named setAuth1Identity() and setAuth2_Password(). The trick to the authenticateMe() method is finding these methods and invoking them. Lines 255 through 275 make up the authenticateMe() method.

Line 256 builds an array of all of the methods exposed by the authenticator class designed as part of the membership service. The class is defined by the code

```
public class PasswdAuthenticator implements Authenticator
```

in the membership service code, Line 256 will return all of the methods defined in the class. However, we don't want all of the methods—we only want the two mentioned previously.

Line 259 loops through all of the methods in the array. Lines 260 through 264 check the name of the current method against the string "setAuth1Identity". If the condition is true, meaning the string matches "setAuth1Identity", the string value passed to the authenticateMe() method as the login is put into an array and the method is invoked, sending the current authenticator object and the login value.

Lines 265 through 269 check the name of the current method against the string "setAuth2_Password". If the condition is true, meaning the string matches "setAuth2_Passwood", the string value passed to the authenticateMe() method as the password is put into an array and the method is invoked, sending the current authenticator object and the password value.

Since this is a simple password membership service, only these two methods have to be called to set up a successful join.

Client for the Secure Peer Group

The code for the client portion of this code—the code that finds the peer group advertisement and joins the group—is basically the same as the code in Listing 12.10. The only change involves putting the new authenticateMe() method into the code and selecting the correct username and password.

Summary

In this chapter, we built three comprehensive applications, showing all of the key features of the JXTA system. Before you move on to the other chapters in this book, we recommend that you either type in the code or download it from the site listed in Appendix A, and then build and execute the applications. If you can understand how the code works, you will be well on your way to building robust JXTA applications. In the next chapter, the topic of JXTA pipes is covered. Pipes are the fundamental component for transferring information from one peer to another. There are a number of different types including one-way, secure, bi-directional, and reliable.

CHAPTER 13

JXTA Pipes

In Chapter 12, "Developing a JXTA Application," we used pipes to send data between peers in a peer group. The pipes were of the Unicast type, which means information can be sent in only one direction between peers. In this chapter, we discuss in detail all the pipes available in the current specification and Java reference implementation. The pipes we focus on are

Unicast—One-way pipe for sending non-secure data over an unreliable channel

UnicastSecure—One-way pipe for sending secure data over an unreliable channel

Propagate—One-to-many pipe for sending non-secure data over an unreliable channel

Bidirectional—Two-way pipe for sending non-secure data over an unreliable channel

Reliable—Pipe that builds on the bidirectional pipe for reliable communication (this type is still being developed in the JXTA platform)

We examine the characteristics of each pipe, and show how to build input and output pipes, how to use the publish/discovery mechanism, and how to transfer data through each pipe. This chapter also provides all the code necessary to use the pipes, and demonstrates how to swap various types of pipes in and out of JXTA peers with very little recoding.

Publishing and Discovering Pipes

Several of the code examples from previous chapters demonstrated how to build pipes, and how to advertise and discover them in the context of simple JXTA peers. This chapter builds on those examples to give you a full understanding of how pipes function; this is critical because pipes are the sole medium for JXTA peer communication.

Publishing

The purpose of publishing a pipe advertisement is to let all the peers in a group know of the pipe's existence. The discovery service offers two publish methods: publish() and remotePublish(). The publish() method lets peers that are directly accessible to the advertising peer know about the new pipe. The remotePublish() takes the publishing one step further by trying to use all available transports, such as TCP/IP and HTTP, in order to get the widest distribution.

As we discussed in Chapter 5, "JXTA Advertisements," one way to let other peers know about a pipe's availability is through the use of a module class advertisement. While this is a good way of providing a high level of documentation and making comprehensive services available to other peers, it isn't always necessary. If you have a pipe that you want to make available just as a singleton device, you can publish the advertisement of the pipe directly. For example, the following code will create a pipe advertisement for a Unicast, or one-way, pipe, and publish the advertisement to all local peers:

```
PipeAdvertisement pipeAdv = (PipeAdvertisement)
  AdvertisementFactory.newAdvertisement(
  PipeAdvertisement.getAdvertisementType());
pipeAdv.setName("JXTA:KEYRECEIVE");
pipeAdv.setType(PipeService.UnicastType);
pipeAdv.setPipeID((ID) net.jxta.id.IDFactory.
  newPipeID(netPeerGroup.getPeerGroupID()));

discoveryService.publish(pipeAdv, DiscoveryService.ADV);
```

Discovery

Once a peer has placed an advertisement into the system, it must be discovered. In Chapter 6, "Peer Discovery Protocol," we discussed using the discovery service to find advertisements, and in the previous chapter we used the discovery service to locate module class advertisements and extract an associated pipe. However, it is a simpler process to design your peer to look for new pipe advertisements as they are published by remote peers. There are basically two ways to find advertisements: through the use of callbacks and by utilizing the local cache.

Using Callbacks

In the case of a callback, a listener object is associated with a discovery attempt. When the discovery service is contacted with advertisements from remote peers, the listener object will be passed the advertisements for processing. Listing 13.1 contains code that will attempt to discover pipe advertisements with a name matching the text DSS*, where * is a wildcard.

```
public class localDiscoveryListener implements DiscoveryListener {
   public void discoveryEvent(DiscoveryEvent e) {
      DiscoveryResponseMsg myMessage = e.getResponse();
      Enumeration enum = myMessage.getResponses();
      while (enum.hasMoreElements()) {
        try {
           String str = (String)enum.nextElement();
           PipeAdvertisement pipeAdvt = (PipeAdvertisement)
             AdvertisementFactory.newAdvertisement(
             new MimeMediaType( "text/xml" ),,
             new ByteArrayInputStream(str.getBytes()));
           // do something with pipe advertisement
}
      catch(Exception ee) {
        // not a pipe advertisement
      }
       }
}

localDiscoveryListener pipeListener = new
  localDiscoveryListener();

discoveryServer.getRemoteAdvertisements(null,
  DiscoveryService.ADV, "Name", "DSS*", 50, pipeListener);
```

Listing 13.1 Using a callback to locate new pipe advertisements.

In Listing 13.1, a listener object is created that defines the discoveryEvent() method required by the DiscoveryListener interface. When the method is called, the parameter will contain all of the advertisements found with a Name key having a value of DSS*. An attempt is made to cast each of the found advertisements to a PipeAdvertisement object. If the cast is successful, the pipe advertisement can be used; otherwise, an exception is thrown and basically ignored because we don't care about the advertisement if it isn't a pipe.

In the last statement in the code, the DiscoveryService object is instructed to attempt to find advertisements. As you can see, a total of 50 are requested from each peer. As all of the advertisements are returned, they are placed in the local cache for further or later consideration.

One of the problems with advertisement is their age. Many times, advertisements returned from a remote query will be old, and they will not work when an attempt is made to connect with a pipe. In addition, you will most definitely receive duplicate pipe advertisements, which isn't very useful.

Filtering Through the Local Cache

When obsolete advertisements are returned from remote queries, one solution is to use the local cache as the primary place to look for advertisements. This concept works by configuring the discovery service to find all remote advertisements, but not to call a listener object. Instead, the service can dump any remote advertisements into the local cache for later processing. At various times, a call can be made to gather the advertisements found in the local cache. A data structure can keep track of those advertisements already seen; dead advertisements can be handled using a connection timeout.

Listing 13.2 contains code that will launch a remote discovery and then call the getLocalAdvertisements() method to handle pipe processing. The example uses bidirectional pipes, which we discuss later in this chapter. Further, the code uses a timer to launch the processing of the local cache.

```
public static void main (String [] args) {

  Java.util.timer databaseConnectionTimerTask = new
    FindDatabaseTimerTask();
  PublishDatabaseTimerTask  databaseConnectionTimer = new
    java.util.Timer();
  databaseConnectionTimer.schedule(databaseConnectionTimerTask,
    15*1000, 5*60*1000);

  discoveryService.getRemoteAdvertisements(null,
DiscoveryService.ADV,
    "Name", "DSS*", 50);
  run();
}


  private class FindDatabaseTimerTask extends TimerTask {
```

Listing 13.2 Filtering advertisements through a peer's local cache. (continues)

```
    private Hashtable databaseConnectionIDs = new Hashtable();

    public FindDatabaseTimerTask() {
      super();
    }

    public void run() {
      try {
        Enumeration localEnum = discoveryService.getLocalAdvertisements(
          DiscoveryService.ADV, "Name", "DSS*");

        while (localEnum.hasMoreElements()) {
          PipeAdvertisement aPipeAdv =
           (PipeAdvertisement)localEnum.nextElement();
          String pipeName = aPipeAdv.getName();
          String pipeID = aPipeAdv.getID().toString();

          if ((pipeName.indexOf("DSSDatabaseQueryInputBiPipe") != -1) &&
             (!databaseConnectionIDs.containsKey(pipeID))        ) {
            try {
              BidirectionalPipeService.Pipe pipe =
                bidirectionalService.connect(aPipeAdv, 10000);
              if (pipe != null) {
                databaseSender.addToDatabaseTable(pipeID, pipe);
                databaseConnectionIDs.put(pipeID, pipeID);
                displayText(aPipeAdv.getID().toString(), databaseText);
              }
            } catch(Exception e) {
            }
          }
        }
      } catch(Exception e) {
      }
    }
  }
```

Listing 13.2   Filtering advertisements through a peer's local cache.

In this code, a timer task is set up to find pipe advertisements in the local cache at 15-minute intervals. When the timer is set off, the run() method of the timer task will fire. All of the local advertisements are obtained and placed into an Enumeration object. The object is looped through to extract each of the pipe advertisements from the cache. If the advertisement found in the cache isn't a pipe advertisement, it is skipped, and the next one is attempted. If the advertisement is a pipe, the code checks the full name of the advertisement, and determines if the ID of the pipe advertisement has already been seen. This is accomplished by using a hashtable data structure.

Unicast Pipes

The most basic type of pipe, Unicast allows communication from one peer to another in a single direction. If information has to be passed between peers in both directions, both of the peers need to publish pipe advertisements, or one of the peers can pass pipe information through the one Unicast pipe. When the other peer receives the pipe advertisement, it will create another pipe.

Although the Java reference implementation builds JXTA pipes on top of TCP/IP (which is a reliable protocol), the Unicast pipe is considered an unreliable means of communication. This is because the JXTA specification defines the Unicast pipe as a one-way and unreliable form of communication. Any implementation of the Unicast pipe is able to build the pipe at this lowest denominator. If a particular implementation chooses to use a "better-quality" vehicle such as TCP/IP for the Unicast pipe, it can; however, no implementation can change the JXTA specification's definition of the pipe type. The pipe is defined as unreliable in the specification, and that fact isn't changed by the physical implementation, even though in reality the pipe might be reliable as a side effect of the implementation.

Here are the steps required to implement a Unicast pipe between two peers.

- On a local peer:
  - Build an input pipe advertisement.
  - Publish the advertisement.
  - Create an input pipe.
  - Wait for data using either polling or a listener.

- On a remote peer:
  - Discover the pipe advertisement.
  - Build the output pipe.
  - Send data through the pipe.

Unicast Pipes on a Local Peer

In the local peer, an input pipe advertisement needs to be built. One of the simplest ways to build the advertisement is programmatically, as shown in Listing 13.3.

```
PipeAdvertisement pipeAdv =
  (PipeAdvertisement)AdvertisementFactory.newAdvertisement(
  PipeAdvertisement.getAdvertisementType());
pipeAdv.setName("JXTA:KEYRECEIVE");
pipeAdv.setType(PipeService.UnicastType);
pipeAdv.setPipeID((ID) net.jxta.id.IDFactory.
  newPipeID(netPeerGroup.getPeerGroupID()));
```

Listing 13.3 Creating an advertisement for a Unicast input pipe.

Next, the advertisement has to be published to other peers. For example:

```
DiscoveryService discoveryService =
  netPeerGroup.getDiscoveryService();
discoveryService.remotePulish(pipeAdv,
DiscoveryService.ADV);
```

Now the input pipe must be built, as shown in Listing 13.4. For most input pipes, a listener object will be used, although you can use the poll() method when an application has the luxury of blocking while it waits for incoming data. Before the code can create the input pipe, it must create a listener object. In the following code, the listener object is created as an anonymous class.

```
PipeMsgListener myService1Listener = new PipeMsgListener() {
        public void pipeMsgEvent(PipeMsgEvent event) {
          Message myMessage = null;
          try {
            myMessage = event.getMessage();

            String myMessageContent;

            myMessageContent = myMessage.getString("DataTag");
            if (myMessageContent != null) {
              System.out.println("Message received: " +
                myMessageContent + "\n");
              return;
            }
          } catch (Exception ee) {
              ee.printStackTrace();
              return;
          }
        }
    };

  InputPipe myPipe = null;
  try {
    myPipe = myPipeService.createInputPipe(pipeAdv,
      myService1Listener);
  } catch (Exception e) {
      System.out.println("Error creating Input Pipe");
      e.printStackTrace();
      System.exit(-1);
  }
```

Listing 13.4 Building a Unicast input pipe.

At this point in the peer application, a run() method could be called, so the peer just waits until a message is received. For the listener, all of the processing is handled asynchronously. All messages received by the input pipe will be checked for a message associated with the DataTag parameter of the message.

Remote Peers

For a remote peer to be able to communicate with another peer through an already established pipe, it must discover a published pipe advertisement. To do this, the peer will initiate a search using both the getLocalAdvertisements() and getRemoteAdvertisements() methods, as shown in Listing 13.5.

```
void findAdvertisements() {
    Enumeration advEnum = null;
    try {
      advEnum = myDiscoveryService.getLocalAdvertisements(
        DiscoveryService.ADV, "Name", "DSS*");

      while (advEnum.hasMoreElements()) {
        try {
          PipeAdvertisement pipeAdv =
           (PipeAdvertisement)advEnum.nextElement();
          createOutputPipe(pipeAdv);
        } catch (Exception e) {
          // not a pipe advertisement — skip it
        }
      }
      else {
        //Attempt a remote discovery
        //Build DiscoveryListener
        DiscoveryListener discoveryListener = new
          DiscoveryListener() {
          public void discoveryEvent(DiscoveryEvent e) {
            Enumeration advEnum;

            DiscoveryResponseMsg message = e.getResponse();
            advEnum = myMessage.getResponses();

            while (advEnum.hasMoreElements()) {
              try {
                String str = (String)enum.nextElement();
              pipeAdv = (PipeAdvertisement)
                AdvertisementFactory.newAdvertisement(XMLMIMETYPE,
                new ByteArrayInputStream(str.getBytes()));
                createOutputPipe(pipeAdv);
              } catch (Exception e) {
                // not a pipe advertisement — skip it
              }
            }
          }
        };
        //Launch the discovery
```

Listing 13.5   Initiating a search for a pipe advertisement. (continues)

```
        discoveryService.getRemoteAdvertisements(null,
          DiscoveryService.ADV, "Name", "DSS*", 10,
          discoveryListener);
    }
  } catch (Exception e) {
    System.out.println("Error during advertisement
      search");
    System.exit(-1);
  }
}
```

Listing 13.5   Initiating a search for a pipe advertisement. (continued)

The code in Listing 13.5 will first check to find a pipe advertisement in the local cache with a Name value of DSS*, where * is a wildcard. If a pipe advertisement is found and successfully cast into a PipeAdvertisement object, the createOutputPipe() method is called with the pipe advertisement. If a pipe advertisement matching the search isn't found in the local cache, a Discovery Listener object is created and passed to the getRemoteAdvertisements() method.

When remote peers provide their advertisements matching the search criteria, the same code used in the local search is executed, and acceptable pipe advertisements are passed to the createOutputPipe() method:

```
private void createOutputPipe(PipeAdvertisement pipeAdv) {
    outputPipe = null;
    try {
        outputPipe = pipeService.createOutputPipe(pipeAdv,
          100000);
    } catch (Exception e) {
        System.out.println("Unable to create output pipe");
        System.exit(-1);
    }
}
```

In this code, the pipe advertisement is passed to the createOutputPipe() method of the pipe service. The class member variable, outputPipe, is set to the return value of the createOutputPipe() method, which is called against the previously defined pipeService variable. If the call is successful, a new pipe will be available where information can be sent using the following code:

```
String data = "Hello my friend!";

    Message msg = pipeService.createMessage();
    msg.setString("DataTag", data);

    try {
      outputPipe.send (msg);
```

```
        } catch (Exception e) {
            System.out.println("Unable to send data");
            e.printStackTrace();
            System.exit(-1);
        }
```

In this code, a message object is created and provided with the data to send to the pipe and the key value DataTag. The message is sent to the pipe through its send() method.

UnicastSecure Pipes

The UnicastSecure pipe ensures that all data sent through it is encrypted. The data sent through the pipe is encrypted by using the Transport Layer Security (TLS) protocol. TLS can be thought of as an extension or second-generation protocol over the Secure Sockets Layer (SSL). Believe it or not, to change the code listed in the previous section from sending non-secure data to sending secure data, we simply have to change the Type element of the pipe advertisement. The code for building the pipe advertisement would look like this:

```
PipeAdvertisement pipeAdv =
  (PipeAdvertisement)AdvertisementFactory.
  newAdvertisement(PipeAdvertisement.getAdvertisementType());
pipeAdv.setName("JXTA:KEYRECEIVE");
pipeAdv.setType(PipeService.UnicastSecureType);
pipeAdv.setPipeID((ID) net.jxta.id.IDFactory.
  newPipeID(netPeerGroup.getPeerGroupID()));
```

Propagate Pipes

In some application designs, a single peer will need the ability to send information to a number of different peers at the same time. One way to handle this design is to create a data structure, such as an array, to hold a number of pipes, each specified as type Unicast. When the peer needs to send data to each peer, it could loop through the data structure and send the same message to each remote peer.

Of course, this isn't a very efficient solution because there could be a large number of pipes, and the housekeeping would be complex. The JXTA specification and Java implementation can handle this type of design easily through the use of the JxtaPropagate pipe type. Listing 13.6 shows an example of a pipe advertisement that supports propagate pipes.

To demonstrate how propagate pipes work, Listings 13.7 and 13.8 show simple peers with the primary jobs of sending and receiving messages, respectively.

The code in Listing 13.7 publishes and builds an output pipe using the pipe advertisement from Listing 13.6. In most cases, an output pipe is created in response to the receipt of an input pipe advertisement. However, when a propagate pipe advertisement is used, the output pipe doesn't require an immediate input pipe in order to be created; the code will create an output pipe, and wait for an input pipe connection for about 1 second. After this time frame, the system will enter a loop, which pauses and then sends a message about the output pipe. Any clients currently attached to the output pipe will receive the message.

The code in Listing 13.8 attempts to find the advertisement published by the code discussed in Listing 13.5. When the advertisement is found, an input pipe is created using the found advertisement. The new pipe is built using a listener, which will be called when a new message is received. The contents of the message are displayed in the terminal window where the application is launched.

The code in Listing 13.8 can be executed any number of times concurrently. Each of the instances of the code will connect with the output pipe from the code in Listing 13.7. The message sent out the pipe will be received by all of the connected peers. The use of a propagate pipe is the only difference in this code.

```
<?xml version="1.0" encoding="UTF-8"?>
<jxta:PipeAdvertisement xmlns:jxta="http://jxta.org">
    <Name>PropOutput</Name>
    <Id>urn:jxta:uuid-094AB61B99C14AB694D
      5BFD56C66E512FF7980EA1E6F4C238A26BB362B34D1F104</Id>
    <Type>JxtaPropagate</Type>
</jxta:PipeAdvertisement>
```

Listing 13.6 Propagate pipe advertisements.

```
import java.io.*;
import java.util.Enumeration;
import net.jxta.document.*;
import net.jxta.peergroup.*;
import net.jxta.exception.*;
import net.jxta.impl.peergroup.*;
import net.jxta.id.*;
import net.jxta.discovery.*;
import net.jxta.pipe.*;
import net.jxta.protocol.*;
import net.jxta.platform.*;
import java.net.MalformedURLException;
```

Listing 13.7 The propagate sending peer. (continues)

```java
import java.net.URL;
import net.jxta.endpoint.Message;


public class sender {
   static  PeerGroup          netPeerGroup = null;
   private DiscoveryService          myDiscoveryService = null;
   private PipeService                 myPipeService = null;
   private PipeAdvertisement myDBPipeAdvertisement = null;
   private OutputPipe         myOutputPipe = null;

   private final static          MimeMediaType XMLMIMETYPE = new
     MimeMediaType("text/xml");

   public sender() {
      launchJXTA();
      getServices();
      buildAndPublishOutputPipe();

      Message msg = myPipeService.createMessage();
      msg.setString("DataTag", "Our Message");

      while (true) {
        try {
          Thread.sleep(3000);
          System.out.println("Sending Message");
          myOutputPipe.send(msg);
        } catch(Exception e) {}
      }
   }

   static public void main(String[] args) {
      new sender();
   }

   private void launchJXTA() {
     try {
       netPeerGroup = PeerGroupFactory.newNetPeerGroup();
     } catch (PeerGroupException e) {
        System.out.println("Unable to create PeerGroup -
          Failure");
        e.printStackTrace();
        System.exit(1);
     }
   }
```

Listing 13.7 The propagate sending peer. (continues)

```
    private void getServices() {
      myDiscoveryService = netPeerGroup.getDiscoveryService();
      myPipeService = netPeerGroup.getPipeService();
    }

    private void buildAndPublishOutputPipe() {
      PipeAdvertisement aPipeAdv = null;

      try {
        FileInputStream is =
          new FileInputStream("outputpipe.adv");
        aPipeAdv =
        (PipeAdvertisement)AdvertisementFactory.newAdvertisement(
         new MimeMediaType("text/xml"), is);
      } catch (Exception e) {
        System.out.println("failed to read/parse pipe
          advertisement");
         e.printStackTrace();
        System.exit(-1);
      }
      try {
        myDiscoveryService.publish(aPipeAdv,
          DiscoveryService.ADV);
        myDiscoveryService.remotePublish(aPipeAdv,
          DiscoveryService.ADV);
      } catch (Exception e) {
        e.printStackTrace();
        System.exit(-1);
      }
      createOutputPipe(aPipeAdv);
    }

    private void createOutputPipe(PipeAdvertisement
      myPipeAdvertisement) {
      try {
        myOutputPipe =
          myPipeService.createOutputPipe(myPipeAdvertisement,
          1000);
        System.out.println("Output Pipe Created");
      } catch (Exception e) {
          e.printStackTrace();
          System.exit(-1);
      }
    }
  }
```

Listing 13.7 The propagate sending peer. (continued)

```
import java.io.*;
import java.awt.*;
import java.awt.event.*;
import javax.swing.*;
import java.util.Enumeration;
import net.jxta.document.*;
import net.jxta.peergroup.*;
import net.jxta.exception.PeerGroupException;
import net.jxta.impl.peergroup.Platform;
import net.jxta.impl.peergroup.GenericPeerGroup;
import net.jxta.id.*;
import net.jxta.discovery.*;
import net.jxta.pipe.*;
import net.jxta.protocol.*;
import java.net.MalformedURLException;
import java.net.URL;
import net.jxta.endpoint.Message;

public class receiver{

    static  PeerGroup         netPeerGroup = null;
    private DiscoveryService  myDiscoveryService = null;
    private PipeService       myPipeService = null;
    private PipeAdvertisement myPipeAdvertisement = null,
                              myInputPipeAdvertisement = null;
    private InputPipe         myInputPipe;
    private final static      MimeMediaType XMLMIMETYPE =
      new MimeMediaType("text/xml");

    public static void main(String args[]) {
        receiver myapp = new receiver();
    }

    public receiver() {
      launchJXTA();
      getServices();
      findAdvertisement("Name", "PropOutput");
      run();
    }

    public void run() {
      while (true) {
        try { Thread.sleep(300); } catch(Exception e) {}
      }
    }

    private void launchJXTA() {
```

Listing 13.8 The propagate receiving peer. (continues)

```
        System.out.println("Launching Peer into JXTA
          Network...\n");
        try {
            netPeerGroup = PeerGroupFactory.newNetPeerGroup();
        } catch (PeerGroupException e) {
            System.out.println("Unable to create PeerGroup -
              Failure");
            e.printStackTrace();
            System.exit(1);
        }
    }

private void getServices() {
  System.out.println("Getting Services...\n");
  myDiscoveryService = netPeerGroup.getDiscoveryService();
  myPipeService = netPeerGroup.getPipeService();
}

private void createInputPipe(PipeAdvertisement pipeAdv) {
  System.out.println("Creating Input Pipe....\n");

  PipeMsgListener myService1Listener = new PipeMsgListener() {
    public void pipeMsgEvent(PipeMsgEvent event) {
      Message myMessage = null;
      try {
        myMessage = event.getMessage();

        System.out.println(myMessage.getString("DataTag"));
        return;
      } catch (Exception ee) {
          ee.printStackTrace();
          return;
      }
    }
  };

  try {
    myInputPipe = myPipeService.createInputPipe(pipeAdv,
      myService1Listener);
  } catch (Exception e) {
      System.out.println("Error creating Input Pipe");
      e.printStackTrace();
      System.exit(-1);
  }
}
```

Listing 13.8   The propagate receiving peer. (continues)

```
private void findAdvertisement(String searchKey, String
    searchValue) {
  Enumeration myLocalEnum = null;
  System.out.println("Trying to find advertisement...\n");

  try {
    myLocalEnum = myDiscoveryService.getLocalAdvertisements(
      DiscoveryService.ADV, searchKey, searchValue);

    if ((myLocalEnum != null) &&
     myLocalEnum.hasMoreElements()) {
      System.out.println("Found Local Advertisement...\n");
      myPipeAdvertisement =
       (PipeAdvertisement)myLocalEnum.nextElement();
      createInputPipe(myPipeAdvertisement);
    }
    else {
      DiscoveryListener myDiscoveryListener =
        new DiscoveryListener() {
        public void discoveryEvent(DiscoveryEvent e) {
          Enumeration enum;

          System.out.println("Found Remote
            Advertisement...\n");
          DiscoveryResponseMsg myMessage = e.getResponse();
          enum = myMessage.getResponses();
          while (enum.hasMoreElements()) {
            try {
              String str = (String)enum.nextElement();
              myPipeAdvertisement = (PipeAdvertisement)
                AdvertisementFactory.newAdvertisement(
                XMLMIMETYPE, new
                ByteArrayInputStream(str.getBytes()));
              System.out.println("Trying to build pipe");
              createInputPipe(myPipeAdvertisement);
            } catch(Exception ee) {
              ee.printStackTrace();
            }
          }
        }
      };

      System.out.println("Launching Remote Discovery
        Service...\n");
      myDiscoveryService.getRemoteAdvertisements(null,
        DiscoveryService.ADV, searchKey, searchValue, 1,
        myDiscoveryListener);
```

Listing 13.8 The propagate receiving peer. (continues)

```
    }
  } catch (Exception e) {
    System.out.println("Error during advertisement
      search");
    System.exit(-1);
  }
}


}
```

Listing 13.8 The propagate receiving peer. (continued)

Bidirectional Pipes

Although Unicast pipes are effective, they are not efficient because two-way communication requires that two pipes be created and all necessary house-keeping handled. Fortunately, the Java binding of the JXTA protocol adds a bidirectional pipe. Bidirectional pipes are not considered part of the JXTA specification; only the Unicast, UnicastSecure, and propagate pipes are part of the Pipe Binding Protocol (which we discussed in Chapter 10). Software developers can create bidirectional pipes by using two Unicast pipes and hiding all of the details from the application; in this way, most of the housekeeping details are contained within the implementation classes. The bidirectional pipe works like this:

1. A peer publishes a pipe (Unicast) advertisement.

2. A remote peer discovers the pipe advertisement, and initiates a connection to the pipe advertisement.

3. Once the connection is made, the original peer will transmit information about a second pipe, which is used for communication in the other direction, thus establishing a bidirectional pipe.

The Bidirectional Pipe Code

Listing 13.9 implements a peer that will publish a bidirectional input pipe, also called an accept pipe. This peer does the job of publishing the pipe advertisement. Later, in Listing 13.10, we implement a peer that will discover the advertisement and begin communication. Using this approach, the discovery peer sends a message through the bidirectional pipe, and receives a response. The peer created in Listing 13.9:

1. Creates a bidirectional pipe.

2. Advertises the pipe's existence.

3. Accepts a connection for the pipe.

4. Accepts data from the pipe and sends a response.

The basic functionality of this application is the same as that found in the examples from Chapter 12. The GUI is created in the same way, and the peer is "connected" to the default peer group. In the following sections, we explain the differences involved in using bidirectional pipes.

```
Line 1: import java.io.*;
import java.awt.*;
import java.awt.event.*;
import javax.swing.*;

import net.jxta.document.*;
import net.jxta.peergroup.*;
import net.jxta.exception.*;
import net.jxta.impl.peergroup.*;
Line 10: import net.jxta.id.*;
import net.jxta.discovery.*;
import net.jxta.pipe.*;
import net.jxta.protocol.*;
import net.jxta.platform.*;
import net.jxta.endpoint.*;
import net.jxta.impl.util.BidirectionalPipeService;

public class server extends JFrame {

Line 20:    static PeerGroup netPeerGroup = null;
    private DiscoveryService myDiscoveryService = null;
    private BidirectionalPipeService myBiPipeService = null;
    private PipeService myPipeService = null;
    private ModuleClassID myService1ID = null;
    private InputPipe myPipe = null;
    private JTextArea displayArea;

    public static void main(String args[]) {
        server myapp = new server();
Line 30:
        myapp.addWindowListener (
          new WindowAdapter() {
            public void windowClosing(WindowEvent e) {
              System.exit(0);
```

Listing 13.9 The bidirectional pipe server application. (continues)

```
                }
              }
          );

          myapp.run();
Line 40:      }

      public server() {
        super("Server");

        Container c = getContentPane();

        displayArea = new JTextArea();
        c.add (new JScrollPane(displayArea), BorderLayout.CENTER);

Line 50:      setSize(300,150);
        show();

        launchJXTA();
        getServices();
      }

      public void run() {
        try {
          BidirectionalPipeService.AcceptPipe incomingAcceptPipe =
            myBiPipeService.bind("bipipe");
Line 60:          displayArea.append("Pipe Bind...\n");

        while (true) {
          try {
          BidirectionalPipeService.MessageListener
            myListenerService =
            new BidirectionalPipeService.MessageListener () {
          public void messageReceived (Message msg, OutputPipe
          responsePipe) {
            String myMessageContent;
            myMessageContent = msg.getString("DataTag");
            Message sendMsg = null;

Line 70:              if (myMessageContent != null) {
              displayArea.append("Message received: " +
                myMessageContent + "\n");
              displayArea.append("Sending Response...");

              try {
                sendMsg = myPipeService.createMessage();
                sendMsg.setString("DataTag", "Here's your
```

Listing 13.9 The bidirectional pipe server application. (continues)

```
                                response");
                                responsePipe.send(sendMsg);
                            } catch(Exception e) {}

Line 80:                    displayArea.append("Waiting for message...\n");
                        return;
                    } else {
                        displayArea.append("Invalid tag\n");
                        return;
                    }
                }
                };

                BidirectionalPipeService.Pipe newPipe =
                    incomingAcceptPipe.accept(30000, myListenerService);
Line 90:            displayArea.append("Accepted a pipe
                    connection\n");

            } catch(Exception e) {}
        }
    } catch(Exception e) {}
}

private void launchJXTA() {
    displayArea.append("Launching Peer into JXTA
        Network...\n");
    try {
Line 100:           netPeerGroup =
            PeerGroupFactory.newNetPeerGroup();
    } catch (PeerGroupException e) {
        System.out.println("Unable to create PeerGroup -
          Failure");
        e.printStackTrace();
        System.exit(1);
    }
}

private void getServices() {
    displayArea.append("Obtaining Discovery and Pipe
        Services....\n");
Line 110:       myDiscoveryService =
            netPeerGroup.getDiscoveryService();
    myBiPipeService = new
        BidirectionalPipeService(netPeerGroup);
    myPipeService = netPeerGroup.getPipeService();
}
}
```

Listing 13.9 The bidirectional pipe server application. (continued)

Initializing the Publishing Peer

Bidirectional pipes don't use the standard PipeService class; instead, they have a class called BidirectionalPipeService. In the getServices() method on line 111, an object of type BidirectionalPipeService is instantiated. Within the service object, the current peer's discovery and normal pipe services are referenced for the purposes of advertising the pipes and creating the Unicast pipes. Thus, it is important that the bidirectional service is not instantiated before the peer is put into the group that will host the application.

Waiting for Acceptance of the Pipe

The most important method in the server peer is the run() method. This method includes most of the functionality necessary for the server.

Lines 57 through 95 implement the run() method. Line 59 creates an Accept-Pipe object, using the bidirectionalPipeService object and bind() method. This is a Unicast input pipe with a name based on the single parameter to the bind() method. The bind() method automatically publishes an advertisement for the pipe using the discovery service of the peer's current group.

Line 62 begins a loop that will check for a pipe connection. Lines 64 through 87 implement a pipe input message listener in the same fashion as those found in Chapter 12.

Line 66 contains the method required to be implemented in a bidirectional pipe listener. This method is passed the message received on the pipe as well as an output pipe, which can be used to send a response to the peer who sent the original message.

Line 77 uses the response pipe to send a message to the peer that sent the original message. Line 89 waits for 30,000 seconds or until a peer attempts to create a connection with the peer's input pipe. Once a connection is accepted, an object instance for the pipe is created, and the input pipe message listener is activated for the input pipe. Any message sent up the input pipe will be processed by lines 64 through 87.

The Bidirectional Pipe Discovery Code

The bidirectional pipe code in Listing 13.10 is based on the examples in Chapter 12, and includes the same code for the GUI and for advertisement discovery. The code attempts to discover a pipe advertisement based on the name of the pipe and the string *bipipe*. If an acceptable advertisement is found, a connection is made to the pipe. The user can click a button to send data to the pipe's originator. The peer will wait on the input pipe of the connection for a response from the originator.

```
Line 1: import java.io.*;
import java.awt.*;
import java.awt.event.*;
import javax.swing.*;
import java.net.MalformedURLException;
import java.net.URL;

import java.util.Enumeration;
import net.jxta.document.*;
Line 10: import net.jxta.peergroup.*;
import net.jxta.exception.*;
import net.jxta.impl.peergroup.*;
import net.jxta.id.*;
import net.jxta.discovery.*;
import net.jxta.pipe.*;
import net.jxta.protocol.*;
import net.jxta.endpoint.Message;
import net.jxta.impl.util.BidirectionalPipeService;

Line 20: public class client extends JFrame {

    static  PeerGroup        netPeerGroup = null;
    private DiscoveryService        myDiscoveryService = null;
    private BidirectionalPipeService        myBiPipeService = null;
    private PipeService myPipeService = null;
    private PipeAdvertisement myPipeAdvertisement = null;
    private BidirectionalPipeService.Pipe myPipe;
    private JTextArea        displayArea;
    private JButton          sendButton;
Line 30:    private String          valueString = "bipipe";

    private final static        MimeMediaType XMLMIMETYPE = new
      MimeMediaType("text/xml");


    public static void main(String args[]) {
        client myapp = new client();

        myapp.addWindowListener (
        new WindowAdapter() {
Line 40:             public void windowClosing(WindowEvent e) {
            System.exit(0);
          }
        }
      );

        myapp.run();
```

Listing 13.10 The bidirectional pipe discovery application. (continues)

```
    }

    public client() {
Line 50:        super("client");

        Container c = getContentPane();

        sendButton = new JButton("Send Data");
        sendButton.addActionListener(
          new ActionListener() {
            public void actionPerformed(ActionEvent e) {
              sendData();
            }
Line 60:          }
        );
        c.add(sendButton, BorderLayout.NORTH);

        displayArea = new JTextArea();
        c.add(new JScrollPane(displayArea), BorderLayout.CENTER);

        setSize(300,150);
        show();

Line 70:        launchJXTA();
        getServices();
        findAdvertisement("Name", "bipipe");

    }

    public void run() {
        displayArea.append("Click on Button to send data...\n");
    }

Line 80:     private void launchJXTA() {
        displayArea.append("Launching Peer into JXTA
          Network...\n");
        try {
            netPeerGroup = PeerGroupFactory.newNetPeerGroup();
        } catch (PeerGroupException e) {
            System.out.println("Unable to create PeerGroup -
              Failure");
            e.printStackTrace();
            System.exit(1);
        }
    }
Line 90:
    private void getServices() {
        displayArea.append("Getting Services...\n");
```

Listing 13.10   The bidirectional pipe discovery application. (continues)

```
        myDiscoveryService = netPeerGroup.getDiscoveryService();
        myBiPipeService = new BidirectionalPipeService(netPeerGroup);
        myPipeService = netPeerGroup.getPipeService();
    }

    private void findAdvertisement(String searchKey, String
      searchValue) {
        Enumeration myLocalEnum = null;
Line 100:       displayArea.append("Trying to find
          advertisement...\n");

        try {
          myLocalEnum = myDiscoveryService.getLocalAdvertisements(
            DiscoveryService.ADV, searchKey, searchValue);

          if ((myLocalEnum != null) &&
            myLocalEnum.hasMoreElements()) {
            displayArea.append("Found Local Advertisement...\n");
            PipeAdvertisement myAdv =
              (PipeAdvertisement)myLocalEnum.nextElement();

            createPipe(myAdv);
Line 110:         }
          else {
            DiscoveryListener myDiscoveryListener =
              new DiscoveryListener() {
                public void discoveryEvent(DiscoveryEvent e) {
                  Enumeration enum;
                  PipeAdvertisement pipeAdv = null;
                  String str;

                  displayArea.append("Found Remote
                   Advertisement...\n");
                  DiscoveryResponseMsg myMessage = e.getResponse();
Line 120:           enum = myMessage.getResponses();
                  str = (String)enum.nextElement();

                  try {
                    pipeAdv = (PipeAdvertisement)
                      AdvertisementFactory.newAdvertisement(
                      XMLMIMETYPE, new
                      ByteArrayInputStream(str.getBytes()));

                    createPipe(pipeAdv);
                  } catch(Exception ee) {
                      ee.printStackTrace();
                      System.exit(-1);
```

Listing 13.10 The bidirectional pipe discovery application. (continues)

```
Line 130:                    }
              }
              };

              displayArea.append("Launching Remote Discovery
                 Service...\n");
              myDiscoveryService.getRemoteAdvertisements(null,
                 DiscoveryService.ADV, searchKey, searchValue, 1,
                 myDiscoveryListener);
          }
      } catch (Exception e) {
          System.out.println("Error during advertisement
             search");
          System.exit(-1);
Line 140:         }
      }

      private void createPipe(PipeAdvertisement
       myPipeAdvertisement) {
        try {
          myPipe = myBiPipeService.connect(myPipeAdvertisement,
             30000);
        } catch(Exception e) {}
      }

      private void sendData() {
Lien 150:         String data = "Hello my friend!";

        Message msg = myPipeService.createMessage();
        msg.setString("DataTag", data);

        try {
          myPipe.getOutputPipe().send(msg);
          displayArea.append("message \"" + data + "\" sent to the
             Server\n");

          msg = myPipe.getInputPipe().poll(30000);
Line 160:          displayArea.append("From SErver: " +
              msg.getString("DataTag"));

        } catch (Exception e) {
            System.out.println("Unable to print output pipe");
            e.printStackTrace();
            System.exit(-1);
        }

      }
}
```

Listing 13.10 The bidirectional pipe discovery application. (continued)

Creating a Connection to the Pipe

Once a pipe advertisement has been found based on the name of the pipe, a call is made to the createPipe( ) method. Lines 143 through 147 implement the method.

Line 145 does all of the work inside a try block. A call is made to the connect( ) method of the BidirectionalPipeService object with the provided discovered pipe advertisement and a timeout value. If a successful connection is made, the myPipe attribute will contain an object for the bidirectional pipe.

Sending Data

Once the pipes have been established, the user can click the Send Data button to transfer data from the client peer to the server peer. Clicking this button calls the sendData( ) method, which appears in lines 149 through 168.

Lines 152 and 153 create the message that will be sent to the server object. Notice that the non-bidirectional pipe service is used to build the message object.

Line 156 obtains the output pipe from the bidirectional pipe created by the createPipe( ) method. This output pipe's send( ) method is called using the message object as its parameter. The message is then sent to the remote peer.

Line 159 obtains the input pipe of the BidirectionalPipe object, and waits for a total of 30,000 seconds or until a message appears on the input pipe to the current client peer. Once the message is received, the information from the server is printed to the GUI's text area.

Reliable Pipes

A quick look through the source code can yield all kinds of information. Notice the implementation of a service called ReliablePipeService. This pipe service is based on the BidirectionalPipeService presented in the previous section. The basic idea is to build a reliable connection mechanism to go along with the Unicast and unreliable connection located in the JXTA specification. For the most part, the ReliablePipeService and its related pipes aren't documented in the JXTA specification and Java implementation; the pipes are an add-on you'll find referenced in the Java source and in a tutorial on the JXTA web site.

The code in Listing 13.11 and Listing 13.12 (in the next section) implement a sender and a receiver, respectively, for the reliable pipes. However, note that although the code is accurate and the pipe might be reliable, the service isn't. Some of the time the service will actually connect two peers and pass information; other times, the service will fail to connect. The JXTA team continues to work on this issue, so by the time this book is published, the service should be more reliable.

```
Line 1: import java.io.*;
import java.awt.*;
import java.awt.event.*;
import javax.swing.*;

import net.jxta.impl.util.*;
import net.jxta.document.*;
import net.jxta.peergroup.*;
import net.jxta.exception.*;
Line 10: import net.jxta.impl.peergroup.*;
import net.jxta.id.*;
import net.jxta.discovery.*;
import net.jxta.pipe.*;
import net.jxta.protocol.*;
import net.jxta.platform.*;
import net.jxta.endpoint.*;

public class server extends JFrame {

Line 20:    static PeerGroup netPeerGroup = null;
    private DiscoveryService myDiscoveryService = null;
    private ReliablePipeService myReliablePipeService = null;
    private PipeService myPipeService = null;
    private ModuleClassID myService1ID = null;
    private InputPipe myPipe = null;
    private JTextArea displayArea;

    public static void main(String args[]) {
        server myapp = new server();
Line 30:
        myapp.addWindowListener (
         new WindowAdapter() {
            public void windowClosing(WindowEvent e) {
               System.exit(0);
            }
          }
        );

        myapp.run();
Line 40:     }

    public server() {
      super("Server");

      Container c = getContentPane();

      displayArea = new JTextArea();
      c.add (new JScrollPane(displayArea), BorderLayout.CENTER);
```

Listing 13.11 The sending peer code. (continues)

```
Line 50:        setSize(300,150);
        show();

        launchJXTA();
        getServices();
    }

    public void run() {
        try {
          ReliablePipeService.AcceptPipe incomingAcceptPipe =
            myReliablePipeService.bind("bipipe2");
Line 60:          displayArea.append("Pipe Bind...\n");

        while (true) {
          try {
          ReliablePipeService.Pipe newPipe =
            incomingAcceptPipe.accept(30000);
          displayArea.append("Accepted a pipe connection\n");

          Message msg = newPipe.getInputPipe().poll (30000);
          InputStream in2 = msg.getElement ("DataTag").getStream ();
          byte[] buf = new byte[8192];
Line 70:          int r = in2.read (buf);
          displayArea.append("Message = " + buf);

          Message sendMsg = myPipeService.createMessage();
          sendMsg.setString("DataTag", "Here's your response");
          newPipe.getOutputPipe().send(sendMsg);

          } catch(Exception e) {}
        }
      } catch(Exception e) {}
Line 80:    }

    private void launchJXTA() {
        displayArea.append("Launching Peer into JXTA
          Network...\n");
        try {
            netPeerGroup = PeerGroupFactory.newNetPeerGroup();
        } catch (PeerGroupException e) {
            System.out.println("Unable to create PeerGroup -
              Failure");
            e.printStackTrace();
            System.exit(1);
Line 90:        }
    }
```

Listing 13.11   The sending peer code. (continues)

```
    private void getServices() {
      displayArea.append("Obtaining Discovery and Pipe
        Services....\n");
      myDiscoveryService = netPeerGroup.getDiscoveryService();
      myReliablePipeService = new ReliablePipeService (
        new BidirectionalPipeService (netPeerGroup));
      myPipeService = netPeerGroup.getPipeService();
    }
}
```

Listing 13.11 Sending peer code. (continued)

Sender Code

The sender code is based on the bidirectional server code with a few changes.

Sender Initialization

The sender for the reliable server needs a different service for the pipes. Line 96 of Listing 13.12 creates an object for the ReliablePipeService class. Notice the use of the BidirectionalPipeService class as a parameter to the method call.

Waiting for a Connection

The code for a connection is a little different in that the reliable pipes don't allow the use of a message listener.

Lines 57 through 91 implement a basic run() method for the server. Line 59 creates an accept pipe for the reliable service just as the bidirectional example did. In this case, the bind() method is called using a pipe name of bipipe2. Within the code, the name of the pipe is provided to the internal bidirectional pipe service.

Line 62 begins a loop for accepting connection on the reliable pipes. Line 64 calls the accept() method of the pipe created in line 59. The system will wait for 30 seconds, or until a remote peer connects to the pipe.

Line 67 calls the getInputPipe() method of the connected bidirectional pipe in order to check for a message. The system will wait for 30 seconds to receive a message from the input pipe.

Lines 68 through 71 pull the data from the message and displays it on the GUI. Lines 73 through 75 create a new message to send back to the client. Line 75 obtains the output pipe of the bidirectional pipe and calls the send() method to send the message object to the client.

```
Line 1: import java.io.*;
import java.awt.*;
import java.awt.event.*;
import javax.swing.*;
import java.net.MalformedURLException;
import java.net.URL;


import java.util.Enumeration;
import net.jxta.document.*;
Line 10: import net.jxta.peergroup.*;
import net.jxta.exception.*;
import net.jxta.impl.peergroup.*;
import net.jxta.id.*;
import net.jxta.discovery.*;
import net.jxta.pipe.*;
import net.jxta.protocol.*;
import net.jxta.endpoint.Message;
import net.jxta.impl.util.BidirectionalPipeService;
import net.jxta.impl.util.ReliablePipeService;
Line 20:
public class client extends JFrame {

    static  PeerGroup        netPeerGroup = null;
    private DiscoveryService      myDiscoveryService = null;
    private ReliablePipeService  myReliablePipeService = null;
    private PipeService myPipeService = null;
    private PipeAdvertisement myPipeAdvertisement = null;
    private ReliablePipeService.Pipe myPipe;
    private JTextArea        displayArea;
Line 30:    private JButton          sendButton;
    private String       valueString = "bipipe2";

    private final static      MimeMediaType XMLMIMETYPE =
      new MimeMediaType("text/xml");

    public static void main(String args[]) {
        client myapp = new client();

      myapp.addWindowListener (
       new WindowAdapter() {
Line 40:             public void windowClosing(WindowEvent e) {
           System.exit(0);
        }
      }
     );
     myapp.run();
  }
```

Listing 13.12 The reliable receiver application. (continues)

```
      public client() {
         super("client");
Line 50:
         Container c = getContentPane();

         sendButton = new JButton("Send Data");
         sendButton.addActionListener(
           new ActionListener() {
             public void actionPerformed(ActionEvent e) {
               sendData();
             }
           }
Line 60:        );
         c.add(sendButton, BorderLayout.NORTH);

         displayArea = new JTextArea();
         c.add(new JScrollPane(displayArea), BorderLayout.CENTER);

         setSize(300,150);
         show();

         launchJXTA();
Line 70:       getServices();
         findAdvertisement("Name", "bipipe2");
      }

      public void run() {
         displayArea.append("Click on Button to send data...\n");
      }

      private void launchJXTA() {
          displayArea.append("Launching Peer into JXTA
            Network...\n");
Line 80:         try {
             netPeerGroup = PeerGroupFactory.newNetPeerGroup();
          } catch (PeerGroupException e) {
             System.out.println("Unable to create PeerGroup -
               Failure");
             e.printStackTrace();
             System.exit(1);
          }
      }

      private void getServices() {
Line 90:        displayArea.append("Getting Services...\n");
         myDiscoveryService = netPeerGroup.getDiscoveryService();
         myReliablePipeService = new ReliablePipeService (
           new BidirectionalPipeService (netPeerGroup));
```

Listing 13.12   The reliable receiver application. (continues)

```
          myPipeService = netPeerGroup.getPipeService();
      }

  private void findAdvertisement(String searchKey, String
    searchValue) {
        Enumeration myLocalEnum = null;
        displayArea.append("Trying to find advertisement...\n");

Line 100:      try {
          myLocalEnum = myDiscoveryService.getLocalAdvertisements(
            DiscoveryService.ADV, searchKey, searchValue);

          if ((myLocalEnum != null) &&
           myLocalEnum.hasMoreElements()) {
            displayArea.append("Found Local Advertisement...\n");
            PipeAdvertisement myAdv =
              (PipeAdvertisement)myLocalEnum.nextElement();

            createPipe(myAdv);
          }
          else {
LIne 110:          DiscoveryListener myDiscoveryListener =
              new DiscoveryListener() {
              public void discoveryEvent(DiscoveryEvent e) {
                Enumeration enum;
                PipeAdvertisement pipeAdv = null;
                String str;

                displayArea.append("Found Remote
                  Advertisement...\n");
                DiscoveryResponseMsg myMessage = e.getResponse();
                enum = myMessage.getResponses();
                str = (String)enum.nextElement();
 Line 120:
                try {
                  pipeAdv = (PipeAdvertisement)
                  AdvertisementFactory.newAdvertisement(
                  XMLMIMETYPE, new
                  ByteArrayInputStream(str.getBytes()));

                  createPipe(pipeAdv);
                } catch(Exception ee) {
                  ee.printStackTrace();
                  System.exit(-1);
                }
              }
Line 130:          };
```

Listing 13.12 The reliable receiver application. (continues)

```
        displayArea.append("Launching Remote Discovery
          Service...\n");
        myDiscoveryService.getRemoteAdvertisements(null,
          DiscoveryService.ADV, searchKey, searchValue, 1,
          myDiscoveryListener);
      }
    } catch (Exception e) {
        System.out.println("Error during advertisement
          search");
        System.exit(-1);
    }
  }
Line 140:

    private void createPipe(PipeAdvertisement
     myPipeAdvertisement) {
      try {
       displayArea.append("Tying to connect...\n");
        myPipe = myReliablePipeService.connect(
          myPipeAdvertisement,30000);
       displayArea.append("Connected...\n");
      } catch (Exception e) {}
    }

Line 150:    private void sendData() {
      String data = "Hello my friend!";

     Message msg = myPipeService.createMessage();
      msg.setString("DataTag", data);

      try {
        myPipe.getOutputPipe().send(msg);
        displayArea.append("message \"" + data + "\" sent to the
          Server\n");

Line 160:         msg = myPipe.getInputPipe().poll (30000);
         InputStream in2 = msg.getElement ("DataTag").getStream ();
          byte[] buf = new byte[8192];
          int r = in2.read (buf);
          displayArea.append("Message = " + buf);

      } catch (Exception e) {
          System.out.println("Unable to print output pipe");
          e.printStackTrace();
          System.exit(-1);
Line 170:      }
    }
}
```

Listing 13.12   The reliable receiver application. (continued)

The Receiver Code

The receiver code begins by trying to find a pipe advertisement with the name bipipe2. Once it's found, a connection will be established with the peer who advertised the pipe. When the user clicks the Send Data button, a message will be sent to the sender, and the receiver will wait for a message to be sent back.

Lines 142 through 148 implement the createPipe() method, which is called when a pipe advertisement is found that matches the name bipipe2.

Lines 150 through 171 are called when the user clicks the Send Data button. The code obtains the output pipe of the reliable bidirectional pipe, and sends a message to the server. After the message is sent, the input pipe is obtained and the poll() method is called to wait for a message to appear in the pipe.

Summary

This chapter has taken a look at the many different pipes available with the Java binding of the JXTA specification. Along with the pipes, some different mechanisms are provided for publishing and discovering advertisements for various application demands. In the next chapter, the pipes used for communicating between peers in the JXTA network will be utilized within the Content Management System for sharing all kinds of content.

CHAPTER 14

Content Sharing and the Content Management Service (CMS)

U p to this point, we have discussed how to publish advertisements about peers, peer groups, and pipes. The Content Management Service (CMS) enables a peer to share data—such as text documents, graphics files, sound files, and other media—with remote peers. To maintain consistency with the specification, the CMS relies on advertisements to provide information about the media or files a peer is going to share, and relies on JXTA pipes to transfer the content.

The CMS is an excellent example of a service that has been built into the JXTA system. A peer can choose to use the service or not, depending on its desire to share content within a peer group. By using the CMS, the peer is relieved of the housekeeping details behind sharing the content and making it available for discovery and transfer.

Overview of the CMS

The purpose of the CMS is to keep an accurate record of all media files stored on the local peer that are eligible to be shared. To optimize the use of system resources, the CMS requires that the shared content remain on the file system. The CMS does not cache or make copies of these files; instead, it creates a store that includes information about the shared content, such as advertisements for the content. This store is used for quick access to the list of shared content on the local peer.

Each shared file must have a unique advertisement that describes its content. The format of the advertisement appears in Listing 14.1; the elements are as follows:

Name—The filename of the media being shared

cid—The content ID unique to the shared file; used to request the download of a file

Type—A MIME type for the shared file: jpg, gif, and text are common examples

Length—The length of the media file (in bytes)

Description—An optional description of the shared file

```
    <?xml version="1.0">
    <!doctype jxta:contentAdvertisement>
    <jxta:contentAdvertisement>
    <name>ship.html</name>
    <cid> md5:2b9cbd6ab82c8fee8fe2a2b9e7eab7a85</cid>
    <type>text/html</type>
    <length>1234</length>
<description>Page for Displaying Model Ships</description>
    </jxta:contentAdvertisement>
```

Listing 14.1 An example of a CMS content advertisement.

The CMS doesn't reinvent the wheel when it comes to retrieving the content from a remote peer. The JXTA pipes are used for receiving requests, queries, and content; a single initial pipe is opened for each CMS instantiation. This single pipe allows the system to receive pipe advertisements for opening additional connections, as needed.

All of the content searching is accomplished on top of the traditional JXTA services, including pipes and messages. When a query is required, a LIST_REQ message is sent to remote peers to obtain a list of the currently shared media. All of the remote peers will respond with a LIST_RES message containing one or more content advertisements.

When the local peer picks one of the files to download, a GET_REQ message is sent to a specific remote peer based on the information found in its content advertisement. All of the communication is accomplished using the JXTA protocols.

Implementing the CMS in Peers

The CMS peers we build in this chapter define files to be shared, and they search for additional files being shared by other peers. For simplicity, the code presented in Listing 14.2 can be executed by two different peers. When the application is executed, a small GUI will appear, as shown in Figure 14.1. Upon execution, the peer will initialize itself into the JXTA network and create the necessary CMS objects. A single file called image.jpg is shared.

At this point, the application waits for the user to click a button presented at the top of the GUI. Clicking the button causes a CMS search to be performed, using the text "jpg" as the search criterion. All peers with executing CMS services will respond with their shared filenames. In our sample code, all files that are found are automatically downloaded, so it's a good idea to test this peer on a single machine without the HTTP transport enabled. When a second peer is executed with the code in Listing 14.2, both of the peers will have shared a file and wait for the user to click a button.

When the user clicks the button of one of the peers, a search will be sent and the appropriate file downloaded for the other peer. In our case, the file shared is called image.jpg, and the application will write the newly downloaded image to a file called fileimage.jpg. Figure 14.2 shows the output of the GUI when the button is clicked.

In the following sections, we describe how to implement the individual functions of the CMS.

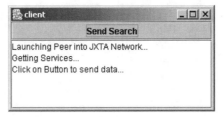

Figure 14.1   CMS peer opening window.

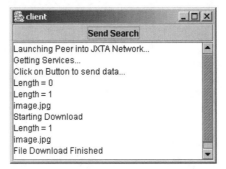

Figure 14.2   CMS peer when the user clicks a button.

```java
import java.io.*;
import java.awt.*;
import java.awt.event.*;
import javax.swing.*;
import java.util.Enumeration;
import net.jxta.document.*;
import net.jxta.peergroup.*;
import net.jxta.exception.*;
import net.jxta.impl.peergroup.*;
import net.jxta.id.*;
import net.jxta.discovery.*;
import net.jxta.pipe.*;
import net.jxta.protocol.*;
import java.net.MalformedURLException;
import java.net.URL;
import net.jxta.endpoint.*;
import net.jxta.discovery.*;
import java.lang.reflect.InvocationTargetException;
import net.jxta.share.*;
import net.jxta.share.client.*;

public class Example1 extends JFrame {

    static  PeerGroup            netPeerGroup = null;
    private DiscoveryService     myDiscoveryService = null;
    private PipeService          myPipeService = null;
    private JTextArea            displayArea;
    private JButton              sendButton;
    private CMS                  myCms = null;
    private ListRequestor        myListRequestor = null;

    private final static   MimeMediaType XMLMIMETYPE = new
      MimeMediaType("text/xml");

    public static void main(String args[]) {
        Example1 myapp = new Example1();

        myapp.addWindowListener (
         new WindowAdapter() {
            public void windowClosing(WindowEvent e) {
               System.exit(0);
            }
          }
        );

        myapp.launchJXTA();
        myapp.getServices();
        myapp.run();
```

Listing 14.2 Peer with CMS capabilities. (continues)

```
  }


  public Example1() {
    super("client");

    Container c = getContentPane();

    sendButton = new JButton("Send Search");
    sendButton.addActionListener(
      new ActionListener() {
        public void actionPerformed(ActionEvent e) {
          sendData();
        }
      }
    );
    c.add(sendButton, BorderLayout.NORTH);

    displayArea = new JTextArea();
    c.add(new JScrollPane(displayArea), BorderLayout.CENTER);

    setSize(300,150);
    show();
  }

  public void run() {
    displayArea.append("Click on Button to send data...\n");

    try {
     myCms.getContentManager().share(new File("image.jpg"));
    } catch (IOException ex) {
      System.out.println("Share command failed.");
    }
  }

  private void launchJXTA() {
      displayArea.append("Launching Peer into JXTA
        Network...\n");
      try {
          netPeerGroup = PeerGroupFactory.newNetPeerGroup();
      } catch (PeerGroupException e) {
          System.out.println("Unable to create PeerGroup -
            Failure");
          e.printStackTrace();
          System.exit(1);
      }
  }
```

Listing 14.2   A peer with CMS capabilities. (continues)

```
private void getServices() {
  displayArea.append("Getting Services...\n");
  myDiscoveryService = netPeerGroup.getDiscoveryService();
  myPipeService = netPeerGroup.getPipeService();

  try {
    myCms = new CMS();
    myCms.init(netPeerGroup, null, null);

    if(myCms.startApp(new File("client")) == -1) {
      System.out.println("CMS initialization failed");
      System.exit(-1);
    }
  } catch (Exception e) {
    System.out.println("CMS init failure");
    System.exit(-1);
  }
}

public interface ContentListener {
  public void finishedRetrieve(String url);
}

class GetRequestor extends GetContentRequest {
  private ContentAdvertisement searchResult = null;
  private String url = null;
  private ContentListener listener;

  public GetRequestor( PeerGroup pg, ContentAdvertisement
      res, File tmpFile, ContentListener listener )
      throws InvocationTargetException {
    super( pg, res, tmpFile );
    searchResult = res;
    url = tmpFile.getAbsolutePath();
    this.listener = listener;
  }

  public ContentAdvertisement getContentAdvertisement() {
    return searchResult;
  }

  public void notifyDone() {
    listener.finishedRetrieve( url );
  }
}

class ListRequestor extends CachedListContentRequest {
```

Listing 14.2 Peer with CMS capabilities. (continues)

```
      boolean gotOne = false;
      public ListRequestor( PeerGroup group, String inSubStr ) {
        super( group, inSubStr );
      }

      public void notifyMoreResults() {
        System.out.println("Search Done");

        ContentAdvertisement[] result =
          myListRequestor.getResults();
        if ( result != null ) {
          displayArea.append("Length = " + result.length + "\n");
          for (int i=0;i<result.length;i++) {
            ContentAdvertisement myAdv = result[i];
            displayArea.append(myAdv.getName() + "\n");

            if (!gotOne) {
              displayArea.append("Starting Download\n");
              File tmpFile = new File( "file" + myAdv.getName()
            )

            ContentListener myListener = new ContentListener() {
              public void finishedRetrieve(String url) {
                displayArea.append("File Download Finished\n");
              }
            };

            try {
              GetRequestor request = new GetRequestor(
               netPeerGroup, result[i], tmpFile, myListener );
            } catch ( InvocationTargetException e ) {
              e.printStackTrace();
            }
            gotOne = true;
          }
        }
      }
      else {
       System.out.println("No results");
      }
    }

  private void sendData() {
    myListRequestor = new ListRequestor( netPeerGroup, "jpg" );
    myListRequestor.activateRequest();
  }
}
```

Listing 14.2   Peer with CMS capabilities. (continued)

Initializing the CMS

The first step in using CMS is to instantiate the service. The code necessary to perform the instantiation is shown in Listing 14.3. For any peer code that requires CMS capability, two imports are necessary:

```
import net.jxta.share.*;
import net.jxta.share.metadata.*;
```

The first line in the code snippet instantiates a new CMS object, which contains the service itself. Next, the service is initialized using the init() method. The init() method accepts three parameters: the peer group that the peer wants to have the content management system associated with, a specific peer ID, and an advertisement for the peer. In most cases, the only information needed is the peer group.

The fourth line makes a call to the method startApp(). This method will start the service itself using the parameters supplied. The method is overloaded to accept either an array of name-value pairs or a File object. In our case, a File object is passed to the method containing the name of a directory that CMS can use as a persistent store when results are returned from a query, or to hold information about any content being shared on the local peer.

```
CMS cms = new CMS();
cms.init(netPeerGroup, null, null);

if(cms.startApp(new File("Client")) == -1) {
  System.out.println("CMS initialization failed");
  System.exit(-1);
}
```

Listing 14.3 TCMS object instantiation code.

Sharing Content

After the CMS service has been started, two operations are possible: sharing content and querying other peers for content. The following line of code is all that it takes to share a file on the local file system with an entire peer group:

```
myCms.getContentManager().share(new File("image.jpg"));
```

Two operations are necessary for sharing content. The first is to obtain the Content Manager of the CMS service. To share a file, the share() method is used, which contains a total of four parameters. The prototype for the method is

```
share(java.io.File file, java.lang.String name, java.lang.String type,
java.lang.String desc)
```

The share( ) method's four parameters are the following:

File object—The file to be shared

name—A name to use for the file, possibly other than the filename; this is optional

type—The MIME type; this parameter is optional

desc—An optional description of the file

In its most simple form, the method provides a File object, as the previous code snippet shows. If the peer desires more search words to be available for the shared file, both the name and description should be provided.

Viewing the Shared Content List

The CMS also has the ability to provide a list of all the files currently shared on the current peer. The code you can use to display all of the names of the files currently shared is shown in Listing 14.4. The first line of the code pulls an array of Content objects. The Content object contains, among other things, a ContentAdvertisement. The ContentAdvertisement contains information about the file being shared, as well as a PipeAdvertisement, which a remote peer can use to obtain the shared file. The getName( ) method is used to pull the filename from the ContentAdvertisement.

```
Content[] content = cms.getContentManager().getContent();
fileList.removeAll();
for (int i=0; i<content.length; i++) {
  System.out.println(content[i].getContentAdvertisement().getName())
;}
```

Listing 14.4   Shared content list.

Searching For and Getting Content

After content is shared, a peer can perform a query for shared content, and download any of the content needed. Quite a bit of code is involved in the query and download. Some of the following code is adapted from demonstration code in the myJXTA application, as well as from the searchDemo and shareDemo files that accompany the CMS source code. The code for the query and download is shown in Listing 14.5.

The query begins when the statement in line 68 is executed. This statement will instantiate a new ListRequestor( ) object that passes the current peer group and the search string. The ListRequestor() class is a private class defined in lines 26–65 and is a derived class from CachedListContentRequest, which is defined in the CMS package.

The derived class overrides the notifyMoreResults() method and defines a constructor for the class. In the constructor, the peer group and search string are passed to the parent class in anticipation of the query. When the query is started in line 69, each time a peer returns results to the query peer, the notifyMoreResults() method will be called.

The notifyMoreResults() method starts in line 33. It begins by building an array of ContentAdvertisements, which are sent from a remote peer. The advertisements are loaded by calling the getResults() method of the ListRequestor object. If there are no advertisements from a remote peer, no additional work is done.

If there are advertisements, a loop is entered where the names of the files found are displayed and the first remote file is downloaded. The download is accomplished in line 54. The peer group, the advertisement of the file to download, a File object used to store the data when retrieved, and a listener object based on the ContentListener object are built in lines 47 through 50. The listener object will allow the application to know when the download has finished.

```
Line 1:    public interface ContentListener {
      public void finishedRetrieve(String url);
   }

   class GetRequestor extends GetContentRequest {
      private SearchResult searchResult = null;
      private String url = null;
      private ContentListener listener;

Line 10:       public GetRequestor( PeerGroup pg, SearchResult
res, File tmpFile, ContentListener listener )
                              throws InvocationTargetException
{
      super( pg, res.contentAdv, tmpFile );
      searchResult = res;
      url = tmpFile.getAbsolutePath();
      this.listener = listener;
   }

   public ContentAdvertisement getContentAdvertisement() {
      return searchResult.contentAdv;
   }
```

Listing 14.5 Query and download code. (continues)

```
Line 20:
      public void notifyDone() {
         listener.finishedRetrieve( url );
      }
   }

   class ListRequestor extends CachedListContentRequest {

      boolean gotOne = false;
      public ListRequestor( PeerGroup group, String inSubStr ) {
Line 30:         super( group, inSubStr );
      }

      public void notifyMoreResults() {
         System.out.println("Search Done");

         ContentAdvertisement[] result =
myListRequestor.getResults();
         if ( result != null ) {
            displayArea.append("Length = " + result.length + "\n");
            for (int i=0;i<result.length;i++) {
Line 40:             ContentAdvertisement myAdv =
result[i].getContentAdvertisement();
               displayArea.append(myAdv.getName() + "\n");

               if (!gotOne) {
                  displayArea.append("Starting Download\n");
                  File tmpFile = new File( "file" + myAdv.getName() );
                   ContentListener myListener = new ContentListener()
{
                      public void finishedRetrieve(String url) {
                         displayArea.append("File Download
Finished\n");
                      }
Line 50:                };

                  try {
                    GetRequestor request = new GetRequestor(
netPeerGroup, result[i], tmpFile, myListener );
                  } catch ( InvocationTargetException e ) {
                        e.printStackTrace();
                  }
                  gotOne = true;
               }
            }
Line 60:      }
         else
```

Listing 14.5   Query and download code. (continues)

```
        System.out.println("No results");
    }
}

private void sendData() {
    myListRequestor =  new ListRequestor( netPeerGroup, "jpg" );
    myListRequestor.activateRequest();
```

Listing 14.5   Query and download code. (continued)

Summary

In this chapter, we showed you how to use the Content Management System built into the JXTA system. The peer code we presented illustrates how you can initialize the CMS service, share files on the local file system, query for remote files, and allow the files to be downloaded. In Chapter 15, we look at the security capabilities of the JXTA specification and Java Reference Implementation. Topics covered include how to encrypt data sent to another peer and how to implement a better secure peergroup.

CHAPTER 15

Implementing Security

With the increasing number of viruses, hacks, and other attacks occurring on the Internet, it is vital that any distributed system implement robust security. In this chapter, we examine two different security issues: login protection and transport security.

To address the issue of login security, we will build our own version of the password membership service used in Chapter 12 "Developing a JXTA Application." Some of the keys issues we want to address in the service are

- Encrypting passwords
- Storing username/passwords on the server peer
- Allowing automatic signups

For all of these issues, we have to build a new skeleton membership service. For the task of transport security, we examine using secure pipes and encrypting message data independent of the pipe connection.

JXTA Security Toolkit

One of the primary projects in the JXTA community focuses on security—you can track this project's progress at http://security.jxta.org/Security-project.html. The site provides an overview of the JXTA Security Toolkit, and contains all the relevant source code. If you download the JXTA installer (as described in Appendix A), the security code will be installed automatically with the system. The security project has three goals:

To provide secure JXTA pipes—We can create secure JXTA input and output pipes by using the JxtaUnicastSecure option, which ensures that all communication between peers will be encrypted. A form of SSL/TLS encryption, this approach provides a transparent secure connection.

To ensure authenticity and integrity—This functionality is provided by the encryption algorithms and various methods of checksum administration.

To provide unrepudiated transactions—Having peers sign all messages being sent to other peers satisfies this goal. The JXTA Security Toolkit provides the ability to digitally sign data.

The goals of the Security Toolkit are accomplished using both RSA public-key encryption and a number of independent ciphers, such as RC4. Both of the techniques provide the necessary encryption mechanisms to accomplish the project's goals. In the remainder of this section, we describe the major components of the JXTA Security Toolkit. Later in this chapter, we use the components to encrypt data flowing through secure and unsecured pipe connections.

Building Keys

In Public Key Infrastructure (PKI) and the independent ciphers, the concept of a key is paramount. The key holds the information necessary to both encrypt and decrypt an array of bytes. For PKI, which requires two keys, one of the keys will be used for encryption. If the other key isn't available, the data will remain encrypted.

The parent class for keys in the toolkit is called key, from which two classes are derived:

- SecretKey—Used for independent ciphers such as RC4 or DES
- RSAKey—Used for RSA and further derived as follows:
  - RSAPrivateKey—Used for RSA
  - RSAPublicKey for RSA

A factory class called KeyBuilder is used to instantiate necessary key objects. The prototype for the key factory is

```
Key KeyBuilder.buildKey(byte KEYTYPE,
                        short KEYLENGTH,
                        boolean UNUSEDPARAMETER);
```

The code behind the buildKey() method is quite simple and uses a compound IF statement to instantiate either a SecretKey or a RSAKey. The values of KEY-TYPE currently recognized are

- TYPE_RSA

- TYPE_RSA_PUBLIC

- TYPE_RSA_PRIVATE

- TYPE_RC4

Note that the code indicates the existence of a DES cipher; however, the current buildKey() method does not recognize the type. All three of the RSA constants will produce a RSAKey object. For the KEYLENGTH parameter, the available values are

- LENGTH_RC4—The default value of 128

- LENGTH_RSA_MIN—The default value of 384

- LENGTH_RSA_512—The default value of 512

The third parameter to the buildKey() method is currently unused, but is required to be a Boolean value.

Using the Toolkit

The Security Toolkit itself is contained in a "suite," as explained on the project's web site. A suite is similar to a factory but can be extended without changing factory code. The suite class, called JxtaCryptoSuite, produces a new suite based on a predefined security profile. The profiles currently available are

- PROFILE_RSA_RC4_SHA1

- PROFILE_RSA_RC4_MD5

- PROFILE_RSA_RC4_SHA1_MD5

- MEMBER_RC4

If a developer wants to use message authentication to ensure message integrity, the following profiles are available:

- ALG_RC4_SHA1

- ALG_RC4_MD5

And if message signing is desired:

- ALG_RSA_SHA1_PKCS1

- ALG_RSA_MD5_PKCS1

The JxtaCryptoSuite suite is created using a number of overloaded and defaulted constructors. The prototype is

```
JxtaCryptoSuite(ENCRYPTIONPROFILE, key, SIGNATUREPROFILE, MACPROFILE);
```

There are three ways to use the algorithms in the Security Toolkit:

- Instantiate a JxtaCryptoSuite object with all algorithms.

- Instantiate a JxtaCryptoSuite object with select algorithms.

- Bypass the JxtaCryptoSuite, and instantiate independent algorithms.

The following code will instantiate a suite object with three encryption algorithms available:

```
RSAKey suiteKey = (RSAKey)KeyBuilder.buildKey(KeyBuilder.TYPE_RSA,
                            KeyBuilder.LENGTH_RSA_512,
                            false);
JxtaCrypto encryptionSuite = new
JxtaCryptoSuite(JxtaCrypto.PROFILE_RSA_RC4_MD5,
            suiteKey,
            Signature.ALG_RSA_MD5_PKCS1,
            MAC.ALG_RC4_MD5);
```

Once instantiated, the encryptionSuite object can be used to obtain specific algorithms. For example:

```
Cipher cipherAlgorithm = encryptionSuite.getJxtaCipher();
```

The cipherAlgorithm object will contain an RC4 algorithm, which can be used to encrypt and decrypt data, as we'll see in a moment. The other algorithms can be obtained using the following code:

```
Signature signatureAlgorithm = encryptionSuite.getJxtaSignature();
MAC authenticationAlgorithm = encryptionSuite.getJxtaMAC();
```

Encrypting Data

After a JxtaCryptoSuite object has been instantiated, the various algorithms can be used to encrypt data for transmission over an non-secure or even a secure connection path. In this section, we look at using the suite algorithms for RSA and RC4. For both encryptions, the steps are basically the same:

1. Obtain a JxtaCryptoSuite object.

2. Pull out the necessary encryption algorithm.

3. Encrypt the data.

In the next few sections, we discuss the details of using the Security Toolkit for encrypting data, providing authentication, and signing.

Using RSA for Data Encryption

Listing 15.1 contains basic code for using the Security Toolkit to encrypt and decrypt data. This code follows the steps we outlined earlier for building an RSA cipher using the JXTA Security Toolkit. After we initialize the toolkit, we extract the RSA cipher from the toolkit suite object, and use it for both the encryption and decryption of an array of data.

```
Line 1:RSAKey  rsaKey = (RSAKey)KeyBuilder.buildKey(
  KeyBuilder.TYPE_RSA, KeyBuilder.LENGTH_RSA_512, false);
JxtaCrypto suite = new
   JxtaCryptoSuite(JxtaCrypto.PROFILE_RSA_SHA1, rsaKey,
   (byte)0, (byte)0);


PublicKeyAlgorithm rsa = suite.getJxtaPublicKeyAlgorithm();


rsa.setPublicKey();
rsa.setPrivateKey();
RSAPublickeyData rPublicD = (RSAPublickeyData)rsa.getPublickey();
RSAPrivatekeyData rPrivateD =
  (RSAPrivatekeyData)rsa.getPrivatekey();
Line 10:
//Encrypt the Data
byte[] X = new byte[rsa.getMaxInputDataBlockLength()];
for (int i = 0; i < X.length; i++) X[i] = (byte)0xCC;
rsa.setPrivateKey(rPrivateD);
byte[] Y = rsa.Algorithm(X, 0, X.length,
  KeyBuilder.TYPE_RSA_PRIVATE, true);


//Decrypt the Data
rsa.setPublicKey(rPublicD);
byte[] Z = rsa.Algorithm(Y, 0, Y.length,
  KeyBuilder.TYPE_RSA_PUBLIC, false);
```

Listing 15.1 Using the JXTA Security Toolkit to encrypt and decrypt code.

Line 1 instantiates a Key object to use in the suite. The key will be 512 bits, and is an RSA key. Notice the use of the cast for the object returned by the method.

Line 2 instantiates an object for holding the suite created based on the Key object generated in line 1 and for utilizing the RSA algorithm. Notice that the third and fourth parameters are null; this tells the suite generator that no authentication or signing algorithm will be needed.

Line 4 obtains the specific RSA encryption/decryption algorithm created for the suite. Lines 6 and 7 set the public and private keys to be used in all encryption and decryption. Of particular importance is the fact that there are no parameters to the methods. The methods are overloaded, and the no-parameter versions generate random keys.

Lines 8 and 9 pull the keys from the suite, and store them in the local object for later use. Lines 12 and 13 obtain a byte array of the largest size available for RSA encryption, and fill the array with sample data. Line 14 sets the private key of the algorithm to be the private key we stored earlier (just in case it had been changed).

Line 15 performs the encryption. The first parameter to the method is the byte array, the second parameter is the byte to begin the encryption, the third parameter is the length of the byte array, the fourth parameter is the key to use in the encryption, and the fifth parameter tells the algorithm to perform an encryption. The fifth parameter is set to true for encryption and false for decryption. Line 18 begins the process of decryption, and sets the public key to be the public key stored earlier.

Line 19 performs the decryption (notice the false value for the fifth parameter), and stores the new bytes in the returned array.

Using RC4 for Data Encryption

Listing 15.2 contains code for encryption using the RC4 algorithm. This code is very similar to Listing 15.1 (for using the RSA cipher); however, the RC4 cipher can be used to encrypt and decrypt a very large array of data, whereas the RSA cipher must be used against a specific size array.

```
Line 1: JxtaCrypto suite =
new JxtaCryptoSuite(JxtaCrypto.MEMBER_RC4, null, (byte)0, (byte)0);
Cipher rc4 = suite.getJxtaCipher();

byte[] password = new byte[KeyBuilder.LENGTH_RC4 >>> 3];
SecretKey key1 = (SecretKey)KeyBuilder.buildKey(
  KeyBuilder.TYPE_RC4, KeyBuilder.LENGTH_RC4, false);

byte[] ibuf = new byte[256];
key1.setKey(password, 0);
rc4.init(key1, Cipher.MODE_ENCRYPT);
Line 10:
// Encrypt the Data
byte[] obuf = new byte[ibuf.length];
rc4.doFinal(ibuf, 0, ibuf.length, obuf, 0);

// Decrypt the Data
byte[] clearText = new byte[obuf.length];//
rc4.init(key1, Cipher.MODE_DECRYPT);
rc4.doFinal(obuf, 0, obuf.length, clearText, 0);
```

Listing 15.2 Encryption using the RC4 algorithm.

Line 1 obtains an object containing the JxyaCryptoSuite utilizing the RC4 cipher and no authenticator or signature functionality. Line 2 pulls the RC4 cipher from the suite for later use.

Line 4 builds a password to use in the RC4 algorithm. There should be a value in the password array—it can be either random or specific values.

Line 5 builds an RC4 key. Notice the key was not necessary when the suite was initialized in line 1.

Line 7 creates a byte array to hold the data to be encrypted. Just after line 7, data should be placed in the array.

Line 8 sets the value of the key obtained from the KeyBuilder class to be the password built in line 4. Line 9 initializes the RC4 cipher using the key built in line 8 and a modifier telling the algorithm to use the key for encryption.

Line 10 performs the actual encryption. RC4 does not have the size restriction of RSA, and therefore a large array of bytes can be encrypted.

Line 13 starts the decryption process. First, a byte array is built as large as the input array. Line 14 initializes the RC4 algorithm using our key as well as a modifier that lets the algorithm know to perform a decryption. Line 15 performs the decryption.

Authenticating Data

The JXTA Security Toolkit contains the algorithms necessary for authenticating data. By authenticating data, you ensure that bits are not changed—either maliciously or accidentally—during data transfer. The authentication works by building the necessary authentication object within the toolkit, extracting it, and then applying the encrypt() method of the authenticator to an array of data. When the data arrives at a specific location, the verify() method is used to authenticate the data. If the result of the verify() method is true, the data is original. Listing 15.3 contains the code necessary for providing this level of authentication.

```
Line 1: SecretKey sKey =    (SecretKey)KeyBuilder.buildKey(
  KeyBuilder.TYPE_RC4, KeyBuilder.LENGTH_RC4, false);
JxtaCrypto suite = new JxtaCryptoSuite(
  JxtaCrypto.PROFILE_RC4_SHA1, null,(byte)0, MAC.ALG_RC4_SHA1);
MAC mac = suite.getJxtaMAC();

// authenticate it
byte[] privateKey = new byte[sKey.getLength()];
byte[] ibuf = new byte[1024];
byte[] macBuf = new byte[ibuf.length];
mac.init(MAC.MODE_ENCRYPT, (Key)sKey, privateKey);
Line 10: int macLength = mac.encrypt(ibuf, 0, ibuf.length,
   macBuf, 0);

//Verify
mac.init(MAC.MODE_VERIFY, (Key)sKey, privateKey);
boolean verified = mac.verify(ibuf, 0, ibuf.length,
   macBuf, 0, macBuf.length);
```

Listing 15.3 Authenticating an RC4 encrypted key.

Lines 1 and 2 obtain a key object and a suite object, as in previous examples. Notice that the last parameter of line 2 indicates which cipher should be used for the authentication.

Line 3 obtains an object representing the MAC algorithm. Line 6 creates a private key to be used for the MAC algorithm—in practice, a value should be placed in the array, either known or random.

Line 7 creates an array for the input bytes to be authenticated. This array would be used for the actual data. Line 8 creates an array to hold the authenticated bytes

Line 9 initializes the MAC algorithm with the key created in line 1 and the private key created in line 6. Line 10 performs the encryption of the input buffer. The fourth parameter is the new byte array where the encrypted data will be stored after encryption.

Line 13 begins the process of verifying the authentication of the bytes by initializing the MAC algorithm with a modifier in the first parameter set to VERIFY. Line 14 performs the actual verification based on the original bytes before signing and the bytes after signing. A value of true indicates that the bytes are authentic.

Signing Data

Listing 15.4 contains the code necessary to use the Security Toolkit for signing data. You can use the process of signing data to tell a remote recipient that you are the one who sent the data. The data is signed and the signature of the sender is embedded in the data. When the data arrives at a remote site, the verify() method is used to determine whether the code is signed appropriately.

```
Line 1: RSAKey rsaKey = (RSAKey)KeyBuilder.buildKey(
  KeyBuilder.TYPE_RSA, KeyBuilder.LENGTH_RSA_512, false);
JxtaCrypto suite = new JxtaCryptoSuite(
  JxtaCrypto.PROFILE_RSA_SHA1, rsaKey,
  Signature.ALG_RSA_SHA_PKCS1, (byte)0);
Signature sig = suite.getJxtaSignature();

// Sign the Data
byte[] ibuf = new byte[1024];
sig.init(Signature.MODE_SIGN);
byte[] sigBuf = sig.sign(ibuf, 0, ibuf.length);
Line 10:
// Check the Sign
sig.init(Signature.MODE_VERIFY);
boolean  verified = sig.verify(ibuf, 0, ibuf.length, sigBuf, 0,
   sigBuf.length);
```

Listing 15.4   Signing data and verifying the signature.

Lines 1 and 2 build our RSAKey object, and obtain a suite object with both an RSA encryption algorithm and a signing algorithm available. Line 3 pulls the signing algorithm from the suite.

Line 6 builds an input buffer that will store the data to be signed. Line 8 initializes the signing algorithm by using a modifier value of MODE_SIGN. Line 9 signs the data, and returns an array of bytes representing the signed data.

Line 12 initializes the signing algorithm by using a modifier value of MODE_VERIFY to start the process of verifying that the bytes received are signed appropriately. A value of true indicates a successful verification.

Secure Membership Service

In Chapter 12, we wrote a simple application that both constructed a secure peer group and allowed others to join the group. As a quick reminder, the necessary steps for joining a peer group are

1. Build an authenticated credential.

2. Obtain the membership service from the peer group.

3. Apply for membership using the membership service's authenticator.

4. Check to see if everything was filled out in our credentials.

5. Join the group.

The code we used in Chapter 12 for accomplishing the above steps follows:

```
StructuredDocument myCredentials = null;
    try {
      AuthenticationCredential myAuthenticationCredential =
       new AuthenticationCredential(myLocalGroup, null,
       myCredentials);
      MembershipService myMembershipService =
        myLocalGroup.getMembershipService();
      net.jxta.membership.Authenticator myAuthenticator =
       myMembershipService.apply(myAuthenticationCredential);

     authenticateMe(myAuthenticator, "username", "password");

     if (!myAuthenticator.isReadyForJoin()) {
       displayArea.append("Authenticator is not
         complete\n");
       return;
     }
     myMembershipService.join(myAuthenticator);
     displayArea.append("Group has been joined\n");
   } catch (Exception e) {
     displayArea.append("Authentication failed - group not
```

```
        joined\n");
    e.printStackTrace();
    System.exit(-1);
}
```

When we used this code to obtain membership into the secure peer group, the only thing we supplied was a specific username and password provided by the peer group. We actually needed to know the username and password before-hand in order to join the group. This isn't very practical; we should have the ability to create a username and password, if the group allows, and have the information stored by the group.

If you look at the preceding code and read the description for the Authentica-tionCredential, you will find that the second parameter to the class's construc-tor is supposed to be the method of authentication the membership service should use to authenticate this peer; the credentials parameter should contain identity information.

As you can see, the examples in Chapter 12 and the default membership ser-vices provided with JXTA don't use either a method or the Credentials object. Note that the method is just a string and that the credentials are an XML-based document (or it appears the intent is for the credentials to be an XML docu-ment). When the apply() method of the membership service is called, the cre-dentials and the method are supposed to be used for the membership.

In the remainder of this section, we deal with changing the password member-ship service provided with the JXTA system to allow the use of the credentials and the storing of the username and password.

Building a New Membership Service

Several areas should be changed in the password membership service code provided with the JXTA toolkit to make it more useful for a peer group:

- Using a XML credential from the peers who want to join the group
- Allowing passwords to be stored in a database
- Creating the potential to use the JXTA Security Toolkit for encryption

Listing 15.5 contains new membership service code that provides this function-ality. The code class, called UpdatedPasswdMembershipService.java, can be compiled using the compile command we discussed in Chapter 12. Once com-piled, the classes generated are stored in a JAR file using the following com-mand:

```
jar cvf passwordmem.jar ./net/jxta/impl/membership/*.class
```

The resulting JAR, called passwordmem.jar, can be placed in the /lib directory that was created when you first installed the JXTA system. The JAR will have to be added to all compile and run commands found in Chapter 12. Before diving into the code, a short explanation of how to use the service is in order.

In Chapter 12, we used the membership service passwdMembershipService to allow secure (password-protected) access to a peer group. The JXTA code for using the membership service didn't use all of the capabilities of the JXTA class (including a credential created by the client who wanted to join the group). In addition, we had to search for specific methods to call in order to set up the join process. The new membership service in Listing 15.5 creates a credential with the following elements:

<Identity>

    <login>

        login value

    </login>

    <password>

        password encrypted value

    </password

</Identity>

When the apply() method of the membership service is called, the credential is passed to an authenticator, which pulls the login and password values from the credential, and stores them locally. The credential is checked to be sure a join can occur. The join() method is then called, and the login/password values are compared to the hard-coded value (we will discuss changing this later in this chapter). The login and password values are no longer kept in the peer group advertisement. The idea for this password membership service is to have one or more server peers that have access to a secure database storing unique login/password values. We could expand the service to allow the creation of login/password combinations by the peers themselves. The potential exists to create a PassPort type system like the one we find in the Microsoft arena.

In Listing 15.5, all code comments have been removed to save space in this book, but you can see the comments in the appropriate files in the source code download.

```
Line 1: package net.jxta.impl.membership;

import java.net.URL;
import java.util.Enumeration;
```

Listing 15.5 Code for the UpdatedPasswdMembership Service. (continues)

```
import java.util.Vector;
import java.util.Hashtable;
import java.net.MalformedURLException;
import java.net.UnknownServiceException;
import org.apache.log4j.Category;
Line 10: import org.apache.log4j.Priority;
import net.jxta.credential.*;
import net.jxta.document.*;
import net.jxta.protocol.*;
import net.jxta.id.*;
import net.jxta.membership.*;
import net.jxta.peer.*;
import net.jxta.peergroup.*;
import net.jxta.platform.*;
import net.jxta.service.Service;
Line 20:
import net.jxta.exception.*;

public class UpdatedPasswdMembershipService extends
  MembershipService {
    private static final Category LOG = Category.getInstance(
      UpdatedPasswdMembershipService.class.getName());

    private class PasswdCredential implements Credential {

        UpdatedPasswdMembershipService source;
Line 30:        String whoami;
        ID peerid;
        String signedPeerID;

        protected PasswdCredential(
          UpdatedPasswdMembershipService source,
          String whoami, String signedPeerID ) {
            this.source = (UpdatedPasswdMembershipService) source;
            this.whoami = whoami;
            this.peerid = source.getPeerGroup().getPeerID();
            this.signedPeerID = signedPeerID;
        }
Line 40:
        protected PasswdCredential(
          UpdatedPasswdMembershipService source, PeerGroupID
          peergroup, PeerID peer, String whoami, String
          signedPeerID ) throws PeerGroupException {
        this.source = (UpdatedPasswdMembershipService) source;

        if( !source.getPeerGroup().getPeerGroupID().equals(
         peergroup ) )
```

Listing 15.5 Code for the UpdatedPasswdMembership Service. (continues)

```
                  throw new PeerGroupException( "Cannot credential
                    for a different peer group." );

              this.whoami = whoami;
              this.peerid = peer;
              this.signedPeerID = signedPeerID;
          }
Line 50:
          public MembershipService getSourceService() {
              return source;
          }

          public ID getPeerGroupID() {
              return source.getPeerGroup().getPeerGroupID();
          }

          public ID getPeerID() {
Line 60:          return peerid;
          }

          public StructuredDocument getDocument(MimeMediaType as)
           throws Exception {
              StructuredDocument doc =
              StructuredDocumentFactory.newStructuredDocument( as,
                "PasswdCredential" );

              Element e = doc.createElement( "PeerGroupID",
               peergroup.getPeerGroupID().toString() );
              doc.appendChild( e );

              e = doc.createElement( "PeerID",
                peergroup.getPeerID().toString() );
Line 70:          doc.appendChild( e );

              e = doc.createElement( "Identity", whoami );
              doc.appendChild( e );

              e = doc.createElement( "ReallyInsecureSignature",
                signedPeerID );
              doc.appendChild( e );

              return doc;
          }

Line 80:      public String getIdentity() {
              return whoami;
          }
```

Listing 15.5 Code for the UpdatedPasswdMembership Service. (continues)

```
            }


        public class PasswdAuthenticator implements Authenticator {
            MembershipService source;
            AuthenticationCredential application;

Line 90:           String whoami = null;
            String password = null;

            PasswdAuthenticator( MembershipService source,
             AuthenticationCredential application ) {
                this.source = source;
                this.application = application;

               try {
                 StructuredTextDocument credentialsDoc =
                   (StructuredTextDocument)
                   application.getDocument(new
                   MimeMediaType("text/xml"));

Line 100:      Enumeration elements =
                 credentialsDoc.getChildren("IdentityInfo");
                 elements = ((TextElement)
                 elements.nextElement()).getChildren();
               elements = ((TextElement)
                 elements.nextElement()).getChildren();
              while (elements.hasMoreElements()) {
                TextElement elem = (TextElement)
                  elements.nextElement();
                String nm = elem.getName();
                if(nm.equals("login")) {
                  whoami = elem.getTextValue();
                    continue;
Line 110:     }

                if(nm.equals("password")) {
                  password = elem.getTextValue();
                  continue;
                }
                }
              } catch(Exception e) {
                e.printStackTrace();
                System.exit(-1);
Line 120:          }
            }
```

Listing 15.5   Code for the UpdatedPasswdMembership Service. (continues)

```
        public MembershipService getSourceService() {
            return source;
        }

        synchronized public boolean isReadyForJoin() {
            return ( (null != password) && (null != whoami) );
        }
Line 130:
        public String getMethodName() {
            return "PasswdAuthentication";
        }

        public void setAuth1Identity( String who ) {
            whoami = who;
        }

        public String getAuth1Identity() {
Line 140:            return whoami;
        }

        public void setAuth2_Password( String secret ) {
            password = secret;
        }

        private String getAuth2_Password() {
            return password;
        }
Line 150:
        public AuthenticationCredential
          getAuthenticationCredential() {
            return application;
        }
    }

    static class IdMaker {
        static ID mkID( String s ) {
            try {
                return IDFactory.fromURL(new URL( "urn", "",
                  "jxta:uuid-" + s));
Line 160:              } catch (MalformedURLException absurd) {
                } catch (UnknownServiceException absurd2) {
                }
            throw new JxtaError("Hardcoded Spec and Class IDs are
              malformed.");
        }
    }
```

Listing 15.5 Code for the UpdatedPasswdMembership Service. (continues)

```
      public static final ModuleSpecID passwordMembershipSpecID =
        (ModuleSpecID)
        IdMaker.mkID( "DeadBeefDeafBabaFeedBabe00000005"
        + "02"
        + "06" );

      private PeerGroup peergroup = null;
Line 170:
       private Vector principals = null;
      private Vector authCredentials = null;
      private ModuleImplAdvertisement implAdvertisement = null;
      private Hashtable logins = null;

      public void init(PeerGroup group, ID assignedID,
        Advertisement impl)
        throws PeerGroupException {
           peergroup = group;
           implAdvertisement = (ModuleImplAdvertisement) impl;
           PeerGroupAdvertisement configAdv =
     (PeerGroupAdvertisement)
group.getPeerGroupAdvertisement();
Line 180:
           resign();
      }

      public Service getInterface() {
           return this;
      }

      public Advertisement getImplAdvertisement() {
           return implAdvertisement;
Line 190:    }

      public int startApp(String[] arg) {
           return 0;
      }

      public void stopApp() {
      }

      public PeerGroup getPeerGroup() {
Line 200:        return peergroup;
      }

      public Authenticator apply(AuthenticationCredential
        application) throws PeerGroupException,
```

Listing 15.5 Code for the UpdatedPasswdMembership Service. (continues)

```
          ProtocolNotSupportedException {

            String method = application.getMethod();

            if( (null != method) &&
              !"UpdatedPasswdAuthentication".equals( method ) )
                throw new ProtocolNotSupportedException(
                "Authentication method not recognized" );
            return new PasswdAuthenticator( this, application );
Line 210:      }

       public synchronized Enumeration getCurrentCredentials()
        throws PeerGroupException {
            return principals.elements();
       }

       public synchronized Enumeration getAuthCredentials() throws
PeerGroupException {
            return authCredentials.elements();
       }

Line 220:      public synchronized Credential join(Authenticator
             authenticated) throws PeerGroupException {

           if( !(authenticated instanceof PasswdAuthenticator) )
               throw new ClassCastException( "This is not my
                   authenticator!" );

           if( !authenticated.isReadyForJoin() )
               throw new PeerGroupException( "Not Ready to join!" );

           if( !checkPasswd(
           ((PasswdAuthenticator)authenticated).getAuth1Identity(),
           ((PasswdAuthenticator)authenticated).getAuth2_Password() ) )
Line 230:            throw new PeerGroupException( "Incorrect Password!" );

           Credential newCred = new PasswdCredential( this,
           ((PasswdAuthenticator)authenticated).getAuth1Identity(),
             "blah" );

           principals.addElement( newCred );

           authCredentials.addElement(
             authenticated.getAuthenticationCredential() );

           return newCred;
       }
```

Listing 15.5 Code for the UpdatedPasswdMembership Service. (continues)

```
Line 240:
    public synchronized void resign() throws PeerGroupException {
        principals = new Vector();
        authCredentials = new Vector();

        principals.addElement( new PasswdCredential( this,
          "nobody", "blah" ) );
    }


    public Credential makeCredential(Element element) throws
      PeerGroupException, Exception {
        Object rootIs = element.getKey();
Line 250:
        if( !"PasswdCredential".equals(rootIs) )
            throw new PeerGroupException( "Element does not
              contain a recognized credential format" );

        Enumeration children = element.getChildren(
          "PeerGroupID");
        if( !children.hasMoreElements() )
            throw new RuntimeException( "Missing PeerGroupID
              Element" );

        PeerGroupID peergroup = (PeerGroupID) IDFactory.fromURL(
          new URL( (String) ((Element)
          children.nextElement()).getValue() ) );
        if( children.hasMoreElements() )
Line 260:           throw new RuntimeException( "Extra
                    PeerGroupID Elements" );

        children = element.getChildren( "PeerID" );
        if( !children.hasMoreElements() )
            throw new RuntimeException(
              "Missing PeerID Element" );

        PeerID peer = (PeerID) IDFactory.fromURL( new URL(
          (String) ((Element) children.nextElement()).getValue() )
          );
        if( children.hasMoreElements() )
            throw new RuntimeException( "Extra PeerID Elements" );

Line 270:       children = element.getChildren( "Identity" );
        if( !children.hasMoreElements() )
          throw new RuntimeException("Missing PeerID Element");

        String whoami = (String) ((Element)
          children.nextElement()).getValue();
```

Listing 15.5 Code for the UpdatedPasswdMembership Service. (continues)

```
            if( children.hasMoreElements() )
                throw new RuntimeException( "Extra Identity Elements" );

            children = element.getChildren( "ReallyInsecureSignature" );
            if( !children.hasMoreElements() )
Line 280:                  throw new RuntimeException( "Missing
                            'ReallyInsecureSignature' Element" );

            String signedPeerID = (String) ((Element)
             children.nextElement()).getValue();
            if( children.hasMoreElements() )
                throw new RuntimeException( "Extra
                   'ReallyInsecureSignature' Elements" );

            return new PasswdCredential( this, peergroup, peer,
              whoami, signedPeerID );
        }

    private boolean checkPasswd( String identity, String passwd ) {
Lien 290:        boolean result;

        result = passwd.equals(makePsswd("password"));

        return result;
        }

    public static String makePsswd( String source ) {

        final String xlateTable = "DQKWHRTENOGXCVYSFJPILZABMU";
Line 300:
        StringBuffer work = new StringBuffer( source );

        for( int eachChar = work.length() - 1; eachChar >=0;
         eachChar- ) {
            char aChar = Character.toUpperCase(
              work.charAt(eachChar) );
            int replaceIdx = xlateTable.indexOf( aChar );
            if( -1 != replaceIdx )
                work.setCharAt( eachChar, (char) ('A' +
                replaceIdx) );
        }

Line 310:        return work.toString();
        }


    }
```

Listing 15.5   Code for the UpdatedPasswdMembership Service. (continued)

Changing the Name of the Class

If you are working from the code in Chapter 12, all references to the class name passwdMembershipService must be changed to UpdatedPasswdMembershipService.

Updating the PasswdAuthenticator Constructor

When the membership service instantiates a new authenticator object, the object expects to receive an AuthenticationCredential. The credential is sent to the membership service by the client wanting to join the peer group. In the constructor for the AuthenticationCredential, the calling object, a membershipService, and the AuthenticationCredential object are stored in object attributes. In the default password membership service code, the credential is simply stored and never used. In the new code, the login and password values are extracted from the credential and stored as well.

Lines 93 through 121 of Listing 15.5 represent the new authenticator class constructor. Lines 98 through 120 pull the login and password elements from the credential document. The entire AuthenticationCredential XML structure is

```
<?xml version="1.0"?>

<!DOCTYPE AuthenticationCredential>

<AuthenticationCredential>
       <Method>
               UpdatedPasswdAuthentication
       </Method>
       <PeerGroupID>
               urn:jxta:uuid-DCEF4386EAED4908BE25CE5019EA02
       </PeerGroupID>
       <PeerID>
               urn:jxta:uuid-
59616261646162614A787461503250335CC7FEC3CCB14C3984E9B261BF19BE6803
       </PeerID>
       <IdentityInfo>
               <Identity>
                       <login>
                               username
                       </login>
                       <password>
                               SWPPDJFA
                       </password>
               </Identity>
       </IdentityInfo>
</AuthenticationCredential>
```

Line 100 pulls the <Identity> element from the full XML document. Line 101 pulls all of the children for the <Identity> element. Each element is compared to the string's login and password. When the login and password are found, the respective values are stored in object attributes for later use.

Changing the init() method of the Membership Service Class

When the default password membership service is first initialized, the login and password for the peer group is pulled from the peer group advertisement. We will no longer need the values in the advertisement, so we can remove the code for pulling the values from the init() method. The new init() method appears in lines 175 through 182.

Changing the checkPasswd() Method

The other code change needed for the password membership service is comparing the password sent by the peer and the password for the secure peer group. Since we pulled the login and password value from the advertisement, it needs to be located in another location. The checkPasswd() method handles the comparison (the current code is located in lines 289 through 295). For our example, the password is hard-coded; however, this method is a good example of where a call to a database would be useful. The authenticator has the current login and password, and the password is encrypted and secure. A secure call could be made to the database to obtain the necessary login information. By adding information to the credential, we could instruct the system to place a new login and password if one is not found in the database.

Changing the Peer Group Creator Code

The new membership service isn't useful without a peer group. In the directory chapter 18/example1/creator located in the downloaded source code, you'll find an application called Example1.java. This code is identical to the code in Chapter 12 for creating and using a secure peer group, except that the new code uses the UpdatedPasswdMembershipService class instead of PasswdMembershipService. Several important changes occur in the joinGroup() method as well.

Creating a Credential

The code in the joinGroup() method is responsible for handling and making the necessary calls to the membership service of a particular peer group. The code for the method is:

```
Line 1:    void joinGroup(PeerGroup myLocalGroup) {
      try {
```

```
        MembershipService myMembershipService =
          myLocalGroup.getMembershipService();

        StructuredTextDocument myCredentials =
          (StructuredTextDocument)
      StructuredDocumentFactory.new          StructuredDocument(
          new MimeMediaType("text/xml"), "Identity");
        myCredentials.appendChild(myCredentials.createElement("login",
  "username"));
        myCredentials.appendChild(myCredentials.createElement("password
  ", UpdatedPasswdMembershipService.makePsswd("password")));

Line 10:        AuthenticationCredential
                  myAuthenticationCredential
                  = new AuthenticationCredential(myLocalGroup,
                  "UpdatedPasswdAuthentication",
                  myCredentials);
        net.jxta.membership.Authenticator myAuthenticator =
          myMembershipService.apply(myAuthenticationCredential);

        if (!myAuthenticator.isReadyForJoin()) {
          displayArea.append("Authenticator is not
            complete\n");
          return;
        }
        myMembershipService.join(myAuthenticator);
        displayArea.append("Group has been joined\n");
      } catch (Exception e) {
Line 20:          displayArea.append("Authentication failed -
              group not joined\n");
        e.printStackTrace();
        System.exit(-1);
      }
    }
```

Line 3 obtains the membership service associated with the peer group sent to the method. You'll recall that the peer group sent to the method is the new group we have created and now want to join. Lines 4 through 8 build the credential XML document necessary for this peer. Notice that the password is encrypted before being placed in the credential.

Line 10 obtains an AuthenticationCredential, which will contain the name of the method the membership service we should use for joining the group as well as the credential necessary for the join. The AuthenticationCredential is really just an XML container document, as described earlier.

Line 11 attempts to apply to the membership service for access to the peer group. The membership service code will instantiate a new authenticator object and extract the information we put in our credential. When the apply() method of the membership service is called, the authentication method given in line 10 will be checked in an IF statement. If the method isn't named Updated-PasswdAuthentication, an error will occur. This adds another level of protection to the system, and allows different methods to be used for different peers.

Line 13 will request that the authenticator check to be sure all necessary information is available to attempt a join. Line 17 will attempt a join to the peer group. The join is accomplished in the join() method of the membership service. The password of the peer group or a password located in a database is checked against the password provided by the peer trying to access the new peer group. If the check is successful, the peer will have joined the group; otherwise, an exception will be thrown.

The new membership service and the code for creating and joining a new peer group provide another skeleton for building robust and secure systems.

Secure Transport

If two peers have gone through all the trouble of using password protection to join a common peer group, it is a good bet that they will also want to be sure that information transferred via a pipe is also secure. In this section, we consider three ways to build that secure pipe between peers:

- Using unicast and secure pipes as defined by JXTA
- Using JXTASPEC from the JXTA Security Toolkit
- Using our own encryption for data

JxtaUnicastSecure Pipes

If you look back at the examples in Chapter 12 and Chapter 13, the pipe advertisement used to let peers know about an available input pipe is

```
<?xml version="1.0" encoding="UTF-8"?>
<jxta:PipeAdvertisement>
    <Name>JXTA-CH15EX2</Name>
    <Id>urn:jxta:uuid-
9CCCDF5AD8154D3D87A391210404E59BE4B888209A2241A4A162A10916074A9504
</Id>
    <Type>JxtaUnicast</Type>
</jxta:PipeAdvertisement>
```

The element <Type> represents the type of pipe being advertised. The JXTA Pipe Service allows three different types of pipes:

JxtaUnicast—Unicast, unreliable, and non-secure pipe

JxtaUnicastSecure—Unicast and secure pipe

JxtaPropagate—Propagated, unreliable, and non-secure pipe

A quick and easy way to provide encrypted data transfer between clients is to use a pipe defined as JxtaUnicastSecure. The process is very simple; just change the <Type> element from JxtaUnicast to JxtaUnicastSecure, and the pipe is instantly encrypted. Note that using a secure pipe for all communication slows performance because the system has to encrypt and decrypt all of the data sent through the pipe.

The code for using a JxtaUnicastSecure pipe is identical to that found in the examples from Chapter 12, except that the advertisement has been changed to

```xml
<?xml version="1.0" encoding="UTF-8"?>
<jxta:PipeAdvertisement>
      <Name>JXTA-CH15EX2</Name>
      <Id>urn:jxta:uuid-9CCCDF5AD8154D3D87A39
          1210404E59BE4B888209A2241A4A162A10916074A9504</Id>
      <Type>JxtaUnicastSecure</Type>
</jxta:PipeAdvertisement>
```

The process of building a secure pipe is so simple that it you might question its effectiveness, so a quick view of the code is warranted to explain how the pipe is secured. The code for a secure output pipe is located in a file called Secure-OutputPipe.java, which builds a new class representing the secure pipe. After looking through the code, you will find a method called mkAddress(), which is responsible for building the endpoint address of the destination peer. Within the method are two key statements:

```java
PeerID asID = (PeerID) IDFactory.fromURL(new
  URL(destPeer));
String asString = "jxtatls://" +
  asID.getUniqueValue().toString();
EndpointAddress addr =
  endpoint.newEndpointAddress(asString);
```

The first statement of this code snippet builds a PeerID object from the URL of the destination peer. The second statement creates a string to be used in the third statement, which creates an EndpointAddress. Of particular importance is the use of the jxtatls qualifier; this qualifier dictates whether or not the pipe is secure. Before we get into the specifics of what this qualifier does, a quick look at the code for a secure input pipe finds the same qualifier used when a message is received through the pipe:

```java
if (!proto.equals ("jxtatls")) {
```

When a new message is received through the secure pipe, one of the first statements encountered is this if statement. If the message received through the pipe was not received using the JXTATLS protocol, the message is discarded.

TLS/SSL

The natural question to ask at this point is: What does the JXTATLS protocol do? TLS is an Internet specification for ensuring the secure transfer of data across unsecured lines. The most common form of this type of security is SSL—TLS is a newer specification and an implementation of SSL.

JXTATLS is built using the PureTLS system, developed by Claymore Systems, which implements the SSLv3 and TLSv1 protocols with the following cipher suites:

- TLS_DHE_DSS_WITH_DES_CBC_SHA
- TLS_DHE_DSS_WITH_3DES_EDE_CBC_SHA
- TLS_RSA_WITH_DES_CBC_SHA
- TLS_RSA_WITH_RC4_128_MD5
- TLS_RSA_WITH_RC4_128_SHA
- TLS_RSA_EXPORT_WITH_RC4_40_MD5
- TLS_RSA_EXPORT_WITH_RC2_CBC_40_MD5
- TLS_RSA_EXPORT_WITH_DES40_CBC_SHA

By using the PureTLS system, we ensure that all of the details for certificate generation and subsequent encryption of our data is solved for us. Again, looking through the JXTA source code, we find that the cipher used for the certs and encryption in JXTA is TLS_RSA_WITH_RC4_128_SHA encryption, which provides a high level of encryption.

Separately Encrypted Data

The JXTA Security Project allows for the encrypting of data to be sent from peer to peer without relying on a secure channel. By using the toolkit, you can determine how data is encrypted before being sent to another peer. The encrypted data can be sent along a secure pipe or an non-secure pipe, as needed by the application. The code, which we will present here using the JXTA Security Toolkit, also shows how to create dynamic pipes between peers in a group and how to use those pipes for bi-directional communication. For our purposes, we will use the RSA public key portion of the toolkit. Because of the nature of RSA encryption, only 53 bytes of space are available for each "packet" to be encrypted; the other 11 bytes are used for padding and other purposes. Keep this limitation in mind when designing your application. If larger buffers are necessary, use one of the other ciphers in the toolkit.

Our example includes two applications: a server and a client. The server application publishes an advertisement about a pipe it has available and creates two

RSA public-key encryption keys. The pipe accepts two different commands: RequestKey and EncryptedData. The client will send two messages when buttons are pressed—first to request a public encryption key and second to send encrypted data to the server.

The process begins with the execution of the server. Figure 15.1 shows the execution, security key creation, and publishing of the pipe advertisement. After the pipe advertisement is published, the server creates an input pipe and waits for messages to be received. Next, the client connects to the JXTA network and finds the pipe advertisement. Once the pipe advertisement is found (either locally or remotely), the client builds an output pipe and attempts the connection to the server's input pipe.

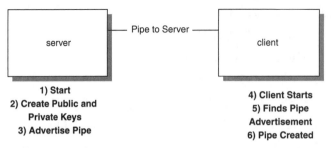

Figure 15.1 Server and client execution.

When the user clicks the Send Key Request button on the client's GUI, several tasks are fulfilled by the client. First, a dynamic pipe advertisement is created; then an input pipe is created. This new pipe will allow the server application to send the requested public encryption key to the peer. Second, the pipe advertisement is bundled into a message along with a tag value of *RequestedKey*. Third, the message is sent to the server, as shown in Figure 15.2.

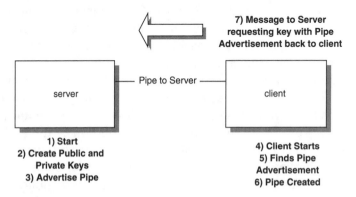

Figure 15.2 Key request from the client.

Figure 15.3 shows the remainder of the process. The server will receive the message from the client. The pipe advertisement from the message is extracted, and an output pipe is connected to the client's new input pipe. The public encryption key previously created by the server is "serialized" and sent to the client. The client receives the public encryption key over its new input pipe and builds a valid RSA public key out of the serialized data. A test byte string is encrypted and sent to the server in a message with a tag value of *Encrypted-Data*.

Finally, the server application receives the encrypted data over its previously published pipe, and decrypts the data using its private key. It then displays the data.

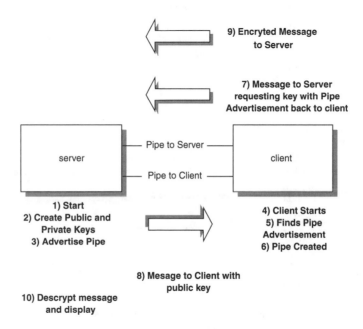

Figure 15.3 The public key is sent to the client and used to encrypt data; the server decrypts data with the private key.

The code in Listing 15.6 illustrates how to handle the reception of data on a pipe that needs to be both plain and encrypted text. We could change the code to open a secure pipe between the peers as well. In the remainder of this section, we discuss the code in detail.

The Server Code

The code for the server appears in Listing 15.6. The base code in this example was taken from the code found in Chapter 12. The code discussion that follows the code listing will highlight those changes necessary for using the JXTA Security Project and the data exchange between the peers.

```
Line 1: import java.io.*;
import java.awt.*;
import java.awt.event.*;
import javax.swing.*;

import net.jxta.document.*;
import net.jxta.peergroup.*;
import net.jxta.exception.PeerGroupException;
import net.jxta.impl.peergroup.Platform;
Line 10: import net.jxta.impl.peergroup.GenericPeerGroup;
import net.jxta.id.*;
import net.jxta.discovery.DiscoveryService;
import net.jxta.protocol.*;
import net.jxta.platform.ModuleClassID;
import net.jxta.endpoint.Message;
import net.jxta.pipe.*;

import jxta.security.exceptions.CryptoException;
import jxta.security.util.Util;
Line 20: import jxta.security.util.GetOpt;
import java.lang.IllegalArgumentException;
import jxta.security.publickey.RSAPublickeyData;
import jxta.security.publickey.RSAPrivatekeyData;

import jxta.security.impl.publickey.RSAKey;
import jxta.security.impl.publickey.RSA;
import jxta.security.impl.cipher.KeyBuilder;


Line 30:public class Example3 extends JFrame {

    static  PeerGroup netPeerGroup = null;
    private DiscoveryService myDiscoveryService = null;
    private PipeService myPipeService = null;
    private ModuleClassID myService1ID = null;
    private InputPipe myPipe = null;
    private OutputPipe myOutputPipe = null;
    private JTextArea displayArea;

Line 40:    private final static     MimeMediaType XMLMIMETYPE =
        new MimeMediaType("text/xml");

    RSAKey rKey;
    RSA rsa;
    RSAPublickeyData rPublicD;
    RSAPrivatekeyData rPrivateD;

    public static void main(String args[]) {
```

Listing 15.6 The server code for encrypted data and the dynamic pipe example. (continues)

```
        Example3 myapp = new Example3();

Line 50:          myapp.addWindowListener (
          new WindowAdapter() {
             public void windowClosing(WindowEvent e) {
                System.exit(0);
             }
           }
         );

         myapp.run();
      }
Line 60:
      public Example3() {
         super("Server");

         Container c = getContentPane();

         displayArea = new JTextArea();
         c.add (new JScrollPane(displayArea), BorderLayout.CENTER);

         setSize(300,150);
Line 70:        show();

         launchJXTA();
         getServices();
         doSecurity();
         buildModuleAdvertisement();
         buildModuleSpecificationAdvertisement(
           createPipeAdvertisement());


      }

Line 80:    public void run() {
         displayArea.append("Waiting for message...\n");
      }

      private void launchJXTA() {
         displayArea.append("Launching Peer into JXTA
            Network...\n");
         try {
            netPeerGroup = PeerGroupFactory.newNetPeerGroup();
         } catch (PeerGroupException e) {
            System.out.println("Unable to create PeerGroup -
               Failure");
Line 90:             e.printStackTrace();
            System.exit(1);
         }
```

Listing 15.6 The server code for encrypted data and the dynamic pipe example. (continues)

```
      }

   private void getServices() {
      displayArea.append("Obtaining Discovery and Pipe
        Services....\n");
      myDiscoveryService = netPeerGroup.getDiscoveryService();
      myPipeService = netPeerGroup.getPipeService();
   }
Line 100:
   private void doSecurity() {
      try {
        rKey = (RSAKey)KeyBuilder.buildKey(KeyBuilder.TYPE_RSA,
          KeyBuilder.LENGTH_RSA_512, false);
        rsa = new RSA(rKey);
        rsa.setPublicKey();
        rsa.setPrivateKey();
        rPublicD = (RSAPublickeyData)rsa.getPublickey();
        rPrivateD = (RSAPrivatekeyData)rsa.getPrivatekey();

Line 110:    } catch (Exception e) {
         System.out.println("Error during RSA initialization");
         System.exit(-1);
      }
   }


   private void buildModuleAdvertisement() {
      ModuleClassAdvertisement myService1ModuleAdvertisement =
        (ModuleClassAdvertisement)
        AdvertisementFactory.newAdvertisement(
        ModuleClassAdvertisement.getAdvertisementType());

      myService1ModuleAdvertisement.setName("JXTAMOD:JXTA-
        CH18EX3");
Line 120: myService1ModuleAdvertisement.setDescription("Service 1
        of Chapter 18 example 3");

      myService1ID = IDFactory.newModuleClassID();
   myService1ModuleAdvertisement.setModuleClassID(myService1ID);
      displayArea.append("Publishing our Module
        Advertisement....\n");
      try {
         myDiscoveryService.publish(myService1ModuleAdvertisement,
  DiscoveryService.ADV);
myDiscoveryService.remotePublish(myService1ModuleAdvertisement,
  DiscoveryService.ADV);
      } catch (Exception e) {
Line 130:         System.out.println("Error during publish of
    Module Advertisement");
```

Listing 15.6 The server code for encrypted data and the dynamic pipe example. (continues)

```
            System.exit(-1);
          }
      }

      private PipeAdvertisement createPipeAdvertisement() {
        PipeAdvertisement myPipeAdvertisement = null;

        try {
          FileInputStream is = new FileInputStream("service1.adv");
Line 140:          myPipeAdvertisement =
            (PipeAdvertisement)AdvertisementFactory.newAdvertisement(
   new MimeMediaType("text/xml"), is);
        } catch (Exception e) {
            System.out.println("failed to read/parse pipe
   advertisement");
              e.printStackTrace();
            System.exit(-1);
        }

        return myPipeAdvertisement;
      }

Line 150:     private void
buildModuleSpecificationAdvertisement(PipeAdvertisement
   myPipeAdvertisement) {

      ModuleSpecAdvertisement myModuleSpecAdvertisement =
        (ModuleSpecAdvertisement)
        AdvertisementFactory.newAdvertisement(
        ModuleSpecAdvertisement.getAdvertisementType());

      myModuleSpecAdvertisement.setName("JXTASPEC:JXTA-CH18EX3");
      myModuleSpecAdvertisement.setVersion("Version 1.0");
      myModuleSpecAdvertisement.setCreator("gradecki.com");
      myModuleSpecAdvertisement.setModuleSpecID(
          IDFactory.newModuleSpecID(myService1ID));
      myModuleSpecAdvertisement.setSpecURI(
          "<http://www.jxta.org/CH18EX3>");
myModuleSpecAdvertisement.setPipeAdvertisement(
   myPipeAdvertisement);
Line 160:        displayArea.append("Publishing Module
     Specification Advertisement....\n");
      try {
        myDiscoveryService.publish(myModuleSpecAdvertisement,
            DiscoveryService.ADV);
        myDiscoveryService.remotePublish(myModuleSpecAdvertisement,
   DiscoveryService.ADV);
      } catch (Exception e) {
```

Listing 15.6 The server code for encrypted data and the dynamic pipe example. (continues)

```
              System.out.println("Error during publish of Module
                Specification Advertisement");
              e.printStackTrace();
              System.exit(-1);
          }
Line 170:
          createInputPipe(myPipeAdvertisement);
      }

      private void createInputPipe(PipeAdvertisement
       myPipeAdvertisement) {
        displayArea.append("Creating Input Pipe....\n");

        PipeMsgListener myService1Listener = new PipeMsgListener() {
          public void pipeMsgEvent(PipeMsgEvent event) {
            Message myMessage = null;
            try {
Line 180:            myMessage = event.getMessage();

            String myMessageContent;

            myMessageContent = myMessage.getString("RequestKey");
            if (myMessageContent != null) {
              createOutputPipe(myMessageContent);
              sendKey();
              return;
            }
Line 190:            myMessageContent =
                      myMessage.getString("EncryptedData");
            if (myMessageContent != null) {
              byte[] encryptedBytes =
                 myMessageContent.getBytes();
              byte[] decryptedBytes;

              try {
                rsa.setPrivateKey(rPrivateD);
                decryptedBytes = rsa.Algorithm(encryptedBytes, 0,
                  encryptedBytes.length,
                  KeyBuilder.TYPE_RSA_PRIVATE, false);
              } catch (Exception eee) {
                eee.printStackTrace();
Line 200:              System.out.println("Unable to
                              decrypt\n");
                return;
              }
              String newString = new String(decryptedBytes);
              displayArea.append("Message received: " + newString
              + "\n");
```

Listing 15.6 The server code for encrypted data and the dynamic pipe example. (continues)

```
                        return;
                } else {
                        displayArea.append("Invalid tag\n");
                        return;
                }
Line 210:              } catch (Exception ee) {
                        ee.printStackTrace();
                        return;
                }
             }
         };

        try {
          myPipe =
             myPipeService.createInputPipe(myPipeAdvertisement,
             myService1Listener);
        } catch (Exception e) {
Line 220:            System.out.println("Error creating Input
                        Pipe");
             e.printStackTrace();
             System.exit(-1);
        }
      }

    private void createOutputPipe(String
      myPipeAdvertisementString) {
       boolean noPipe = true;
       int count = 0;

Line 230:      PipeAdvertisement myOutputPipeAdvertisement = null;
        try {
          myOutputPipeAdvertisement = (PipeAdvertisement)
           AdvertisementFactory.newAdvertisement(XMLMIMETYPE,
           new ByteArrayInputStream(
           myPipeAdvertisementString.getBytes()));
        } catch (Exception e) {
            System.out.println("Error creating output Pipe");
            e.printStackTrace();
            System.exit(-1);
        }

Line 240:      myOutputPipe = null;
        while (noPipe && count < 10) {
          count++;
          try {
            myOutputPipe =
             myPipeService.createOutputPipe(
```

Listing 15.6 The server code for encrypted data and the dynamic pipe example. (continues)

```
                    myOutputPipeAdvertisement, 100000);
                displayArea.append("Output Pipe Created...\n");
                noPipe = false;
              } catch (Exception e) {
                System.out.println("Unable to create output pipe");
                System.exit(-1);
Line 250:         }
          }

          if (count >= 10) {
            System.out.println("no Pipe");
            System.exit(-1);
          }
        }

        private void sendKey() {
Line 260:
          byte[] myBytes = rPublicD.getModulus();
          ByteArrayOutputStream myStream = null;
          try {
            myStream = (ByteArrayOutputStream) new
                ByteArrayOutputStream();
            myStream.write(myBytes, 0, myBytes.length);
          } catch (Exception e) {
            System.out.println("Unable encode public key");
            e.printStackTrace();
            System.exit(-1);
Line 270:     }

          Message msg = myPipeService.createMessage();
          msg.setString("RequestedKey", myStream.toString() );

          try {
            myOutputPipe.send (msg);
          } catch (Exception e) {
            System.out.println("Unable to print output pipe");
            e.printStackTrace();
Line 280:         System.exit(-1);
          }

          displayArea.append("key sent to the Server\n");
        }
      }
```

Listing 15.6 The server code for encrypted data and the dynamic pipe example. (continued)

Security ToolKit Initialization

Before any of the Security Toolkit methods can be used, the toolkit itself must be initialized. For our current example, only the RSA Public Encryption functionality will be used.

Lines 18 through 27 list the required imports for the toolkit functionality required in the application. The actual code for the toolkit is found in the security JAR file. The JAR file has been listed in the compile and run commands for all of our previous examples, so no change needs to occur when compiling and executing the server application.

Line 74 makes a call to the doSecurity() method from the constructor. Lines 101 through 108 build the doSecurity() method.

Line 103 executes the buildKey() method of the KeyBuilder class, which creates a new object of type RSAKey and sets the desired length of RSA keys to be 512 bits using the constant identifier LENGTH_RSA_512.

Line 104 instantiates a RSA object using the RSAKEY object instantiated from line 103. The RSA object is needed for all subsequent encryption operations.

Lines 105 and 106 call methods to build dynamic public and private keys. Methods are available in the RSA object for setting the public and private keys to values previously calculated, but our intent is to have secure data that is built using different keys each time the server is executed. We can change the code so that a new private and public key are generated each time a client requests the key. To do this, move the setPublicKey() and setPrivateKey() methods found in lines 105 and 106 to the pipe listener code.

Lines 107 and 108 extract the private and public keys for later reference. In our case, the public key will be serialized and sent to the client peer so it can encrypt its data for our eyes only.

Of course, if any of these operations fail, an exception will be thrown and the application halted.

Advertised Pipe Message Reception

Most all of the work for the server occurs in the listener handler for its input pipe. All messages received will be filtered by two tags and actions will be taken when the appropriate tag is received.

Lines 177 through 215 build the listener class for the input pipe. Line 184 pulls any data associated with the key tag labeled RequestKey. The getString() method will check the tag value for the current message and return a string if the tag is the same as the tag. Otherwise, the method will return null.

Lines 185 through 189 check the value of the returned string, and execute if the value is not null. If the value is not null, then a message has been received from a client requesting the server send its public key. The idea is that the client wants to send encrypted data to the server, but needs its public key first. Now, we certainly have room to expand the application at this point. Can we trust the client? What if the client wants to send us illegal information? Right now, let's just assume the client has good intentions. In addition to the basic request for the server's public key (as noted by the tag value of *RequestKey*), the information in the message must be a pipe advertisement. The call on line 186 will send the message string to the method createOutputPipe() in order to build an output pipe with the requesting client.

Lines 226 through 257 represent the code for the createOutputPipe() method, and build the output pipe by creating a PipeAdvertisement object and passing the object to the createOutputPipe() method of the PipeService on line 244. If the pipe advertisement sent from the client is valid, a new pipe connection will have been established.

Once the output pipe has been created, a call is made to the sendKey() method.

Sending the Public Key

When the client requests the public key from the server, it will send a pipe advertisement, and the server will build a pipe connection. Once the pipe connection is created, the server will send the actual public key. Because the public key is a Java object, it will need to be converted in some way to allow it to be sent down the pipe connection. Obviously, the most appropriate way would have been to use an ObjectOutputStream; however, the public key object wasn't built to implement the serializable interface. Fortunately, the modulus associated with the public can be grabbed since it is just an array of bytes and can be used to fully reconstruct the public key. The modulus can also be used to build the public key by the recipient.

Lines 259 through 285 define the sendKey() method for the server. Line 261 pulls the modulus from the public key and places it in an array of bytes. Lines 262 through 270 convert the bytes into a string, which can be sent to the client. A ByteArrayOutputStream is used for the conversion.

Lines 272 through 273 create a message and populate the message with the serialized public key. The RequestedKey tag is used for the message since this is what the client is expecting to receive. Line 276 sends the public key to the client.

As mentioned earlier, if we wanted to build a new private and public key each time a client peer requested a key, we could call the setPublicKey() and setPrivateKey() methods of the RSA object here before pulling the modulus from the public key.

Handling the Encrypted Data

The last process the server will need to handle is decrypting data that has been previously encrypted by a client. The current code expects to decrypt data based on the public key sent, and thus isn't designed to handle decrypting data based on multiple public/private key pairs. The code for handling the decryption is located in the input pipe listener class. Recall that the same code also obtains the request from a client for a public key. The code will check for a string associated with the RequestKey tag first. If the method returns a value of null, the code will check for a tag with a value of *EncryptedData*.

Lines 190 through 205 handles the decryption of client data. Line 190 attempts to pull any data string associated with the EncryptedData tag. Line 191 checks for a valid string from the method in line 190. If the value is not null, an attempt is made to decrypt the string.

Lines 192 through 204 do the encryption process. The first step is to convert the string into a byte string. Line 193 does this using the getBytes() method of the string we received from the client. A new byte array variable is created to hold the newly encrypted bytes.

The real work occurs in line 197 with a call to the Algorithm() method of the RSA object. The method takes the encrypted bytes and the type of key to use for the decryption. Since the public key was used for the encryption, we have to state that the private key should be used for the decryption.

The last parameter in the method is a Boolean that indicates whether the algorithm should be used for encryption or decryption. A value of *false* is used for decryption. The result of the method is a byte array, which we hope are the original bytes encrypted by the client.

The Client Code

The client is the controller application for our security communication example. Activities occur in the client until the user clicks the Send Key Request or Send Encrypted Data button. Just as in the server application, the code was taken from Chapter 12. Additional button code was added for the Send Encrypted Data functionality, and the code necessary to receive and process a serialized public key. The code for the client is shown in Listing 15.7.

```
import java.io.*;
import java.awt.*;
import java.awt.event.*;
import javax.swing.*;


import java.util.Enumeration;
import net.jxta.document.*;
import net.jxta.peergroup.*;
Line 10: import net.jxta.exception.PeerGroupException;
import net.jxta.impl.peergroup.Platform;
import net.jxta.impl.peergroup.GenericPeerGroup;
import net.jxta.id.*;
import net.jxta.discovery.*;
import net.jxta.pipe.*;
import net.jxta.protocol.*;
import java.net.MalformedURLException;
import java.net.URL;
import net.jxta.endpoint.Message;
Line 20:
import jxta.security.exceptions.CryptoException;
import jxta.security.util.Util;
import jxta.security.util.GetOpt;
import java.lang.IllegalArgumentException;
import jxta.security.publickey.RSAPublickeyData;
import jxta.security.publickey.RSAPrivatekeyData;

import jxta.security.impl.publickey.RSAKey;
import jxta.security.impl.publickey.RSA;
Line 30: import jxta.security.impl.cipher.KeyBuilder;

public class Example3 extends JFrame {

    static  PeerGroup                netPeerGroup = null;
    private DiscoveryService          myDiscoveryService = null;
    private PipeService        myPipeService = null;
    private PipeAdvertisement myPipeAdvertisement = null,
                              myInputPipeAdvertisement = null;
    private OutputPipe        myOutputPipe;
Line 40:    private InputPipe       myInputPipe;
    private JTextArea          displayArea;
    private JButton         sendButton;
    private String          valueString = "JXTA-CH15EX2";

    private final static      MimeMediaType XMLMIMETYPE =
      new MimeMediaType("text/xml");
```

Listing 15.7 The client code for encrypted data and the dynamic pipe example. (continues)

```
    RSAKey rKey;
    RSA rsa;
    RSAPublickeyData rPublicD;
Line 50:

    public static void main(String args[]) {
        Example3 myapp = new Example3();

        myapp.addWindowListener (
         new WindowAdapter() {
            public void windowClosing(WindowEvent e) {
              System.exit(0);
            }
Line 60:            }
        );

        myapp.launchJXTA();
        myapp.getServices();
        myapp.createInputPipe();
        myapp.findAdvertisement("Name",
          "JXTASPEC:JXTA-CH18EX3");
        myapp.run();
    }

Line 70:
    public Example3() {
      super("client");

      Container c = getContentPane();

      sendButton = new JButton("Send Key Request");
      sendButton.addActionListener(
        new ActionListener() {
          public void actionPerformed(ActionEvent e) {
Line 80:            sendKeyRequest();
          }
        }
      );
      c.add(sendButton, BorderLayout.NORTH);

      sendButton = new JButton("Send encrypted data");
      sendButton.addActionListener(
        new ActionListener() {
          public void actionPerformed(ActionEvent e) {
Line 90:            sendEncryptedData();
          }
        }
```

Listing 15.7 The client code for encrypted data and the dynamic pipe example. (continues)

```
        );
      c.add(sendButton, BorderLayout.SOUTH);


      displayArea = new JTextArea();
      c.add(new JScrollPane(displayArea), BorderLayout.CENTER);

Line 100:        setSize(300,150);
      show();
    }

    public void run() {
      displayArea.append("Click on Button to send data...\n");
    }

    private void launchJXTA() {
        displayArea.append("Launching Peer into JXTA
          Network...\n");
Line 110:          try {
            netPeerGroup = PeerGroupFactory.newNetPeerGroup();
        } catch (PeerGroupException e) {
          System.out.println("Unable to create PeerGroup -
            Failure");
          e.printStackTrace();
          System.exit(1);
        }
    }

    private void getServices() {
Line 120:        displayArea.append("Getting Services...\n");
      myDiscoveryService = netPeerGroup.getDiscoveryService();
      myPipeService = netPeerGroup.getPipeService();
    }


    private void createInputPipe() {
      displayArea.append("Creating Input Pipe....\n");

      myInputPipeAdvertisement = (PipeAdvertisement)
        AdvertisementFactory.newAdvertisement(
        PipeAdvertisement.getAdvertisementType());
Line 130:        myInputPipeAdvertisement.
              setName("JXTA:KEYRECEIVE");
      myInputPipeAdvertisement.setType("JxtaUnicast");
      myInputPipeAdvertisement.setPipeID((ID)
        net.jxta.id.IDFactory.newPipeID(
        netPeerGroup.getPeerGroupID()));
```

Listing 15.7 The client code for encrypted data and the dynamic pipe example. (continues)

```
        PipeMsgListener myService1Listener = new PipeMsgListener() {
          public void pipeMsgEvent(PipeMsgEvent event) {
            Message myMessage = null;
            try {
              myMessage = event.getMessage();
Line 140:
              String myMessageContent;

              myMessageContent =
                myMessage.getString("RequestedKey");
              if (myMessageContent != null) {
                doSecurity(myMessageContent);
                return;
              } else {
                displayArea.append("Invalid tag\n");
                return;
Line 150:             }
            } catch (Exception ee) {
                ee.printStackTrace();
                return;
            }
          }
        };

        try {
          myInputPipe = myPipeService.createInputPipe(
            myInputPipeAdvertisement, myService1Listener);
Line 160:      } catch (Exception e) {
            System.out.println("Error creating Input Pipe");
            e.printStackTrace();
            System.exit(-1);
        }
      }


    private void findAdvertisement(String searchKey,
      String searchValue) {
      Enumeration myLocalEnum = null;
Line 170:        displayArea.append("Trying to find
                advertisement...\n");

        try {
          myLocalEnum = myDiscoveryService.
            getLocalAdvertisements(DiscoveryService.ADV,
            searchKey, searchValue);
```

Listing 15.7 The client code for encrypted data and the dynamic pipe example. (continues)

```
        if ((myLocalEnum != null) &&
         myLocalEnum.hasMoreElements()) {
          displayArea.append("Found Local Advertisement...\n");
          ModuleSpecAdvertisement myModuleSpecAdv =
            (ModuleSpecAdvertisement)myLocalEnum.nextElement();

          myPipeAdvertisement =
            myModuleSpecAdv.getPipeAdvertisement();
Line 180:         createOutputPipe(myPipeAdvertisement);
        }
        else {
          DiscoveryListener myDiscoveryListener =
          new DiscoveryListener() {
            public void discoveryEvent(DiscoveryEvent e) {
              Enumeration enum;
              PipeAdvertisement pipeAdv = null;
              String str;

              displayArea.append("Found Remote
                Advertisement...\n");
Line 190:           DiscoveryResponseMsg myMessage =
                      e.getResponse();
              enum = myMessage.getResponses();
              str = (String)enum.nextElement();

              try {
                ModuleSpecAdvertisement myModSpecAdv =
                  (ModuleSpecAdvertisement)
                  AdvertisementFactory.  newAdvertisement(
                  XMLMIMETYPE,
                  new ByteArrayInputStream(str.getBytes()));
                myPipeAdvertisement =
                  myModSpecAdv.getPipeAdvertisement();

                createOutputPipe(myPipeAdvertisement);
              } catch(Exception ee) {
Line 200:                 ee.printStackTrace();
                System.exit(-1);
              }
            }
          };

          displayArea.append("Launching Remote Discovery
            Service...\n");
          myDiscoveryService.getRemoteAdvertisements(null,
            DiscoveryService.ADV, searchKey, searchValue, 1,
            myDiscoveryListener);
```

Listing 15.7 The client code for encrypted data and the dynamic pipe example. (continues)

```
                }
            } catch (Exception e) {
Line 210:              System.out.println("Error during
                          advertisement search");
              System.exit(-1);
            }
        }

    private void createOutputPipe(PipeAdvertisement
      myPipeAdvertisement) {
        boolean noPipe = true;
        int count = 0;

        myOutputPipe = null;
Line 220:       while (noPipe && count < 10) {
            count++;
            try {
              myOutputPipe = myPipeService.createOutputPipe(
                myPipeAdvertisement, 100000);
              displayArea.append("Output Pipe Created...\n");
              noPipe = false;
            } catch (Exception e) {
                System.out.println("Unable to create output pipe");
                System.exit(-1);
            }
Line 230:        }

        if (count >= 10) {
            System.out.println("no Pipe");
            System.exit(-1);
        }
    }

    private void sendKeyRequest() {

Line 240:       ByteArrayOutputStream myStream =
                  (ByteArrayOutputStream)
                  new ByteArrayOutputStream();
        StructuredTextDocument paramDoc =
          (StructuredTextDocument)myInputPipeAdvertisement.
          getDocument(new MimeMediaType("text/xml"));
        try {
          paramDoc.sendToStream(myStream);
        } catch (Exception e) {
            System.out.println("Unable to print output pipe");
            e.printStackTrace();
            System.exit(-1);
```

Listing 15.7 The client code for encrypted data and the dynamic pipe example. (continues)

```
        }

Line 250:   Message msg = myPipeService.createMessage();
        msg.setString("RequestKey", myStream.toString() );

        try {
          myOutputPipe.send (msg);
        } catch (Exception e) {
            System.out.println("Unable to print output pipe");
            e.printStackTrace();
            System.exit(-1);
        }
Line 260:     }

      private void sendEncryptedData() {
        String sendString = null;

        try {
          byte[] plainBytes =
            new byte[rsa.getMaxInputDataBlockLength()];
          for (int i=0;i<plainBytes.length;i++)
            plainBytes[i] = (byte)0xCC;

          byte[] encryptedBytes = rsa.Algorithm(plainBytes, 0,
            plainBytes.length, KeyBuilder.TYPE_RSA_PUBLIC, true);
Line 270:          sendString = new String(encryptedBytes);
        } catch (Exception e) {
            System.out.println("Unable to encrypted string");
            e.printStackTrace();
            System.exit(-1);
        }

        Message msg = myPipeService.createMessage();
        msg.setString("EncryptedData", sendString );

Line 280:     try {
          myOutputPipe.send (msg);
        } catch (Exception e) {
            System.out.println("Unable to print output pipe");
            e.printStackTrace();
            System.exit(-1);
        }

        displayArea.append("message \"" + sendString + "\" sent to
          the Server\n");
      }
Line 290:
```

Listing 15.7 The client code for encrypted data and the dynamic pipe example. (continues)

```
    void doSecurity(String myPublicKeyString) {

      try {
        rKey = (RSAKey)KeyBuilder.buildKey(KeyBuilder.TYPE_RSA,
          KeyBuilder.LENGTH_RSA_512, false);
        rsa = new RSA(rKey);
        rsa.setPublicKey(myPublicKeyString.getBytes());
      } catch (Exception e) {
          System.out.println("Unable to do client security\n");
          System.exit(-1);
      }
Line 300:    }
  }
```

Listing 15.7 The client code for encrypted data and the dynamic pipe example. (continued)

Public Key Request

When the user clicks the client button labeled Send Key Request, the client application will call the sendKeyRequest() method. This method creates a message containing the pipe advertisement for the input pipe that the client has created in order to receive the public key.

Lines 239 through 260 contain the code for the sendKeyRequest() method. Line 240 creates a stream object, which will be used to print the pipe advertisement for the client's input pipe. Line 241 obtains a document object containing an XML view of the pipe advertisement

Line 243 uses the sendToStream() method of the StructuredTextDocument object to move the text from the pipe advertisement to the output stream. Lines 250 and 251 create a message with a tag value of RequestKey and a string based on the output stream from the work done in lines 240 and 241.

Line 254 sends the request to the server. If and when the server responds to our request, the response will be caught by the client's input pipe listener, as we discuss in the next section.

Public-Key Reception

The client is designed to only process public key messages sent by the server over its input pipe. As in all JXTA applications we've built so far, the input pipe processing occurs in a listener object.

Lines 134 through 156 create the listener object for the client's input pipe. Lines 134 and 142 obtain any string value associated with the RequestedKey tag from a pipe message. If a value is available using this tag value (a potential public key string), the client will process the value using a method called doSecurity(). If the message received doesn't have the required tag, the message is ignored.

Once the security system has been initialized with the public key string received by the client, the system is ready to send encrypted data to the server.

Lines 290 through 301 represent the doSecurity() method. Lines 293 through 294 initialize the RSA objects, just as we did with the server. Line 295 sets the public key of the RSA system using the modules bytes found in the string from the server.

If any of the security initialization steps fail, an exception will occur and the application will be terminated.

Data Encryption

The final piece of the client that we should discuss involves the sending of encrypted data. The user clicks a button on the client's GUI when he or she wants to send encrypted data to the server. A method called sendEncrypted-Data() does the work of encrypting some sample data and sending the data to the server.

Lines 263 through 290 are the statements for the sendEncryptedData() method. Line 267 creates an array whose size is based on the largest position data block for the RSA system.

Line 268 fills the block with sample data. Line 269 calls the Algorithm() method to encrypt the data. As in the server code, the RSA algorithm requires the key to be used in the algorithm, and determines whether the code should encrypt or decrypt. A value of true indicates that the algorithm will encrypt the data.

Line 270 converts the bytes to a string. Lines 277 and 278 build a pipe message with a tag value of EncryptedData and a string representing the encrypted data.

Line 281 sends the message to the server,

Summary

In this chapter, we have taken a look at the ever-evolving issue of security with the JXTA network. Security is an important issue when client peers will be executing on remote machines. The new membership service built in this chapter provides the necessary foundation for a truly secure peer group. In the next chapter, we examine how individual peers in the JXTA network can query other peers about their state. Using the Peer Information Protocol, peers are able to respond automatically to such requests.

CHAPTER 16

Peer Monitoring and Metering

In a comprehensive peer-to-peer system, it is a good idea to build a peer that keeps track of the health and status of the network. The goal need not be the recording of IP information or other functions that raise privacy issues, but simply a way of providing network performance statistics. In this chapter, we discuss monitoring and metering between peers in a peer group. At the time of this writing, the Peer Information Protocol is in a state of flux and all of its functionality isn't in place. Unfortunately, this is the protocol used to obtain information about peers in your local peer group. On a positive note, there is enough functionality in the current protocol to pull valuable information from clients.

Finding Peers in a Group

Finding other peers in a peer group is a fundamental operation in JXTA, and specific discovery types are available to make the process as painless as possible. Most of the code for finding a peer on the local network is similar to the code for finding a pipe or a group to join. In this section, we present the code you need to use to find peers.

Building the Peer Discovery Listener

The process of discovering peers in a specific peer group is accomplished by sending a discovery message to the JXTA network specifying the advertisements that should be discovered. In previous chapters, we used the discovery service to accomplish this, and we will use it in this case as well.

Recall the method getRemoteAdvertisements() discussed in Chapter12. The purpose of this method is to send a query on the network. The type of query we want to perform is provided as the second parameter. To discover other peers, we must use the type DiscoveryService.PEER. We have the option of specifying a search parameter, such as "education", to find peers with a name containing the string "education". Or we can use the value null to find all peers on the network. The following is a sample method call:

```
myDiscoveryService.getRemoteAdvertisements(null,DiscoveryService.PEER,
        null, null, 5, peerDiscoveryListener);
```

When a peer is found, its peer advertisement will be returned and the listener provided by the last parameter, peerDiscoveryListener, will be activated to interpret the listener event.

Interpreting Events

When the listener is triggered, its primary responsibility is to interpret the event sent to it. In the case of the peer discovery event, a message will be found that contains the peer advertisement of discovered peers. The advertisements might appear as shown in Listing 16.1:

```
<?xml version="1.0"?>

<!DOCTYPE jxta:PA>

<jxta:PA xmlns:jxta="http://jxta.org">
        <PID>
                urn:jxta:uuid-
59616261646162614A787461503250337CE1ACE17356403D8EECBE6B9D25351303
        </PID>
        <GID>
                urn:jxta:jxta-NetGroup
        </GID>
        <Name>
                JosephGradeckiServer
        </Name>
        <Svc>
                <MCID>
                        urn:jxta:uuid-
DEADBEEFDEAFBABAFEEDBABE0000000805
                </MCID>
                <Parm>
                        <Addr>
```

Listing 16.1   Sample PeerInfoAdvertisement. (continues)

```
                              tcp://12.254.21.182:9701/
                    </Addr>
                    <Addr>
                              jxtatls://uuid-
59616261646162614A787461503250337CE1ACE17356403D8EECBE6B9D253513
03/TlsTransport/jxta-WorldGroup
                    </Addr>
                    <Addr>
                              jxta://uuid-
59616261646162614A787461503250337CE1ACE17356403D8EECBE6B9D25351303/
                    </Addr>
                    <Addr>
                              http://JxtaHttpClientuuid-
59616261646162614A787461503250337CE1ACE17356403D8EECBE6B9D25351303/
                    </Addr>
               </Parm>
        </Svc>
        <Svc>
             <MCID>
                    urn:jxta:uuid-
DEADBEEFDEAFBABAFEEDBABE0000000105
             </MCID>
             <Parm>
                    <RootCert>
MIICVDCCAb2gAwIBAgIBATANBgkqhkiG9w0BAQUFADByMRUw
EwYDVQQKEwx3d3cuanh0YS5vcmcxCzAJBgNVBAcTAlNGMQswCQYDVQQGEwJVUzEg
MB4GA1UEAxMXSm9zZXBoR3JhZGVja2IlTZXJ2ZXItQ0ExHTAbBgNVBAsTFDNFNjE3
OEQ4OTM5RTEzQkFDNjU3MB4XDTAyMDExMzE3MjYyMloXDTEyMDExMzE3MjYyMlow
cjEVMBMGA1UEChMMd3d3Lmp4dGEub3JnMQswCQYDVQQHEwJTRjELMAkGA1UEBhMC
VVMxIDAeBgNVBAMTF0pvc2VwaEdyYWRlY2tpU2VydmVyLUNBMR0wGwYDVQQLExQz
RTYxNzhEODkzOUUxM0JBQzY1NzCBmzALBgkqhkiG9w0BAQEDgYsAMIGHAoGBAKqJ
kZr0Ke3T3ZPNsmp/i1t3HYBVKVp4dMOKsDh0RDC3w3xt/LZ0LYA++ekBBUObNBUR
x7TYoTGXmEYWrVr0eYBbq4YUH4bfIARSs+VKoYxP0G0NrhaVt85rKuTmWHuLgHJQ
9G/rn8c3d/lXJktjRm6KkiNxMHBtY/D24wt0fG1AgERMA0GCSqGSIb3DQEBBQUAA
4GBAKWl2u21lQ/Taxv5vbeN7nxj500FUOfwz+ugG5Q6DKKiU39SgSyuCdB6PhI8A
FQhNuiXG5NkP7vtOieClfOvQ83VSxqxP1YUZiJvrzAu8/Sz87FtY4NK31HX0wdd0
QiTL4a8eyqO/7wV
NjvdobfrODaCWfkx4z81QfiV9ByYV8j3
                    </RootCert>
             </Parm>
        </Svc>
</jxta:PA>
```

Listing 16.1   Sample PeerInfoAdvertisement. (continued)

The code listed in the next section will pull the name of the peer from the advertisement using the method getName().

The Discovery Code

The code in Listing 16.2 is all we need to find peers in a peer group.

```
Line 1:  private void findPeers() {

    displayArea.append("Sending Peer Discovery...\n");

    DiscoveryListener peerDiscoveryListener = new
DiscoveryListener() {
       public void discoveryEvent (DiscoveryEvent ev) {
        PeerAdvertisement localPeerAdv = null;
        DiscoveryResponseMsg localResource = ev.getResponse();
        String localAdv = localResource.getPeerAdv();
Line 10:
         try {
           InputStream localIS = new
ByteArrayInputStream(localAdv.getBytes());
           localPeerAdv =
(PeerAdvertisement)AdvertisementFactory.newAdvertisement(new
MimeMediaType("text/xml"), localIS);
           displayArea.append("Discovery Event from peer: " +
localPeerAdv.getName() + " with " +
localResource.getResponseCount() + " peers\n");
         } catch (Exception e) {
            System.out.println("Error during Peer Discovery\n");
            e.printStackTrace();
            return;
         }
Line 20:
         Enumeration localEnum = localResource.getResponses();
         String tempString = null;
         while (localEnum.hasMoreElements()) {
           try {
             tempString = (String)localEnum.nextElement();
             localPeerAdv =
(PeerAdvertisement)AdvertisementFactory.newAdvertisement(new
MimeMediaType("text/xml"), new
ByteArrayInputStream(tempString.getBytes()));
             displayArea.append("Peer Name = " +
localPeerAdv.getName() + "\n");
             displayArea.append("Sending Peer Info Discovery for
" + localPeerAdv.getID() + "\n");
```

Listing 16.2 Locating peers in a peer group. (continues)

```
            } catch (Exception e) {
Line 30:          System.out.println("Error during Peer
Discovery\n");
            e.printStackTrace();
          continue;
          }
        }
      }
    };

    myDiscoveryService.getRemoteAdvertisements(null,
DiscoveryService.PEER, null, null, 5, peerDiscoveryListener);
```

Listing 16.2 Locating peers in a peer group. (continued)

Lines 1–40 build a method that can be called to begin the process of finding peers in a peer group. The code will create a discovery listener and launch the remote discovery process. Lines 5–37 instantiate a DiscoveryListener object for asynchronously handling any peers discovered.

Line 11 creates a PeerAdvertisement object from the bytes found in the message sent to the listener. Since the code is located within a try block, an exception will be thrown if the advertisement sent to the listener isn't a peer advertisement. When an advertisement is received that isn't a peer, the application shouldn't end but should instead display a message indicating that an error has occurred; however, it should continue executing the application so that other real peers can be found. The first peer advertisement the code pulls isn't a real peer advertisement; it is a reference advertisement to let the receiver code know what is located with the message.

Lines 21–26 do the actual work of pulling individual peer advertisements from the message received. Each message response is converted to a PeerAdvertisement object. Line 28 uses the getName() method to display the name of the peer associated with the current peer advertisement.

Line 39 begins the entire discovery process by calling the getRemoteAdvertisements() method of the current peer group's discovery process.

Local Peers versus Remote Peers

You can control the process of locating peers in your current group by entering values into the configuration window when the discovery code is first executed. When the code in Listing 16.2 is executed, the peers located might look like those in Figure 16.1.

The peers found in Figure 16.1 are all of the JXTA peers that we could find using only the TCP transport and no outside rendezvous peers. The code will perform only a local TCP multicast to find peers. Because the peer executing the code is the only peer on the local network, no others peers are found.

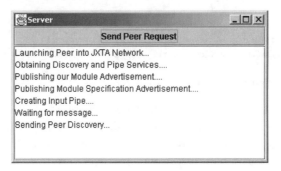

Figure 16.1 Locating peers locally.

In Figure 16.2, an additional peer is started on the local network; the peers found will be the client peers as well as the server because the client peer also knows about the server peer.

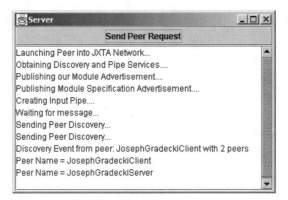

Figure 16.2 Additional local peers.

In Figure 16.3, we changed the values in the configuration window to allow both TCP and HTTP protocols for discovery and rendezvous peers. Quite a number of additional peers are found in the NetPeerGroup peer group.

Figure 16.3 Full peer discovery.

Obtaining Information about a Peer

Once a peer is located, we can find more information about that peer by checking the PeerInfoAdvertisement. Here is some of the information contained in the advertisement:

- Uptime of the peer
- Travel bytes transferred
- The date of last message sent
- The date of last message received

A peer requests a PeerInfoAdvertisement directly by using the peer ID. The peer ID can be found in the peer advertisement received during the discovery process, which we described earlier. A sample PeerInfoAdvertisement is shown in Listing 16.3.

```xml
<?xml version="1.0"?>

<!DOCTYPE jxta:PeerInfoAdvertisement>

<jxta:PeerInfoAdvertisement xmlns:jxta="http://jxta.org">
        <sourcePid>
                urn:jxta:uuid-
59616261646162614A787461503250337CE1ACE17356403D8EECBE6B9D25351303
        </sourcePid>
        <targetPid>
                urn:jxta:uuid-
59616261646162614A787461503250337CE1ACE17356403D8EECBE6B9D25351303
        </targetPid>
        <uptime>
                22642
        </uptime>
        <timestamp>
                1010872452153
        </timestamp>
        <traffic>
                <in>
                </in>
                <lastIncomingMessageAt>
                        0
                </lastIncomingMessageAt>
                <out>
                </out>
                <lastOutgoingMessageAt>
                        0
                </lastOutgoingMessageAt>
        </traffic>
</jxta:PeerInfoAdvertisement>
```

Listing 16.3 A sample PeerInfoAdvertisement.

Of particular importance are the <in> and <out> elements. Reading the source code indicates these elements should contain the number of bytes into and out of the peer. The bytes are tabulated based on channels that appear to be based on pipe or other transmission avenues. However, the code below in Listing 16.4, which pulls PeerInfo advertisements, never produces any values for the bytes in and out of a peer. As we mentioned early in this chapter, the Peer Information Protocol is still a work in progress and we hope the bytes will become valid soon.

A Sample Application for Discovering Peers

Listing 16.4 contains a stand-alone application that submits peer-discovery queries when a user clicks the button at the top of the GUI. The application should compile and execute in the same manner as other JXTA applications. Of particular significance is how you set up the configuration window. If you want to discover all peers in the network, it is important that you provide the addresses of known rendezvous peers and enable the HTTP protocol. Once the application has logged into the JXTA network, a user can simply click the top button to send a peer query; the GUI will display the results of the query. In the next section, we discuss the details of this code.

```java
import java.io.*;
import java.awt.*;
import java.awt.event.*;
import javax.swing.*;

import net.jxta.document.*;
import net.jxta.peergroup.*;
import net.jxta.exception.*;
import net.jxta.impl.peergroup.*;
import net.jxta.id.*;
import net.jxta.discovery.*;
import net.jxta.pipe.*;
import net.jxta.protocol.*;
import net.jxta.platform.*;
import net.jxta.endpoint.Message;
import java.util.Enumeration;
import net.jxta.peer.*;

public class Example1 extends JFrame {

    static PeerGroup netPeerGroup = null;
    private DiscoveryService myDiscoveryService = null;
    private PipeService myPipeService = null;
    private PeerInfoService myPeerInfoService = null;
    private ModuleClassID myService1ID = null;
    private InputPipe myPipe = null;
    private JTextArea displayArea;
    private JButton sendButton;

    public static void main(String args[]) {
        Example1 myapp = new Example1();

        myapp.addWindowListener (
```

Listing 16.4 Code for peer and peer info discovery. (continues)

```
      new WindowAdapter() {
         public void windowClosing(WindowEvent e) {
            System.exit(0);
         }
       }
    );

    myapp.run();
}

public Example1() {
  super("Server");

  Container c = getContentPane();

  sendButton = new JButton("Send Peer Request");
  sendButton.addActionListener(
    new ActionListener() {
      public void actionPerformed(ActionEvent e) {
        findPeers();
      }
    }
  );
  c.add(sendButton, BorderLayout.NORTH);


  displayArea = new JTextArea();
  c.add (new JScrollPane(displayArea), BorderLayout.CENTER);

  setSize(300,150);
  show();

  launchJXTA();
  getServices();
  buildModuleAdvertisement();
  buildModuleSpecificationAdvertisement(createPipeAdvertisement());
}

public void run() {
  displayArea.append("Waiting for message...\n");
}

private void launchJXTA() {
    displayArea.append("Launching Peer into JXTA Network...\n");
    try {
        netPeerGroup = PeerGroupFactory.newNetPeerGroup();
    } catch (PeerGroupException e) {
        System.out.println("Unable to create PeerGroup -
```

Listing 16.4 Code for peer and peer info discovery. (continues)

```
Failure");
            e.printStackTrace();
            System.exit(1);
        }
    }

    private void getServices() {
        displayArea.append("Obtaining Discovery and Pipe
Services....\n");
        myDiscoveryService = netPeerGroup.getDiscoveryService();
        myPipeService = netPeerGroup.getPipeService();
        myPeerInfoService = netPeerGroup.getPeerInfoService();
    }

    private void buildModuleAdvertisement() {
        ModuleClassAdvertisement myService1ModuleAdvertisement =
(ModuleClassAdvertisement) AdvertisementFactory.newAdvertisement(ModuleClas-
sAdvertisement.
getAdvertisementType());

        myService1ModuleAdvertisement.setName("JXTAMOD:JXTA-
CH19EX1");
        myService1ModuleAdvertisement.setDescription("Service 1 of
Chapter 19 example 1");

        myService1ID = IDFactory.newModuleClassID();
        myService1ModuleAdvertisement.setModuleClassID(myService1ID);

        displayArea.append("Publishing our Module
Advertisement....\n");
        try {
            myDiscoveryService.publish(myService1ModuleAdvertisement,
DiscoveryService.ADV);
            myDiscoveryService.remotePublish(myService1ModuleAdvertisement,
DiscoveryService.ADV);
        } catch (Exception e) {
            System.out.println("Error during publish of Module
Advertisement");
            System.exit(-1);
        }
    }

    private PipeAdvertisement createPipeAdvertisement() {
        PipeAdvertisement myPipeAdvertisement = null;

    try {
        FileInputStream is = new FileInputStream("service1.adv");
            myPipeAdvertisement = (PipeAdvertisement)AdvertisementFactory.newAd-
```

Listing 16.4 Code for peer and peer info discovery. (continues)

```
vertisement(new
MimeMediaType("text/xml"), is);
      } catch (Exception e) {
        System.out.println("failed to read/parse pipe
advertisement");
          e.printStackTrace();
        System.exit(-1);
    }

    return myPipeAdvertisement;
    }

    private void buildModuleSpecificationAdvertisement(PipeAdvertisement
myPipeAdvertisement) {
      ModuleSpecAdvertisement myModuleSpecAdvertisement =
(ModuleSpecAdvertisement) AdvertisementFactory.newAdvertisement(
ModuleSpecAdvertisement.
getAdvertisementType());

    myModuleSpecAdvertisement.setName("JXTASPEC:JXTA-CH19EX1");
    myModuleSpecAdvertisement.setVersion("Version 1.0");
    myModuleSpecAdvertisement.setCreator("gradecki.com");
    myModuleSpecAdvertisement.setModuleSpecID(IDFactory.
newModuleSpecID(myService1ID));
    myModuleSpecAdvertisement.setSpecURI("<http://www.jxta.org/CH19EX1>");
      myModuleSpecAdvertisement.setPipeAdvertisement(myPipeAdvertisement);

      displayArea.append("Publishing Module Specification
Advertisement....\n");
      try {
        myDiscoveryService.publish(myModuleSpecAdvertisement,
DiscoveryService.ADV);
        myDiscoveryService.remotePublish
(myModuleSpecAdvertisement, DiscoveryService.ADV);
      } catch (Exception e) {
        System.out.println("Error during publish of Module
Specification Advertisement");
        e.printStackTrace();
        System.exit(-1);
      }
    createInputPipe(myPipeAdvertisement);
    }

    private void createInputPipe(PipeAdvertisement
myPipeAdvertisement) {
      displayArea.append("Creating Input Pipe....\n");

      PipeMsgListener myService1Listener = new PipeMsgListener() {
```

Listing 16.4 Code for peer and peer info discovery. (continues)

```
        public void pipeMsgEvent(PipeMsgEvent event) {
          Message myMessage = null;
          try {
            myMessage = event.getMessage();

            String myMessageContent;

            myMessageContent = myMessage.getString("DataTag");
            if (myMessageContent != null) {
              displayArea.append("Message received: " +
myMessageContent + "\n");
              displayArea.append("Waiting for message...\n");
              return;
            } else {
              displayArea.append("Invalid tag\n");
              return;
            }
          } catch (Exception ee) {
            ee.printStackTrace();
            return;
          }
        }
      };

      try {
        myPipe = myPipeService.createInputPipe(myPipeAdvertisement,
myService1Listener);
      } catch (Exception e) {
          System.out.println("Error creating Input Pipe");
          e.printStackTrace();
          System.exit(-1);
      }
    }

  private void findPeers() {

    displayArea.append("Sending Peer Discovery...\n");

    DiscoveryListener peerDiscoveryListener = new
DiscoveryListener() {
        public void discoveryEvent (DiscoveryEvent ev) {
          PeerAdvertisement localPeerAdv = null;
          DiscoveryResponseMsg localResource = ev.getResponse();
          String localAdv = localResource.getPeerAdv();

          try {
            InputStream localIS = new
ByteArrayInputStream(localAdv.getBytes());
```

Listing 16.4 Code for peer and peer info discovery. (continues)

```
            localPeerAdv = (PeerAdvertisement)AdvertisementFactory.
newAdvertisement(new
MimeMediaType("text/xml"), localIS);
            displayArea.append("Discovery Event from peer: " +
localPeerAdv.getName() + " with " +
localResource.getResponseCount() + " peers\n");
        } catch (Exception e) {
            System.out.println("Error during Peer Discovery\n");
            e.printStackTrace();
            return;
        }

        Enumeration localEnum = localResource.getResponses();
        String tempString = null;
        while (localEnum.hasMoreElements()) {
          try {
            tempString = (String)localEnum.nextElement();
            localPeerAdv =
(PeerAdvertisement)AdvertisementFactory.newAdvertisement(new
MimeMediaType("text/xml"), new
ByteArrayInputStream(tempString.getBytes()));
            displayArea.append("Peer Name = " +
localPeerAdv.getName() + "\n");
            displayArea.append("Sending Peer Info Discovery for
" + localPeerAdv.getID() + "\n");
            getPeerInfo(localPeerAdv.getID());
          } catch (Exception e) {
            System.out.println("Error during Peer Discovery\n");
            e.printStackTrace();
            continue;
          }
        }
      }
    };

    myDiscoveryService.getRemoteAdvertisements(null,
DiscoveryService.PEER, null, null, 5, peerDiscoveryListener);
  }

Line 233:  private void getPeerInfo(ID localPeerID) {
    displayArea.append("Sending Peer Info Request for " +
localPeerID + "\n");

    PeerInfoListener peerInfoListener = new PeerInfoListener() {
      public void peerInfoResponse(PeerInfoEvent e) {
        PeerInfoResponseMessage adv =
e.getPeerInfoResponseMessage();
        displayArea.append("Total Uptime in milliseconds = " +
```

Listing 16.4 Code for peer and peer info discovery. (continues)

```
adv.getUptime() + "\n");

        Enumeration localInEnum = adv.getIncomingTrafficChannels();
        if (localInEnum.hasMoreElements()) {
          String inChannelName = (String)localInEnum.nextElement();
          displayArea.append("Incoming Channel Bytes = " +
adv.getIncomingTrafficOnChannel(inChannelName) + "\n");
        }
        Enumeration localOutEnum = adv.getOutgoingTrafficChannels();
        if (localOutEnum.hasMoreElements()) {
          String outChannelName =
(String)localOutEnum.nextElement();
          displayArea.append("Outgoing Channel Bytes = " +
adv.getOutgoingTrafficOnChannel(outChannelName) + "\n");
        }
      }
    };

  myPeerInfoService.getRemotePeerInfo(localPeerID,
peerInfoListener);
Line 255:  }


}
```

Listing 16.4 Code for peer and peer info discovery. (continued)

Explaining the Code

The code in Listing 16.4 is based on the peer code from Chapter 12. The code builds a GUI, advertises an input pipe, and displays a button. When the button is clicked, the code found in Listing 16.2 will be executed. The method, called findPeers(), is responsible for building a listener object and submitting the peer query. When a peer is found, a call is made to the getPeerInfo() method.

Lines 233–255 build the getPeerInfo() method for finding information about a peer. The method requires a string that represents the peer ID of the peer for which the information is needed.

Lines 236–252 instantiate a PeerInfoListener object to handle the asynchronous reception of PeerInfo messages. Line 238 pulls the PeerInfoAdvertisement from the event object passed to the listener. The remaining code pulls information about the advertisement by using the methods associated with the advertisement object.

Line 254 sets the query of a specific peer for a PeerInfoAdvertisement. When the peer returns the information, the object built earlier will be executed.

Code Output

When the code is executed, information for the peers will be displayed, as shown in Figure 16.4. It should be noted that peers aren't required to respond to peer information requests. There are times when a request will be made and no response received.

Figure 16.4 The PeerInfo application.

Summary

In this chapter, we discussed how to find peers in a group by using the discovery service and a listener object. Once a peer is found—either a specific one or all peers in the group—we can find information about the peer by executing the getRemotePeerInfo() method. We can further expand the functionality of an administrator peer by creating a list of the peers and displaying updated information in either a list or a graphical representation of the network.

Sometimes it is useful to keep track of bytes going into and out of a peer. If an administrator peer sees that another peer is using a proportionally large amount of bandwidth, it could take action to govern the peer. When the JXTA Peer Information Protocol matures, this type of functionality may be built into peers.

In the next chapter, the topic of peers existing behind firewalls and using Network Address Translation is covered. The discussion focuses on how to configure peers to relay messages and find Rendezvous peers out on the open Internet.

CHAPTER 17

Configuring NAT and Firewall Peers

Not all JXTA peers will be attached directly to the Internet—some may reside behind a firewall or use Network Address Translation (NAT). As far as the JXTA network is concerned, these peers do not exist since they cannot be directly contacted. In this chapter, we discuss how to configure peers so that they can be accessed and connect to the outside world. We build a simple application that can be used as a router by itself, as a rendezvous peer by itself, or as both a router and a rendezvous peer.

The JXTA Network Topology

The JXTA network consists of a disparate topology in which peers can exist independently or as part of a group of peers. Theoretically, each peer has direct access to all other peers in the JXTA network. However, there are two situations that can put a wrinkle in this topology. The first is when a peer is located behind a firewall. A *firewall* is designed to limit communication in and out of a private network. This means that the ports used by a JXTA peer will be unable to pass information back and forth. In most cases where a firewall is in place, we can still gain access by using the HTTP protocol and port 80. A JXTA peer can take advantage of this by enabling the transport of information using HTTP through the Configurator dialog box presented when the peer is first executed.

Another problem with firewalls and the HTTP protocol is the fact that HTTP is a *push/pull* protocol. A peer on the outside of a firewall will be unable to "see" or use a peer behind the firewall because it needs to send an HTTP request through the firewall, and most firewalls will only allow a response message through. To handle this, a router or relay peer can be used to handle the relay of information between the two peers.

In addition, discovery of advertisements is complicated because of the lack of complete communication through the firewall. A rendezvous peer can be used in this case. The rendezvous peer acts as a common peer with a large cache of advertisements. A peer behind a firewall can designate one or more rendezvous peers for use when publishing and discovering advertisements.

The second problem that needs to be considered is Network Address Translation (NAT). If a network is using NAT, all internal IP addresses aren't visible to the outside world. The only IP address visible is the server machine that handles all requests on behalf of the machines in the internal network that have a NAT IP address. Both the rendezvous and router/relay peers can be used to solve the problem of peers having internal IP addresses.

Running a Peer Behind a Firewall/NAT

Let's look at an example in which a peer is behind a firewall and has an IP address assigned through NAT. Within the network is a gateway peer, which the client will use to join the JXTA network and WorldNetPeer peer group. The gateway machine has been seeded with the static rendezvous peers in the JXTA network as well as another one of our own peers, called a *communication peer*. This peer has been configured as a rendezvous peer and has also published a pipe advertisement. The code for all three clients can be found on the book's Web site at www.wiley.com/compbooks/gradecki, and is based on the code from Chapter 15 and the previous router/rendezvous peer code. Figure 17.1 shows how the network is currently set up.

Communication Peer Configuration

The communication peer is executing on a machine located on the Internet, implying that it has a static IP address. The peer has a single input pipe, which will be advertised locally and remotely to the entire JXTA network. The remote advertisement is possible because the communication peer is configured to be

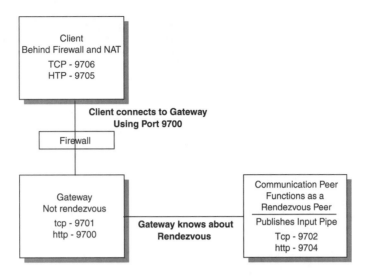

Figure 17.1 A client behind a firewall and that uses a NAT address.

a rendezvous peer and has the JXTA network rendezvous peers loaded as well. When the server peer executes, the pipe advertisement will be propagated through the entire network.

Figure 17.2 shows the Advanced tab for the communication peer. Since the peer is located on the Internet, both the TCP and HTTP protocols are checked so that the peer has complete access to all other peers. It is also important that the different protocols are using different ports. If you don't specify different ports, one of the protocols will be unable to bind a socket for communication. Unfortunately, no application error is created that can be caught, but the error can be seen in the debug information (which we discuss later in this chapter under the section "Using the Configurator's Debug Option").

Figure 17.3 shows the Rendezvous/Routers tab. The most important thing to note on this screen is that the Act As Rendezvous checkbox is enabled, allowing the peer to act as a rendezvous for advertisements and such. To be truly effective as a rendezvous, the peer also needs to have a list of other rendezvous peers in the network. The list is pulled from one of the JXTA servers on the network.

Once configured, the server will execute, publish its pipe advertisement, and wait for both a connection to its pipe and the receipt of information from clients.

Figure 17.2   The Advanced tab for the communication peer.

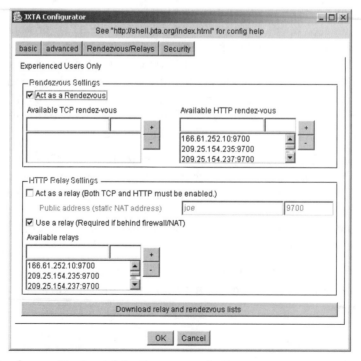

Figure 17.3   The Rendezvous/Routers tab for the communication peer.

Gateway Configuration

The gateway peer is based on the code in Listing 17.1. The peer itself doesn't have any functionality, but will be configured to act as a router or gateway for peers behind firewalls and peers that use NAT addresses. Figure 17.4 shows the Advanced tab for the gateway machine. The gateway machine is also directly connected to the Internet, and has both the TCP and HTTP protocols configured. Again, notice the port values are different for the protocols. Although the values aren't 9700 and 9701 (the default for JXTA), they are still in the range of ports that applications can use on a machine.

Figure 17.5 shows the Rendezvous/Routers tab of the gateway machine. To make the peer a gateway, the system requires that the checkbox labeled "Act as a Gateway" be enabled and that the peer have both the TCP and HTTP protocols checked. We can use the edit line under the checkbox to list the IP address that internal peers should use for contacting this gateway peer. Because we want this gateway peer to have direct access to the server/rendezvous peer created earlier, we added its IP and HTTP port value to the Available HTTP Rendezvous list box. Notice that port 9704 is listed, which matches the port specified in the HTTP protocol section of the server machine.

Once executed, the gateway peer will start the appropriate gateway services and contact the rendezvous peer to be sure it exists on the network.

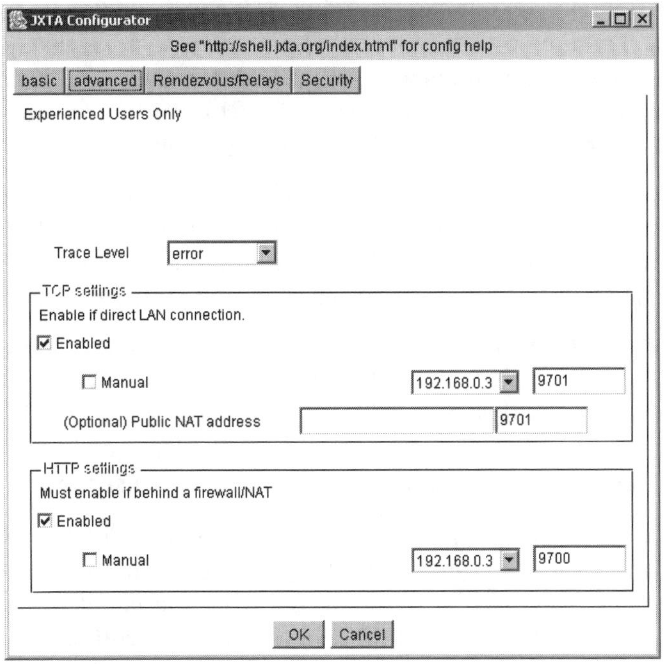

Figure 17.4   The Advanced tab for the gateway.

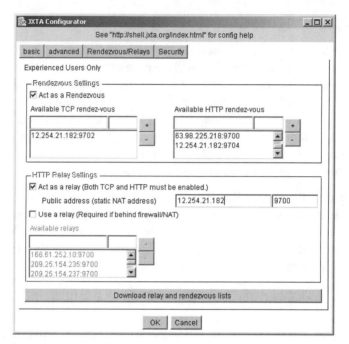

Figure 17.5 The Rendezvous/Routers tab for the gateway.

The Discovery Peer Configuration

The final peer in our sample network is the discovery peer. This peer performs a local and remote discovery to locate the pipe advertisement created and published by the communication peer. Unfortunately, the discovery peer is behind a firewall and uses a NAT address. For this reason, we must configure the peer to use the gateway peer as its portal to the network.

Figure 17.6 shows the Advanced tab of the client peer. The client peer is executing on a RedHat Linux box on an internal network. Both the TCP and HTTP protocols are configured with appropriate port values, but they won't actually be used because we will instruct the peer to use a gateway peer instead.

Figure 17.7 shows the Rendezvous/Routers tab, with the Use A Gateway option enabled. The value in the Public Address (static NAT address) edit line is the gateway peer's IP and port. The system will require that this port value be open through the firewall. If this port isn't available, select another port, such as port 80. You also need to modify the gateway peer to use port 80 instead of port 9700.

Once executed, the discovery peer contacts the gateway peer for access to the network. The discovery peer then requests a remote discovery for a pipe advertisement. The discovery propagates from the client to the gateway peer and finally to the communication peer. Once the advertisement is found, appropriate connections are made, and data is sent to the communication peer from the discovery peer.

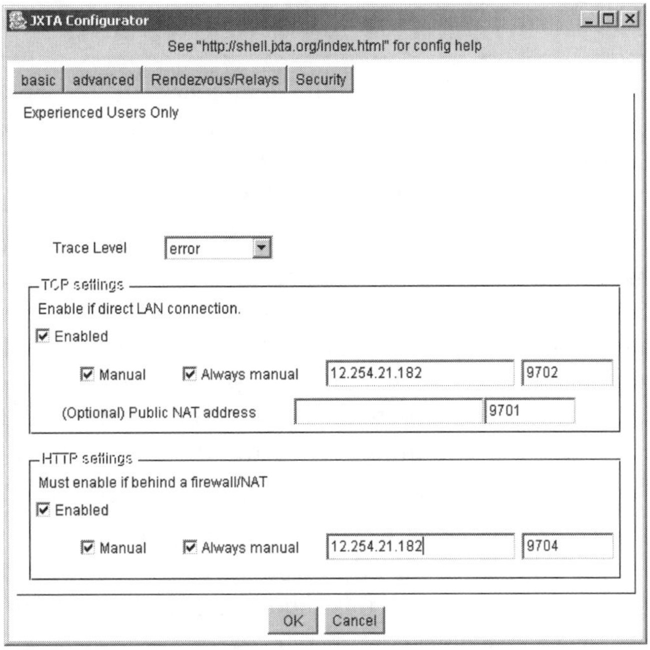

Figure 17.6 The discovery peer's Advanced tab.

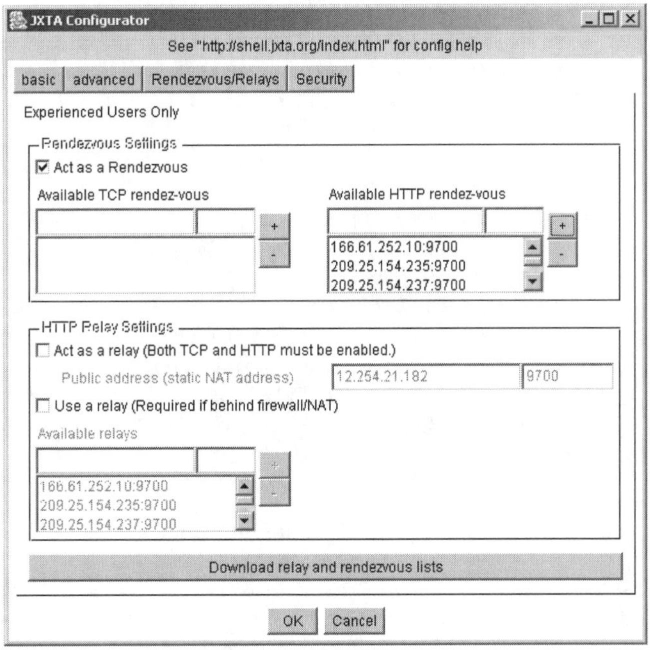

Figure 17.7 The discovery peer's Rendezvous/Routers tab.

Using the Configurator's Debug Option

If you are interested in seeing the details behind the various "hidden" services being used by a peer, you can use the Configurator to set the debug option. Click on the Configurator's Advanced tab and select the Trace Level drop-down box (see Figure 17.6). You'll see several choices, among them the debug option.

For an example of the output from a debug option, look at Listing 17.1. This output is from a normal peer that has been given a specific rendezvous peer to access. Unfortunately, the rendezvous peer is not available. There is really nothing in the application GUI to show a problem, but in Listing 17.1 we see the rendezvous peer wasn't found. This specific peer had been instructed via the Configurator screen to contact a rendezvous peer using the HTTP protocol at port 9700 and the TCP protocol at port 9701, but neither had a peer available.

After a few moments, the peer tries to find a local advertisement for an input pipe; it doesn't find one, so it then tries to send out a remote discovery. However, since no rendezvous peers were available to handle the remote discovery, the peer ends. You can see this sequence of errors in Listing 17.2.

```
<DEBUG 20:45:41,074 HttpClientMessageSender:170> Ping result to
   http://12.254.21.182:9700/ping: false
<DEBUG 20:45:41,074 RendAddrCompactor:197> Cannot connect to
   Rendezvous at http://12.254.21.182:9700:java.io.IOException:
   Cannot ping rendezvous
<DEBUG 20:45:41,074 RendezVousServiceImpl:487>
   connectToRendezVous with EndpointAddress
<DEBUG 20:45:41,084 RendezVousServiceImpl:496>      to =
   tcp://12.254.21.182:9701
<DEBUG 20:45:41,084 TcpTransport:817> ping to
   tcp://12.254.21.182:9701/
<DEBUG 20:45:42,076 TcpTransport:777> Ping
   [tcp://12.254.21.182:9701/] exception
   java.net.ConnectException: Connection refused: connect
<DEBUG 20:45:42,076 TcpTransport:841> ping returns false
<DEBUG 20:45:42,076 RendAddrCompactor:197> Cannot connect to
   Rendezvous at tcp://12.254.21.182:9701:java.io.IOException:
   Cannot ping rendezvous
```

Listing 17.1   Debug errors from an invalid rendezvous peer.

```
<DEBUG 20:47:21,018 PipeResolver:261> findLocal urn:jxta:uuid
 -CCCDF5AD8154D3D87A391210404E59BE4B888209A2241A4A162
```

Listing 17.2   Failed discovery attempts. (continues)

```
 A10916074A9504
<DEBUG 20:47:21,018 PipeResolver:733> findCached urn:jxta:uuid
 -9CCCDF5AD8154D3D87A391210404E59BE4B888209A2241A4A162
  A10916074A9504
<DEBUG 20:47:21,018 PipeResolver:733> findCachedurn:jxta:uuid
  9CCCDF5AD8154D3D87A391210404E59BE4B888209A2241A4A162
  A10916074A9504
<DEBUG 20:47:21,018 PipeResolver:816> findRemote waiting...
<DEBUG 20:47:21,018 PipeResolver:828> findRemote timeout.
<DEBUG 20:47:21,018 NonBlockingOutputPipe:132> Constructor: no
  macthing InputPipe for urn:jxta:uuid-9CCCDF5AD815
    4D3D87A391210404E59BE4B888209A2241A4A162A10916074A9504
Unable to create output pipe
```

Listing 17.2 Failed discovery attempts. (continued)

Building a Router/Rendezvous Peer

If you have a peer behind a firewall, it will need access to a rendezvous peer outside the firewall in order to gain access to the JXTA network. As we've seen, you can configure a peer to access the known JXTA network rendezvous peers or you can build your own. The application code in Listing 17.3 provides a simple peer that can be executed as a rendezvous peer, a router peer, or both simultaneously.

```java
import java.io.*;
import java.awt.*;
import java.awt.event.*;
import javax.swing.*;

import net.jxta.document.*;
import net.jxta.peergroup.*;
import net.jxta.exception.*;
import net.jxta.impl.peergroup.*;
import net.jxta.id.*;
import net.jxta.protocol.*;
import net.jxta.platform.*;
import net.jxta.endpoint.*;

public class Example1 extends JFrame {

    static PeerGroup netPeerGroup = null;
    private JTextArea displayArea;
```

Listing 17.3 The router/rendezvous peer code. (continues)

```
    public static void main(String args[]) {
        Example1 myapp = new Example1();

        myapp.addWindowListener (
         new WindowAdapter() {
            public void windowClosing(WindowEvent e) {
               System.exit(0);
            }
          }
        );

        myapp.launchJXTA();
        myapp.run();
    }

    public Example1() {
      super("Router/Rendezvous Peer");

      Container c = getContentPane();

      displayArea = new JTextArea();
      c.add (new JScrollPane(displayArea), BorderLayout.CENTER);

      setSize(300,150);
      show();
    }

    public void run() {
        displayArea.append("Just a Router/Rendezvous Peer");
    }

    private void launchJXTA() {
        displayArea.append("Launching Peer into JXTA
          Network...\n");
        try {
           netPeerGroup = PeerGroupFactory.newNetPeerGroup();
        } catch (PeerGroupException e) {
           System.out.println("Unable to create PeerGroup -
             Failure");
           e.printStackTrace();
           System.exit(1);
        }
    }
}
```

Listing 17.3 The router/rendezvous peer code. (continued)

As you can see, the code appears to be very simple; it builds a peer, starts the JXTA service, and waits for the application to be stopped. Behind the scenes, though, various services are being started. When the code is compiled and executed, two additional libraries must be linked into the code:

- org.mortbay.jetty.jar

- javax.servlet.jar

These two additional libraries provide the HTTP servlet functionality for the rendezvous functionality. You can find the files on the JXTA web site at www.jxta.org on the downloads page. Pull down the all.zip of the binaries section to find the files. Upon execution, the application will produce the following on the command screen (be sure you have trace debugging turned on):

```
15:20:08.458 EVENT   Starting Jetty/3.1.1
15:20:08.528 EVENT   Started ServletHandler in HandlerContext[/]
15:20:08.758 EVENT   Started SocketListener on
  12.254.21.182:9700
15:20:08.768 EVENT   Started org.mortbay.http.HttpServer@2001ff
15:20:10.220 EVENT
  net.jxta.impl.endpoint.servlethttp.HttpRelayServlet: init
15:20:59.201 EVENT
  net.jxta.impl.endpoint.servlethttp.HttpMessageReceiverServlet:
  init
```

These lines indicate to the user that the services have started properly. At this point, how do you activate the rendezvous and router functionality? All of the switches for the functionality are found on the Configurator screen, as described previously.

This screen allows us to set up the current peer to use a combination of the TCP and HTTP protocols. If the peer is to be a rendezvous or router, then more than likely the peer is directly connected to the Internet through a dedicated or dial-up connection. Restrictions to the flow of information don't exist, which is why this peer is a good candidate to have special functionality. Remember that peers behind firewalls or peers that have a NAT IP address will use a router peer that must have unrestricted access to the network. For a rendezvous peer, you will want to have as many protocols available for message passing as possible.

The TCP and HTTP checkboxes should be enabled. Notice the use of different ports since the protocols will need to have independent paths for passing data. The Configurator will pick the current IP address of the computer it is being executed on. If you have multiple IP addresses assigned to a box, enable the Manual checkbox, and an IP address will appear automatically in the edit line. In this way, a different IP address can be specified for both the HTTP and IP protocols.

Once the protocol ports and options are set, click on the Rendezvous/Router tab to display the screen shown previously in Figure 17.7. This tab contains two important checkboxes:

- Act As A Rendezvous
- Act As A Gateway (both TCP and HTTP must be enabled)

If you want the peer to act as a rendezvous, simply check the Act As A Rendezvous checkbox. In order to be an effective rendezvous peer, it should have other rendezvous peers to communicate with. At the bottom of the screen, you see a button called Download Gateways And Rendezvous Lists. When you click this button, a dialog box will appear that allows you to enter three URLs. The URLs are hard-coded into the dialog box for each new release of the JXTA Java reference implementation. If different URLs are available (usually found on the mailing lists for JXTA), you should enter them. It is the goal of the JXTA project to keep these URLs static and not change them, so the hard-coded values should work correctly.

Once you've entered the URLs, click the Load button to contact the network machines and download a list of rendezvous and router peers. These lists will allow the current rendezvous peer to have other peers to pass information and advertisements to.

If you want the peer to act as a gateway/router, click the button at the bottom of the screen. Notice the note associated with the checkbox for a gateway: To be a gateway, you must have both the TCP and HTTP protocol checkboxes enabled on the Advanced tab. Now your peers that have NAT addresses or that are behind your firewall can use the router peer to gain access to the broader JXTA network.

Summary

In this chapter, we showed you a number of different network configurations using both peers in the clear and peers that are behind firewalls or that use NAT addresses. We presented the code for building simple rendezvous and router peers along with the options for allowing all the peers to communicate effectively.

In the next chapter, we look at how low-level communication services can be used to send data from one peer to another without relying on a pipe for the communication channel. This enables you to build your own communication protocol, if needed.

CHAPTER 18

Using Endpoints for Low-Level Communication

In the first part of this book, we discussed the many protocols that make up the JXTA specification, including the endpoint service and its associated protocols. The endpoint service enables a JXTA peer to exchange data using an established transport protocol, such as TCP/IP or HTTP. The endpoint service can be expanded to include other transport mechanisms, such as Bluetooth for wireless communication.

One of the fundamental components of the endpoint service is the endpoint itself. In the case of TCP/IP, an endpoint consists of a peer's IP address and port number. In most situations, two peers will exchange information by using a pipe that hides all the communication details. One of these hidden details involves the routing of a message from one peer to another when the peers aren't on the same network. The Java reference implementation allows developers to bypass the use of pipes and built-in routing if they wish, and communicate directly with peers at a lower level. In this chapter, low-level communication channels will be built between peers using the endpoint service in the Java Reference Implementation.

The Endpoint Service

The endpoint service is the mechanism used for building communication channels between peers. Pipes will use the endpoint service implemented as part of the Peer Endpoint Protocol to logically connect any two peers. If we don't want to utilize the features of a pipe, we can use the endpoint service directly. A peer can use the service to build its own networks and to set up a specific topology, if necessary. For example, we could design an application that has individual peers communicating in a tree with a single root node propagating information to a second level, and have each level send data to another level.

Although it is not expected that traditional P2P systems will need to use this low-level communication—pipes provide almost all of the necessary functionality—it is good to know about the service. We could use the endpoint service instead of a pipe, for example, if the specification of a system requires that all communication occur between two peers only. Because a pipe might route information using intermediary peers, the endpoint service can be used instead to enable communication directly from one peer to another.

To illustrate how to use the endpoint service, let's consider an example. We build two peers. One peer, the receiving peer, will launch itself into the JXTA network and display all of the current endpoints associated with the peer. The other peer will be a sender; it will accept the endpoint of a peer, and use it to build a communication channel through which data will be sent.

All peers are started with several different endpoints, depending on how they were configured when first executed. As you recall, the Configurator, which executes when a peer is first run, includes the option of allowing both TCP/IP and HTTP communication. Each of these communication types will build an endpoint on the peer. Listener objects can be built and attached to the endpoints to process incoming data through the endpoint service based on a specific service name and parameter value. When data comes through the endpoints, the service name and parameter value are checked by the code to determine whether a listener is available to process the incoming data.

To help with the assignment of endpoints, the receiving peer, when executed, displays on its GUI all of the endpoints and their associated IDs available for this peer. A sending peer uses these IDs for the communication hookup. In Figure 18.1, the receiving peer is started and shows three different endpoints available for use. The endpoints defined on the receiving peer shown in Figure 18.1 are

- A secure endpoint using TLS transport
- A TCP/IP endpoint
- An endpoint defined using a JXTA ID

The code in Listing 18.1 registers a listener to determine whether any messages arrive on the endpoints that should be processed. The listener is designed to monitor messages based on an endpoint service name and parameter value. These two values are strings concatenated together and sent with all messages to a peer. Once the listener has been set up, the peer can continue with other

Figure 18.1 The receiving peer shows three endpoints..

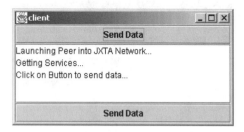

Figure 18.2 The sending peer has two buttons.

tasks because the listener will be triggered asynchronously when an appropriate message is received.

When the listener is triggered, the listener method will receive both the source and destination addresses of the communication, as well as a message object. The string associated with the message can be extracted and processed. We can be sure that the message is appropriate for the peer because it was sent using a specific service name and parameter value.

As Figure 18.2 shows, the sending peer has two buttons on its GUI with a text area between them. The button at the top is designed to send a message to an endpoint directly. When a user clicks that button, a dialog box will appear, prompting the user to enter an endpoint address to be used for communication. The system will build a connection to that address, and send a test message using a service name and parameter value known to exist on the receiving peer.

The user clicks the bottom button to send a message using propagation and the service name and parameter value. The user does not enter a specific endpoint in this case because the system will send the message to allowed peers, and only those who recognize the service name and parameter value will process the information.

Figure 18.3 The receiving peer's view of a message sent directly.

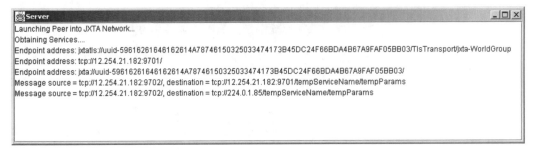

Figure 18.4 The receiving peer's view of a message sent using propagation.

Figure 18.3 shows what happens when a user clicks the top button on the sending peer. The endpoint used for our example is the TCP endpoint defined on the receiving peer. If the user clicks the Send Data button at the bottom, a message will be sent using propagation to all peers that can be contacted using the endpoint service of the host peer. The result of clicking the bottom button is shown in Figure 18.4.

Code for the Endpoint Receiving Peer

Listing 18.1 contains the code necessary to execute a peer that creates an endpoint handler capable of receiving messages addressed to a specific service name and parameter. The service name and parameter are simple strings used to create unique channels of communication using a single endpoint service.

```
Line 1: import java.io.*;
import java.awt.*;
import java.awt.event.*;
import javax.swing.*;
```

Listing 18.1 Endpoint receiving code. (continues)

```
import net.jxta.document.*;
import net.jxta.peergroup.*;
import net.jxta.exception.*;
import net.jxta.impl.peergroup.*;
line 10: import net.jxta.id.*;
import net.jxta.discovery.*;
import net.jxta.pipe.*;
import net.jxta.protocol.*;
import net.jxta.platform.*;
import net.jxta.endpoint.*;
import java.util.Enumeration;

public class receiving extends JFrame {

Line 20:    static PeerGroup netPeerGroup = null;
    private DiscoveryService myDiscoveryService = null;
    private EndpointService myEndpointService = null;
    private JTextArea displayArea;

    public static void main(String args[]) {
        receiving myapp = new receiving();

        myapp.addWindowListener (
          new WindowAdapter() {
Line 30:            public void windowClosing(WindowEvent e) {
              System.exit(0);
            }
          }
        );
        myapp.run();
    }

    public receiving() {
      super("Receiving");
Line 40:
      Container c = getContentPane();

      displayArea = new JTextArea();
      c.add (new JScrollPane(displayArea), BorderLayout.CENTER);

      setSize(300,150);
      show();

      launchJXTA();
Line 50:     getServices();
    }

    public void run() {
```

Listing 18.1 Endpoint receiving code. (continues)

```
            EndpointListener objectEndpointListener =
             new EndpointListener() {
              public void processIncomingMessage(Message message,
                EndpointAddress source, EndpointAddress destination)
              {
                displayArea.append("Message source = " + source + ",
                  destination = " + destination + "\n");
                displayArea.append("Message = " +
                  message.getString("MessageText"));
Line 60:        }
            };

            EndpointProtocol tempInst = null;
            Enumeration currentProtocols =
              myEndpointService.getEndpointProtocols();
            while (currentProtocols.hasMoreElements())
            {
              tempInst = (EndpointProtocol)
                currentProtocols.nextElement();
              displayArea.append("Endpoint address: " +
                tempInst.getPublicAddress().toString() + "\n");
            }
Line 70:        myEndpointService.addListener(
                  "tempServiceName"+"tempParams",
                  objectEndpointListener);
        }

        private void launchJXTA() {
          displayArea.append("Launching Peer into JXTA
            Network...\n");
          try {
            netPeerGroup = PeerGroupFactory.newNetPeerGroup();
          } catch (PeerGroupException e) {
            System.out.println("Unable to create PeerGroup -
              Failure");
Line 80:        e.printStackTrace();
            System.exit(1);
          }
        }

        private void getServices() {
          displayArea.append("Obtaining Services....\n");
          myDiscoveryService = netPeerGroup.getDiscoveryService();
          myEndpointService = netPeerGroup.getEndpointService();
        }
}
```

Listing 18.1 Endpoint receiving code. (continued)

The code consists of a GUI with a single display text area. When the application begins, the peer will connect to the default JXTA peer group and obtain a local object representing the peer group's endpoint service (on line 87).

Lines 55 through 61 define an Endpoint listener anonymous inner class and associated object. For this listener, the only method needed is processIncomingMessage(). The method accepts the message that has been sent to this peer, the address of the source peer, and the address of the destination. For our example, the string associated with the message is pulled out in line 59 and displayed in the GUI. The endpoint addresses are also displayed.

Lines 63 through 69 run through all of the endpoint addresses available on the current peer. This step is necessary so that the user can type one of the addresses into the dialog box of the client. The getEndpointProtocols() method associated with the endpoint service returns an Enumeration object consisting of elements for each of the addresses.

Line 71 calls the addListener() method of the endpoint service to associate the listener object previously built with a specific handler name. The handler name is made through a concatenation of the serviceName and the serviceParam values. In our case, sample strings are used. The remote or client peer will need to address messages to this handler name specifically.

Once the various methods are called, the peer will enter its run() method and begin the execution of the application event loop. A remote peer or peers can address messages to the peer and cause the listener to trigger.

Code for the Endpoint Sending Peer

As you read this chapter, you will quickly realize that using the endpoint service and related functionality isn't the best way to communicate because the client needs to know specific information about the server. In this case, the sending peer needs to know an exact endpoint address to begin communicating with the receiving peer.

The code in Listing 18.2 builds a peer with a GUI containing a text area and two buttons. Just as the receiving peer did, the sending peer connects to the JXTA network and allocates an endpoint service to begin the communication process with the server.

```
Line 1: import java.io.*;
import java.awt.*;
import java.awt.event.*;
```

Listing 18.2   Endpoint sending code. (continues)

```
import javax.swing.*;
import java.net.MalformedURLException;
import java.net.URL;

import java.util.Enumeration;
import net.jxta.document.*;
Line 10: import net.jxta.peergroup.*;
import net.jxta.exception.*;
import net.jxta.impl.peergroup.*;
import net.jxta.id.*;
import net.jxta.discovery.*;
import net.jxta.pipe.*;
import net.jxta.protocol.*;
import net.jxta.endpoint.*;

public class sending extends JFrame {
Line 20:
    static  PeerGroup              netPeerGroup = null;
    private DiscoveryService       myDiscoveryService = null;
    private EndpointService  myEndpointService = null;
    private JTextArea              displayArea;
    private JButton                sendButton;
    private JButton           sendButton2;

    private final static       MimeMediaType XMLMIMETYPE =
      new MimeMediaType("text/xml");

Line 30:    public static void main(String args[]) {
        sending myapp = new sending();

        myapp.addWindowListener (
         new WindowAdapter() {
            public void windowClosing(WindowEvent e) {
              System.exit(0);
            }
          }
        );
Line 40:        myapp.run();
    }


    public sending() {
      super("Sending");

      Container c = getContentPane();

      sendButton = new JButton("Send Data");
```

Listing 18.2 Endpoint sending code. (continues)

```
Line 50:       sendButton.addActionListener(
          new ActionListener() {
            public void actionPerformed(ActionEvent e) {
              sendData();
            }
          }
        );
        c.add(sendButton, BorderLayout.NORTH);

        sendButton2 = new JButton("Send Data");
Line 60:       sendButton2.addActionListener(
          new ActionListener() {
            public void actionPerformed(ActionEvent e) {
              sendData2();
            }
          }
        );
        c.add(sendButton2, BorderLayout.SOUTH);

        displayArea = new JTextArea();
Line 70:       c.add(new JScrollPane(displayArea),
                BorderLayout.CENTER);

        setSize(300,150);
        show();

        launchJXTA();
        getServices();
    }

    public void run() {
Line 80:       displayArea.append("Click on Button to send
                data...\n");
    }

    private void launchJXTA() {
        displayArea.append("Launching Peer into JXTA
          Network...\n");
        try {
            netPeerGroup = PeerGroupFactory.newNetPeerGroup();
        } catch (PeerGroupException e) {
            System.out.println("Unable to create PeerGroup -
              Failure");
            e.printStackTrace();
Line 90:            System.exit(1);
        }
    }
```

Listing 18.2   Endpoint sending code. (continues)

```
      private void getServices() {
        displayArea.append("Getting Services...\n");
        myDiscoveryService = netPeerGroup.getDiscoveryService();
        myEndpointService = netPeerGroup.getEndpointService();
      }

Line 100:    private void sendData() {

        String toAddress = JOptionPane.showInputDialog("Enter
          Address to Send String:");

        EndpointAddress endpointAddress =
          myEndpointService.newEndpointAddress(toAddress);
        endpointAddress.setServiceName("tempServiceName");
        endpointAddress.setServiceParameter("tempParams");

        if (myEndpointService.ping(endpointAddress)) {
          Message message = myEndpointService.newMessage();
Line 110:        message.setString("MessageText", "Just a
                   String");

          try {
            EndpointMessenger messenger =
              myEndpointService.getMessenger(endpointAddress);
            messenger.sendMessage(message);
          } catch (IOException e) {
            System.out.println("Error sending to endpoint");
          }
        } else {
          displayArea.append("No Endpoint Available\n");
Line 120:        }
      }

      private void sendData2() {
        Message message = myEndpointService.newMessage();

        message.setString("MessageText", "Just a propagated
          string");
        try {
          myEndpointService.propagate(message, "tempServiceName",
            "tempParams");
        } catch (IOException e) {
Line 130:            System.out.println("Error sending to
                     endpoint");
        }
      }
    }
```

Listing 18.2 Endpoint sending code. (continued)

Each button has a listener method associated with it, so the only work to be performed after joining the JXTA network is to display a message to the user to click a button and enter the application event loop. Clicking the top button creates a direct connection between the sending and receiving peers, and sends a message. Users wishing to use the propagate() method of the endpoint service to send a message should click the bottom button.

Lines 100 through 121 implement the functionality for the top button. When the user clicks the button, a dialog box is created (see line 102) to receive an endpoint address from the user. The user enters one of the endpoint addresses listed by the receiving peer. As mentioned earlier, all messages sent with the endpoint service are addressed to a specific handler created through the concatenation of the serviceName and serviceParam strings. On line 104, an EndpointAddress object is created using the address entered by the user. Lines 105 and 106 set the serviceName and serviceParm values of the endpoint address.

On line 108, the ping() method is used to ensure that the remote peer is available to receive a message. This is very important; the system will be unable to build a connection without the server available. Line 109 creates a message object to hold the information being sent to the server, and line 110 attaches a string to the object.

Lines 112 through 117 attempt to build a connection between the peers and send the message. The connection is built when the getMessenger() method is called on line 113. The method will do all of the dirty work associated with building the connection to the remote peer based on the protocol of the endpoint address passed to the method. Once the messenger is successfully instantiated, the message is sent.

Lines 123 through 133 implement the functionality of the second button. The code begins by instantiating a message object and populating it with a string. Next, the propagate() method is called, and passes the message to be sent on the JXTA network and the serviceName and serviceParm strings. Notice that no endpoint address is passed to the method; the system will send the message to all available peers on the network. Once peers have implemented the tempServiceNametempParams handler, they will process the message.

Summary

The endpoint service provides a low-level communication mechanism that can be used to bypass the JXTA pipes. By using this service, an application can bypass the default JXTA topology and build its own by manually sending messages. When using endpoints, a sending peer needs to know specific information about an endpoint on the remote peer, and listener objects are used to catch messages sent to peer handlers.

In the next chapter, we put to use all of the knowledge you gained from this chapter. We build a framework and sample application that allows algorithms to be passed to remote peers in an effort to build a comprehensive distributed system.

CHAPTER 19

Building a Generic Framework for Distributed Computing

One of the most popular uses for peer-to-peer applications in recent years has been to solve complex computational problems. Applications such as distributed.net and SETI use the idle CPU cycles of thousands of computers connected to the Internet in order to break encryption codes and find signs of intelligent life in outer space. The underlying foundation for this type of application is parallel processing—breaking a large problem into smaller pieces, distributing those pieces to an array of processors, and then combining the small solutions to solve the larger problem. Parallel machines are very expensive to build and maintain, so why not take advantage of smaller existing machines?

In this chapter, we build a generic distributed computational framework capable of utilizing the idle CPU cycles of any Internet computer that the peer is installed on. This framework can be easily extended with your own computational code. To accomplish this, we need to build the following components:

Computation code—The code that will be executed by the remote peers

Master peer—A peer that remote peers can contact to obtain the computation code as well as data to work with using the code

Worker peer—A peer that resides on multiple remote computers, requests work, solves it, and sends the results back to the master peer

Conclusion peer—An optional peer that can be contacted to return results from the computations

In this chapter, we discuss the first three components of the framework. The fourth component, the conclusion peer, is a good follow-up project to try on your own—its functionality has been incorporated into the master peer for this application. The master peer is responsible for accepting messages from the worker peers. The messages have two functions: to request code and data to work on and to deliver the results from the computation. As long as the master has data available, it will provide that information upon request.

The worker peer requests work as well as data from the master. In our example, the worker receives an object for the actual computation, and the necessary data is embedded in the object. The worker calls an appropriate method of the object and returns the results.

The computation code component is a class used to build objects for computation. This component follows a framework necessary for serialization and reconstruction on the worker peer. To show how the computational objects can be used to execute real problems, the Mandelbrot algorithm is used as an example.

Master Code

The master code for our generic distributed computation framework provides functionality for the following:

- Launching into the JXTA network
- Building an input pipe to receive work requests
- Building and instantiating work objects
- Gathering work results

The master peer will advertise a pipe for receiving work and result requests. The peer expects to receive a JXTA message with the type element defined. If the type element has a value of *results*, the message will also contain an element called results. This element could contain a value, a string, or a serialized object—it all depends on the complexity of the results.

If the type element has any other value, the master will assume that the remote peer is looking for new work. In this case, the message from the worker peer should contain an element called pipe that contains an input pipe advertisement for the worker. The worker will receive the work from the master over this pipe. The return message from the master will contain the element work. The content of the element consists of a serialized work class object, which we discuss later in this chapter.

The master peer is designed in the same fashion as other JXTA peers in this book. The most important part of the code is the listener for the input pipe. Listing 19.1 contains the code for the master.

```
Line 1: import java.awt.*;
import java.io.*;
import java.util.Enumeration;
import net.jxta.document.*;
import net.jxta.peergroup.*;
import net.jxta.exception.*;
import net.jxta.impl.peergroup.*;
import net.jxta.id.*;
import net.jxta.discovery.*;
Line 10: import net.jxta.pipe.*;
import net.jxta.protocol.*;
import net.jxta.platform.*;
import java.net.MalformedURLException;
import java.net.URL;
import net.jxta.endpoint.Message;

public class master {
    static  PeerGroup           netPeerGroup = null;
    private DiscoveryService     myDiscoveryService = null;
Line 20:    private PipeService             myPipeService = null;
    private PipeAdvertisement   myDBPipeAdvertisement = null;
    private InputPipe           myPipe = null;
    private OutputPipe          myOutputPipe = null;

    private final static     MimeMediaType XMLMIMETYPE =
      new MimeMediaType("text/xml");
    private Queue   resultsQueue = new Queue();

    private int x=150,
              y=0;
Line 30:    private int resolution = 300;
    private double xmin = -2.25,
                 xmax = 0.75,
                 ymin = -1.5,
                 ymax = 1.5,
                 xgap = (xmax - xmin) / (double)resolution,
                 ygap = (ymax - ymin) / (double)resolution;

    public master() {
      launchJXTA();
```

Listing 19.1 Master peer code. (continues)

```
Line 40:       getServices();
      buildAndPublishInputPipe();

  }

  static public void main(String[] args) {
     new master();
  }

  private void launchJXTA() {
Line 50:      try {
        netPeerGroup = PeerGroupFactory.newNetPeerGroup();
     } catch (PeerGroupException e) {
        System.out.println("Unable to create PeerGroup -
          Failure");
        e.printStackTrace();
        System.exit(1);
     }
  }

  private void getServices() {
Line 60:      myDiscoveryService =
             netPeerGroup.getDiscoveryService();
     myPipeService = netPeerGroup.getPipeService();
  }

  private void buildAndPublishInputPipe() {
     PipeAdvertisement aPipeAdv = null;

     try {
       FileInputStream is =
         new FileInputStream("inputpipe.adv");
       aPipeAdv = (PipeAdvertisement)AdvertisementFactory.
       newAdvertisement(new MimeMediaType("text/xml"), is);
Line 70:       } catch (Exception e) {
         System.out.println("failed to read/parse pipe
           advertisement");
         e.printStackTrace();
         System.exit(-1);
     }
     try {
       myDiscoveryService.publish(aPipeAdv,
         DiscoveryService.ADV);
       myDiscoveryService.remotePublish(aPipeAdv,
         DiscoveryService.ADV);
     } catch (Exception e) {
       e.printStackTrace();
```

Listing 19.1   Master peer code.   (continues)

```
Line 80:          System.exit(-1);
      }
    createInputPipe(aPipeAdv);
  }

  private void createInputPipe(PipeAdvertisement
    myPipeAdvertisement) {
    PipeMsgListener myService1Listener = new PipeMsgListener() {
      public void pipeMsgEvent(PipeMsgEvent event) {
        Message myMessage = null;
Line 90:        Integer intValue = null;
        try {
          myMessage = event.getMessage();
          if (myMessage.getString("type").equals("results")) {

            valueContainer result = new
              valueContainer(Integer.parseInt(
              myMessage.getString("result")),
              Integer.parseInt(
              myMessage.getString("x")),
              Integer.parseInt(
              myMessage.getString("y")));
            synchronized (resultsQueue) {
            resultsQueue.queueValue(result);
Line 100:            }
            System.out.println("From worker and queued: " +
              result.getResults() + " X:= " + result.getX() + "
              Y:= " + result.getY());
          } else {
            createOutputPipe(myMessage.getString("pipe"));

            work tempWork = new work(x, y, xmin, ymin, xgap, ygap);
            if ((y++) == resolution) {
              if ((x++) == resolution) {
                System.exit(0);
              }
Line 110:              y=0;
            }
            Message tempMessage =
              myPipeService.createMessage();

            ByteArrayOutputStream myStream =
              (ByteArrayOutputStream) new
              ByteArrayOutputStream();
            ObjectOutputStream s = new
              ObjectOutputStream(myStream);
            s.writeObject(tempWork);
```

Listing 19.1 Master peer code. (continues)

```
                    tempMessage.setString("work", myStream.toString());
                    myOutputPipe.send(tempMessage);
Line 120:                 }
            return;
        } catch (Exception ee) {
            ee.printStackTrace();
            return;
        }
      }
    };

    try {
Line 130:        myPipe = myPipeService.createInputPipe(
                    myPipeAdvertisement, myService1Listener);
        System.out.println("Input Pipe Created");
    } catch (Exception e) {
        e.printStackTrace();
        System.exit(-1);
    }
  }

  private void createOutputPipe(String
    myPipeAdvertisementString) {
    PipeAdvertisement myOutputPipeAdvertisement = null;
Line 140:      try {
        myOutputPipeAdvertisement = (PipeAdvertisement)
        AdvertisementFactory.newAdvertisement(XMLMIMETYPE, new
        ByteArrayInputStream(
        myPipeAdvertisementString.getBytes()));
    } catch (Exception e) {
        System.out.println("Error creating output Pipe");
        e.printStackTrace();
        System.exit(-1);
    }

    myOutputPipe = null;
    try {
Line 150:        myOutputPipe = myPipeService.createOutputPipe(
                    myOutputPipeAdvertisement, 100000);
    } catch (Exception e) {
        System.exit(-1);
    }
  }
}
```

Listing 19.1 Master peer code. (continued)

The input pipe listener is defined in lines 88 through 128. The code begins by checking the value contained in the message's type element. If the value is *results*, the framework code pulls the value for the elements results, x, and y; converts them to integers; encapsulates them into an object called valueContainer; and queues the object for later processing. Another thread should execute on the master peer to pull values from the queue and process them.

We would have to modify our code if more than one integer had to be returned as a result. It is still a good idea to have a queue in place to receive the results in the event they cannot be processed quickly enough.

The master next instantiates a new object based on the work class (defined later in the chapter). This class expects to have data provided to the object for processing through its constructor. Once the object is fully initialized, it is serialized into an ObjectOutputStream using the writeObject() method. The ObjectOutputStream is fed into a ByteArrayOutputStream. Finally, the work object is put into a String and placed in the work element of the message being sent to the worker peer.

Worker Code

The worker in the framework has two primary responsibilities: to request work and to return results to the master peer. Work is requested through an output pipe, which the worker peer discovers and then connects with. The worker will send a message with a type element having a value of *work*. Also included in the message is an advertisement for a pipe the worker has created to receive the work message from the master. Both the pipe and the advertisement are created dynamically when the worker peer is executed. Listing 19.2 contains the code for the worker peer.

```
Line 1: import java.io.*;
import java.awt.*;
import java.awt.event.*;
import javax.swing.*;
import java.util.Enumeration;
import net.jxta.document.*;
import net.jxta.peergroup.*;
import net.jxta.exception.PeerGroupException;
import net.jxta.impl.peergroup.Platform;
Line 10: import net.jxta.impl.peergroup.GenericPeerGroup;
import net.jxta.id.*;
```

Listing 19.2 Worker peer code. (continues)

```
import net.jxta.discovery.*;
import net.jxta.pipe.*;
import net.jxta.protocol.*;
import java.net.MalformedURLException;
import java.net.URL;
import net.jxta.endpoint.Message;

public class worker{
Line 20:
    static  PeerGroup            netPeerGroup = null;
    private DiscoveryService       myDiscoveryService = null;
    private PipeService       myPipeService = null;
    private PipeAdvertisement myPipeAdvertisement = null,
                           myInputPipeAdvertisement = null;
    private OutputPipe         myOutputPipe;
    private InputPipe          myInputPipe;
    private JTextArea          displayArea;
    private boolean            notDone;
Line 30:    private final static     MimeMediaType XMLMIMETYPE =
            new MimeMediaType("text/xml");

    public static void main(String args[]) {
        worker myapp = new worker();
    }

    public worker() {
      launchJXTA();
      getServices();
      createInputPipe();
Line 40:     findAdvertisement("Name", "JXTA:RequestInput");
      run();
    }

    public void run() {
      while (myOutputPipe == null) {
        try { Thread.sleep(300); } catch(Exception e) {}
      }
      while (true) {
        getWork();
Line 50:        while (notDone) {
          try {Thread.sleep(5);} catch(Exception e){}
        }
      }
    }

    private void launchJXTA() {
        System.out.println("Launching Peer into JXTA Network...\n");
```

Listing 19.2 Worker peer code. (continues)

```
          try {
              netPeerGroup = PeerGroupFactory.newNetPeerGroup();
Line 60:        } catch (PeerGroupException e) {
              System.out.println("Unable to create PeerGroup -
                Failure");
              e.printStackTrace();
              System.exit(1);
          }
      }

    private void getServices() {
        System.out.println("Getting Services...\n");
        myDiscoveryService = netPeerGroup.getDiscoveryService();
Line 70:        myPipeService = netPeerGroup.getPipeService();
    }


    private void createInputPipe() {
        System.out.println("Creating Input Pipe....\n");

        myInputPipeAdvertisement =
          (PipeAdvertisement)AdvertisementFactory.
          newAdvertisement(PipeAdvertisement.
          getAdvertisementType());
        myInputPipeAdvertisement.setName("JXTA:valueGet");
        myInputPipeAdvertisement.setType("JxtaUnicast");
        myInputPipeAdvertisement.setPipeID((ID)
          net.jxta.id.IDFactory.newPipeID(
          netPeerGroup.getPeerGroupID()));
Line 80:
        PipeMsgListener myService1Listener = new PipeMsgListener() {
          public void pipeMsgEvent(PipeMsgEvent event) {
            Message myMessage = null;
            try {
              myMessage = event.getMessage();

              String myMessageContent;

              StringBufferInputStream myStream =
                (StringBufferInputStream) new
                StringBufferInputStream(myMessage.getString(
                "work"));
Line 90:            ObjectInputStream s = new
                    ObjectInputStream(myStream);
              Object tempWork = s.readObject();
              ((work)tempWork).run();

              sendResults(((work)tempWork).getResult(),
```

Listing 19.2 Worker peer code. (continues)

```
                        ((work)tempWork).getX(), ((work)tempWork).getY());

                notDone = false;
                return;
            } catch (Exception ee) {
                ee.printStackTrace();
Line 100:               return;
            }
        }
    };

    try {
        myInputPipe = myPipeService.createInputPipe(
            myInputPipeAdvertisement, myService1Listener);
    } catch (Exception e) {
        System.out.println("Error creating Input Pipe");
        e.printStackTrace();
Line 110:           System.exit(-1);
    }
}

private void findAdvertisement(String searchKey, String
searchValue) {
    Enumeration myLocalEnum = null;
    System.out.println("Trying to find advertisement...\n");

    try {
        myLocalEnum = myDiscoveryService.getLocalAdvertisements(
            DiscoveryService.ADV, searchKey, searchValue);
Line 120:
        if ((myLocalEnum != null) &&
          myLocalEnum.hasMoreElements()) {
            System.out.println("Found Local Advertisement...\n");
            myPipeAdvertisement =
                (PipeAdvertisement)myLocalEnum.nextElement();
            createOutputPipe(myPipeAdvertisement);
        }
        else {
            DiscoveryListener myDiscoveryListener = new
              DiscoveryListener() {
                public void discoveryEvent(DiscoveryEvent e) {
                    Enumeration enum;
Line 130:               String str;

                    System.out.println("Found Remote
                        Advertisement...\n");
                    DiscoveryResponseMsg myMessage = e.getResponse();
```

Listing 19.2 Worker peer code. (continues)

```
                    enum = myMessage.getResponses();
                    str = (String)enum.nextElement();

                    try {
                      myPipeAdvertisement = (PipeAdvertisement)
                        AdvertisementFactory.newAdvertisement(
                        XMLMIMETYPE, new
                        ByteArrayInputStream(str.getBytes()));
                      createOutputPipe(myPipeAdvertisement);
Line 140:                 } catch(Exception ee) {
                      ee.printStackTrace();
                      System.exit(-1);
                    }
                 }
              };

            System.out.println("Launching Remote Discovery
              Service...\n");
            myDiscoveryService.getRemoteAdvertisements(null,
              DiscoveryService.ADV, searchKey, searchValue, 1,
              myDiscoveryListener);
          }
Line 150:       } catch (Exception e) {
            System.out.println("Error during advertisement
              search");
            System.exit(-1);
          }
       }

    private void createOutputPipe(PipeAdvertisement
      myPipeAdvertisement) {
      myOutputPipe = null;
      try {
          myOutputPipe = myPipeService.createOutputPipe(
            myPipeAdvertisement, 100000);
          System.out.println("Output Pipe Created...\n");
Line 160:     } catch (Exception e) {
            System.out.println("Unable to create output pipe");
            System.exit(-1);
          }
       }

    private void getWork() {
      ByteArrayOutputStream myStream = (ByteArrayOutputStream)
        new ByteArrayOutputStream();
      StructuredTextDocument paramDoc = (StructuredTextDocument)
        myInputPipeAdvertisement.getDocument(new
```

Listing 19.2   Worker peer code. (continues)

```
                MimeMediaType("text/xml"));
          try {
Line 170:          paramDoc.sendToStream(myStream);
          } catch (Exception e) {
             System.out.println("Unable to print output pipe");
             e.printStackTrace();
             System.exit(-1);
          }

          Message msg = myPipeService.createMessage();
          msg.setString("type", "work");
          msg.setString("pipe", myStream.toString());
Line 180:
          try {
            notDone = true;
            myOutputPipe.send(msg);
          } catch (Exception e) {
             System.out.println("Unable to print output pipe");
             e.printStackTrace();
             System.exit(-1);
          }
       }
Line 190:
       private void sendResults(int result, int x, int y) {
          Message msg = myPipeService.createMessage();

          msg.setString("type", "results");
          msg.setString("result", ""+result);
          msg.setString("x", ""+x);
          msg.setString("y", ""+y);
          try {
            myOutputPipe.send(msg);
          } catch (Exception e) {
Line 200:          System.out.println("Unable to print output
                     pipe");
             e.printStackTrace();
             System.exit(-1);
          }
       }
}
```

Listing 19.2   Worker peer code. (continued)

In the following sections, we discuss the two important parts of the worker peer: setup and work.

Setup

The setup of the worker peer is found in lines 37 through 41. Once the peer has been launched into the JXTA network, it will attempt to find and connect to the pipe advertised by the master peer. Before the connection is made to the pipe, no additional activity can occur on the worker. Within the run() method, the code uses a loop and the sleep() method to wait until the myOutputPipe variable has a value other than null. When the variable has an instantiated object associated with it, the worker will attempt to obtain and execute while there is work available. The code is designed to execute one piece of work at a time. This is accomplished by checking for a variable called notDone. If notDone is true, this indicates that the object sent from the master is still executing and that another one should not be obtained.

Work

The worker peer obtains work by calling the getWork() method, which is defined in lines 166 through 189. In this method, the peer sends a message to the master that has a type element with the value *work* and a pipe element that contains the pipe advertisement of the input pipe to the peer. The master will use the pipe to send the work to the worker peer. With the message sent to the master, the variable notDone is set to true, causing the loop in the run() method to execute, and preventing the system from requesting another piece of work.

The work is received by the listener for the worker peer's input pipe (defined in lines 83 through 103). When a message is received from the master, the worker peer extracts the string from the work element and converts it back into a Java object using an ObjectInputStream and the readObject() method. The instantiated and reincarnated object is executed by calling the run() method. Calling this method should cause the object to perform calculations on values provided to the object by the master. The run() method should block until it has populated the appropriate result attributes of the work object.

When control returns from the run() method, a call is made to the sendResults() method defined in lines 191 through 204. This method builds a message with the type, results, x, and y elements. The type element holds a value of *results* to let the master peer know that it is receiving results from a peer, and that the other elements hold the actual results.

The current framework returns just three results to the master. We must modify the sendResults() method if more than these integers have to be provided to the master peer. A further enhancement might be the inclusion of a result class, which the worker peer could populate and send to the master. If the result class was defined appropriately, the work class we discuss next might be able to populate it generically, thus allowing the peer to instantiate the result and send it.

Computational Code

The distributed computation framework requires a class that can be distributed to idle and willing machines on the Internet. The class designed for this distributed is called work, and Listing 19.3 contains the code for it.

The work class is very basic, and can be expanded as needed for a specific application such as distributed.net or SETI. The class is designed to be instantiated into an object; the object is then initialized and sent to a worker peer in a JXTA message. The worker peer receives the object and executes the run() method. The results from the work object are packaged into a JXTA message and sent to a master peer that gathers all the results. (The master peer's input pipe could have been sent in the original message with the work object or hardcoded into an idle peer's code.)

The process of sending the instantiated work object to a worker peer sounds simple, but there are a few things to keep in mind. First, the work class must implement the Java Serializable interface. In order to implement the interface, the text "implements Serializable" must be found after the class's definition line. If there are no special requirements for serialization of the class, no additional work has to occur in order for the Java system to be able to serialize an object of the class.

With the basic serialization code in place, the system will be able to serialize the work object using the code described in Listing 19.1 and put it into a JXTA message. When the worker peer receives the object and converts it back into a normal Java object, the Java runtime will throw an exception. The exception will state that the objects have different version IDs (which are assigned when the Java class is compiled). Because the work class file will be compiled in both the master and worker peer classes, the objects will have different version IDs. Fortunately, there is a workaround.

You will notice in the work class code a statement called

```
static final long serialVersionUID = 152024149877783929L;
```

This code tells the Java compiler to use a specific version ID when compiling and using the class. Both the master and worker peers will have the same class code using the same version ID, and no exception will be thrown when the object is reincarnated on the worker peer.

For our example, the Mandelbrot algorithm is executed, and each peer is responsible for calculating a single point. Obviously, this consumes quite a bit of network traffic. A more realistic work object would require much more in the way of computation. The work is performed in lines 42 through 64, which define the doMandel() method. The values needed in the algorithm can be found in the object's private variables. All of the variables were set when the work object was instantiated by the master peer.

```
Line 1: import java.io.*;

    public class work implements Serializable {
      private int result;
      private int i;
      private int j;
      private double xmin;
      private double ymin;
      private double xgap;
Line 10:      private double ygap;

      static final long serialVersionUID = 152024149877783929L;

      public work() {
      }

      public void run() {
        result = doMandel();
      }
Line 20:
      public work(int inx, int iny, double inxmin, double inymin,
        double inxgap, double inygap) {
        i = inx;
        j = iny;
        xmin = inxmin;
        ymin = inymin;
        xgap = inxgap;
        ygap = inygap;
      }

Line 30:      public int getX() {
        return i;
      }

      public int getY() {
        return j;
```

Listing 19.3 Distributed work class. (continues)

```
            }

         public int getResult() {
           return result;
Line 40:          }

         private int doMandel() {
           double x, y, sx2;
           double rad;
            int count;
           double savex, savey;
           x = xmin + (double)(i) * xgap;
           y = ymin + (double)(j) * ygap;
           savex = x;
Line 50:          savey = y;
           rad = 0.0;
           count = 0;
           while ((rad < 5.0) && (count < 1000)){
               sx2 = x;
               x = x * x - y * y + savex;
               y = 2.0 * sx2 * y + savey;
               rad = x * x + y * y;
               count++;
           }
Line 60:          if (rad >= 5.0)
               return count % 256;
           else
               return 0;
        }
}
```

Listing 19.3 Distributed work class. (continued)

Summary

In this chapter, we discussed a framework for allowing computations to be distributed to JXTA peers executing on the network. The framework allows an entire object based on a work class to be distributed, and encapsulates the computations necessary to solve a problem. As mentioned at the beginning of the chapter, you could add a conclusion component to the system that acts as a repository for results from the computations and works to produce a report or some other type of output.

In the next chapter, we continue the theme of developing JXTA applications by examining the development of a storage system. Our storage system uses encryption and multiple peers to provide fault tolerance.

CHAPTER 20

Building an Encrypted, Highly Available Storage System

In this chapter, we bring together many of the features of JXTA to build an *encrypted and highly available storage system (EHASS)*. This system accepts for safekeeping data in the form of images. The EHASS stores the images in one or more databases, and makes those images available for retrieval through a GUI client application.

System Architecture

The EHASS is based on a three-tier architecture, as shown in Figure 20.1. The four main components of the architecture are

databasePeer—This peer is responsible for all database access and control. Data is received by the peer and placed in one database associated with the peer. Depending on needs, the database can be either on the same node as the peer or on a different one.

businessPeer—This peer is responsible for acting as a buffer between the databasePeer and the gatheringPeer. The peer simply receives a packet and forwards it to the databasePeer, but additional logic could be incorporated.

gatheringPeer—This peer is responsible for gathering any data that needs to be saved in the EHASS and forwarding that data to a businessPeer. The peer could be a spider that looks at web sites for data, as described later in this chapter, or an application that parses e-mail, for example.

clientPeer—This peer is responsible for requesting an image from the database to be displayed. The clientPeer will typically be a GUI-based application that a person will use to request data from the data. The peer will interact with a businessPeer, which will in turn attempt to communicate with a databasePeer.

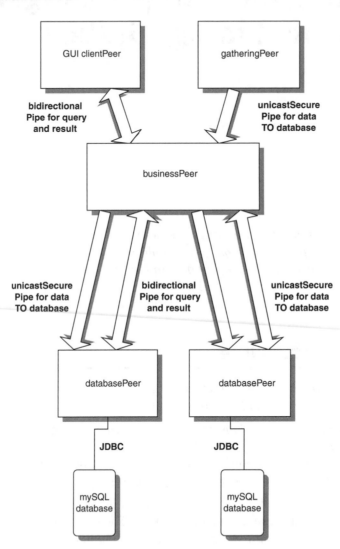

Figure 20.1 The basic architecture of an EHASS.

As you can see, this system is designed to be expandable in several different ways. First, multiple databasePeers can be in the system at one time. Each of the databasePeers will be discovered as needed by the businessPeers. Using more than one databasePeer ensures that all data stored in the EHASS will be replicated and highly available. Second, multiple businessPeers can be instantiated to handle the specific needs of a clientPeer or to provide redundancy. Finally, the gatheringPeers in the system are unlimited—all that is required is that a JXTA interface be built into the user. The JXTA system handles locating a businessPeer and the actual transport of the data.

Our Example

For the purposes of explaining an EHASS, the peers in our example are designed to handle a particular solution. The code you'll find in the Chapter 20 directory of the download source features a system that allows image data to be stored in a database using the EHASS.

In the test architecture, you will find two databasePeers, one businessPeer, and a gatheringPeer, all distributed across three different machines. The databasePeers are located on one machine that executes the Mandrake Linux 8.2 beta. One of the databasePeers communicates with a MySQL database executing on the same box through a JDBC connection. The other databasePeer has a connection to another MySQL database executing on a remote Linux box running Caldera 2.3. The databasePeer connecting to the remote database doesn't store all data it receives—it is executed with a command-line option limiting the category of image it should store. The idea is that the remote database is replicating only the most important images. As you might expect, we could use the latest MySQL version to perform database replication as well.

The businessPeer executes on a second machine, running Windows 2000. The businessPeer is designed to locate both of the databasePeers. The primary purpose of the businessPeer is to act as the middle tier in a three-tier architecture. The businessPeer will receive data from a gatheringPeer and store it in a database. Based on the data contents, the businessPeer can decide where and how to store the information. The businessPeer will also receive requests from a gatheringPeer for information from the database. Again, the businessPeer could be coded with functionality to check for authentication or other logging purposes.

The gatheringPeer is located on a third machine, also running Windows 2000. This gatheringPeer is a modified version of the open-source application called WebLech. The WebLech application takes a URL, pulls all pages and images on the site, and saves them to the local hard drive. We changed the application's source code to put all images into a message and ship the image to the businessPeer. The domain, path, and filename of the image are sent as well. We could assign an optional category to provide some level of filtering at the database. All of the image data is encrypted by the gatheringPeer before being sent to the database.

The client is also a JXTA peer executing on a fourth machine in the network. Queries are executed from the client, and the resulting images are displayed. We tested the code for the system components on a combination of machines; all of the components can execute solely on a Linux box, a Windows machine, or a combination as described above.

Database Schema

The database used in our example is MySQL. A basic MySQL installation is all you need. The database in the example is called pics; you should create it within MySQL by using either a SQL interface to MySQL or the mysql administrator application. The steps for creating the database are as follows:

1. Launch the mysql administrator by issuing the command mysql.

2. Build a new database called pics with the command

   ```
   create database pics;
   ```

3. Once the database is created, build a table with the following command:

   ```
   create table main ( ID int not null auto_increment
                       primary key,
                       name      varchar(128),
                       data      mediumblob,
                       ts        timestamp,
                       domain    varchar(128),
                       path      varchar(128),
                       category  varchar(32),
                       size      int);
   ```

The same table exists on both the database machines. Because there is always the potential to store duplicate data, the database code will execute a SELECT query to check for the same name, domain, and path in the database. The current code uses the username *spider* and the password *spider* to access the MySQL database. You could change these names in both the databasePeer and the spider peer, if necessary.

Message Schema

For this application, a specific message schema is used. The elements available are

   Filename—The name of the data to save

   Data—The binary data

   Domain —The domain of the source of the data

   Path—The path associated with the domain and name

Category—A category to assign the data

Size—The size of the data (or image in this case)

You can change the message to be specific to an application or more generalized.

Executing the System

Executing the EHASS requires only a few steps. First, execute all of the databasePeers in the system, and make sure the appropriate database connections are created. Figure 20.2 shows the execution of a database connection on a Linux box. There are a few System.out.println() methods in the peer code so you can see what is occurring interactively.

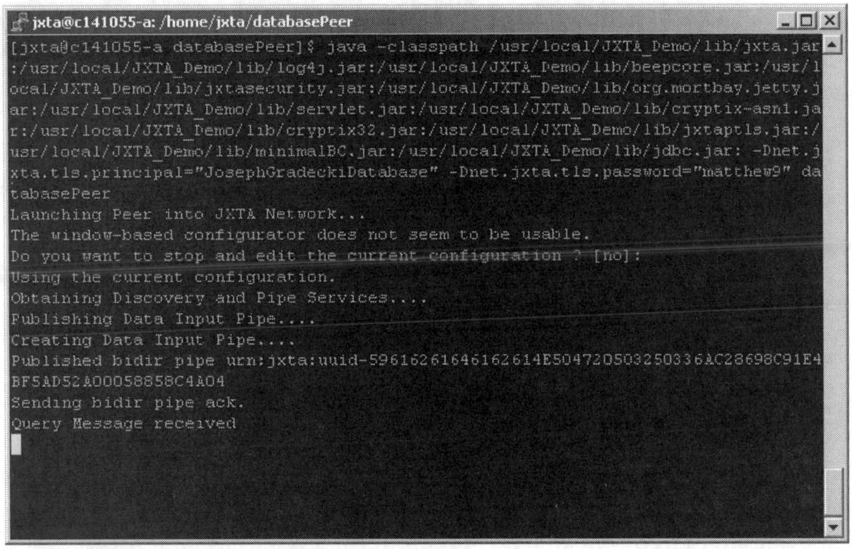

Figure 20.2 Execution of the databasePeer.

Once the databasePeers are fully launched, execute the businessPeers. After a few moments, the businessPeers will discover the databasePeers in the network and create output pipes to them. Figure 20.3 shows the execution of a businessPeer. Of particular note is the output showing the businessPeer's attempt to find and connect with the databasePeers.

With the businessPeers connected to the databasePeers, the gatheringPeers can be executed. These source peers will discover the businessPeers and begin the process of sending data to be stored in the underlying databases (somewhere in the network). The gatheringPeers will execute based on their programmed functionality—to "spider" the web or look through e-mail messages, for example.

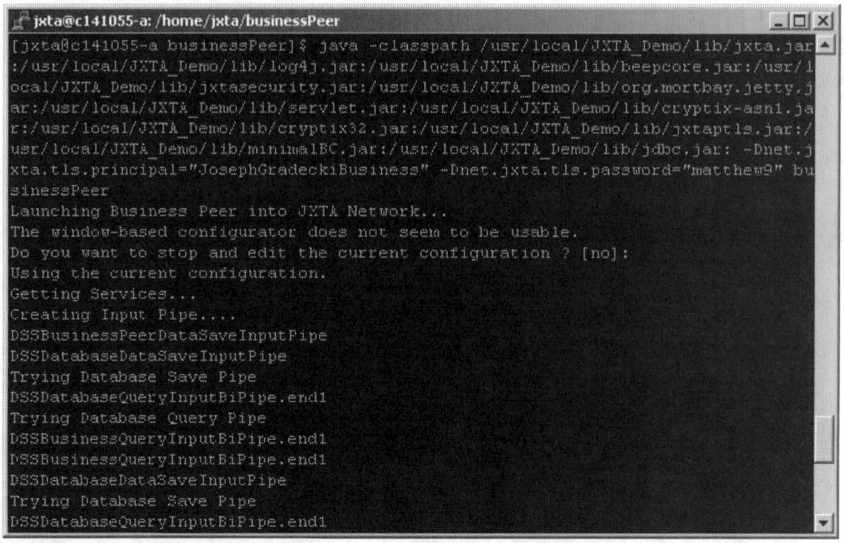

Figure 20.3 Execution of the businessPeer.

The gatheringPeer provided with the code for this chapter is called spider, and it operates by pulling a URL from a file called links.dat. The format of the links.dat file is

```
DatabaseTableName
URL
```

For example,

```
Main
http://www.yahoo.com
```

It should be noted that multiple URLs can appear in the links.dat file as needed. Figure 20.4 shows the execution of the spider peer. This gatheringPeer will send data to the businessPeer and ultimately to the database.

At the same time the gatheringPeers are executing, a client can be executed to retrieve information from the database. Figure 20.5 shows an example of submitting a query to the EHASS. Notice the list of pictures returned in the file list at the bottom of the GUI. Figure 20.6 shows what happens when we double-click one of the filenames.

```
jxta@c141055-a: /home/jxta/oldspider                        _ □ X
usr/local/JXTA_Demo/lib/cryptix32.jar:/usr/local/JXTA_Demo/lib/jxtaptls.jar:/usr
/local/JXTA_Demo/lib/minimalBC.jar:/usr/local/JXTA_Demo/lib/jdbc.jar: -Dnet.jxta
.tls.principal="JosephGradeckiDatabase" -Dnet.jxta.tls.password="matthew9" weble
ch.spider.Spider config/Spider.properties
category
.....Updated 1row(s) in primary DB
......Updated 1row(s) in primary DB
.......................Updated 1row(s) in primary DB
.Updated 1row(s) in primary DB
.Updated 1row(s) in primary DB
.Updated 1row(s) in primary DB
.Updated 1row(s) in primary DB
.Updated 1row(s) in primary DB
.Updated 1row(s) in primary DB
.Updated 1row(s) in primary DB
.Updated 1row(s) in primary DB
.Updated 1row(s) in primary DB
.Updated 1row(s) in primary DB
.Updated 1row(s) in primary DB
..Updated 1row(s) in primary DB
.........Bailing
Total Count = 67
[jxta@c141055-a oldspider]$
```

Figure 20.4   The spider gatheringPeer.

Figure 20.5   A list of images requested from the database.

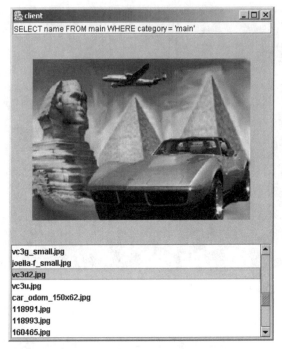

Figure 20.6 Displaying an image found in the database.

DatabasePeer

The databasePeer is responsible for storing data in the database. The features of the databasePeer include:

- JDBC connection to an ODBC-compliant database
- Command-line category filtering
- Command-line database domain/IP selection
- An option for local file system saves
- An option for local decryption of image data

The databasePeer is executed using the Java commands found in Appendix A. A few additional options are available. If the command line includes the –d option followed by a domain or IP address, this domain or IP will be used to contact a remote database. If the option is not present, the IP of 127.0.0.1 will be used. This IP is equivalent to the localhost. The domain or IP of 127.0.0.1 is used to build a connection string for the JDBC connection.

If the command-line option –s is used, a filter value can be assigned for the category column of the database. The databasePeer will use the value to determine whether or not an image is stored in the database. If this switch does not appear in the execution of the databasePeer or the option *–s all* is used, all images sent to this databasePeer will be stored. If the value of the option is something like *–s cars*, only data sent to this databasePeer will be saved in the database when the value of the category field of a message matches.

The code for the databasePeer is shown in Listing 20.1.

```
Line 1: import java.io.*;
import java.awt.*;
import java.awt.event.*;
import javax.swing.*;

import java.util.*;
import net.jxta.document.*;
import net.jxta.peergroup.*;
import net.jxta.exception.*;
Line 10: import net.jxta.impl.peergroup.*;
import net.jxta.id.*;
import net.jxta.discovery.*;
import net.jxta.pipe.*;
import net.jxta.protocol.*;
import net.jxta.platform.*;
import java.net.*;
import net.jxta.endpoint.*;
import java.sql.*;
import net.jxta.impl.util.BidirectionalPipeService;
Line 20:

public class databasePeer {

    static  PeerGroup netPeerGroup = null;
    private DiscoveryService myDiscoveryService = null;
    private PipeService myPipeService = null;

    private BidirectionalPipeService myBiPipeService = null;
    private BidirectionalPipeService.Pipe myQueryPipe = null;
Line 30:     private BidirectionalPipeService.AcceptPipe
                incomingAcceptPipe = null;
    private BidirectionalPipeService.MessageListener
      myListenerService;

    private InputPipe myBusinessDataSaveInputPipe = null;
    private Connection conn = null;
    static  String database = new String("127.0.0.1");
    static  String categorySwitch = new String("all");
```

Listing 20.1 The databasePeer code. (continues)

```
      static  String DBUrl1 = "jdbc:mysql://";
      static  String DBUrl2 = "/pics?user=root&password=";
Line 40:
      private final static MimeMediaType XMLMIMETYPE =
        new MimeMediaType("text/xml");

      public static void main(String args[]) {
          databasePeer myapp = new databasePeer();
       if (args.length > 0) {
            for (int i=0;i<args.length;i++) {
              if (args[i].equals("-d")) {
              database = args[i+1];
              break;
Line 50:             }

            if (args[i].equals("-s")) {
            categorySwitch = args[i+1];
            break;
          }
        }
      }
    }

Line 60:    public databasePeer() {
        run();
    }

    public void run() {

      try {
        Class.forName("org.gjt.mm.mysql.Driver").newInstance();
        conn =
          DriverManager.getConnection(DBUrl1+database+DBUrl2);
      } catch (Exception E) {
Line 70:          System.out.println("JDBC Driver error");
      }

      launchJXTA();
      getServices();
      publishDataInputPipe();
      buildQueryPipe();

      while (true) {
        try {
Line 80:          Thread.sleep(500);
        if (myQueryPipe == null) {
```

Listing 20.1 The databasePeer code. (continues)

```
          myQueryPipe = incomingAcceptPipe.accept(
            3000, myListenerService);
      }
    } catch(Exception e) {}
    }


    }

    private void launchJXTA() {
Line 90:        System.out.println("Launching Peer into JXTA
                Network...");
        try {
            netPeerGroup = PeerGroupFactory.newNetPeerGroup();
        } catch (PeerGroupException e) {
            System.out.println("Unable to create PeerGroup -
                Failure");
            e.printStackTrace();
            System.exit(1);
        }
    }

Line 100:    private void getServices() {
        System.out.println("Obtaining Discovery and Pipe
          Services....");
        myDiscoveryService = netPeerGroup.getDiscoveryService();
        myPipeService = netPeerGroup.getPipeService();
        myBiPipeService =
          new BidirectionalPipeService(netPeerGroup);
    }

    private void publishDataInputPipe() {
        System.out.println("Publishing Data Input Pipe....");
        try {
Line 110:      PipeAdvertisement aPipeAdv =
  (PipeAdvertisement)AdvertisementFactory.
   newAdvertisement(PipeAdvertisement.getAdvertisementType());
        aPipeAdv.setName("DSSDatabaseDataSaveInputPipe");
        aPipeAdv.setType("JxtaUnicastSecure");
        aPipeAdv.setPipeID((ID) net.jxta.id.IDFactory.newPipeID(
          netPeerGroup.getPeerGroupID()));
        myDiscoveryService.publish(aPipeAdv,
          DiscoveryService.ADV);
        myDiscoveryService.remotePublish(aPipeAdv,
          DiscoveryService.ADV);
      createInputPipe(aPipeAdv);
        } catch (Exception e) {
          System.out.println("Error during publish of Module
```

Listing 20.1 The databasePeer code. (continues)

```
                Specification Advertisement");
Line 120:            e.printStackTrace();
          System.exit(-1);
      }
    }

    private void createInputPipe(PipeAdvertisement
      myPipeAdvertisement) {
      System.out.println("Creating Data Input Pipe....");

      PipeMsgListener myService1Listener =
        new PipeMsgListener(){
        public void pipeMsgEvent(PipeMsgEvent event) {
Line 130:            Message myMessage = null;
            try {
              myMessage = event.getMessage();

            if (myMessage.getString("filename") != null) {
                System.out.println("Message Received - Checking
                  database");

                if (categorySwitch.equals("all") ||
                  categorySwitch.equals(
                  myMessage.getString("category"))) {
                  Statement stmt = conn.createStatement();
                  ResultSet rs = stmt.executeQuery("SELECT name,
                    domain, path FROM main WHERE name = '" +
                    myMessage.getString("filename") + "' AND
                    domain = '" + myMessage.getString("domain") +
                    "' AND path = '" + myMessage.getString("path")
                    + "'");
Line 140:
                  if (!rs.next()) {
                  PreparedStatement pstmt =
                    conn.prepareStatement("INSERT INTO main
                    VALUES (null, '" +
                    myMessage.getString("filename") + "',?,
                    now(), '" + myMessage.getString("domain") +
                    "', '" + myMessage.getString("path") + "', '"
                    + myMessage.getString("category") + "', " +
                    myMessage.getString("size") + " )");
                  pstmt.setBytes(1, myMessage.getBytes("data"));
                  pstmt.execute();

                  int rowsUpdated = pstmt.getUpdateCount();
                  System.out.println("Updated " + rowsUpdated +
                    "row(s)");
```

Listing 20.1 The databasePeer code. (continues)

```
                                 }
                             }
Line 150:                          return;
                       } else {
                           System.out.println("Invalid tag\n");
                           return;
                       }
                   } catch (Exception ee) {
                       ee.printStackTrace();
                       return;
                   }
               }
           };
Line 160:
           try {
               myBusinessDataSaveInputPipe =
                   myPipeService.createInputPipe(myPipeAdvertisement,
                   myService1Listener);
           } catch (Exception e) {
               System.out.println("Error creating Input Pipe");
               e.printStackTrace();
               System.exit(-1);
           }
       }

Line 170:    private void buildQueryPipe() {
           try {
               incomingAcceptPipe =
                   myBiPipeService.bind("DSSDatabaseQueryInputBiPipe");

               myListenerService =
                new BidirectionalPipeService.MessageListener () {
                public void messageReceived (Message msg, OutputPipe
                 responsePipe) {

                   if (msg.getString("action").equals("QUERY")) {
                     System.out.println("Query Message received");

Line 180:             try {
                       Statement stmt = conn.createStatement();
                       ResultSet rs =
                        stmt.executeQuery(msg.getString("SQL"));
                       String results = new String();

                       while (rs.next()) {
                         results = results + rs.getString("name") +
                         "|";
```

Listing 20.1   The databasePeer code. (continues)

```
                }

                Message sendMsg = myPipeService.createMessage();
Line 190:            sendMsg.setString("action", "QUERY");
                sendMsg.setString("results", results);
                responsePipe.send(sendMsg);
            } catch(Exception e) {}
            return;
          } else {
            try {
              Statement stmt = conn.createStatement();
              ResultSet rs = stmt.executeQuery("SELECT data
                FROM main WHERE name = '" +
                msg.getString("name") + "'");

Line 200:              if (rs.next()) {
                Message sendMsg =
                  myPipeService.createMessage();
                sendMsg.setString("action", "GET");
                sendMsg.setBytes("result",
                  rs.getBytes("data"));
                responsePipe.send(sendMsg);
              }
            } catch(Exception e) {}
            return;
          }
        }
Line 210:        };
      } catch(Exception e) {
        e.printStackTrace();
    System.exit(-1);
      }
    }
}
```

Listing 20.1 The databasePeer code. (continued)

The code for the databasePeer is based on the same code as the other peers in this book, and can be broken down into four key areas: setting up, publishing a data input pipe, publishing a query input pipe, and processing input.

DatabasePeer Connectivity

The databasePeer has several different connections to external components. The first connection is to the storage device, which in most cases will be a database. The database is required to follow the ODBC protocol.

A second connection is a single JxtaUnicastSecure input pipe that will receive data to be saved in the database. The name of the pipe is DSSDatabase-DataSaveInputPipe, and it is published using a pipe advertisement to the local and remote JXTA network. This connection is made between a businessPeer and a databasePeer, and relies on a message with this format:

```
filename - string
domain - string
path - string
category - string
size - int
data - bytes
```

The third connection is a bidirectional pipe that will receive queries from a client application. The name of the pipe is DSSDatabaseQueryInputBiPipe, and it is also published using a pipe advertisement to the local and remote JXTA network. This connection is made between a businessPeer and a databasePeer. Two messages are transferred between a clientPeer and the databasePeer. The first is a query for the names of files in the database based on a specific criteria. The message's elements are

action—The value of QUERY

SQL—The SQL statement passed from the client; it is assumed to be in the form

```
SELECT name FROM main WHERE category = '<value>'
```

The results from the query are placed in a string delimited by the character |. The entire string is placed in a message with these elements:

action—The value of QUERY

results—An element that contains the delimited string of names found in the database

The second message used between the businessPeer and the databasePeer is sent when the data from a single image needs to be extracted from the database. The elements in this message are

action—The value of GET

name—The name of the file to pull from the database

When the data from the file is pulled from the database, it is returned in a message with these elements:

action—The value of GET

results—Bytes from the database

Setup

Many of the peers in our previous examples have had a GUI to display information produced by the peer. The architecture of the system dictates that the databasePeer and businessPeer execute in a minimalist way, so no GUI is attached to the peer. Any output needed from the peer should be displayed either in the command window or, better yet, through a series of log files. For the databasePeer code, the primary class is called databasePeer.

The main( ) method instantiates a new application object and checks on the two possible command-line options—as you'll recall, –d designates a domain for the database connect, and –s designates a category string to filter image data placed in the database. The string associated with either option is stored in a static string variable to be used by the application object.

The constructor for the application object consists of a call to the run( ) method. The run( ) method starts on line 64, and performs a number of operations for launching the peer.

Line 66 gets the JDBC driver necessary for our database connection; then, the code attempts to connect to the database specified by the combination of the DBUrl1, database, and DBUrl2 strings. Notice that the peer will not fail if the database connection isn't made. If this isn't what you want, you can add the statement System.exit(-1); to halt the peer.

Lines 73 and 74 should look familiar; this is where the peer is launched in the JXTA network, and the necessary discovery and pipe services are obtained. On line 75, a call is made to create and publish the pipe used to receive data destined for the database. On line 76, the bidirectional pipe is created to receive queries from a clientPeer.

Finally, an infinite loop is defined to keep the databasePeer executing continuously. In order to keep the CPU from executing at 100 percent, the application will be forced to sleep for a half-second at a time. Within the infinite loop is code that attempts to connect using the bidirectional pipe, but only if a connection isn't already assigned. In the bidirectional code, the parameters to the accept( ) method found in line 82 specify the number of milliseconds to wait for a connection and the listener to use once a connection is made. The source code for the bidirectional pipe should allow a value of 0 for the wait time, and it does with the anticipated result of blocking until a connection is made. However, if a value of 0 is used, the system isn't able to obtain a connection with any clients. This appears to be a bug in the bidirectional code. Nevertheless, the workaround is to just call the accept( ) method periodically to find a connection from a client.

Publishing a Data Input Pipe

One of the most important jobs of the databasePeer is to publish the pipe advertisement so that businessPeers can find and connect with it. The databasePeer advertises a pipe using an advertisement like the following:

```
<?xml version="1.0" encoding="UTF-8"?>
<jxta:PipeAdvertisement>
    <Name>DSSDatabaseDataSaveInputPipe</Name>
        <Id>urn:jxta:uuid-CE19C9353ED641B6A1
            879527667BBC32699352C32E0D40579C17A7CCB7CE781C04</Id>
        <Type>JxtaUnicastSecure</Type>
</jxta:PipeAdvertisement>
```

Because all databasePeers will be publishing a pipe, it is critical that each of the pipe advertisements have a unique ID. For this reason, the code in lines 110 through 113 builds a pipe dynamically, and publishes it locally and remotely. Using code to generate the pipe advertisement ensures that the databasePeers can be distributed without worrying about a remote advertisement file that has be updated.

The code for creating and publishing the pipe advertisement is found on lines 105 through 162. Unlike other applications we have built, the code doesn't rely on module class and module specification advertisements to publish the existence of a pipe, but simply publishes the pipe advertisement itself.

Publishing a Query Bidirectional Pipe

Lines 170 through 213 handle the creation of the bidirectional pipe. A bidirectional pipe is a little different from the traditional JXTA pipe in that a preliminary pipe is created to listen for remote connections. Once a connection to the listening pipe is made, a series of input and output pipes are created between the local and remote peer. As we noted earlier, the code for accepting a connection with the bidirectional pipe is found in the run() method.

Processing Input

Both the data input and query input pipes accept messages that must be processed. For the data input pipe, the messages will contain information to be placed in the database associated with this peer. The query input pipe will have messages requesting information from the database. In both cases, the processing is handled by a listener attached to the respective pipes.

Data Input Processing

Lines 127 through 159 establish a listener object for the data input pipe. Recall from an earlier discussion that the data input pipe will receive a message from a businessPeer, which contains an image to be placed in the database. Line 131 determines if anything should occur within this databasePeer. The variable categorySwitch is set when the databasePeer is executed and defaults to a value of *ALL*. This means that all images received by the peer will be placed in the database. You can use a command-line option to change the value to reflect a specific category to place in the database. This option allows some databases to hold only sensitive or important data, not common data.

For logical reasons, the same image shouldn't be placed in the database, if possible. To help facilitate keeping duplicate images out of the database, the listener code will execute a SELECT query using the name of the image, the domain and path where the image came from, or values placed in these message entries. The SELECT query is performed on lines 137 and 138; line 140 checks the result of the query. If the ResultSet returned from the query is empty, the databasePeer will attempt to place the image in the database.

The code uses a PreparedStatement to handle the insertion of binary data into the database. On line 141, the PreparedStatement is created using most of elements in the message received from the businessPeer. Notice the use of the ? in the statement—this is a placeholder that will receive the binary data inserted from line 142.

Finally, the statement is executed against the database. Line 145 executes the code against the statement to return the number of rows affected by the insert.

Query Processing

The processing for a query message received from the bidirectional pipe is handled in lines 175 through 205. There are two possible options for a message received on the pipe: QUERY or GET. Line 177 checks the action element of the message to determine the option needed in this specific case. Lines 178 through 194 will process a QUERY message. It is assumed that the message element SQL contains a SELECT statement in the form

```
SELECT name FROM main WHERE category = 'value'
```

The SQL is executed against the database on line 182. Lines 185 through 187 loop through the names returned by the query. The names are placed in a string delimited by the | character. The final string is placed in a new message under the element *results*. On line 192, the message is sent down the response pipe that was defined when this bidirectional pipe's listener was called.

The processing for a GET message is handled in lines 196 through 207. A SELECT command is created using the filename found in the name element. On line 200, the ResultSet from the query is checked for a result. If a result is found, the bytes are placed in a message element called *result* using the setBytes() method instead of setString() because the image data consists of raw bytes and we don't want them to be converted to characters. Finally, the message with the data from the query is returned to the calling peer.

BusinessPeer

The businessPeer acts as an intermediary between the databasePeer and any potential users of the system (for example, sourcePeers and clientPeers). All of the messages received from a user application will arrive at the businessPeer and be forwarded to 0 or more databasePeers.

The businessPeer in this example will transfer all messages to databasePeers automatically. However, the underlying purpose of a businessPeer is to implement business rules of an organization. The rules are placed between the receipt of the message and the subsequent transfer to the databasePeers. The code for the businessPeer is shown in Listing 20.2.

Because the businessPeer will be connecting two different types of sources to the database, there are two different pipes. The first pipe is Unicast, and transfers data from a gatheringPeer to the databasePeer. Data is placed in the pipe and ultimately stored in the database. The second pipe is a bidirectional pipe designed to handle query requests from a clientPeer. The clientPeer will expect a response, either as a list of names found in the database or as data from a specific image when a message is sent to the businessPeer through the bidirectional pipe.

What makes the businessPeer unique is the use of code to discover remote advertisements for both of the pipes we need to connect to from the databasePeer. The remote discovery is accomplished by looking for all advertisements with a name value of *DSS**. Obviously, this will bring in a number of responses. For the bidirectional query pipe, only a single connection is made to a databasePeer. It really doesn't matter what databasePeer gets the connection.

```
Line 1: import java.io.*;
import java.awt.*;
import java.awt.event.*;
import javax.swing.*;
```

Listing 20.2 The businessPeer Code. (continues)

```
import java.util.Enumeration;
import net.jxta.document.*;
import net.jxta.peergroup.*;
import net.jxta.exception.*;
import net.jxta.impl.peergroup.*;
Line 10: import net.jxta.id.*;
import net.jxta.discovery.*;
import net.jxta.pipe.*;
import net.jxta.protocol.*;
import net.jxta.platform.*;
import java.net.MalformedURLException;
import java.net.URL;
import net.jxta.endpoint.Message;
import net.jxta.impl.util.BidirectionalPipeService;
import java.util.Hashtable;
Line 20:
public class businessPeer {
  static  PeerGroup          netPeerGroup = null;
  private DiscoveryService       myDiscoveryService = null;
  private PipeService       myPipeService = null;
  private PipeAdvertisement   myDBPipeAdvertisement = null;
  private PipeAdvertisement   myPipeAdvertisement = null;
  private OutputPipe myDBOutputPipe[] = new OutputPipe[10];
  private int               myDBOutputPipeCount = 0;
  private InputPipe         myPipe = null;
Line 30:  private BidirectionalPipeService
            myBiPipeService = null;
  private BidirectionalPipeService.Pipe
    myClientQueryPipe = null;
  private BidirectionalPipeService.Pipe
    myDatabaseQueryPipe = null;
  private BidirectionalPipeService.AcceptPipe
    incomingAcceptPipe;
  private BidirectionalPipeService.MessageListener
    myListenerService;
  private final static    MimeMediaType XMLMIMETYPE =
    new MimeMediaType("text/xml");

  private boolean haveDatabaseDataInputPipe = false;
  private boolean allowMultipleDatabase = false;
  private Hashtable currentOutputAdv = new Hashtable();
Line 40:
  public static void main(String args[]) {
    businessPeer myapp = new businessPeer();
    myapp.run();
  }
```

Listing 20.2 The businessPeer Code. (continues)

```
  public businessPeer() {
  }

  public void run() {
Line 50:    launchJXTA();
    getServices();
    buildAndPublishInputPipe();

    launchRemoteDiscovery("Name", "DSS*");

    while ((myDatabaseQueryPipe == null) &&
          (myDBOutputPipeCount == 0))    {
      findLocalAdvertisements("Name", "DSS*");
    }

Line 60:    getClientPipe();
    while (true) {
      try {
        Thread.sleep(500);
        if (myClientQueryPipe == null) {
         myClientQueryPipe = incomingAcceptPipe.accept(10000,
         myListenerService);
        }
        if (allowMultipleDatabase == true) {
          findLocalAdvertisements("Name", "DSS*");
        }
Line 70:        } catch(Exception e) {}
    }
  }

    private void launchJXTA() {
      System.out.println("Launching Business Peer into JXTA
        Network...");
      try {
        netPeerGroup = PeerGroupFactory.newNetPeerGroup();
      } catch (PeerGroupException e) {
        System.out.println("Unable to create PeerGroup -
        Failure");
Line 80:        e.printStackTrace();
        System.exit(1);
      }
    }

    private void getServices() {
      System.out.println("Getting Services...");
      myDiscoveryService = netPeerGroup.getDiscoveryService();
      myPipeService = netPeerGroup.getPipeService();
```

Listing 20.2   The businessPeer Code. (continues)

```
          myBiPipeService =
            new BidirectionalPipeService(netPeerGroup);
Line 90:      }

      private void launchRemoteDiscovery(String searchKey,
        String searchValue) {
        try {
          myDiscoveryService.getRemoteAdvertisements(null,
            DiscoveryService.ADV, searchKey, searchValue, 50);
        } catch (Exception e) {
          System.out.println("Error during remote advertisement
            discovery");
          System.exit(-1);
        }
      }
Line 100:

      private void sendData(Message aMsg) {
        try {
          if (myDBOutputPipeCount > 0)
          for (int i=0;i<myDBOutputPipeCount;i++) {
            myDBOutputPipe[i].send (aMsg);
          }
        } catch (Exception e) {
          System.out.println("Unable to print output pipe");
Line 110:        }
      }

      private void buildAndPublishInputPipe() {
        try {
          FileInputStream is = new
            FileInputStream("businessPeerDataSaveInputPipe.adv");
          PipeAdvertisement aPipeAdv =
            (PipeAdvertisement)AdvertisementFactory.
            newAdvertisement(new MimeMediaType("text/xml"), is);

          myDiscoveryService.publish(aPipeAdv,
            DiscoveryService.ADV);
          myDiscoveryService.remotePublish(aPipeAdv,
            DiscoveryService.ADV);
Line 120:          createInputPipe(aPipeAdv);

        } catch (Exception e) {
          System.out.println("Error during publish of Module
            Specification Advertisement");
          e.printStackTrace();
          System.exit(-1);
```

Listing 20.2 The businessPeer Code. (continues)

```
        }
    }

    private void createInputPipe(PipeAdvertisement
     myPipeAdvertisement) {
Line 130:        System.out.println("Creating Input Pipe....");
      PipeMsgListener myService1Listener = new PipeMsgListener()
      {
        public void pipeMsgEvent(PipeMsgEvent event) {
          Message myMessage = null;
          try {
            myMessage = event.getMessage();
            sendData(myMessage);
            return;
          } catch (Exception ee) {
            ee.printStackTrace();
Line 140:            return;
          }
        }
      };
      try {
        myPipe = myPipeService.createInputPipe(
          myPipeAdvertisement, myService1Listener);
      } catch (Exception e) {
        System.out.println("Error creating Input Pipe");
        e.printStackTrace();
        System.exit(-1);
      }
Line 150:    }

    private void findLocalAdvertisements(String searchKey,
     String searchValue) {
      try {
        Enumeration LocalEnum =
          myDiscoveryService.getLocalAdvertisements(
          DiscoveryService.ADV, searchKey, searchValue);

        if (LocalEnum != null) {
          while (LocalEnum.hasMoreElements()) {
            PipeAdvertisement aPipeAdv =
              (PipeAdvertisement)LocalEnum.nextElement();
            String pipeName = aPipeAdv.getName();
            System.out.println(pipeName);
Line 160:
            if ((myDatabaseQueryPipe == null) &&
              (pipeName.indexOf("DSSDatabaseQueryInputBiPipe")
                != -1)) {
```

Listing 20.2 The businessPeer Code. (continues)

```
            try {
              System.out.println("Trying Database Query
                Pipe");
              myDatabaseQueryPipe = myBiPipeService.connect(
                aPipeAdv, 10000);
              System.out.println("Got Database Query Pipe");
            } catch(Exception e) {
        continue;
            }
          }
Line 170:
          if (pipeName.equals("DSSDatabaseDataSaveInputPipe"))
          {
            if (currentOutputAdv.containsValue(aPipeAdv) ==
             false) {
              try {
                System.out.println("Trying Database Save
                  Pipe");
                myDBOutputPipe[myDBOutputPipeCount] =
                  myPipeService.createOutputPipe(aPipeAdv,
                  10000);
                currentOutputAdv.put(new
                  Integer(myDBOutputPipeCount), aPipeAdv);
                System.out.println("Got Database Data Input
                  Pipe");
              } catch (Exception e) {
                continue;
Line 180:              }
              myDBOutputPipeCount++;
            }
          }
        }
      } catch(Exception e) {
      }
    }

Line 190:
    private void getClientPipe() {
      try {
        incomingAcceptPipe =
          myBiPipeService.bind("DSSBusinessQueryInputBiPipe");

        myListenerService = new
          BidirectionalPipeService.MessageListener () {
        public void messageReceived (Message msg, OutputPipe
          responsePipe) {
```

Listing 20.2 The businessPeer Code. (continues)

```
            try {
              myDatabaseQueryPipe.getOutputPipe().send(msg);
              Message aMsg =
                myDatabaseQueryPipe.getInputPipe().
                poll(30000);
Line 200:                   responsePipe.send(aMsg);
            } catch(Exception e) {}
            return;
          }
        };
      } catch(Exception e) {}
    }
  }
```

Listing 20.2   The businessPeer Code. (continued)

Setup

In the same manner as the databasePeer, the businessPeer doesn't have a GUI for the display of output messages; instead, it relies on the command window where it was launched. The application will contact the JXTA network and obtain the necessary services.

On line 52, a call is made to establish the data input pipe and publish a pipe advertisement for any source peers that need to send data to the database. The businessPeer next executes a call to a method called launchRemoteDiscovery() on line 54. As we will see shortly, this method starts a remote discovery for all advertisements with a name having a string of DSS* where * is a wildcard.

Lines 56 through 59 make up a loop that executes until both a query pipe and a data pipe have been established with at least one databasePeer. The call to findLocalAdvertisements() does all of the work in processing any advertisements returned from the remote discovery. Recall that the remote discovery service is responsible for finding advertisements and putting them in the local cache.

Once the pipes have been connected, the bidirectional query pipe for a clientPeer is created on line 60. Finally, an infinite loop is entered for handling a connection on the client query pipe. If there is no connection from a client querying the database, a call is made on line 65 to listen for a connection. Only one query connection is allowed, so the statement to accept a connection will be called only once. Finally, a check is made to determine if multiple database connections can be created for this businessPeer. If they can, a call is made to findLocalAdvertisements() and additional connections are created.

Discovery

When a call is made to findLocalAdvertisements(), the code in lines 152 through 188 is called. This code is designed to be called periodically, and additional advertisements are processed from the local cache. The code will check for advertisements through a call on line 154 to the getLocalAdvertisements() method of the discovery service object. This method will return all of the advertisements found based on a search criterion of *Name* and a value of *DSS**.

If advertisements are available, a loop is entered on line 157 to process those advertisements. The first step in the process is converting the advertisement to a PipeAdvertisement object, which occurs on line 158. The name associated with the pipe is obtained on line 159; the name is used to determine which pipe advertisement has been found.

The first check comes on line 162, where the name of the advertisement is checked against the string "DSSDatabaseQueryInputBiPipe". This is the bidirectional pipe from the database where queries can be directed from a client. If the current pipe advertisement is for the query pipe, and the pipe hasn't been previously connected, an attempt is made to connect to the remote pipe. If the attempt is successful, the connection is stored in an object, and processing continues with the next advertisement. If the attempt is not successful, the pipe object remains null, and another connection can be created when an appropriate advertisement is found.

If the name of the pipe is DSSDatabaseDataSaveInputPipe, the code on line 171 will be executed. This code attempts to build a pipe between the businessPeer and the databasePeer for transferring information to be placed in the database. The code will attempt the connection, and place a successful one into an array of output pipes. This all occurs on line 176. If the connection isn't successful, processing continues with the next advertisement found in the local cache.

For both of the pipes, there is the possibility that the remote peer won't be available. The code will handle this situation by simply ignoring the error produced when a connection fails.

Processing Input

The third part of the businessPeer is the portion that handles the transfer of the message from the user of the system to the databasePeer. When the input pipe handler of the businessPeer fires, a call is made to the sendData() method. This method is defined in lines 102 through 111.

The code itself is quite simple. A message is received and passed to the sendData() method. This message is forwarded using a FOR loop to each of the outputPipes discovered by the peer.

GatheringPeers

With the databasePeer ready to put data into a database, and the businessPeers are ready to transfer information, all that's left is some sort of user peer to pass information. A source application needs to implement some of the basic JXTA functionality, including launching into the JXTA network, as well as the ability to discover advertisements and establish a pipe connection. A gatheringPeer called a spider is provided with the code for this chapter. The spider pulls images from a URL and sends them to the database. The code for the spider is based on the WebLech open-source project, but we made significant changes for JXTA and database access. You can find all of the peers for this chapter at www.wiley.com/books/Gradecki.

The spider application takes a URL and pulls all of the images at various depths within the site. When the application starts, it accesses the JXTA network, and a businessPeer advertisement is discovered. Once the advertisement is discovered, an output pipe is created between the businessPeer and the spider application. As each image is found using a URL, the image is encrypted and packaged into a message. The code to handle this functionality is found within a method called writeToFile():

```
public void writeToFile(String fileName, OutputPipe
  outPipe, int pipeCount, PipeService pipeService, String
  category, Cipher rc4)
{

    byte[] encryptedData = new byte[content.length];
    try {
      rc4.doFinal(content, 0, content.length,
        encryptedData, 0);
    } catch (Exception e) {
      System.out.println("Error during encryption");
    }

      if (pipeCount > 0) {
        Message msg = pipeService.createMessage();
        findParts();

        msg.setString("filename", fileName);
        msg.setBytes("data", content); //encryptedData);
        msg.setString("domain", domain);
        msg.setString("path", path);
        msg.setString("category", category);
        for (int i=0;i<pipeCount;i++) {
          try {
            outPipe.send(msg);
          } catch (Exception e) {
```

```
            System.out.println("Unable to send data down
              pipe");
            e.printStackTrace();
            System.exit(-1);
        }
      }
    }
  }
```

The code begins by encrypting the image into an array of bytes. The doFinal() method of the cipher is used to perform the encryption. Once the data has been encrypted, the code checks to be sure that the application has a pipe connection to the businessPeer.

ClientPeer

A storage system without the ability to retrieve stored information isn't of much use. We developed a sample clientPeer to allow images stored in the database to be retrieved effectively. Figure 20.7 shows an example of the client application after it queries for results and requests an image to be displayed.

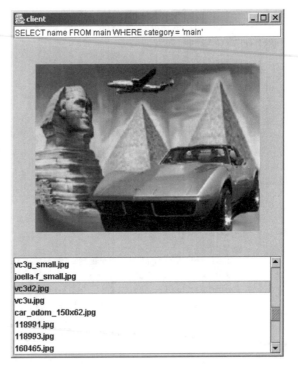

Figure 20.7 An example of a clientPeer.

The client works by discovering the bidirectional pipe advertised by a businessPeer. The user of the client will update the SQL string displayed at the top of the GUI. When the user presses Enter, the peer will build a message with an element called action and a value of QUERY along with the SQL statement. This message will be delivered to the businessPeer, which will forward it to the databasePeer. The response will consist of the filename found in the database relating to the specified column. The user double-clicks on one of the filenames to start the process again, but the action element will have a value of GET. The message will be delivered to the businessPeer and then the databasePeer. The bytes making up the image will be returned and subsequently displayed on the GUI. Listing 20.3 contains the code for the clientPeer.

```
Line 1: import java.util.*;
import java.io.FileInputStream;
import java.io.FileNotFoundException;
import java.io.IOException;
import java.net.URL;

import java.io.*;
import java.awt.*;
import java.awt.event.*;
Line 10: import java.awt.geom.AffineTransform;
import java.awt.image.BufferedImage;
import javax.swing.*;
import java.util.*;
import net.jxta.document.*;
import net.jxta.peergroup.*;
import net.jxta.exception.*;
import net.jxta.impl.peergroup.*;
import net.jxta.id.*;
import net.jxta.discovery.*;
Line 20: import net.jxta.pipe.*;
import net.jxta.protocol.*;
import java.net.MalformedURLException;
import java.net.URL;
import net.jxta.endpoint.Message;
import net.jxta.discovery.*;
import net.jxta.peer.*;
import net.jxta.impl.util.BidirectionalPipeService;
import jxta.security.publickey.*;
import jxta.security.impl.cipher.*;
Line 30: import jxta.security.impl.crypto.*;
import jxta.security.cipher.*;

public class client extends JFrame
```

Listing 20.3 The client code. (continues)

```
{
    private JTextArea   displayArea = null;
    private JTextField input = null;
    private final JList fileList = new JList();
    private ImageIcon icon = null;
    private ImageIcon iconThumbnail = null;
Line 40:
    private Vector filesFound = new Vector();
    JLabel photographLabel;

    private JxtaCryptoSuite   suite = null;
    private Cipher rc4;
    private String password = "This is the string";
    private SecretKey encryptKey;
    private boolean gotImage;

Line 50:    private int gettingBusinessPipe = 0;
    private PeerGroup  netPeerGroup = null;
    private BidirectionalPipeService myBiPipeService = null;
    private BidirectionalPipeService.Pipe myBusinessQueryPipe =
      null;
    private DiscoveryService        myDiscoveryService = null;
    private PipeService        myPipeService = null;
    private PipeAdvertisement   myPipeAdvertisement = null;
    private PipeAdvertisement   myInputPipeAdvertisement = null;
    private OutputPipe          myOutputPipe = null;
    private InputPipe           myInputPipe = null;
    private Integer  pipeSemaphore = new Integer(1);

Line 60:    private final static       MimeMediaType XMLMIMETYPE
                = new MimeMediaType("text/xml");

    public client()
    {
      super("client");

      Container c = getContentPane();

      displayArea = new JTextArea();
      c.add(new JScrollPane(displayArea), BorderLayout.CENTER);
Line 70:
      input = new JTextField("SELECT name FROM main WHERE
        CATEGORY = '<@@>'");
      input.addActionListener (new ActionListener() {
        public void actionPerformed (ActionEvent e) {
        try {
          Message msg = myPipeService.createMessage();
```

Listing 20.3 The client code. (continues)

```
             msg.setString("action", "QUERY");
             msg.setString("SQL", input.getText());

          myBusinessQueryPipe.getOutputPipe().send(msg);
Line 80:          Message aMsg =
             myBusinessQueryPipe.getInputPipe().poll(300000);

          String results = aMsg.getString("results");
          filesFound.clear();
          int index = 0;
          while (results != "") {
            index = results.indexOf("|");
            if (index>=0) {
              filesFound.add(results.substring(0, index));
              results = results.substring(index+1);
Line 90:          } else {
              break;
            }
          }
          fileList.setListData(filesFound);
        } catch(Exception ee) {
          ee.printStackTrace();
        }
      }});
      c.add (input, BorderLayout.NORTH);
Line 100:
      JScrollPane pane = new JScrollPane(fileList);
      MouseListener mouseListener = new MouseAdapter() {
       public void mouseClicked(MouseEvent e) {
         if (e.getClickCount() == 2) {
             int index = fileList.locationToIndex(e.getPoint());
             try {
               Message msg = myPipeService.createMessage();
               msg.setString("action", "GET");
               msg.setString("name",
                 (String)filesFound.get(index));

Line 110:                myBusinessQueryPipe.getOutputPipe().
               send(msg);
               Message aMsg =
                 myBusinessQueryPipe.getInputPipe().
                 poll(300000);

               byte[] buf = aMsg.getBytes("result");
               rc4.init(encryptKey, Cipher.MODE_DECRYPT);
               byte[] decryptBuf = new byte[buf.length];
               rc4.doFinal(buf, 0, buf.length, decryptBuf, 0);
```

Listing 20.3   The client code. (continues)

```
                    icon = new ImageIcon(decryptBuf);
                    createThumbnail();
Line 120:                     photographLabel.setIcon(iconThumbnail);
                } catch(Exception ee) {}
            }
        }
    };
    fileList.addMouseListener(mouseListener);
    c.add(pane, BorderLayout.SOUTH);

    photographLabel = new JLabel();
    photographLabel.setHorizontalAlignment(JLabel.CENTER);
Line 130:       photographLabel.setVerticalAlignment(
                JLabel.CENTER);
    photographLabel.setVerticalTextPosition(JLabel.CENTER);
    photographLabel.setHorizontalTextPosition(JLabel.CENTER);

    c.add(photographLabel, BorderLayout.CENTER);

    setSize(450,600);
    show();

    launchJXTA();
Line 140:       getServices();

    try {
      suite = new JxtaCryptoSuite(JxtaCryptoSuite.MEMBER_RC4,
        null, (byte)0, (byte)0);
      rc4 = suite.getJxtaCipher();
      encryptKey = (SecretKey)KeyBuilder.buildKey(
        KeyBuilder.TYPE_RC4, KeyBuilder.LENGTH_RC4, false);
      encryptKey.setKey(password.getBytes(), 0);
      rc4.init(encryptKey, Cipher.MODE_DECRYPT);
    } catch(Exception e) {
      System.out.println("Trouble with security setup");
Line 150:       System.exit(-1);
    }

    findAdvertisement("Name", "DSSBusinessQueryInputBiPipe");
    }

    private void launchJXTA() {
        displayArea.append("Launching Peer into JXTA
          Network...\n");
        try {
            netPeerGroup = PeerGroupFactory.newNetPeerGroup();
```

Listing 20.3 The client code. (continues)

```
Line 160:         } catch (PeerGroupException e) {
            System.out.println("Unable to create PeerGroup -
              Failure");
            e.printStackTrace();
            System.exit(1);
        }
    }

    private void getServices() {
      displayArea.append("Getting Services...\n");
      myDiscoveryService = netPeerGroup.getDiscoveryService();
Line 170:     myPipeService = netPeerGroup.getPipeService();
      myBiPipeService = new
        BidirectionalPipeService(netPeerGroup);
    }


    private void findAdvertisement(String searchKey, String
      searchValue) {
        try {
          DiscoveryListener myDiscoveryListener = new
            DiscoveryListener() {
            public void discoveryEvent(DiscoveryEvent e) {
              Enumeration enum;
Line 180:            String str;

              synchronized (pipeSemaphore){
                if (myBusinessQueryPipe == null) {
                  System.out.println("Found Remote
                    Advertisement...\n");
                  DiscoveryResponseMsg myMessage =
                    e.getResponse();
                enum = myMessage.getResponses();
                  while (enum.hasMoreElements()) {
                  str = (String)enum.nextElement();

Line 190:                 try {
                    PipeAdvertisement pipeAdv =
                    (PipeAdvertisement)
                    AdvertisementFactory.newAdvertisement(
                    XMLMIMETYPE, new
                    ByteArrayInputStream(str.getBytes()));
                    myBusinessQueryPipe =
                    myBiPipeService.connect(pipeAdv, 30000);
                  } catch(Exception ee) {
                  }
                }
```

Listing 20.3 The client code. (continues)

```
                        }
                    }
                }
            };
Line 200:
            System.out.println("Launching Remote Discovery
                Service...\n");
            myDiscoveryService.getRemoteAdvertisements(null,
                DiscoveryService.ADV, searchKey, searchValue, 10,
                myDiscoveryListener);
        } catch (Exception e) {
            System.out.println("Error during advertisement search");
        }
    }

    public void run() {
    }
Line 210:
    public static void main(String[] args){
        client cli = new client();

        cli.addWindowListener(
            new WindowAdapter() {
                public void windowClosing(WindowEvent e) {
                    System.exit(0);
                }
Line 220:          }
        );
        cli.run();
    }

    private void createThumbnail() {
        int maxDim = 350;
        try {
            Image inImage = icon.getImage();

            double scale = (double)maxDim/(double)inImage.getHeight(null);
Line 230:             if (inImage.getWidth(null) >
                    inImage.getHeight(null)) {
                scale =
                (double)maxDim/(double)inImage.getWidth(null);
            }

            int scaledW = (int)(scale*inImage.getWidth(null));
            int scaledH = (int)(scale*inImage.getHeight(null));

            BufferedImage outImage = new BufferedImage(scaledW,
```

Listing 20.3   The client code. (continues)

```
                scaledH, BufferedImage.TYPE_INT_RGB);

Line 240:               AffineTransform tx = new AffineTransform();

        if (scale < 1.0d) {
            tx.scale(scale, scale);
        }

        Graphics2D g2d = outImage.createGraphics();
        g2d.drawImage(inImage, tx, null);
        g2d.dispose();

        iconThumbnail = new ImageIcon(outImage);
Line 250:
    } catch (Exception e) {
        e.printStackTrace();
    }
  }

}
```

Listing 20.3 The client code. (continued)

The code for the client can be broken down into four main areas: setup, pipe discovery, query request, and image request.

Setup

The clientPeer is a GUI application that extends the JFrame class and has a number of GUI components attached to it. The components include

JTextField—This component allows the input of a SQL string.

JTextArea—This component displays the location in the middle of the GUI.

ImageIcon/JLabel—An image icon is attached to a label, also placed in the middle of the GUI.

JList—This component is a scrollable list for holding filenames returned from a query.

All of these components and the basic JXTA services are set up in the constructor (defined in lines 64 through 156) of the application class. Some of the code in the constructor defines handlers for the JTextField and the JList; we discuss this functionality next.

Lines 142 and 143 put the peer into the JXTA network, and obtain the discovery and bidirectional pipe service necessary for the functionality of the peer. Lines

145 through 154 perform the setup of the JxtaCryptoSuite needed for the decryption of the image data returned from the database. The decryption code begins with an instantiation of the JxtaCryptoSuite on line 146. The only parameter to the constructor of the class is the type of cipher needed: RC4. The constructor of the suite will instantiate the necessary code behind the scenes based on the cipher specified. Line 147 extracts the cipher from the suite for use, and line 148 builds a key for use in the data encryption. This line only builds a key container with no passcode; the passcode for the key is assigned on line 149. The bytes of the *password* variable are passed to the key through its setKey() method. These bytes will be used in the RC4 decryption of the image data from the database.

Finally, line 150 initializes the RC4 cipher using the key and a parameter specifying the cipher to be used for decryption of data. If any of the operations fail, the application will halt because the decryption functionality is a vital part of the application.

The last operation for the constructor is found on line 156, where the system attempts to find the bidirectional pipe advertisement from a businessPeer.

Pipe Discovery

As we just explained, the last operation for the initialization of the peer is an attempt to find a bidirectional pipe from a businessPeer. The pipe is the only way the code can transfer a QUERY or image GET request to the database. The code for the pipe discovery is the same used in our other peer applications, except the peer doesn't look in its cache for a pipe advertisement. The only reason for this is to show a different way of finding advertisements. By not checking the local cache, the peer has a better chance of finding a valid pipe through which it can make a request. A remote discovery process is less likely to return an advertisement that is stale.

The code for finding a businessPeer pipe is found in lines 178 through 209. In most of the applications built before this chapter, the peer just tried to make a pipe connection with the first advertisement it found. This isn't very realistic because a pipe advertisement might be old. The findAdvertisement() method in the client goes about the discovery and connection processes a little differently. On line 205, the remote discovery process is started using the name and value of the pipes we want to discover. Notice that the second parameter to the method now has a value of 10; this means we will allow any peer to return up to 10 different advertisements, matching our search key and value, to the discovery listener code.

The discovery listener code is defined in line 180 through 202. When a call to the listener code occurs, the code will immediately hit a critical region of code.

This critical region is signified by the synchronized(pipeSemaphore) statement. If any other peers send results to the clientPeer, they will be "blocked" until the current peer's response messages are processed. This ensures that the code cannot be corrupted by an asynchronous call to the listener.

Within the critical code, the advertisements returned are processed using a while loop. Each pipe advertisement is used in an attempt to create a pipe to a businessPeer that published the advertisement. In some cases, the businessPeer might not be available. When this occurs, the connection attempt to the remote pipe will fail, and the code will proceed to the next advertisement. Once a pipe is connected to a businessPeer, all remaining advertisements will be skipped.

The Query Request

The client functionality begins with the user entering a category value in the SQL at the top of the GUI. When the user presses the Enter key, the JTextField listener code will execute on lines 74 through 99. The code starts by creating a message to send to the businessPeer. This message includes two elements: action and SQL. The action element contains a value of QUERY, and the SQL element contains the actual SQL string to be processed.

The output pipe is obtained from the bidirectional pipe on line 81, and the message is sent to the businessPeer. Unlike other peers, the client will sit and poll for a response from the businessPeer. The polling occurs on line 82 after the input pipe is obtained.

When a response is received from the businessPeer, the filenames from the query need to be extracted from the delimited string found in the results element. The code in lines 83 through 93 pulls all of the filenames, and places them in a list called filesFound. The vector is fed to the JList GUI control on line 96. The statement setListData() will have the result of placing all of the filenames on the GUI.

The Image Request

Once all of the filenames are displayed in the list box on the GUI, a user can double-click a filename to see the image. The code in lines 105 through 126 will be called. The code represents a listener for the list box. When a user double-clicks a filename, the code will determine which filename was clicked by using a reference from the list box into the filesFound list object. The filename is packaged into a message object and sent to the businessPeer. The businessPeer will forward the message to the databasePeer, where the data for the image will be extracted and placed in a response object.

When the response object is received, the image data will be located in the result element. Since the image data was originally put into the database in encrypted form, the data must be decrypted. This process takes place in lines 115 through 119. The RC4 cipher is used to perform the decryption.

Once the image is back in its original form, it will be reduced in size to fit on the GUI. A call is made to the createThumbnail( ) method on line 122; this method reduces the size of the image before it is placed on the GUI.

Summary

The encrypted and highly available storage system (EHASS) is an example of what we can accomplish in a very short time period using the JXTA system. The EHASS allows image data to be stored in any number of available databases within the JXTA network, without regard to location and database type.

Installing JXTA and Compiling JXTA Applications

In this appendix, we discuss where to download the various builds of JXTA and the steps for installing JXTA on Linux and Windows systems. We also examine how to compile code using both the command-line Java compile and Borland's JBuilder IDE.

Installing JXTA

The primary web site for JXTA is www.jxta.org, where you can find all of the system code and documentation. For information on downloading an easy-install package, go to

```
http://download.jxta.org/easyinstall/install.html
```

and for information on downloading stable and daily builds, go to

```
http://www.jxta.org/project/www/download.html
```

Easy Install

For those of you who want to quickly install the JXTA system, go to http://download.jxta.org/easyinstall/install.html, where numerous downloads are available, based on the platform and whether a Virtual Machine (VM) is needed. Table A.1 lists the available downloads.

Table A.1   Downloads for Installing the JXTA System

PLATFORM	WITH VM	WITHOUT VM
Windows	Available	Available
Max OSX	Not available	Available
Solaris	Available	Available
Linux	Available	Available
Unix	Not available	Available
Other	Not available	Available

Each of these installs includes

- The myJXTA application
- JXTA libraries
- The JXTA shell application

There are two versions for most all of the platforms: one with the JXTA system only, and another that includes JXTA and an appropriate copy of the Java Runtime Environment (JRE). The VM and JRE versions both allow the applications within the installation to execute; however, since neither package includes a Java compiler, you won't be able to write applications. If you plan to develop new applications with JXTA, you'll need to install a Java SDK, which we discuss later in this appendix.

Installing on a Windows System

If the machine you'll use already includes a Java system, click the Without Java VM version; otherwise, choose the Includes Java VM version. The download will begin when you click the appropriate link. Once the package downloads, either click the Open option to immediately execute the file, or click Save and place the file on your local hard drive. If you save the file to your local hard drive, you will have to find the file and then double-click it to begin the installation process.

Once you launch the installation program, a wizard will walk you through a number of screens, including a license agreement and a screen that asks where you want to place the JXTA system (in a default location or in a specific location on your hard drive). Click Next on the various screens to install the program.

Installing on a Linux System

The process for installing the JXTA software on a Linux system is basically the same as for Windows. The JXTA software is contained in an installation application. After you click on the link for the appropriate software (with or without VM), save the file in a convenient place on your system. For the test system used in this book, we installed the software in a directory called /usr/local/jxta, owned by the user jxta and the users group.

When you've downloaded the file, open a terminal window, and change to the directory containing the file. Then, for the file without the VM, type

```
sh ./JXTAInst.bin
```

to start the installation process. If you already have a Java system installed, you'll see an error. If this is the case, you should instead install the file with the Java VM embedded.

To install the file with the embedded VM, use the following command:

```
sh ./JXTAInst_LNX_VM.bin
```

Once you've installed the software, you'll see a lib directory, an InstantP2P directory, and a Shell directory. The lib directory contains the JXTA system JAR files, the Shell directory contains a shell application, and the InstantP2P directory contains the myJXTA application.

JXTA Libraries

Most JXTA applications will require the following libraries to compile and execute correctly:

- beepcore.jar
- cms.jar
- cryptix32.jar
- cryptix-asn1.jar
- insntantp2p.jar
- jxta.jar
- jxtasecurity.jar
- minimalBC.jar

The easy-install files install all the necessary libraries. Developers will typically download newer code if needed, as we discuss in the next section.

Stable Builds

Whether or not you chose the easy-install JXTA files, you can download the individual JXTA JAR files directly and use them. There are two versions of the JAR files: stable and daily. You can find the stable JAR files at

`http://download.jxta.org/stablebuilds/index.html`

Located on this web page are the following:

- Binaries:
    - jxta.jar—The platform infrastructure
    - jxtasecurity.jar—Security files
    - jxme.zip—The J2ME JXTA implementation
    - ms.jar—The Content Management System (CMS)
    - jxtasearch.zip—The distributed search service
    - jxtashell.zip—The command-line shell
    - instantp2p.zip—The myJXTA application
    - all.zip—All build binary JARs
- Documentation:
    - jxta_doc.zip—The platform API
    - jxta_refdoc—The platform reference
    - security_doc.zip—The security API
    - security_refdoc.zip—The security reference
    - jxme_doc.zip—The JXME API
    - cms_doc.zip—The CMS API
    - cms_refdoc.zip-_The CMS reference
    - jxtasearch_doc.zip—The search API
    - shell_refdoc—The shell reference
    - instantp2p_doc—The myJXTA API
    - all_doc.zip—All documentation files
- Source code
    - jxta.zip—The platform infrastructure
    - jxtasecurity.zip—Security files
    - jxme.zip—The J2ME JXTA implementation
    - cms.zip—The Content Management System
    - jxtasearch.zip—The distributed search service

- jxtashell.zip—The command-line shell
- instantp2p.zip—The myJXTA application
- all.zip—All build binary JARs

You can place the binaries JAR directly in the lib directory of the installation. Note that many of the JAR files needed to compile applications with JXTA aren't included in the stable build area—you'll have to install these files by using the easy-install application or by downloading the all*.zip file.

Daily Builds

If you want to remain on the cutting edge with the system's developers, you can download daily builds of the code. The builds are located at

```
http://download.jxta.org/nightlybuilds/index.html
```

The code layout is the same in this area as found in the stable build. You have options for downloading individual JARs or the entire system. Updated documentation is also available.

Compiling the Examples

In order to compile an application using JXTA, you need to install a version of the Java SDK. We built all of the code in this book on both Windows and Linux using the Java SDK version 1.3.1_02. You can download the SDK for both Windows and Linux from www.javasoft.com. As of this writing, Sun has released version 1.4 of the SDK; however, we haven't tested the applications in this book and the JXTA platform with that version.

There are a number of different ways to compile Java applications, including using an IDE such as JBuilder or the command-line tools provided by Sun. Our goal is to introduce JXTA to everyone, so we rely on the command-line tools provided with the Java SDK. In this section, we introduce the command-line tools for both the Windows and the Linux operating systems.

Windows

The Windows test system we used to build and test the applications in this book used JDK 1.3.1.1, installed in the c:\jdk1.3.1_02 directory. We installed the JXTA system using the JXTAInst.exe application and placed it in the c:\program files\jxta_demo directory.

For the compiling phase of development, the Java compiler needs to know where to find the JAR files associated with JXTA. We created a single environment variable called JXTALIB, and gave it the value *c:\program files\jxta_demo\lib*, where the JXTA JAR files were located on our system.

You can compile each of the applications in this book by typing the following at the command line:

```
javac -d . -classpath
%JXTALIB%/jxta.jar;%JXTALIB%/log4j.jar;%JXTALIB%/beepcore.jar;
%JXTALIB%/jxtasecurity.jar;%JXTALIB%/org.mortbay.jetty.jar;
%JXTALIB%/servlet.jar;%JXTALIB%/cryptixasn1.jar;
%JXTALIB%/cryptix32.jar;%JXTALIB%/jxtaptls.jar;
%JXTALIB%/minimalBC.jar <application name>.java
```

The resulting class file will be located in the current directory.

Linux

The same command line will work on Linux; however, you'll need to change the directory where the library files are located and change the ; delimiter (semicolon) between the JARs to change to : (colon).

```
javac -d . -classpath /usr/local/jxta/lib/jxta.jar:
/usr/local/jxta/lib/log4j.jar: /usr/local/jxta/lib
/beepcore.jar: /usr/local/jxta/lib /jxtasecurity.jar:
/usr/local/jxta/lib/org.mortbay.jetty.jar:
/usr/local/jxta/lib/servlet.jar:/usr/local/jxta/lib/cryptixasn1
.jar:/usr/local/jxta/lib/cryptix32.jar:/usr/local/jxta/lib/jxta
ptls.jar: /usr/local/jxta/lib/minimalBC.jar
<application name>.java
```

For both systems, you can create a bat and a sh file to hold the compile text so you won't have to type it when needed; instead, you can just type the name of the bat or sh file.

Running the Examples

This section explains how to execute the code for both the Windows and Linux systems.

Windows

Once you've compiled the application and built the appropriate class files, you must execute the application. To do so, type the following at the command line:

```
java -classpath
%JXTALIB%/jxta.jar;%JXTALIB%/log4j.jar;%JXTALIB%/beepcore.jar;
%JXTALIB%/jxtasecurity.jar;%JXTALIB%/org.mortbay.jetty.jar;
```

```
%JXTALIB%/servlet.jar;%JXTALIB%/cryptix-asn1.jar;
%JXTALIB%/cryptix32.jar;%JXTALIB%/jxtaptls.jar;
%JXTALIB%/minimalBC.jar; Example1
```

Linux

For Linux, use the same command but replace *%JXTALIB%* with the path to the installed JXTA system and replace the ; character with :.

```
java -classpath /usr/local/jxta/lib/jxta.jar:
/usr/local/jxta/lib/log4j.jar: /usr/local/jxta/lib
/beepcore.jar: /usr/local/jxta/lib /jxtasecurity.jar:
/usr/local/jxta/lib/org.mortbay.jetty.jar:
/usr/local/jxta/lib/servlet.jar:/usr/local/jxta/lib/cryptixasn1
.jar:/usr/local/jxta/lib/cryptix32.jar:/usr/local/jxta/lib/jxta
ptls.jar: /usr/local/jxta/lib/minimalBC.jar:
 <application name>
```

JBuilder Compiling and Execution

For those of you who want to use an IDE for your Java work, the following section offers instructions for setting up the Borland JBuilder Personal Edition for compiling and executing JXTA applications. The current version of JBuilder comes with the 1.3.1_B24 version of Java and is an appropriate tool for executing the various examples in this book. Once you download the package from www.borland.com and install it, you need to apply a JXTA-specific configuration.

Launch JBuilder and click Project, Default Project Properties, and then select the Required Libraries tab, shown in Figure A.1.

Figure A.1 The Default Project Properties dialog box.

Click the Add button to open the dialog box shown in Figure A.2. This dialog box allows you to add libraries necessary to compile and execute JXTA applications. The IDE already has the normal Java libraries but not the JXTA JARs.

Figure A.2   This dialog box lets you add libraries.

Click on the entry User Home and then click the New button to bring up the New Library Wizard, shown in Figure A.3.

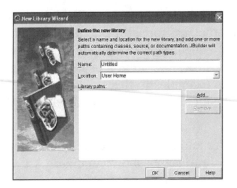

Figure A.3   The New Library Wizard.

Next, enter a name for the libraries, such as *JXTA*. Then, click the Add button to open the Open Files dialog box. Browse to the lib directory where the JXTA JAR library files are located and then click OK. You will be returned to the Add Required Library dialog box. Click OK to continue. The JXTA JARs will now be available for all new projects.

Adding a New JBuilder Project

Now we will start a new JXTA application in a project. Click File, New Project to open the New Project Wizard, shown in Figure A.4.

Figure A.4   The New Project Wizard.

Enter a name for the project, and change the location where the project will be stored (if necessary). Click the Next button, and you'll see a tab called Required Libraries. Click the tab to see the JXTA entry in the list. Then, click Finish to build the project.

At this point, check the JBuilder documentation to see how to add files to the project and to learn about compiling and execution. The JXTA libraries have been added to the project, which means they will be available to the application you are building.

JXTA API

T his appendix consists of a comprehensive summary of the JXTA Java Reference Implementation API. This material is not meant to replace the Javadoc produced by the Reference Implementation but to provide a quick reference when needed during development of applications. Each of the major classes and interfaces are represented in this appendix. You will find a short description of the class/interface, parent and/or derived classes, attribute and method listings and in most cases a short code example.

Class Advertisement

The Advertisement class provides the basis for advertising all peers, peer-groups, pipes, and other JXTA resources.

- **Parent Class:** java.lang.Object
- **Class:** net.jxta.document.Advertisement
- **Derived Classes:**

    EndpointAdvertisement

    ModuleClassAdvertisement

    ModuleImplAdvertisement

    ModuleSpecAdvertisement

    PeerAdvertisement

    PeerGroupAdvertisement

> PipeAdvertisement
>
> RdvAdvertisement
>
> TransportAdvertisement

Field Summary

- protected long expiration: Absolute time at which this advertisement will expire.

Constructor Summary

- Advertisement()

Method Summary

- java.lang.Object clone() static java.lang.String getAdvertisementType(): Returns the identifying type of this advertisement.

- abstract Document getDocument(MimeMediaType asMimeType): returns Document representation o

- abstract ID getID(): Returns advertisement ID.

- long getLocalExpirationTime(): Returns advertisement expiration

Example

In the following code snippet, a Document object is created from a PipeAdvertisement object using the getDocument() method:

```
PipeAdvertisement pipeAdv;
StructuredTextDocument doc = pipeAdv.getDocument(XMLMIMETYPE);
```

Class AdvertisementFactory

The AdvertisementFactory class is a factory for building new advertisements. This factory will build all of the advertisements used in JXTA.

- **Parent Class:** next.jxta.util.ClassFactory
- **Class:** net.jxta.document.AdvertisementFactory
- **Derived Classes:** None

Method Summary

- java.lang.Class getClassForKey(): Used by ClassFactory methods to ensure that all keys used with the mapping are of the correct type.

- java.lang.Class getClassOfInstantiators(): Used by ClassFactory methods to ensure that all of the instance classes that register with this factory have the correct base class.

- static Advertisement newAdvertisement(MimeMediaType mimetype, java.io.InputStream stream): Constructs an instance of Advertisement

- static Advertisement newAdvertisement(MimeMediaType mimetype, java.io.InputStream stream, long timeout): Constructs an instance of Advertisement matching the type specified by the advertisementType parameter.

- static Advertisement newAdvertisement(java.lang.String advertisement-Type): Constructs an instance of Advertisement matching the type specified by the advertisementType parameter.

- static Advertisement newAdvertisement(java.lang.String advertisement-Type, long timeout): Constructs an instance of Advertisement matching the type specified by the advertisementType parameter.

- static Advertisement newAdvertisement(TextElement root): Constructs an instance of Advertisement matching the type specified by the root parameter.

- static Advertisement newAdvertisement(TextElement root, long timeout): Constructs an instance of Advertisement matching the type specified by the root parameter.

- static Boolean registerAdvertisementInstance(java.lang.String rootType, java.lang.Class instanceClass): Register an array of constructor for an ID type to enable IDs of that type to be constructed.

- protected Boolean registerAssoc(java.lang.String className): Registers className class with factory

Example

In the following code snippet, the AdvertisementFactory class is used to build a new advertisement of type PeerGroup.

```
PeerGroupAdvertisement adv = (PeerGroupAdvertisement)
AdvertisementFactory.newAdvertisement(PeerGroupAdvertisement.
getAdvertisementType());
```

Class AuthenticationCredential

The AuthenticationCredential class is a container for holding credential information for a specific peer group. The class encapsulates the methods provided by the peer group to handle the authentication using the credential information within the class.

- **Parent Class:** java.lang.Object
- **Class:** net.jxta.document.AuthenticationCredential
- **Derived Classes:** none

Constructor Summary

- AuthenticationCredential(PeerGroup peergroup, java.lang.String method, Element indentityInfo): Creates new AuthenticationCredential.

Method Summary

- StructuredDocument getDocument(MimeMediaType as): Writes credentials into a document.
- Element getIdentityInfo(): Returns the StructuredDocument Element containing the identity information that was originally provided when this AuthenticationCredential was created.
- java.lang.String getMethod(): Returns the AuthenticationMethod that this AuthenticationCredential will be requesting when it is provided to a MembershipService service during the Apply operation.
- ID getPeerGroupID(): Returns the PeerGroupID associated with this AuthenticationCredential.
- ID getPeerID(): Returns the PeerID associated with this Authentication-Credential.
- MembershipService getSourceService(): Always returns null because this type of credential is not associated with a particular membership service.

Example

In the following code snippet, a new AuthenticationCredential object is created for the group defined in the myLocalGroup object using an authentication class called UpdatedPasswdAuthentication. The newly created AuthenticationCredential object is passed to the Authenticator in the current group.

```
AuthenticationCredential myAuthenticationCredential = new
AuthenticationCredential(myLocalGroup,
"UpdatedPasswdAuthentication", myCredentials);

net.jxta.membership.Authenticator myAuthenticator =
myMembershipService.apply(myAuthenticationCredential);
```

Class Codat

The Codat class is used to hold binary data in the form of an advertisement.

- **Parent Class:** java.lang.Object
- **Class:** net.jxta.codat.Codat
- **Derived Classes:** Metadata

Field Summary

- protected Document doc: A JXTA document that contains the data held by this Codat.
- protected ID id: The ID of this Codat.
- protected ID metaId: The ID of a Codat to which this Codat is related.

Constructor Summary

- Codat(CodatID id, CodatID about, Document document): Makes a new Codat instance from an existing Codat, with a given CodatID and a document.
- Codat(PeerGroupID groupID, ID about, Document document): Makes a new Codat with a new CodatId given a PeerGroupID and a document.

Method Summary

- ID getCodatID(): Returns the Codat ID associated with this Codat.
- Document getDocument(): Returns the document associated with this Codat.
- ID getMetaID(): Returns the ID of related codats associated with this metadata Codat.

Example

The following snippet builds a new Codat object based in the current peer group with a new ID and document:

```
Codat codat = new Codat(netPeerGroup.getPeerID(), newID, advDoc);
```

Class CodatID

The CodatID class represents an ID specific to a Codat.

- **Parent Class:** java.lang.id.ID
- **Class:** net.jxta.codat.CodatID
- **Derived Classes:** none

Constructor Summary

- CodatID()

Method Summary

- abstract ID getPeerGroupID(): Returns the PeerGroupID of the peer group to which this Codat ID belongs.
- abstract Boolean isStatic(): Returns true if this Codat ID is associated with a static Codat.

Example

In the following code snippet, the Codat ID of a Codat object is obtained and its embedded PeerGroupID displayed:

```
CodatID codatID = codat.getCodatID();
System.out.println(codatID.getID().toString());
```

Interface Credential

The credential class is used to contain information that could be used as a credential for a peer group and a membership service.

Method Summary

- StructuredDocument getDocument(MimeMediaType as): Writes credentials into a document.
- ID getPeerGroupID(): Returns the peerGroupID associated with this credential.
- ID getPeerID(): Returns the peerID associated with this credential.
- MembershipService getSourceService(): Returns the service that generated this credential.

Class DiscoveryEvent

The DiscoveryEvent class is used to contain information passed from a peer during a discovery attempt. An object of the class will be passed to a discovery listener if defined.

- **Parent Class:** java.util.EventObject
- **Class:** net.jxta.discovery.DiscoveryEvent
- **Derived Classes:** None

Constructor Summary

- DiscoveryEvent(java.lang.Object source, DiscoveryResponseMsg response, int queryid): Creates a new event.

Method Summary

- int getQueryID(): Returns the query ID associated with the response returned in this event.
- DiscoveryResponseMsg getResponse(): Returns the response associated with the event.

Example

In the following snippet, the DiscoveryEvent is passed to the listener object's callback method. The getResponse() method is used to pull advertisements found during the discovery attempt.

```
DiscoveryListener myDiscoveryListener = new DiscoveryListener() {
  public void discoveryEvent(DiscoveryEvent e) {
    DiscoveryResponseMsg myMessage = e.getResponse();
    Enumeration enum = myMessage.getResponses();
    String str = (String)enum.nextElement();
  }
};
```

Interface DiscoveryListener

The DiscoveryListener interface defines the method necessary to build a listener called when a discovery search is made. The listener can be defined as either an inner class or a separate class.

Method Summary

- void discoveryEvent(DiscoveryEvent event): Returns the discoveryService event.

Example

In the following snippet, a DiscoveryListener object is created to handle the callback necessary when an advertisement discovery is made.

```
DiscoveryListener myDiscoveryListener = new DiscoveryListener() {
  public void discoveryEvent(DiscoveryEvent e) {
    DiscoveryResponseMsg myMessage = e.getResponse();
  }
};
```

Class DiscoveryQueryMsg

The DiscoveryQueryMsg class is an internal class used to build a message sent during a query involving the discovery service.

- **Parent Class:** java.lang.Object
- **Class:** net.jxta.protocol.DiscoveryQueryMsg
- **Derived Classes:** None

Field Summary

- int type

Constructor Summary

- DiscoveryQueryMsg()

Method Summary

- static java.lang.String getAdvertisementType(): All messages have a type (in XML, this is !doctype) that identifies the message.
- java.lang.String getAttr(): Returns the Attr value.
- int getDiscoveryType(): Gets the response type.
- abstract Document getDocument(MimeMediaType asMimeType): Writes an advertisement into a document.
- java.lang.String getPeerAdv(): Returns the responding's peer advertisement.

- int getThreshold( ): Gets the threshold for the number of responses.
- java.lang.String getValue( ): Returns the value of Attr.
- void setAttr(java.lang.String attr): Sets the Attr.
- void setDiscoveryType(int type): Sets the response type, whether it's peer or group discovery.
- void setPeerAdv(java.lang.String peer): Sets the response type, whether it's peer or group discovery.
- void setThreshold(int threshold): Sets the threshold.
- void setValue(java.lang.String value): Sets the query.

Class DiscoveryResponseMsg

The DiscoveryResponseMsg is an internal class defined to contain information returned from one peer to another during a discovery query.

- **Parent Class:** java.lang.Object
- **Class:** net.jxta.protocol.DiscoveryResponseMsg
- **Derived Classes:** None

Field Summary

- int count
- int type

Constructor Summary

- DiscoveryResponseMsg( )

Method Summary

- static java.lang.String getAdvertisementType( ): All messages have a type (in XML, this is !doctype) that identifies the message.
- int getDiscoveryType( ): Gets the response type.
- abstract Document getDocument(MimeMediaType asMimeType): Writes advertisements into a document.
- java.util.Enumeration getExpirations( )
- java.lang.String getPeerAdv( ): Returns the responding's peer advertisement.

- java.lang.String getQueryAttr(): Returns the attributes used by the query.
- java.lang.String
- getQueryValue(): Returns the value used by the query.
- int getResponseCount(): Gets the response count.
- java.util.Enumeration getResponses(): Returns the response(s).
- void setDiscoveryType(int type): Sets the response type, whether it's peer or group discovery.
- void setExpirations(java.util.Vector expirations)
- void setPeerAdv(java.lang.String peer): Sets the response peer advertisement.
- void setQueryAttr(java.lang.String attr): Sets the attribute used by the query.
- void setQueryValue(java.lang.String value): Sets the value used by the query.
- void setResponseCount(int count: Sets the response count in this message.
- void setResponses(java.util.Vector responses): Sets the responses to the query.

Example

In the following snippet, a DiscoveryResponseMsg object is created from the DiscoveryEvent object passed to the DiscoveryListener used for discovery:

```
DiscoveryListener myDiscoveryListener = new DiscoveryListener() {
  public void discoveryEvent(DiscoveryEvent e) {
    DiscoveryResponseMsg myMessage = e.getResponse();
    Enumeration enum = myMessage.getResponses();
    String str = (String)enum.nextElement();
  }
};
```

Interface DiscoveryService

The DiscoveryService interface defines the functionality required of code implementing the discovery service.

Field Summary

- static int ADV: DiscoveryService type advertisement.
- static long DEFAULT_EXPIRATION: Default expiration time for advertisements.

- static long DEFAULT_LIFETIME: Default lifetime time for advertisements.

- static int GROUP: default group for advertisements

- DiscoveryService type Group : associated peer group

- static int PEER : default peer

- DiscoveryService type Peer : associated peer

Method Summary

- void addDiscoveryListener(DiscoveryListener listener): Registers a discovery listener to be notified for discovery events.

- void flushAdvertisements(java.lang.String id, int type): Flushes the stored document.

- java.util.Enumeration getLocalAdvertisements(int type, java.lang.String attribute, java.lang.String value): Retrieves the stored peer, group, and general advertisements.

- int getRemoteAdvertisements(java.lang.String peerid, int type, java.lang.String attribute, java.lang.String value, int threshold): Deprecated.

- void getRemoteAdvertisements(java.lang.String peerid, int type, java.lang.String attribute, java.lang.String value, int threshold, DiscoveryListener listener): Discovers PeerAdvertisements, GroupAdvertisements and JXTA Advertisements.

- void publish(Advertisement advertisement, int type): Publishes an advertisement with a default lifetime of DEFAULT_LIFETIME and default expiration time for "others" of DEFAULT_EXPIRATION.

- void publish(Advertisement adv, int type, long lifetime, long lifetimeForOthers): Publishes an advertisement that will expire after a certain time.

- void remotePublish(Advertisement adv, int type): Attempts to publish an advertisement remotely on all configured transports; the advertisement will carry a lifetime of the Expiration time or *lifetime*, whichever is smaller.

- void remotePublish(Advertisement adv, int type, long lifetime): Attempts to publish an advertisement remotely on all configured transports; the advertisement will carry an expiration of *lifetime*.

- boolean removeDiscoveryListener(DiscoveryListener listener): Removes a discovery listener.

Example

In the following snippet, the DiscoveryService associated with a peer group is obtained. The getLocalAdvertisements() method is called to obtain any advertisements in the local cache that match the provided search key and value.

```
DiscoveryService myDiscoveryService =
netPeerGroup.getDiscoveryService();
myLocalEnum =
myDiscoveryService.getLocalAdvertisements(DiscoveryService.
GROUP, searchKey, searchValue);
```

Interface Document

The Document interface states the functionality required to be implemented when building a document class.

Method Summary

- java.lang.String getFileExtension(): Returns the file extension type used by this document.

- MimeMediaType getMimeType(): Returns the MIME media type of this document per IETF RFC 2046 MIME: Media Types. JXTA does not currently support the Multipart or Message media types.

- java.io.InputStream getStream(): Returns a stream of bytes that represent the content of this document.

- void sendToStream(java.io.OutputStream stream): Rather than returning an InputStream like getStream(), this method sends the document to the specified stream.

Example

The Document interface defines the basic methods of a JXTA document. In the following snippet, a document from a PipeAdvertisement is obtained and output to the screen. The StructuredTextDocument class is used, which implements a Document interface.

```
StructuredTextDocument doc =
(StructuredTextDocument)pipeAdv.getDocument(XMLMIMETYPE);
doc.sendToStream(System.out);
```

Interface Element

The Element interface defines the methods required to be implemented when building an Element class.

Method Summary

- void appendChild(Element element): Adds a child element to this element.
- java.util.Enumeration getChildren(): Returns an enumeration of the immediate children of this element.
- java.util.Enumeration getChildren(java.lang.Object key): Returns an enumeration of the immediate children of this element whose names match the specified string.
- java.lang.Object getKey(): Gets the name associated with an element.
- Element getParent(): Gets the parent element of this element.
- StructuredDocument getRoot(): Gets the root element of the hierarchy this element belongs to.
- java.lang.Object getValue(): Gets the value (if any) associated with an element.

Example

An element is part of a document, usually from the standpoint of an XML document. The following snippet obtains all of the elements from a Structured-TextDocument.

```
StructuredTextDocument doc = (StructuredTextDocument)pipeAd
Enumeration elements = doc.getChildren("row");
while (elements.hasMoreElements()) {
  Element element = elements.next();
}
```

Interface EndpointAddress

The EndpointAddress interface defines the methods necessary when building an EndpointAddress class.

Method Summary

- java.lang.Object clone(): Returns a clone of this object.
- java.lang.String getProtocolAddress(): Returns a String that contains the name of the protocol address embedded in the endpoint address.

- java.lang.String getProtocolName( ): Returns a String that contains the name of the protocol embedded in the endpoint address.

- java.lang.String getServiceName( ): Returns a String that contains the name of the service name embedded in the endpoint address.

- java.lang.String getServiceParameter( ): Returns a String that contains the service parameter embedded in the endpoint address.

- void setProtocolAddress(java.lang.String address): Sets the protocol address.

- void setProtocolName(java.lang.String name): Sets the protocol name.

- void setServiceName(java.lang.String name): Sets the service name.

- void setServiceParameter(java.lang.String name): Sets the service parameter.

Example

The following code snippet builds an endpoint address for a peer in the network. The endpoint address is used to ping the remote peer.

```
EndpointAddress endpointAddress =
myEndpointService.newEndpointAddress(toAddress);
endpointAddress.setServiceName("tempServiceName");
endpointAddress.setServiceParameter("tempParams");

myEndpointService.ping(endpointAddress);
```

Class EndpointAdvertisement

The EndpointAdvertisement class is a derived class from Advertisement with specific methods and attributes appropriate for an Endpoint.

- **Parent Class:** java.lang.document.Advertisement
- **Class:** net.jxta.protocol.EndpointAdvertisement
- **Derived Classes:** None

Constructor Summary

- EndpointAdvertisement( )

Method Summary

- static java.lang.String getAdvertisementType( ): Returns the advertisement type.

- java.lang.String getEndpointAddress(): Returns the endpoint address.
- java.lang.String getKeywords(): Returns the keywords associated with the endpoint.
- java.lang.String getName(): Returns the name of the endpoint.
- TransportAdvertisement getTransportAdvertisement(): Returns the transport advertisement associated with the endpoint.
- boolean isEnabled(): Tells whether specific endpoint is enabled or not.
- void setEnabled(Boolean enabled): Enables or disables this specific endpoint.
- void setEndpointAddress(java.lang.String add): Sets the endpoint address.
- void setKeywords(java.lang.String keywords): Sets the keywords associated with the endpoint.
- void setName(java.lang.String name): Sets the name of the endpoint.
- void setTransportAdvertisement(TransportAdvertisement transport): Sets the transport advertisement.

Interface EndpointFilterListener

The EndpointFilterListener interface defines the methods necessary when building an endpoint filter listener class.

Method Summary

- Message processIncomingMessage(Message message, EndpointAddress srcAddr, EndpointAddress dstAddr): Invoked by the endpoint service for each incoming message that contains a message element associated with this endpoint filter.

Interface EndpointProtocol

The EndpointProtocol interface defines the methods necessary for implementation of an endpoint service.

Method Summary

- boolean allowOverLoad(): Returns true if this protocol accepts to be overloaded.
- boolean allowRouting(): Returns true if the endpoint protocol can be used by the EndpointRouter.

- EndpointMessenger getMessenger(EndpointAddress dest): Creates and returns an EndpointMessenger for sending messages.

- java.lang.String getProtocolName(): Returns a String containing the canonical name of this endpoint protocol, as it appears in an endpoint address.

- EndpointAddress getPublicAddress(): Returns an endpoint address of the local endpoint managed by the endpoint protocol.

- boolean isConnectionOriented(): Returns true if the endpoint protocol can establish connection to the remote host (like TCP).

- boolean ping(EndpointAddress addr): Returns true if the target address is reachable.

- void propagate(Message msg, java.lang.String serviceName, java.lang.String serviceParams, java.lang.String prunePeer): Propagates a message on this endpoint protocol.

Example

The following code sample obtains and displays all of the current endpoint protocols associated with the current peer:

```
EndpointProtocol tempInst = null;
Enumeration currentProtocols = myEndpointService.getEndpointProtocols();
while (currentProtocols.hasMoreElements()) {
  tempInst = (EndpointProtocol)currentProtocols.nextElement();
  System.out.println("Endpoint address: " +
tempInst.getPublicAddress().toString() + "\n");
}
```

Interface EndpointService

The EndpointService Interface defines the API for all endpoint protocols and subsequent services. The EndpointService can be used to directly manipulate the JXTA network topology.

Method Summary

- void addEndpointProtocol(EndpointProtocol proto): Installs the given endpoint protocol in this endpoint.

- void addFilterListener(java.lang.String elementName, EndpointFilterListener listener, boolean incoming): Registers an incoming messages filter listener.

- void addListener(java.lang.String address, EndpointListener listener): Registers an incoming messages listener.

- void demux(Message msg): Handles the given incoming message by calling the listener specified by its destination as returned by the getDestAddress() method of the message.

- EndpointProtocol getEndpointProtocolByName(java.lang.String name): Returns the endpoint protocol registered under the given name.

- java.util.Enumeration getEndpointProtocols(): Returns an enumeration of the endpoint protocols available to this endpoint service.

- PeerGroup getGroup(): Returns the group to which this Endpoint ServiceImpl is attached.

- EndpointMessenger getMessenger(EndpointAddress addr): Builds and returns an EndpointMessager that may be used to send messages via this endpoint to the given destination.

- EndpointAddress newEndpointAddress(java.lang.String Uri): Builds an endpoint address out of the given URI string.

- Message newMessage(): Returns a new Message object suitable for use with this endpoint service.

- boolean ping(EndpointAddress addr): Verifies that the given address can be reached.

- void propagate(Message srcMsg, java.lang.String serviceName, java.lang.String serviceParam): Propagates the given message through all the endpoint protocols that are available to this endpoint.

- void removeEndpointProtocol(EndpointProtocol proto): Removes the given endpoint protocol from this endpoint service.

- void removeFilterListener(java.lang.String address, EndpointFilterListener listener, boolean incoming): Removes the given listener previously registered under the given element name.

- boolean removeListener(java.lang.String address, EndpointListener listener): Removes the given listener previously registered under the given address.

Example

The following snippet obtains the endpoint service associated with the current peer group:

```
EndpointService  myEndpointService =
netPeerGroup.getEndpointService();
```

Interface GenericResolver

- The GenericResolver Interface defines the API for all resolver services.

Method Summary

- void sendQuery(java.lang.String peerId, ResolverQueryMsg query): For services that wish to implement a ResolverService Service, they must implement this interface. Sends query to the specified address.

- void sendResponse(java.lang.String destPeer, ResolverResponseMsg response): Sends a response to a peer.

Class ID

The ID class is the superclass for all identifiers in the JXTA system.

- **Parent Class:** java.lang.Object
- **Class:** net.jxta.id.ID
- **Derived Classes:**

    CodatID

    ModuleClassID

    ModuleSpecID

    PeerGroupID

    PeerID

    PipeID

Field Summary

- static ID nullID: Returns the null ID.

- static java.lang.String URIEncodingName: Defines the URI scheme that we will be using to present JXTA IDs.

- static java.lang.String URNNamespace: Defines the URN Namespace that we will be using to present JXTA IDs.

Constructor Summary

- protected ID(): Constructor for IDs.

Method Summary

- java.lang.Object clone(): Returns a clone of this object.
- abstract java.lang.String getIDFormat(): Returns a string identifier that indicates which ID format is used by this ID instance.
- abstract java.lang.Object getUniqueValue(): Returns an object containing the unique value of the ID.
- abstract java.net.URL getURL(): Returns a URI (URL in Java nomenclature) representation of the ID.
- java.lang.String toString(): Returns a string representation of the ID.

Class IDFactory

The IDFactory class allows for the building of ID objects.

- **Parent Class:** net.jxta.util.ClassFactory
- **Class:** net.jxta.id.IDFactory

Method Summary

- static ID fromURL(java.net.URL source): Constructs a new ID instance from a JXTA ID contained in a URI.
- protected java.util.Hashtable getAssocTable(): Used by ClassFactory methods to get the mapping of ID types to constructors.
- protected java.lang.Class getClassForKey(): Used by ClassFactory methods to ensure that all keys used with the mapping are of the correct type.
- protected java.lang.Class getClassOfInstantiators(): Used by ClassFactory methods to ensure that all of the instance classes that register with this factory have the correct base class.
- static CodatID newCodatID(PeerGroupID groupID): Creates a new CodatID instance.
- static CodatID newCodatID(PeerGroupID groupID, java.io.InputStream in): Creates a new CodatID instance.
- static ModuleClassID newModuleClassID(): Creates a new ModuleClassID instance.
- static ModuleClassID newModuleClassID(ModuleClassID baseClass): Creates a new ModuleClassID instance.
- static ModuleSpecID newModuleSpecID(ModuleClassID baseClass): Creates a new ModuleClassID instance.

- static PeerGroupID newPeerGroupID( ): Creates a new PeerGroupID instance.
- static PeerID newPeerID(PeerGroupID groupID): Creates a new PeerID instance.
- static PipeID newPipeID(PeerGroupID groupID): Creates a new PipeID instance.
- static PipeID newPipeID(PeerGroupID groupID, byte[]seed): Creates a new PipeID instance.
- protected boolean registerAssoc(java.lang.String className): Registers a class with the factory from its class name.
- static boolean registerIDType(int type, java.lang.Class instanceClass): Registers a constructor for an ID type to enable IDs of that type to be constructed.

Example

The following snippet shows how to obtain a new ModuleClassID from the IDFactory:

```
ModuleClassID yServiceID = IDFactory.newModuleClassID();
```

Interface InputPipe

The InputPipe Interface defines the API for the reception of messages through the Pipe Service.

Method Summary

- void close( ): Closes the pipe.
- message poll(int timeout): Polls for a message from the pipe.
- message waitForMessage( ): Waits for a message to be received.

Example

The following code snippet creates a reliable InputPipe object and polls for possible messages:

```
ReliablePipeService.Pipe newPipe =
incomingAcceptPipe.accept(30000);
Message msg = newPipe.getInputPipe().poll (30000);
```

Class JxtaError

The JxtaError class is a high-level exception that can be thrown by any of the JXTA code.

- **Parent Class:** java.lang.Error
- **Class:** net.jxta.exception.JxtaError
- **Derived Classes:** None

Field Summary

- None

Constructor Summary

- JxtaError(): Constructs a new NoResponseException with no detailed message.
- JxtaError(java.lang.String msg)

Method Summary

- None

Class MembershipService

The Membership Service is used by individual peers to join a peer group. The Membership Service is implemented by the peer group.

- **Parent Class:** java.lang.Object
- **Class:** net.jxta.membership.MembershipService
- **Derived Classes:** None

Constructor Summary

- MembershipService()

Method Summary

- abstract Authenticator apply(AuthenticationCredential application): Requests the necessary credentials to join the group with which this service is associated.

- abstract java.util.Enumeration getAuthCredentials(): Returns the current credentials for this peer.

- abstract java.util.Enumeration getCurrentCredentials(): Returns the current credentials for this peer.

- Service getInterface(): Returns the Service object represented by this class.

- java.lang.String getName(): Returns the name of the associated service.

- abstract Credential join(Authenticator authenticated): Joins the group by virtue of the completed authentication provided.

- abstract Credential makeCredential(Element element): Given a fragment of a StructuredDocument, reconstructs a Credential object from that fragment.

- abstract void resign(): Leaves the group to which this service is attached.

Example

In this example, the membership service is used to join a new group:

```
AuthenticationCredential myAuthenticationCredential = new
  AuthenticationCredential(myLocalGroup, null, myCredentials);

MembershipService myMembershipService =
  myLocalGroup.getMembershipService();

net.jxta.membership.Authenticator myAuthenticator =
  myMembershipService.apply(myAuthenticationCredential);

authenticateMe(myAuthenticator, "username", "password");

if (!myAuthenticator.isReadyForJoin()) {
  displayArea.append("Authenticator is not complete\n");
  return;
}

myMembershipService.join(myAuthenticator);
displayArea.append("Group has been joined\n");
```

Interface Message

The Message Interface defines the API necessary for messages sent between peers using the Endpoint and Pipe services.

Method Summary

- void addElement(MessageElement add): Adds a MessageElement into the message.

- java.lang.Object clone( ): Creates a deep copy of the message.

- boolean equals(java.lang.Object o): Checks to see if two messages are equal.

- byte[] getBytes(java.lang.String qname): Gets the named element from the message, and returns the element's byte array.

- EndpointAddress getDestinationAddress( ): Gets the destination address from the message.

- MessageElement getElement(java.lang.String name): Retrieves an element by name from the message.

- MessageElementEnumeration getElements( ): Returns an enumeration of all of the elements contained in this message.

- StringEnumeration getNames( ): Returns a StringEnumeration for all the message element names in this message.

- java.util.Enumeration getNamespaces( ): Returns an Enumeration of all namespace names used in this message.

- EndpointAddress getSourceAddress( ): Gets the source address from the message.

- java.lang.String getString(java.lang.String elementName): Gets the element from the message as a string.

- boolean hasElement(java.lang.String nsname): Checks for a message element with the given name.

- MessageElement newMessageElement(java.lang.String name, MimeMediaType type, byte[] b): Creates a new element, but doesn't add it to the message.

- MessageElement newMessageElement(java.lang.String name, MimeMediaType type, byte[] b, int offset, int len): Creates a new element, but doesn't add it to the message.

- MessageElement newMessageElement(java.lang.String name, MimeMediaType type, java.io.InputStream in): Creates a new MessageElement.

- MessageElement newMessageElement(java.lang.String name, MimeMediaType type, java.io.InputStream in, int len): Creates a new element, but doesn't add it to the message.

- boolean removeElement(MessageElement remove): Removes an element from a message.

- MessageElement removeElement(java.lang.String name): Removes an element from a message by its name.

- void setBytes(java.lang.String name, byte[] bytes): Creates or replaces a MessageElement using the given namespace and name.

- void setBytes(java.lang.String name, byte[] bytes, int offset, int len): Creates or replaces an element, and adds it to the message.

- void setDestinationAddress(EndpointAddress dstAddress): Sets the destination address to the message.

- void setSourceAddress(EndpointAddress srcAddress): Sets the source address to the message.

- void setString(java.lang.String elementName, java.lang.String s): Sets the string to the message.

Example

In this example, a new Message object is created, and data is put into the object and sent through an output pipe:

```
Message msg = myPipeService.createMessage();
msg.setString("DataTag", data);
myOutputPipe.send (msg);
```

Class MessageElement

The MessageElement class is an abstract class for elements within a message.

- **Parent Class:** java.lang.Object
- **Class:** net.jxta.endpoint.MessagesElement

Constructor Summary

- MessageElement()

Method Summary

- abstract java.lang.Object clone(): Makes a clone of this element.

- abstract boolean equals(java.lang.Object target): Compares this MessageElement against another.

- abstract byte[] getBytesOffset(): Returns the byte array that contains the element data.

- abstract int getLength(): Returns the number of bytes used in the array returned by getBytes().

- abstract java.lang.String getName(): Returns the name of the MessageElement.

- abstract int getOffset(): Returns the offset into the array returned by getBytes() of where data used by this element starts.

- abstract java.io.InputStream getStream(): Returns a stream containing the element data.

- abstract MimeMediaType getType(): Returns the type of the MessageElement.

- static java.lang.String[] parseName(java.lang.String name): Parses a name into its two colon-separated components.

Example

The MessageElement is an abstract class. A Message object contains a set of MessageElements private to a message.

The following code shows how the getElement() method of a Message object can be used to obtain a MessageElement. The getStream() method of MessageElement is called immediately.

```
Message msg = newPipe.getInputPipe().poll (30000);
InputStream in2 = msg.getElement ("DataTag").getStream ();
byte[] buf = new byte[8192];
int r = in2.read (buf);
```

Class MimeMediaType

The MimeMediaType class defines the type of stream used in the system.

- **Parent Class:** java.lang.Object
- **Class:** net.jxta.document.MimeMediaType

Constructor Summary

- MimeMediaType(java.lang.String someString): Creates a new MimeMediaType.

- MimeMediaType(java.lang.String type, java.lang.String subtype): Creates a new type/subtype MimeMediaType.

- MimeMediaType(java.lang.String type, java.lang.String subtype, java.lang.String parameters): Creates a new type/subtype MimeMediaType.

- MimeMediaType(java.lang.String type, java.lang.String subtype, java.lang.String[] parameters): Creates a new type/subtype MimeMediaType.

Method Summary

- void addParameter(java.lang.String newParam): Adds a parameter to a mime-type.

- java.lang.Object clone() boolean equals(java.lang.Object obj) java.lang.String getMimeMediaType(): Gets the "root" mime-type/subtype without any of the parameters.

- java.util.Enumeration getParameters(): Gets parameter values of a mime-type.

- java.lang.String getSubtype(): Gets the subtype of the mime-type.

- java.lang.String getType(): Gets the type of the mime-type.

- int hashCode() boolean isExperimentalSubtype(): Checks to see if the mime-type is for debugging.

- boolean isExperimentalType(): Checks to see if the mime-type is for provisional.

- boolean isValid(): Checks to see if the mime-type is valid.

- void setParameters(java.lang.String[] parameters): Sets the parameter to a mime-type.

- void setSubtype(java.lang.String subtype): Sets the subtype of the Mime-MediaType.

- void setType(java.lang.String type): Sets the type of the MimeMediaType.

- java.lang.String toString()

Example

The MimeMediaType is generally used to set the type of document being passed to a method. In the following example, a new PipeAdvertisement object is created with bytes from a string based on an XML document. The MimeMediaType indicates the document type.

```
pipeAdv = (PipeAdvertisement) AdvertisementFactory.newAdvertisement(
  new MimeMediaType("text/xml"),
  new ByteArrayInputStream(str.getBytes()));
```

Class ModuleClassAdvertisement

The ModuleClassAdvertisement class is a specialization of the Advertisement class, and is used for publishing a module class.

- **Parent Class:** net.jxta.document.Advertisement

- **Class:** net.jxta.protocol.ModuleClassAdvertisement

Constructor Summary

- ModuleClassAdvertisement()

Method Summary

- java.lang.Object clone(): Clones this ModuleClassAdvertisement.
- tatic java.lang.String getAdvertisementType(): Returns the advertisement type.
- java.lang.String getDescription(): Returns the keywords/description associated with this class.
- ID getID(): Returns a unique ID for that advertisement (for indexing purposes).
- ModuleClassID getModuleClassID(): Returns the ID of the class.
- java.lang.String getName(): Returns the name of the class.
- void setDescription(java.lang.String description): Sets the description associated with this class.
- void setModuleClassID(ModuleClassID id): Sets the ID of the class.
- void setName(java.lang.String name): Sets the name of the class.

Example

In this code example, a new ModuleClassAdvertisement is created, populated, and published:

```
ModuleClassAdvertisement myService1ModuleAdvertisement =
  (ModuleClassAdvertisement)
AdvertisementFactory.newAdvertisement(
  ModuleClassAdvertisement.getAdvertisementType());

myService1ModuleAdvertisement.setName("JXTAMOD:JXTA-CH18EX3");
myService1ModuleAdvertisement.setDescription("Service 1 of Chapter
  18 example 3");

myService1ID = IDFactory.newModuleClassID();
myService1ModuleAdvertisement.setModuleClassID(myService1ID);

myDiscoveryService.publish(myService1ModuleAdvertisement,
DiscoveryService.ADV);
```

Class ModuleClassID

The ModuleClassID class is used to identify a specific class module.

- **Parent Class:** net.jxta.id.ID
- **Class:** net.jxta.platform.ModuleClassID

Constructor Summary

- ModuleClassID()

Method Summary

- abstract ModuleClassID getBaseClass(): Returns a ModuleClassID of the same base class, but with the role portion set to zero.
- abstract boolean isOfSameBaseClass(ModuleClassID id): Returns true if this ModuleClassID is of the same base class as the given class.
- abstract boolean isOfSameBaseClass(ModuleSpecID id): Returns true if this ModuleClassID is of the same class as the given ModuleSpecID.

Example

In this code example, a new ModuleClassID is obtained from the IDFactory class:

```
ModuleClassID myService1ID = IDFactory.newModuleClassID();
```

Class ModuleImplAdvertisement

The ModuleImplAdvertisement is used to publish the existence of a specific implementation of a class.

- **Parent Class:** net.jxta.document.Advertisement
- **Class:** net.jxta.protocol.ModuleImplAdvertisement

Constructor Summary

- ModuleImplAdvertisement()

Method Summary

- java.lang.Object clone(): Clones this ModuleImplAdvertisement.
- static java.lang.String getAdvertisementType(): Returns the advertisement type.

- java.lang.String getCode(): Returns the code; a reference to or representation of the executable code advertised by this advertisement.

- StructuredDocument getCompat(): Returns the module impl.

- java.lang.String getDescription(): Returns the description.

- ID getID(): Returns the unique ID of that advertisement for indexing purposes.

- ModuleSpecID getModuleSpecID(): Returns the ID of the spec that this implements.

- StructuredDocument getParam(): Returns the param element.

- java.lang.String getProvider(): Returns the provider.

- java.lang.String getUri(): Returns the URI that is a reference to or representation of a package from which the executable code referenced by the getCode() method may be loaded.

- void setCode(java.lang.String code): Sets the code.

- void setCompat(Element compat): Sets the module impl.

- void setDescription(java.lang.String description): Sets the description.

- void setModuleSpecID(ModuleSpecID sid): Sets the ID of the spec that is implemented.

- void setParam(Element param): Sets the module param.

- void setProvider(java.lang.String provider): Sets the provider.

- void setUri(java.lang.String uri): Sets the URI.

Example

This code example builds a new ModuleImplAdvertisement based on a stream called outputter from a parent advertisement.

```
ModuleImplAdvertisement myNewImplAdv =
(ModuleImplAdvertisement)AdvertisementFactory.newAdvertisement(
XMLMIMETYPE, new ByteArrayInputStream(outputter.outputString(
doc).getBytes()));
```

Class ModuleSpecAdvertisement

The ModuleSpecAdvertisement is used to publish a module specification.

- **Parent Class:** net.jxta.document.Advertisement
- **Class:** net.jxta.protocol.ModuleSpecAdvertisement

Constructor Summary

- ModuleSpecAdvertisement()

Method Summary

- java.lang.Object clone(): Clones this ModuleSpecAdvertisement.
- static java.lang.String getAdvertisementType(): Returns the advertisement type.
- ModuleSpecID getAuthSpecID(): Returns the specID of an authenticator module.
- java.lang.String getCreator(): Returns the creator of the module spec.
- java.lang.String getDescription(): Returns the keywords/description associated with this class
- ID getID(): Returns a unique ID for that advertisement for the purpose of indexing.
- ModuleSpecID getModuleSpecID(): Returns the ID of the spec.
- java.lang.String getName(): Returns the name of the module spec.
- StructuredDocument getParam(): Returns the param element.
- PipeAdvertisement getPipeAdvertisement(): Returns the embedded pipe advertisement, if any.
- ModuleSpecID getProxySpecID(): Returns the specID of a proxy module.
- java.lang.String getSpecURI(): Returns the URI.
- java.lang.String getVersion(): Returns the specification version number.
- void setAuthSpecID(ModuleSpecID authSpecID): Sets an authenticator module specID.
- void setCreator(java.lang.String creator): Sets the creator of this module spec.
- void setDescription(java.lang.String description): Sets the description associated with this class.
- void setModuleSpecID(ModuleSpecID id): Sets the ID of the class.
- void setName(java.lang.String name): Sets the name of the module spec.
- void setParam(StructuredDocument param): Sets the param element.
- void setPipeAdvertisement(PipeAdvertisement pipeAdv): Sets an embedded pipe advertisement.
- void setProxySpecID(ModuleSpecID proxySpecID): Sets a proxy module specID.

- void setSpecURI(java.lang.String uri): Sets the URI.

- void setVersion(java.lang.String version): Sets the version of the module.

Example

This code example builds a new ModuleSpecAdvertisement and populates it with appropriate values, including a pipe advertisement:

```
ModuleSpecAdvertisement myModuleSpecAdvertisement =
  (ModuleSpecAdvertisement) AdvertisementFactory.newAdvertisement(
  ModuleSpecAdvertisement.getAdvertisementType());

myModuleSpecAdvertisement.setName("JXTASPEC:JXTA-CH19EX1");
myModuleSpecAdvertisement.setVersion("Version 1.0");
myModuleSpecAdvertisement.setCreator("gradecki.com");
myModuleSpecAdvertisement.setModuleSpecID(IDFactory.newModuleSpecID(
  myService1ID));
myModuleSpecAdvertisement.setSpecURI("<http://www.jxta.org/CH19EX1>");
      myModuleSpecAdvertisement.setPipeAdvertisement
        (myPipeAdvertisement);
```

Class ModuleSpecID

The ModuleSpecID is used to identify a specific Module.

- **Parent Class:** java.jxta.id.ID

- **Class:** net.jxta.platform.ModuleSpecID

Constructor Summary

- ModuleSpecID()

Method Summary

- abstract ModuleClassID getBaseClass(): Returns a ModuleClassID of the same base class, but with the role portion set to zero.

- abstract boolean isOfSameBaseClass(ModuleClassID id): Returns true if this ModuleSpecID is of the same base class as the given class.

- abstract boolean isOfSameBaseClass(ModuleSpecID id): Returns true if this ModuleSpecID is of the same base class as the given ModuleSpecID.

Example

The following code example creates a new ModuleSpecID based on a Module-ClassID defined in the variable.myService1ID.

```
ModuleSpecID = IDFactory.newModuleSpecID( myService1ID)
```

Interface OutputPipe

The InputPipe Interface defines the API for the sending of messages through the Pipe Service.

Method Summary

- void close(): Closes the pipe.
- void send(Message msg): Sends a message through the pipe.

Example

The following example shows how to send a message through an output pipe:

```
try {
  myOutputPipe.send (msg);
} catch (Exception e) {
    System.out.println("Unable to print output pipe");
    e.printStackTrace();
    System.exit(-1);
}
```

Class PeerAdvertisement

The PeerAdvertisement is used to publish and hold information about a peer.

- **Parent Class:** next.jxta.document.Advertisement
- **Class:** net.jxta.protocol.PeerAdvertisement

Constructor Summary

- PeerAdvertisement()

Method Summary

- java.lang.Object clone(): Makes a safe clone of this PeerAdvertisement.
- static java.lang.String getAdvertisementType(): Returns the advertisement type.
- java.lang.String getDebugLevel(): Returns the debugLevel.
- java.lang.String getDescription(): Returns the description.
- ID getID(): Returns a unique ID for that peer X group intersection.
- java.lang.String getName(): Returns the name of the peer.

- PeerGroupID getPeerGroupID(): Returns the ID of the peer group this peer advertisement is for.

- PeerID getPeerID(): Returns the ID of the peer.

- StructuredDocument getServiceParam(ID key): Returns the parameter element that matches the given key from the service parameters table.

- java.util.Hashtable getServiceParams(): Returns the sets of parameters for all services.

- void putServiceParam(ID key, Element param): Puts a service parameter in the service parameters table under the given key.

- StructuredDocument removeServiceParam(ID key): Removes and returns the parameter element that matches the given key from the service parameters table.

- void setDebugLevel(java.lang.String debugLevel): Sets the debugLevel.

- void setDescription(java.lang.String description): Sets the description.

- void setName(java.lang.String name): Sets the name of the peer.

- void setPeerGroupID(PeerGroupID gid): Returns the ID of the peer group this peer advertisement is for.

- void setPeerID(PeerID pid): Sets the ID of the peer.

- void setServiceParams(java.util.Hashtable params): Sets the sets of parameters for all services.

Example

This code example shows how to obtain a peer's PeerAdvertisement and display it to standard output:

```
try {
  PeerAdvertisement myPeerAdv =
    (PeerAdvertisement)netPeerGroup.getPeerAdvertisement();
  StructuredTextDocument myDocument =
    (StructuredTextDocument)myPeerAdv.getDocument(XMLMIMETYPE);
  myDocument.sendToStream(System.out);
} catch(Exception e) {}
```

Interface PeerGroup

The PeerGroup Interface defines the API necessary for all peer group to implement.

- net.jxta.peergroup

Constructor Summary

- static class PeerGroup.IdMaker: An inner class used to create static, well-known identifiers.

Method Summary

- static ModuleSpecID allPurposePeerGroupSpecID: A well-known group specification identifier: an all-purpose peer group specification.

- static ModuleClassID applicationClassID: A well-known module class identifier: application.

- static int Both: Looks for the needed ModuleImplAdvertisement in both this group and its parent.

- static long DEFAULT_EXPIRATION: Default expiration time for discovered group advertisements.

- static long DEFAULT_LIFETIME: Default lifetime for group advertisements in the publisher's cache.

- static ModuleClassID discoveryClassID: A well-known module class identifier: discovery service.

- static ModuleClassID endpointClassID: A well-known module class identifier: endpoint service.

- static int FromParent: Looks for the needed ModuleImplAdvertisement in the parent group of this group.

- static int Here: Looks for the needed ModuleImplAdvertisement in this group.

- static ModuleClassID httpProtoClassID: A well-known module class identifier: HTTP protocol.

- static ModuleClassID membershipClassID: A well-known module class identifier: membership service.

- static ModuleClassID peerGroupClassID: A well-known module class identifier: peer group.

- static ModuleClassID peerinfoClassID: A well-known module class identifier: peer info service.

- static ModuleClassID pipeClassID: A well-known module class identifier: pipe service.

- static ModuleSpecID refDiscoverySpecID: A well-known service specification identifier: the standard discovery.

- static ModuleSpecID refEndpointSpecID: A well-known service specification identifier: the standard endpoint.

- static ModuleSpecID refHttpProtoSpecID: A well-known endpoint protocol specification identifier: the standard HTTP endpoint protocol.

- static ModuleSpecID refMembershipSpecID: A well-known service specification identifier: the standard membership.

- static ModuleSpecID refNetPeerGroupSpecID: A well-known group specification identifier: the NetworkPeerGroup.

- static ModuleSpecID refPeerinfoSpecID: A well-known service specification identifier: the standard peer info.

- static ModuleSpecID refPipeSpecID: A well-known service specification identifier: the standard pipe.

- static ModuleSpecID refPlatformSpecID: A well-known group specification identifier: the platform.

- static ModuleSpecID refRendezvousSpecID: A well-known service specification identifier: the standard rendezvous.

- static ModuleSpecID refResolverSpecID: A well-known service specification identifier: the standard resolver.

- static ModuleSpecID refRouterProtoSpecID: A well-known endpoint protocol specification identifier: the standard router.

- static ModuleSpecID refShellSpecID: A well-known application: the shell.

- static ModuleSpecID refStartNetPeerGroupSpecID: A well-known main application of the platform: startNetPeerGroup.

- static ModuleSpecID refTcpProtoSpecID: A well-known endpoint protocol specification identifier: the standard TCP endpoint protocol.

- static ModuleSpecID refTlsProtoSpecID: A well-known endpoint protocol specification identifier: the standard TLS endpoint protocol.

- static ModuleClassID rendezvousClassID: A well-known module class identifier: rendezvous service.

- static ModuleClassID resolverClassID: A well-known module class identifier: resolver service.

- static ModuleClassID routerProtoClassID: A well-known module class identifier: router protocol.

- static ModuleClassID tcpProtoClassID: A well-known module class identifier: TCP protocol.

- static ModuleClassID tlsProtoClassID: A well-known module class identifier: tlsProtocol.

Example

This code example shows how to obtain a PeerGroup object from the NetPeer-Group and then pull the pipe service from the peer group:

```
PeerGroup netPeerGroup = PeerGroupFactory.newNetPeerGroup();
PipeService pipeService = netPeerGroup.getPipeService();
```

Class PeerGroupAdvertisement

The PeerGroupAdvertisement is used to publish information about a peer group.

- **Parent Class:** net.jxta.document.Advertisement
- **Class:** net.jxta.protocol.PeerGroupAdvertisement

Constructor Summary

- PeerGroupAdvertisement()

Method Summary

- java.lang.Object clone(): Clones this PeerGroupAdvertisement.
- static java.lang.String getAdvertisementType(): Returns the advertisement type.
- java.lang.String getDescription(): Returns the description.
- ID getID(): Returns a unique ID for indexing purposes.
- ModuleSpecID getModuleSpecID(): Returns the ID of the group spec that this uses.
- java.lang.String getName(): Returns the name of the group.
- PeerGroupID getPeerGroupID(): Returns the ID of the group.
- StructuredDocument getServiceParam(ID key): Returns the parameter element that matches the given key from the service parameters table.
- java.util.Hashtable getServiceParams(): Returns the sets of parameters for all services.
- void putServiceParam(ID key, Element param): Puts a service parameter in the service parameters table under the given key.
- StructuredDocument removeServiceParam(ID key): Removes and returns the parameter element that matches the given key from the service parameters table.

- void setDescription(java.lang.String description): Sets the description.
- void setModuleSpecID(ModuleSpecID sid): Sets the ID of the group spec that this uses.
- void setName(java.lang.String name): Sets the name of the group.
- void setPeerGroupID(PeerGroupID gid): Sets the ID of the group.
- void setServiceParams(java.util.Hashtable params): Sets the sets of parameters for all services.

Example

This code example shows how to programmatically build a new PeerGroup Advertisement object:

```
PeerGroupAdvertisement groupAdvertisement =
(PeerGroupAdvertisement)
  AdvertisementFactory.newAdvertisement(
  PeerGroupAdvertisement.getAdvertisementType());

groupAdvertisement.setPeerGroupID(myPeerGroupID);
groupAdvertisement.setModuleSpecID(myGroupImpl.getModuleSpecID());
groupAdvertisement.setName(myPeerGroupName);
groupAdvertisement.setDescription(myPeerGroupDescription);
displayArea.append("New Peer Group Advertisement has been
created\n");
```

Class PeerGroupFactory

The PeerGroupFactory class allows use PeerGroup to be constructed.

- **Parent Class:** java.util.EventObject
- **Class:** net.jxta.peergroup.PeerGroupFactory

Constructor Summary

- PeerGroupFactory()

Method Summary

- static PeerGroup newNetPeerGroup(): Creates a default platform peer group, from which a new NetPeerGroup is created.
- static PeerGroup newNetPeerGroup(PeerGroup pg): Until the concept of *NetPeerGroup* is better integrated, we need something straightforward so that applications that wish to control the start-up process can easily bring up a NetPeerGroup like startNetPeerGroup does.

- static PeerGroup newPeerGroup(): A static method to create a new peer group instance.
- static PeerGroup newPlatform():A static method to create a new peer platform; the init() method is called automatically.
- static void setPlatformClass(java.lang.Class c): A static method to initialize the platform peer group class.
- static void setStdPeerGroupClass(java.lang.Class c): A static method to initialize the std peer group class.

Example

This code obtains the NetPeerGroup using a PeerGroupFactory class:

```
try {
  netPeerGroup = PeerGroupFactory.newNetPeerGroup();
} catch (PeerGroupException e) {
  System.out.println("Unable to create PeerGroup - Failure");
  e.printStackTrace();
  System.exit(1);
}
```

Class PeerGroupID

The PeerGroupID uniquely identifies a peer group.

- **Parent Class:** net.jxta.id.ID
- **Class:** net.jxta.peergroup.PeerGroupID

Field Summary

- static PeerGroupID defaultNetPeerGroupID: The well-known unique identifier of the NetPeerGroup.
- static PeerGroupID worldPeerGroupID: The well-known unique identifier of the WorldPeerGroup.

Constructor Summary

- PeerGroupID()

Example

The following code will obtain the PeerGroupID of the NetPeerGroup:

```
PeerGroupID = netPeerGroup.getPeerGroupID()
```

Class PeerID

The PeerID uniquely identifies a JXTA peer.

- **Parent Class:** next.jxta.id.ID
- **Class:** net.jxta.peer.PeerID

Constructor Summary

- PeerID()

Method Summary

- abstract ID getPeerGroupID(): Returns the PeerGroupID of the peer group to which this peer ID belongs.

Example

This example snippet obtains a new peer ID using the IDFactory:

```
PeerID peerID =
  IDFactory.getPeerID(netPeerGroup.getPeerGroupID());
```

Class PeerInfoEvent

The PeerInfoEvent class is a container for all event returned from a peer info request.

- **Parent Class:** java.util.EventObject
- **Class:** net.jxta.peer.PeerInfoEvent

Constructor Summary

- PeerInfoEvent(java.lang.Object source, PeerInfoResponseMessage piResp, int queryid): Creates a new event.

Method Summary

- PeerInfoResponseMessage getPPeerInfoResponseMessage(): Returns the response associated with the event.
- int getQueryID(): Returns the query ID associated with the response returned in this event.

Example

This code shows how a PeerInfoEvent is passed to an appropriate listener:

```
public void peerInfoResponse(PeerInfoEvent e) {
  PeerInfoAdvertisement adv = e.getPeerInfoAdvertisement();
  displayArea.append("Total Uptime in milliseconds = " +
    adv.getUptime() + "\n");
}
```

Interface PeerInfoListener

The PeerInfoListener interface defines the API that needs to be implemented by a class wishing to receive PeerInfoEvents.

Method Summary

- void peerInfoResponse(PeerInfoEvent event): PeerInfoService Event

Class PeerInfoQueryMessage

The PeerInfoQueryMessage class is an abstract class defining the API for query messages.

- **Parent Class:** java.util.EventObject
- **Class:** net.jxta.protocol.PeerInfoQueryMessage

Constructor Summary

- PeerInfoQueryMessage()

Method Summary

- abstract Document getDocument(MimeMediaType encodeAs) static java.lang.String getMessageType(): Returns the message type.
- Element getRequest(): Returns the request.
- ID getSourcePid(): Returns the sender's PID.
- ID getTargetPid(): Returns the target's PID.
- void setRequest(Element request): Sets the request.
- void setSourcePid(ID pid): Sets the sender's PID.
- void setTargetPid(ID pid): Sets the target's PID.

Example

The following code shows an example of a PeerInfoListener and how it can be used in a remote peer information request:

```
PeerInfoListener peerInfoListener = new PeerInfoListener() {
  public void peerInfoResponse(PeerInfoEvent e) {
    PeerInfoAdvertisement adv = e.getPeerInfoAdvertisement();
    displayArea.append("Total Uptime in milliseconds = " +
      adv.getUptime() + "\n");
  }
};
myPeerInfoService.getRemotePeerInfo(localPeerID,
peerInfoListener);
```

Class PeerInfoResponseMessage

The PeerInfoResponseMessage class is an abstract class defining the API for response messages.

- **Parent Class:** java.lang.Object
- **Class:** net.jxta.protocol.PeerInfoResponseMessage

Constructor Summary

- PeerInfoResponseMessage()

Method Summary

- abstract Document getDocument(MimeMediaType encodeAs) java.util.Enumeration getIncomingTrafficChannels(): Gets an enumeration of incoming traffic channels on this peer.

- long getIncomingTrafficOnChannel(java.lang.String channel): Gets the number of bytes received on the specified channel.

- long getLastIncomingMessageTime(): Gets the time in milliseconds since this peer last received a message in milliseconds since the "epoch," namely January 1, 1970, 00:00:00 GMT.

- long getLastOutgoingMessageTime(): Gets the time in milliseconds since this peer last sent a message in milliseconds since the "epoch," namely January 1, 1970, 00:00:00 GMT.

- static java.lang.String getMessageType(): Returns the message type.

- java.util.Enumeration getOutgoingTrafficChannels(): Gets an enumeration of outgoing traffic channels on this peer.

- long getOutgoingTrafficOnChannel(java.lang.String channel): Gets the number of bytes sent on the specified channel.

- Element getResponse(): Returns the response.
- ID getSourcePid(): Returns the sender's PID.
- ID getTargetPid(): Returns the target's PID.
- long getTimestamp(): Returns the time when this peer was last polled.
- long getUptime(): Returns the number of milliseconds since this peer was started.
- void setIncomingTrafficElement(java.lang.String channel, long bytes): Sets the number of bytes received on the specified channel.
- void setLastIncomingMessageTime(long t): Sets the time in milliseconds since this peer last received a message in milliseconds since the "epoch," namely January 1, 1970, 00:00:00 GMT.
- void setLastOutgoingMessageTime(long t): Sets the time in milliseconds since this peer last sent a message in milliseconds since the "epoch," namely January 1, 1970, 00:00:00 GMT.
- void setOutgoingTrafficElement(java.lang.String channel, long bytes): Sets the number of bytes sent on the specified channel.
- void setResponse(Element response): Sets the request.
- void setSourcePid(ID pid): Sets the sender's PID.
- void setTargetPid(ID pid): Sets the target's PID.
- void setTimestamp(long milliseconds): Sets the time when this peer was last polled.
- void setUptime(long milliseconds): Sets the number of milliseconds since this peer was started.

Class PipeAdvertisement

The PipeAdvertisement class defines information about an input or output pipe.

- **Parent Class:** net.jxta.document.advertisement
- **Class:** net.jxta.protocol.PipeAdvertisement
- **Derived Classes:** None

Field Summary

- static java.lang.String IdTag: XML tag to store the PipeID.
- static java.lang.String NameTag: XML tag to store the name of the pipe.
- static java.lang.String TypeTag: XML tag to store the pipe type.

Constructor Summary

- PipeAdvertisement()

Method Summary

- java.lang.Object clone(): Clones this PipeAdvertisement.
- static java.lang.String getAdvertisementType(): Gets the pipe type.
- ID getID(): Gets an ID for indexing purposes.
- java.lang.String getName(): Gets the symbolic name associated with the pipe.
- ID getPipeID(): Gets the pipe ID.
- java.lang.String getType(): Gets the pipe type.
- void setName(java.lang.String n): Sets the symbolic name associated with the pipe.
- void setPipeID(ID pipeId): Sets the pipe ID.
- void setType(java.lang.String type): Sets the pipe type.

Example

The following code example shows building a new PipeAdvertisement object using a flatfile on the local hard drive and publishing it:

```
PipeAdvertisement aPipeAdv = null;

try {
  FileInputStream is = new FileInputStream("outputpipe.adv");
  aPipeAdv = (PipeAdvertisement)AdvertisementFactory.newAdvertisement(
    new MimeMediaType("text/xml"), is);
} catch (Exception e) {
  System.out.println("failed to read/parse pipe advertisement");
  e.printStackTrace();
  System.exit(-1);
}

try {
  myDiscoveryService.publish(aPipeAdv, DiscoveryService.ADV);
  myDiscoveryService.remotePublish(aPipeAdv, DiscoveryService.ADV);
} catch (Exception e) {
  e.printStackTrace();
  System.exit(-1);
}
```

Class PipeID

The PipeID class uniquely identified a pipe.

- **Parent Class:** net.jxta.id.ID
- **Class:** net.jxta.pipe.PipeID

Constructor Summary

- PipeID()

Method Summary

- abstract ID getPeerGroupID(): Returns the PeerGroupID of the peer group to which this peer ID belongs.

Example

The following code example shows building a PipeAdvertisement programmatically and obtaining a new PipeID from the IDFactory class:

```
displayArea.append("Creating Input Pipe....\n");

myInputPipeAdvertisement =
 (PipeAdvertisement)AdvertisementFactory.newAdvertisement(
  PipeAdvertisement.getAdvertisementType());

myInputPipeAdvertisement.setName("JXTA:valueGet");
myInputPipeAdvertisement.setType("JxtaUnicast");
myInputPipeAdvertisement.setPipeID((ID)
net.jxta.id.IDFactory.newPipeID(netPeerGroup.getPeerGroupID()));
```

Class PipeMsgEvent

The PipeMsgEvent is a container for pipe messages received by a peer.

- **Parent Class:** java.util.EventObject
- **Class:** net.jxta.pipe.PipeMsgEvent

Constructor Summary

- PipeMsgEvent(java.lang.Object source, Message message): Creates a new event.

Method Summary

- Message getMessage(): Returns the message associated with the event.

Example

See the next example in PipeMsgListener

Interface PipeMsgListener

The PipeMsgListener defines the methods that must be implemented by a class wishing to receive asynchronous pipe messages.

Method Summary

- void pipeMsgEvent(PipeMsgEvent event): PipeMsgEvent Event

Example

This code snippet shows a new pipe listener and the required PipeMsgListener() method:

```
PipeMsgListener myService1Listener = new PipeMsgListener() {
  public void pipeMsgEvent(PipeMsgEvent event) {
    Message myMessage = null;
    try {
      myMessage = event.getMessage();
      String myMessageContent;

      myMessageContent = myMessage.getString("DataTag");
      if (myMessageContent != null) {
        displayArea.append("Message received: " + myMessageContent +
"\n");

        displayArea.append("Waiting for message...\n");
        return;
      } else {
        displayArea.append("Invalid tag\n");
        return;
      }
    } catch (Exception ee) {
      ee.printStackTrace();
      return;
    }
  }
};
```

Interface PipeService

The PipeService Interface defines the API that must be implemented by potential pipe services.

Field Summary

- static java.lang.String PropagateType: Propagated, non-secure, and unreliable type of pipe.

- static java.lang.String UnicastSecureType: Unicast and secure type of pipe.

- static java.lang.String UnicastType: Unicast, unreliable, and non-secure type of pipe.

Method Summary

- InputPipe createInputPipe(PipeAdvertisement adv): Creates an InputPipe from a pipe advertisement.

- InputPipe createInputPipe(PipeAdvertisement adv, PipeMsgListener listener): Creates an InputPipe from a pipe advertisement.

- Message createMessage(): Creates a new message.

- OutputPipe createOutputPipe(PipeAdvertisement adv, java.util.Enumeration peers, long timeout): Creates an OutputPipe from the pipe advertisement giving a PeerId(s) where the corresponding InputPipe is supposed to be.

- OutputPipe createOutputPipe(PipeAdvertisement adv, long timeout): Creates an OutputPipe from the pipe advertisement.

- void createOutputPipe(PipeAdvertisement adv, OutputPipeListener listener): Registers a listener for a NetPipe.

- OutputPipeListener removeOutputPipeListener(java.lang.String pipeID, OutputPipeListener listener): Removes an output pipe listener.

Example

This code snippet shows obtaining a PipeService object and creating an output pipe:

```
PipeService myPipeService = netPeerGroup.getPipeService();
myPipe = myPipeService.createInputPipe(myPipeAdvertisement,
  myService1Listener);
```

Interface QueryHandler

- The QueryHandler Interface defines the methods to be implemented by resolver services.

Method Summary

- ResolverResponseMsg processQuery(ResolverQueryMsg query): Processes the resolver query and generates a response.
- void processResponse(ResolverResponseMsg response): The callback method; when messages are received by the resolver service, it calls back this method to deal with received responses.

Interface RendezvousListener

The RendezvousListener interface defines the methods that must be implemented by a class wanting to receive rendezvous events.

Method Summary

- void rendezvousEvent(RendezvousEvent event): The rendezvous event

Interface RendezVousService

The RendezVousService Interface defines the API to be implemented by a potential rendezvous service.

Method Summary

- void addListener(RendezvousListener listener): Adds a listener for RenDezVousEvents.
- void addPropagateListener(java.lang.String name, EndpointListener listener): Clients of the rendezvous service can use this method to receive raw propagation rather than crawling query/responses.
- void connectToRendezVous(EndpointAddress addr): Adds a peer as a new RendezVousService point.
- void connectToRendezVous(PeerAdvertisement adv): Adds a peer as a new RendezVousService point.
- void disconnectFromRendezVous(PeerID peerID): Removes a RendezVousService point.

- java.util.Enumeration getConnectedPeers(): Returns an Enumeration of PeerIDs of the peers that are currently connected.

- java.util.Enumeration getConnectedRendezVous(): Returns an Enumeration of the PeerIDs of all the RendezVous on which this peer is currently connected.

- java.util.Enumeration getDisconnectedRendezVous(): Returns an Enumeration of the PeerIDs of all the RendezVous on which this peer failed to connect.

- boolean isConnectedToRendezVous(): Returns true if connected to a rendezvous.

- boolean isRendezVous(): Tells whether this rendezvous service currently acts as a "super-node", "rendezvous", knowledge hub, influence broker, or whichever higher status applies to the implementation.

- void propagate(Message msg, java.lang.String serviceName, java.lang.String serviceParam, int defaultTTL): Propagates a message onto as many peers on the local network as possible.

- void propagateInGroup(Message msg, java.lang.String serviceName, java.lang.String serviceParam, int defaultTTL, java.lang.String prunePeer): Deprecated.

- void propagateToNeighbors(Message msg, java.lang.String serviceName, java.lang.String serviceParam, int defaultTTL, java.lang.String prunePeer): Deprecated.

- boolean removeListener(RendezvousListener listener): Removes a listener previously added with addListener.

- void removePropagateListener(java.lang.String name, EndpointListener listener): Removes a listener previously added with addPropagateListener.

- void sendRendezVousAdv(PeerAdvertisement destPeer, PeerAdvertisement rendezVous): Sends an advertisement about other RendezVous to a given peer.

- RendezVousMonitor setMonitor(RendezVousMonitor monitor): Registers a notification monitor that is called each time a RendezVous peer is not reachable anymore.

- void startRendezVous(): Starts the local peer as a RendezVous peer with the default manager.

- void startRendezVous(RendezVousManager monitor): Starts the local peer as a RendezVous peer.

- void stopRendezVous(): Stops the RendezVous function on the local peer.

Class ResolverResponseMsg

The ResovlerResponseMsg defines the messages used in a response message from the resolver service.

- **Parent Class:** java.lang.Object
- **Class:** net.jxta.protocol.ResolverResponseMsg

Field Summary

- static int queryid

Constructor Summary

- ResolverResponseMsg()

Method Summary

- static java.lang.String getAdvertisementType(): All messages have a type (in XML, this is !doctype), which identifies the message.
- java.lang.String getCredential(): Returns the credential.
- abstract Document getDocument(MimeMediaType asMimeType): Writes an advertisement into a document.
- java.lang.String getHandlerName(): Returns the handlername.
- int getQueryId(): Returns the queryid value.
- java.lang.String getResponse(): Returns the query.
- void setCredential(java.lang.String cred): Sets the credential.
- void setHandlerName(java.lang.String name): Sets the handlername.
- void setQueryId(int id): Sets the query ID.
- void setResponse(java.lang.String response): Sets the response.

Interface ResolverService

The ResolverService interface defines the API for classes that act as a resolver service.

Method Summary

- QueryHandler registerHandler(java.lang.String name, QueryHandler handler): Registers a given ResolveHandler.

- QueryHandler unregisterHandler(java.lang.String name): Unregisters a given ResolveHandler.

Interface StructuredDocument

The StructuredDocument interface defines the API XML-like message used throughout the JXTA system.

Method Summary

- Element createElement(java.lang.Object key): Creates a new element without a value.

- Element createElement(java.lang.Object key, java.lang.Object value): Creates a new element with a value.

Class StructuredDocumentFactory

The StructuredDocumentFactory allows for the creation of StructuredDocument objects.

- **Parent Class:** net.jxta.util.ClassFactory
- **Class:** net.jxta.document.StructuredDocumentFactory
- **Derived Classes:** None

Method Summary

- protected java.util.Hashtable getAssocTable(): Used by ClassFactory methods to get the mapping of MIME types to constructors.

- protected java.lang.Class getClassForKey(): Used by ClassFactory methods to ensure that all keys used with the mapping are of the correct type.

- protected java.lang.Class getClassOfInstantiators(): Used by ClassFactory methods to ensure that all of the instantiators that are registered with this factory have the correct interface.

- static java.lang.String getFileExtensionForMimeType(MimeMediaType mimetype): Returns the preferred extension for a given mime-type.

- static MimeMediaType getMimeTypeForFileExtension(java.lang.String extension): Returns the preferred mime-type for a given file extension.

- static StructuredDocument newStructuredDocument(MimeMediaType mimetype, java.io.InputStream stream): Constructs an instance of StructuredDocument matching the mime-type specified by the mimetype parameter.

- static StructuredDocument newStructuredDocument(MimeMediaType mimetype, java.lang.String doctype): Constructs an instance of StructuredDocument matching the mime-type specified by the mimetype parameter.

- static StructuredDocument newStructuredDocument(MimeMediaType mimetype, java.lang.String doctype, java.lang.String value): Constructs an instance of StructuredDocument matching the mime-type specified by the mimetype parameter.

- protected boolean registerAssoc(java.lang.String className): Registers a class with the factory from its class name.

- static boolean registerInstantiator(MimeMediaType mimetype, StructuredDocumentFactory.Instantiator instantiator): Registers an instantiator object a mime-type of documents to be constructed.

Example

The following code shows how to use the StructuredDocumentFactory to build a new StructuredTextDocument based with a Parm element in it:

```
StructuredTextDocument paramDoc =
  (StructuredTextDocument)StructuredDocumentFactory.
  newStructuredDocument(new MimeMediaType("text/xml"),"Parm");
```

Interface StructuredTextDocument

The StructuredTextDocument interface defines an extension to the StructuredDocument allowing for String accessors.

Method Summary

- TextElement createElement(java.lang.String name): Creates a new element without a value.

- TextElement createElement(java.lang.String name, java.lang.String value): Creates a new element with a value.

Example

See the example in StructuredDocumentFactory.

Interface TextDocument

The TextDocument extends the Document interface and allows for text output.

Method Summary

- java.lang.String getFileExtension(): Returns the file extension type used by this document.
- java.io.Reader getReader(): Returns a stream of characters that represent the content of this document.
- void sendToWriter(java.io.Writer stream): Rather than returning an Input-Stream, sends the document to the specified stream.

Interface TextElement

The TextElement extends the Element interface with String accessors.

Method Summary

- void appendChild(TextElement element): Adds a child element to this element.
- java.util.Enumeration getChildren(java.lang.String name): Returns an enumeration of the immediate children of this element whose names match the specified string.
- java.lang.String getName(): Gets the name associated with an element.
- java.lang.String getTextValue(): Gets the value (if any) associated with an element

Example

The following code shows how to obtain a TextElement from a Structured-TextDocument:

```
Enumeration elements =
  myParamDoc.getChildren("jxta:PipeAdvertisement");
elements = ((TextElement)
  elements.nextElement()).getChildren();
```

Current Add-on JXTA Services

The JXTA community has spent considerable time coming up with additional services for use by peers in the network. This appendix provides a glimpse of those services and their current status.

caservice

Description: Designed to provide an authority service for certificates and signed data with the JXTA network.

URL: http://caservice.jxta.org/servlets/ProjectHome

Status: There hasn't been much activity in the project since late 2001. Some code is available in the CVS.

cms

Description: We discussed the Content Management System in Chapter 14. The project's goal is to develop a consistent mechanism for document sharing.

URL: http://cms.jxta.org/servlets/ProjectHome

Status: The project is very active.

compute-power-market

Description: The Computer Power Market (CPM) project employs an economics approach to managing computational resource consumers, and provides computations across the work in peer-to-peer computing style.

URL: http://compute-power-market.jxta.org/servlets/ProjectHome

Status: There is currently no activity in this project.

edutella

Description: A multi-staged effort to build a metadata infrastructure that allows highly heterogeneous peers to communicate with each other.

URL: http://edutella.jxta.org/servlets/ProjectHome

Status: This project is very active.

gisp

Description: The Global Information Sharing Protocol (GISP) is designed to provide information sharing using a distributed index.

URL: http://gisp.jxta.org/servlets/ProjectHome

Status: Source code is available for this project.

iPeers

Description: iPeers is an effort to use artificial intelligence (AI) within the JXTA network through Agent technology.

URL: http://ipeers.jxta.org/servlets/ProjectHome

Status: This project is currently not active.

jxrtl

Description: jxrtl is an effort to create a language within JXTA peers for distributing work across the entire network.

URL: http://jxrtl.jxta.org/servlets/ProjectHome

Status: The project has quite a few documents available, as well as some source code for a router.

jxta-rmi

Description: This project enables applications to be developed with the Remote Method Invocation (RMI) API of the Java SDK.

URL: http://jxta-rmi.jxta.org/servlets/ProjectHome

Status: This is an active project, with source code and constant additional work.

jxtaspace

Description: jxtaspace is a project designed to implement distributed shared memory between JXTA peers.

URL: http://jxtaspaces.jxta.org/servlets/ProjectHome

Status: This project is active, with both discussions and source code commits to CVS.

jxtavfs

Description: jxtavfs is a project for building a virtual file system within peers.

URL: http://jxtavfs.jxta.org/servlets/ProjectHome

Status: There hasn't been much activity in this project since 2001.

monitoring

Description: Designed to extend the current core monitoring functionality of the JXTA platform.

URL: http://monitoring.jxta.org/servlets/ProjectHome

Status: This is no activity in this project.

networkservice

Description: networkservice is a project to integrate JXTA and Web services.

URL: http://networkservices.jxta.org/servlets/ProjectHome

Status: There is little activity in this project.

presence

Description: This project provides a software layer to help with the development of applications that need to discover and communicate with other peers in the network.

URL: http://presence.jxta.org/servlets/ProjectHome

Status: There is activity in this project.

replication

Description: The replication project is designed to assist in the replication of files and data across the JXTA network.

URL: http://replication.jxta.org/servlets/ProjectHome

Status: There has been some activity in this project since early 2002.

rrs

Description: A JXTA service designed to run on rendezvous peers. The rendezvous peer operator thus gains the ability to run the peer as a background process, and remotely observe and regulate its configuration.

URL: http://rrs.jxta.org/servlets/ProjectHome

Status: The project had some discussion and activity in early 2002.

search

Description: A distributed search system designed for P2P networks and Web sites.

URL: http://search.jxta.org/servlets/ProjectHome

Status: This is a very active project; source code and discussions are available.

Latest JXTA Projects

T his appendix lists the names, URLs, and descriptions of the current JXTA projects.

allhands

An event-notification infrastructure (http://allhands.jxta.org/servlets/ProjectHome).

brando

The beginnings of a distributed source code control application using JXTA (http://brando.jxta.org/servlets/ProjectHome).

chattutorial

This project implements three simple chat applications (http://chattutorial.jxta.org/servlets/ProjectHome).

chess

A networked chess game between JXTA peers (http://chess.jxta.org/servlets/ProjectHome).

configurator

A GUI configuration tool (http://configurator.jxta.org/servlets/ProjectHome).

di

Implementation of a general-purpose, fully distributed index service
(http://di.jxta.org/servlets/ProjectHome).

fuel-auction

An example of using JXTA for an auction-type system
(http://fuel-auction.jxta.org/servlets/ProjectHome).

gasnet

A GUI and audio demo of JXTA (http://gasnet.jxta.org/servlets/ProjectHome).

gnougat

A decentralized file-caching implementation
(http://gnougat.jxta.org/servlets/ProjectHome).

gnovella

Experimental peers for document storage, retrieval, and indexing of documents using JXTA (http://gnovella.jxta.org/servlets/ProjectHome).

jnushare

A set of applications for file and message sharing
(http://jnushare.jxta.org/servlets/ProjectHome).

juxtaprose

A decentralized open discussion network
(http://juxtaprose.jxta.org/servlets/ProjectHome).

jxauction

A project for building an auction system using JXTA
(http://jxauction.jxta.org/servlets/ProjectHome).

jxta-httpd

A set of applications and tools for web publishing using JXTA (http://jxta-httpd.jxta.org/servlets/ProjectHome).

jxtaview

A graphical demonstration of the JXTA discovery mechanism (http://jxtaview.jxta.org/servlets/ProjectHome).

parlor

A collaborative peer-to-peer space using JXTA (http://parlor.jxta.org/servlets/ProjectHome).

radiojxta

Implementation of a system that distributes audio using JXTA (http://radiojxta.jxta.org/servlets/ProjectHome).

rosettachat

An IRC-like application using JXTA (http://rosettachat.jxta.org/servlets/ProjectHome).

JXTA Resources

The primary Web site for the JXTA platform is www.jxta.org. There, you will find the JXTA specification and the latest information, as well as many projects involving the system. In this appendix, we'll take a look at the available resources.

Mailing Lists

To keep up with the happenings of the system, you can join the following mailing lists.

Discuss Mailing List

This mailing list is designed for messages that discuss the JXTA specification and related implementations; however, the messages are generally not technical in nature.

- The subscribe email is discuss-subscribe@jxta.org.
- The unsubscribe email is discuss-unsubscribe@jxta.org.
- The archive for the mailing list can be found at
  http://www.jxta.org/servlets/SummarizeList?projectName=www&list-Name=discuss.

Announce Mailing List

This mailing list is designed for announcement messages. You will generally find messages from the JXTA group as well as projects that have new information available.

- The subscribe email is announce-subscribe@jxta.org.
- The unsubscribe email is announce-unsubscribe@jxta.org.
- The archive for the mailing list can be found at www.jxta.org/servlets/ SummarizeList?projectName=www&listName=announce.

Dev Mailing List

This mailing list contains messages of the most technical nature. Developers, JXTA team members, and project members post and exchange messages on this list, and it is the most active of all the lists.

- The subscribe email is dev-subscribe@jxta.org.
- The unsubscribe email is dev-unsubscribe@jxta.org.
- The archive for the mailing list can be found at www.jxta.org/servlets/ SummarizeList?projectName=www&listName=dev.

User Mailing List

This mailing list is designed to allow users of the JXTA specification and implementation to post messages when things aren't working quite right.

- The subscribe email is user-subscribe@jxta.org.
- The unsubscribe email is user-unsubscribe@jxta.org.
- The archive for the mailing list can be found at www.jxta.org/servlets/ SummarizeList?projectName=www&listName=user.

JXTA Tutorials

The JXTA Web site, which includes a complete page of tutorials, is located at www.jxta.org/project/www/Tutorials.html. As all developers know, the more source code you can view, the better. These tutorials deal with the basic fundamentals of the JXTA specification and Java implementation.

OpenP2P

The OpenP2P Web site includes a number of topics dealing with peer-to-peer networking, and one of the specific topics is JXTA. You can find the JXTA features at http://openp2p.com/topics/p2p/jxta/. The site includes many articles about using JXTA as well as news about the system.

Sun.com

The original JXTA site is located at www.sun.com/p2p/. This site is updated with news information and spotlight articles.

JXTA Bindings

The original implementation of the JXTA Specification was written in Java, but shortly after its introduction, work began on implementations for other languages. This chapter covers the most recent JXTA specification implementations.

Java

Of course, the reference architecture for the JXTA specification, protocols, and service is Java SE. The project home page is located at http://platform.jxta.org/servlets/ProjectHome, and it contains the latest information on the implementation. Some of the interesting things found on this site include

Programming Resources

- Project Developer Guidelines
- How to Build the Source
- Public API Javadoc
- JXTA on a Yopy

Running JXTA

- Configuration Quick Guide
- Available Rendezvous Peers
- How to Configure a Rendezvous

Protocol Documentation

- JXTA Protocols Docs
- Description of Binary Message Format
- Description of New Adv Format
- Description of Endpoint Service
- Description of Propagate Service
- Description of Endpoint Router Transport

Graphical Examples

- Project JXTA: Discovery Animation
- Project JXTA Connection Scenarios

Articles

- Project JXTA: Setting the P2P Tone
- Making P2P Interoperable: The JXTA Story, by Sing Li
- Making P2P Interoperable: The JXTA Command Shell, by Sing Li

Mailing Lists

- *cvs@platform.jxta.org:* A mailing list for CVS commit messages

To subscribe, send e-mail to cvs-subscribe@platform.jxta.org.

To unsubscribe, send e-mail to cvs-unsubscribe@platform.jxta.org.

- *issues@platform.jxta.org:* A mailing list for issuezilla messages.

To subscribe, send e-mail to issues-subscribe@platform.jxta.org.

To unsubscribe, send e-mail to issues-unsubscribe@platform.jxta.org.

Java ME (JXME)

Outside of the Java SE project, the JXTA project for Java ME (JXME) is very popular. The JXME project is designed to implement the JXTA specification based on the J2ME platform (which is intended to execute on very small devices, such as cell phones). The project home page, at http://jxme.jxta.org, includes a comprehensive discussion of goals, constraints, and features of the implementation. The project currently has code and build instructions available.

The mailing lists for the JXME project are:

- *cvs@jxme.jxta.org*: A mailing list for CVS commit messages.

To subscribe, send e-mail to cvs-subscribe@jxme.jxta.org.

To unsubscribe, send e-mail to cvs-unsubscribe@jxme.jxta.org

- discuss@jxme.jxta.org: A list for the discussion of technical issues related to the JXTA-J2ME project.

To subscribe, send e-mail to discuss-subscribe@jxme.jxta.org.

To unsubscribe, send e-mail to discuss-unsubscribe@jxme.jxta.org.

- *issues@jxme.jxta.org*: A mailing list for issuezilla messages.

To subscribe, send e-mail to issues-subscribe@jxme.jxta.org.

To unsubscribe, send e-mail to issues-unsubscribe@jxme.jxta.org.

jxta-c

The jxta-c project is dedicated to bringing the JXTA specification and protocols to those programmers using C and C++. The home page for the project is http://jxta-c.jxta.org/servlets/ProjectHome. Here, you will find the latest source code for the implementation. At this time, there is no installation for the C implementation, and you will have to obtain source code by joining and using CVS. As of this writing, the jxta-c project is being actively worked and a good section of the specification has been laid out, including protocol APIs and some service code.

Dedicated mailing lists for the jxta-c project are available as well. The primary mailing list, called discuss, is available through the following links:

- To subscribe, send e-mail to discuss-subscribe@jxta-c.jxta.org.
- To unsubscribe, send e-mail to discuss-unsubscribe@jxta-c.jxta.org.

jxtaPerl

The jxtaPerl project is designed to bring the JXTA spec and protocols to users of the Perl language. As of this writing, the members of the project are concentrating on the development of Perl code to handle IDs for peers, peer groups, and codats.

The following mailing lists are currently available for the project (the majority of the traffic in the mailing lists occurs in the CVS commit messages):

- *cvs@jxtaperl.jxta.org*: A mailing list for CVS commit messages.

To subscribe, send e-mail to cvs-subscribe@jxtaperl.jxta.org.

To unsubscribe, send e-mail to cvs-unsubscribe@jxtaperl.jxta.org.

- *issues@jxtaperl.jxta.org*: A mailing list for issuezilla messages.

To subscribe, send e-mail to issues-subscribe@jxtaperl.jxta.org.

To unsubscribe, send e-mail to issues-unsubscribe@jxtaperl.jxta.org.

jxtapy

The purpose of this project (http://jxtapy.jxta.org/servlets/ProjectHome) is to develop a Python language binding of the JXTA core protocols using Jython. The current phases of the project include:

Phase 0: Feasibility via Command Line (Completed): Interface from Jython command line to JXTA class methods.

Phase 1: Python Script: Scripts based on the JXTA Programming Guide

Phase 2: Basics: Implementations of ID, Advertisements, and Resolver base classes

Phase 3: Main Implementation: Implementation of core JXTA protocols

The project has two mailing lists:

- *cvs@jxtapy.jxta.org*: A mailing list for CVS commit messages.

To subscribe, send e-mail to cvs-subscribe@jxtapy.jxta.org.

To unsubscribe, send e-mail to cvs-unsubscribe@jxtapy.jxta.org.

- *issues@jxtapy.jxta.org*: A mailing list for issuezilla messages.

To subscribe, send e-mail to issues-subscribe@jxtapy.jxta.org.

To unsubscribe, send e-mail to issues-unsubscribe@jxtapy.jxta.org.

jxtaruby

The goal of the jxtaruby project (http://jxtaruby.jxta.org/servlets/ProjectHome) is to implement the JXTA spec and protocols using Ruby. No mailing lists have been set up for the project, and little work appears to be occurring at this time.

pocketJXTA

The objective of the pocketJXTA project (http://pocketjxta.jxta.org/servlets/ ProjectHome) is to take the jxta-c project and extend it to a Pocket PC platform. Little work has been done on this project.

The mailing lists for the project are:

- *cvs@pocketjxta.jxta.org*: A mailing list for CVS commit messages.
- To subscribe, send e-mail to cvs-subscribe@pocketjxta.jxta.org.
- To unsubscribe, send e-mail to cvs-unsubscribe@pocketjxta.jxta.org.
- *discuss@pocketjxta.jxta.org*: The pocketJXTA discussion forum.
- To subscribe, send e-mail to discuss-subscribe@pocketjxta.jxta.org.
- To unsubscribe, send e-mail to discuss-unsubscribe@pocketjxta.jxta.org.
- *issues@pocketjxta.jxta.org*: A mailing list for issuezilla messages.
- To subscribe, send e-mail to issues-subscribe@pocketjxta.jxta.org.
- To unsubscribe, send e-mail to issues-unsubscribe@pocketjxta.jxta.org.

Other Peer-to-Peer Implementations and Toolkits

JXTA and its Java implementation are excellent tools for Java developers, but JXTA is by no means the only peer-to-peer (P2P) toolkit available. There are many others, both open-source and commercial. Even if you only intend to use JXTA, it could be worth your while to look at source code from other projects—you may find inspiration or a solution to a problem you're facing in your own work.

IBM BabbleNet

IBM's alphaWorks is an organization that builds and distributes new technologies, primarily for software developers. One of alphaWorks' technologies is BabbleNet, a decentralized, P2P program that allows users to build real-time, on-the-fly chat network without connecting to or installing a central server. The system is built on top of a P2P framework, which supports node-to-node communications and is written in Java.

Once you've installed the software, you can view the Java source used to execute BabbleNet. The documentation is minimal, and comments within the code describe the system. Clearly, the software is in the experimental stage, but it does give developers an idea of what can be accomplished beyond the client-server paradigm. The BabbleNet system appears to follow an open-source license, and you can download it at

```
www.alphaworks.ibm.com/tech/babblenet?open&l=p2pt,t=gr
```

Intel

As you might expect, Intel is also in the P2P business with its Peer-to-Peer Accelerator Kit. The kit is designed to be used with Microsoft .NET, and gives the platform reusable infrastructure middleware. The URL for Intel's P2P web site is

```
http://cedar.intel.com/cgi-bin/ids.dll/topic.jsp?catCode=BYM
```

Microsoft .NET and P2P

Microsoft has created a web site to illustrate how the .NET framework can be used in the development of P2P systems. The web site itself highlights some of the features of the P2P examples:

- All of the P2P code is based on the .NET framework.
- Messages sent between peers is serialized as XML.
- Objects can be shared and accessed by peers.
- A discovery service has been implemented using .NET.

The web site includes examples for peer discovery as well as a simple chat application. Of course, the focus of the Microsoft initiative is the web service, and several examples illustrate building services that peers can use. The URL for Microsoft's .NET P2P initiative is

```
www.gotdotnet.com/team/p2p/
```

The Peer-to-Peer Trusted Library

One of the well-known libraries is called the Peer-to-Peer Trusted Library (PtPTL). This library is open source, and its goal is to provide innovation in the security arena as it relates to P2P systems. The library is designed to provide the following:

- Digital certificates
- Peer authentication
- Secure storage
- Public-key encryption
- Digital signatures
- Digital envelopes
- Symmetric-key encryption

The code is designed to execute on both the Windows and Linux operating systems. Numerous examples are provided, and full API documentation is available. As a replacement to secure communication using SSL, the PtPTL provides support for more than just client-server network topologies. Note that PtPTL is not a P2P system or toolkit—it is designed to add trust to a P2P system. The URL for the library is

```
http://sourceforge.net/projects/ptptl
```

The Bluetooth P2P Toolkit

For those of you interested in the wireless market, Pocit Labs has introduced a P2P toolkit designed specifically for the Bluetooth technology. This toolkit lets you incorporate wireless devices, such as PDAs and cell phones, into a P2P network. The software handles the foundational part of a system, including node creation, network building and network destruction, as well as the publishing of services that might be available on a specific peer. The system provides security features such as authentication and access services, credentials, and security keys. The toolkit, which is a licensed product, costs nearly $5,000, so this kit isn't for the average experimenter. You can find the kit at

```
www.pocitlabs.com
```

Other Tools

A variety of other toolkits and applications are available in the P2P arena. Most of the toolkits aren't generic in nature, but are instead geared toward a specific area, such as distributed computing. Other options you might explore include the following:

Adaptinet—A commercial, Java-based distributed toolkit (www.adaptinet.com/download/)

Buzzpad—A commercial, web-based P2P networking application (www.buzzpad.com)

Frontier—A commercial distributed computing application (www.parabon.com/developers/index.jsp)

Hive—A business P2P system based on JXTA (http://alberg.com/products/hive_download.html)

Ubero—A Java-based distributed toolkit (www.ubero.net/memberdownload.asp)

The Anthill Project—A P2P framework (www.cs.unibo.it/projects/anthill/download.htm)

Sun Gridware—A distributed-computing system for Linux (www.sun.com/software/gridware/download.html)

Index